VICTORIAN LITERATURE AND SOCIETY

VICTORIAN LITERATURE
AND SOCIETY

Essays Presented to Richard D. Altick

Edited by James R. Kincaid
and Albert J. Kuhn

OHIO STATE UNIVERSITY PRESS

Extracts from letters of Charles Dickens, Mary Dickens, and Sydney Smith Haldi-mand Dickens quoted in the essay by Arthur A. Adrian are reproduced by permis-sion of Professor Graham Storey, acting in behalf of the editors of *The Pilgrim Edition of the Letters of Charles Dickens*, edited by Madeline House, Graham Storey, and Kathleen Tillotson, and of Mr. Christopher Dickens. (Two quotations on page 282 are from a letter of 18 September 1865 from Charles Dickens to W. Brackenbury that was formerly in the H. E. House Collection in Cambridge but is now deposited in the Dickens House in London.)

Extracts from *The Pilgrim Edition of the Letters of Charles Dickens* in the Adrian essay are reproduced by permission of the Oxford University Press.

The extracts on page 288 from letters of Charles Dickens and his son Sydney Smith Haldimand Dickens are reproduced by permission of Farrer and Company in Lon-don.

Extracts from three letters in the Huntington Library, San Marino, California—Mary Dickens to Anne Fields, 1 September 1870 (FI 1233), Charles Dickens to Georgina Hogarth, 12 October 1864 (HM 17588), and Charles Dickens to William Henry Wills, 6 June 1867 (HM 18387)—reproduced on pages 285, 287, and 293, respectively, are used by permission of the Library.

The extract on page 276 from a letter from Charles Dickens to George Dolby of 25 September 1868 is reproduced by permission of the Henry W. and Albert A. Berg Collection, The New York Public Library, Astor, Lenox, and Tilden Foundations.

Extracts from letters of Charles Dickens to Angela Burdett Coutts quoted in the essay by Arthur A. Adrian are reproduced by permission of the Pierpont Morgan Library.

Extracts from letters of Kate Dickens (Perugini) to George Bernard Shaw quoted in the essay by Arthur A. Adrian are from ADD MS 50546 in the British Library, and are reproduced by permission of the Library and Mrs. Florence Perugini Kenyon.

The extract on page 293 from the diaries of Mrs. James T. (Anne) Fields is repro-duced by permission of the Massachusetts Historical Society in Boston.

LIBRARY OF CONGRESS CATALOGING IN PUBLICATION DATA

Main entry under title:
Victorian literature and society.
  "Bibliography of the writings of Richard D. Altick": p.
  Includes index.
  1. English literature—19th century—History and criticism—
Addresses, essays, lectures.   2. Literature and society—
Addresses, essays, lectures.   3. Altick, Richard Daniel, 1915-
I. Altick, Richard Daniel, 1915-   .   II. Kincaid, James R.
(James Russell).   III. Kuhn, Albert J., 1926-   .
PR463.V53   1984   820'.9'355   83-13317
ISBN 0-8142-0362-0

CONTENTS

↓ 3-18-11 Includes info on
art, architecture, design, nature
(gardens, property design)
decoration

Foreword

RICHARD D. ALTICK HAS TAUGHT AT THE OHIO STATE UNIVERsity since 1945 and as Regents Professor of English has been one of the most distinguished members of its faculty. He was born in Lancaster, Pennsylvania, in 1915, took his B. A. from Franklin and Marshall College in 1936 and his doctorate from the University of Pennsylvania in 1941. He served as an instructor at Franklin and Marshall from 1941 to 1945. Though he has retired from full-time scheduled teaching this past academic year to give himself wholly to a major work of scholarship, his influence as teacher will continue to be felt in this and many departments of English across the country.

Among a variety of graduate and undergraduate courses which he taught with imagination and impeccable scholarship, for more than twenty years Mr. Altick taught English 980, a graduate seminar in bibliography and methods of research. Many, many students have attested that this has been the single most important course in their graduate program. With exacting standards it introduced them to the worth and work of literary scholarship and to a genuine sense of vocation. It was a vale of soul-making, though a few more ruefully preferred to think of it as a kind of graduate study boot camp. In the preface to the latest edition of a book that is both an inspiration and reflection of the course, *The Art of Literary Research* (1981), Mr. Altick reflects with good humor on the rigors too of teaching it, confiding the sense of constant challenge in keeping a firm creative step ahead of his students. And among his many students, whether they will have remembered it or not, are the great numbers of those at the advanced high school and beginning college levels, all over the country, who are better readers and writers for having used his popular *Preface to Critical Reading* since it was first published in 1946.

Mr. Altick's bibliography included here indicates the range and diversity of his scholarship. Most of his writing has focused on Victorian literature and society, and hence the shape and content of this volume of essays honoring him. He has written with critical freshness on a variety of individual writers, and particularly on Browning and Dickens. He has given us a masterful general survey of the whole period in *Victorian People and Ideas* (1973) and a fascinating social history of Victorian violence in *Studies in Scarlet* (1970). And in *The Scholar Adventurers* (1950) he provided us with a lively and enduring account of some celebrated literary forgeries and mystifications.

But his major achievement, I think, has been as a social and literary historian in *The English Common Reader* (1957), *Lives and Letters* (1965), and *The Shows of London* (1978). These are indispensable studies. Impressive in scope and scholarship, they bring together the great talents of a social and literary historian in illuminating the cultural climate of mass reading, of literary biography, and of popular consciousness and taste, and they trace the changing spirit of the times. And, typical of Richard Altick's scholarly writing, they are uncommonly well written. They are lucid, witty, alive. They instruct and entertain.

Such distinction of course has brought him many academic honors in a wide range of professional recognitions, national and international. These include service to the Conference on British Studies, the National Endowment for the Humanities, and the Library of Congress, and he has been a Fellow of several learned societies and institutions. His recent splendid book, *The Shows of London*, won the George Freedley Memorial Book Award.

But Richard Altick takes a special and rightful pride in the honor of the title Regents Professor conferred by the Ohio State University in 1968 on a select few of its most distinguished teachers and scholars. The contributors to this volume, and the Ohio State University Press, which he has served so generously for so many years, are pleased and proud to present these essays in his honor. For special help with this volume the editors thank the Office of Academic Affairs, Elizabeth Martin, and Charles Zarobila.

Albert J. Kuhn

VICTORIAN LITERATURE
AND SOCIETY

I

PHILIP COLLINS

"Agglomerating Dollars with Prodigious Rapidity": British Pioneers on the American Lecture Circuit

SOME CONTEMPORARY BRITISH AUTHORS, PARTICULARLY POETS, make a substantial income, or even their main livelihood, from regular forays into the American lecture circuit or by short annual spells as campus poet at an American university. One hears of "tarmac professors," too, hopping not unprofitably from campus to campus, conference to conference. Dylan Thomas, whose American tours became sadly legendary, wrote a rumbustious account ("A Visit to America") of the extraordinary number and variety of itinerant British lecturers always criss-crossing the continent and of the capers and misadventures to which they are prone; Kingsley Amis has described the corruptions as well as the gratifications of the trade ("Who Needs No Introduction"); Malcolm Muggeridge, when retiring from his regular connection with this circuit, wrote an ungratefully cruel valediction to the ladies' luncheon clubs and other such audiences that had long been adding goodly supplies of jam to his financial bread and butter. But when did this business start? and why has America proved so attractive to these lecturers, recitalists, celebrities major or minor?

Americans have long gone in for lectures much more than Englishmen have, and have paid much better, being conspicuously readier, years before they overtook Britain in affluence, to pay an economic fee or a temptingly honorific one instead of the nominal fee more common at home. When the scientist Sir Charles Lyell lectured in Boston in 1841, he discovered that the fees were "on a scale more than three times higher than the remuneration awarded to the best literary and scientific lecturers in London."[1] In England, remarked Anthony Trollope in 1861, "lectures are mostly given gratuitously by the lecturer," whereas in America, particularly in New England, "lecturing is 'quite an institution' . . . more popular than either theatres or concerts . . . so that the profession is lucrative. . . . The whole thing is done in great style."[2] Another English author, touring America a few years earlier, noted that lecturing was there "almost as much entitled to be called a learned profession as that of the Law, the Church, or Medicine," and that in Boston, "the great metropolis of lectures," if one met in the street "a gentlemanly-looking person with a decent coat and a clean shirt," it was safe to guess that he was either a lecturer, a Unitarian minister, or a poet (or quite possibly all three). Oscar Wilde's Lord Illingworth guessed further: "All Americans lecture, I believe. I suppose it is something in their climate."[3]

From the 1840s onward, Britons have noted this Yankee passion for lectures with surprise, awe, respect, derision, or opportunistic cupidity. In the 1850s their two leading novelists were among the first prominent Englishmen to realize that this strange but delightful American zest for paying good money to see and hear notabilities might be exploited. William M. Thackeray came in 1852-53, and again in 1855-56, to lecture. He toured Britain first with his earlier series *The English Humourists*, but this was avowedly a rehearsal for the real thing, and within two months of arriving in America he was able to report triumphantly that the real thing had materialized: "I . . . agglomerate dollars with prodigious rapidity." "It actually rains dollars in New-York."[4] Five years later, Charles Dickens was wondering whether to give paid public readings from his works, and his calculations included the hope that, besides what he might earn from short seasons at home, he might earn at least ten thousand pounds from an American tour. Personal problems, and then the Civil War, prevented his going until 1867–68, when in four-and-

4

one-half months he took at the box office nearly a quarter of a million dollars and (all expenses paid and his dollars converted into sterling at a disastrously unfavorable rate) banked in England nearly twenty thousand pounds. And Lyell's equation held true for him too: his average profit in America was just about three times as much as he could, at best, earn from reading in Britain.

This transatlantic "traffic in brains," as it was then called, before the snappier term "brain drain" was devised for a more permanent exodus, is an area of Anglo-American relations that deserves some attention, for it had some importance when the lecture or other form of personal appearance was a prime form of international cultural penetration; in the electronic age it has been supplemented, and largely replaced, by film, radio or television appearances, and recordings. The lecture traffic has always been mostly one-way. In the nineteenth century some famous Americans, such as Ralph Waldo Emerson, lectured in Britain, but few compared with the number of Britons sailing westward with a carpetbag full of scripts. This was partly, then as later, for economic reasons; to quote Thackeray again, "Why, a little New England village in the midst of the snow is more ready with its 100$ than a great bulky Birmingham or Newcastle with its 20£ note."[5] (Five dollars to the pound was the exchange rate during the period I am discussing.) But also American audiences specially welcomed British lecturers. As an English pioneer on this circuit wrote in 1841, "There is a great desire, among all classes in this country, to hear and see everything that is new, especially if it has had any celebrity in England; for with all the jealousy that is felt for foreign superiority, and this is not a little, there is a great deference to English taste."[6] Jealousy, or native protest, was indeed often vigorous: thus, when Thackeray was being lionized in New York and Philadelphia, critics wrote resentfully of "our insane passion for foreign lions," the "toadyism . . . to every foreign celebrity," the national desire to pay "mean flattery to any kind of clap-trap that comes with the stamp of the Old World upon it."[7] The offense was aggravated when (as sometimes happened) the visitors put on superior airs, condescended to or criticized America: so that Walt

Whitman growled, in 1888, "What a damned set of roosters come over here . . . to tell us what we are! . . . Gosse, Matthew Arnold—such fellows!"[8] Still, even Arnold, who gave much offense and was technically inefficient anyway as a lecturer, took home a thousand pounds after five months, and Gosse five hundred pounds in half the time, with an offer too of a Chair at Johns Hopkins at the high salary of five thousand dollars; both of them were received by the president at the White House, and Arnold spent Christmas Day there. As a modern American historian, Louis B. Wright, has remarked:

> The English lecturer's . . . condescension towards American 'colonials'—as he often made them appear—was a constant source of irritation and did much to unsweeten Anglo-American relations, though Americans continued to pay fees to hear Englishmen describe Yankee cultural shortcomings. The persistence of the English lecturer in the West is one of the curious cultural phenomena of the nineteenth and early twentieth centuries. Perhaps the English lecturer's hold on the public lay in the subconscious feeling on the part of Americans that the Englishman had something to impart which was culturally uplifting, however unpalatable it might be to take.[9]

The American reverence for lectures has a long history which is indicated by a fact that many later British visitors recorded with glee: that in the 1790s the Puritan conscience of Boston tried to accommodate itself to the theater by calling plays "moral lectures." The earliest reference by a British visitor to the lecture habit (that I have noticed) is in 1807, when one remarked that "it has become the fashion in New York to attend lectures on moral philosophy, chemistry, mineralogy, botany, mechanics, &c." The ladies in particular had "made considerable progress in those studies," and many young men had been shamed into attending the lecture room by "their more accomplished female companions."[10] The lecture habit became institutionalized through the Lyceums: the first was established in 1826, and within ten years there were three thousand of them. But, though British actors soon saw America as an El Dorado, "the rich and pleasure-loving country, which liberally rewarded every one who succeeded in enlivening it,"[11] lecturers seem not to have done likewise until the middle decades of the nineteenth century. To simplify and to generalize by decades: in the 1830s the British began to realize the possibilities of lecturing in America, and a few tried it. In the forties the first such financial killing was made (by an Irishman), and American zest for lectures became so conspicuous that British travelers (like Charles Dickens in 1842) commented upon it more than their predecessors had done. In the fifties the first big stars entered the business, Thackeray's being the most important name at that time. In the early sixties the Civil War interrupted this development, but Dickens's tour of 1867–68 was the first financial blockbuster.

In the seventies the cultural import trade was really flourishing, so that in the winter season 1872–73, for instance, Britons on circuit included the scientist John Tyndall, the astronomer Richard Proctor, the historian J. A. Froude, the popular novelist George MacDonald, the journalist and author Edmund Yates, and a then-famous recitalist the Reverend Bellew (he managed two seasons running, but it killed him). The following winter lecturers included Wilkie Collins and Charles Kingsley, the artisan-poet Gerald Massey, and the freethinker and republican Charles Bradlaugh on the first of three successive winter tours (which nearly ended him, too). By then, fees had risen sharply, and the financial possibilities were spendid for the big star or for the attractive second-ranker who would work hard. In 1872, for the first time, a lecturer obtained a thousand dollars a night, and T. H. Huxley, Tennyson, and Gladstone soon received (but declined) offers to tour at this magnificent rate. Even a man of moderate fame, like that now-forgotten Reverend Bellew whom I mentioned, could negotiate "an arrangement of one hundred nights for one-half gross receipts, with a guarantee of not less than £6,000. The amount might [he added] reach £8,000 or £10,000."[12] These were enormous sums at a time when many living-in domestic servants in England earned twenty, and many laborers maintained a family on fifty, pounds a year: and in America, in the 1850s when money-values were not greatly different, "Many and many a decent family [wrote Emerson] lives in Boston on a thousand dollars a year, and sends one or two boys to College."[13] This possibility of earning fifty thousand dollars in one winter represented too an extraordinary increase in the fees obtainable. Twenty years

7

earlier the poet Arthur Hugh Clough, investigating ways and means of living in Boston, found that most lecturers got fifteen or twenty dollars plus expenses for a lecture, though the current star, Oliver Wendell Holmes, was said to earn fifteen to eighteen hundred dollars a year through lecturing, and the winter of 1852–53 the great British lion, Thackeray, had earned a comfortable (though by later standards inconsiderable) twelve thousand dollars.[14]

No wonder that, from the 1870s onward, many authors, journalists, scientists, politicians, clerics, explorers, celebrities, and notorieties of every kind were tempted across the Atlantic—not that (as will be seen) financial need or greed was always their main motive. The seventies and eighties seem to have been the climax of the business. By the nineties, according to the leading American lecture-agent, Major J. B. Pond, who had organized many of the most illustrious tours by native and imported speakers, lecturing had fallen into disrepute. "The days of giants are gone, never to return, I fear," he said. "The colleges are in a particularly decadent condition. In the old days they would take only orators and writers. Now they want actors. . . . I am willing to give Irving more than any man living, except Gladstone, for a lecturing tour."[15] Nevertheless, as Pond reports, the demand for quantity, if not quality, was still rising. In the seventies there were five hundred Lyceums to be kept supplied with speakers; in the summer of 1900 over two hundred lecturers had announced their winter season plans for touring one state alone (Illinois). And enough of the beneficiaries of this demand had hailed from Britain for a wag to publish in 1900 the spoof news item that the leading literary men in Britain were erecting a memorial tablet to Major Pond in Westminster Abbey, inscribed "It is he that hath made us, and not we ourselves."[16]

I shall now turn back and consider some of the more significant moments, personalities, and developments in this traffic and try to discern its cultural implications. First, two essential mechanical factors must be noted: transport facilities and lecture agencies. By the mid-century transatlantic steamships and the American railroad system had made such invasions relatively easy, comfortable, and cheap. The voyage could be made, in the right ship and with luck, inside ten days, and trains (happily cheap, by European standards) made one-night stands possible. As Thackeray wrote home after a quick journey of five hundred miles through the snow, "20 years ago that journey wd. have taken a fortnight. Oughtn't I for one to be grateful for railroads, who never could have made all these dollars without 'em?"[17] Thackeray's American publishers gave him some organizational help and guidance, and other British lecturers engaged a local agent or adviser, but the scene was transformed in the late 1860s when the big lecturer agencies were established. In particular, James Redpath in Boston and Major Pond in New York organized the whole business more thoroughly. Fees quickly rose from the fifty or hundred dollars that the stars of the circuit could command to that legendary thousand dollars a go; the demand for lectures was increased tenfold, it was said, and soon the agencies were taking the initiative in obtaining celebrities. Outside America, Britain was the obvious place to seek them, if only for linguistic reasons. Pond, the longest and most active in this field, failed in some of his transatlantic proffers: Tennyson and Sir James Barrie, the great preacher Charles Haddon Spurgeon, the politicians John Bright and Gladstone rejected even the most splendid terms. Other Englishmen who felt disinclined to spend a winter that way, or who replied that they had no talent for lecturing, included Herbert Spencer, Huxley (as was mentioned), and John Ruskin, who had a cast-iron case for rejecting all such invitations: "I could not, even for a couple of months, live in a country so miserable as to possess no castles."[18] Tennyson was tempted, but decided that it was "beneath him." But Pond's haul of British celebrities was impressive: Kingsley, Collins, Charles Bradlaugh, Matthew Arnold, Annie Besant, Hall Caine, Anthony Hope, Israel Zangwill, "Ian Maclaren," George Augustus Sala, Sir Edwin Arnold, H. M. Stanley, the Reverend Bellew, Canon Farrar, Dean Hole, Charles Dickens, Jr., Conan Doyle, and many others more famous then than now. Others lecturing in America at this time, under different auspices, included (besides those mentioned earlier) poets as diverse as Martin

Tupper and Oscar Wilde, politicians such as Justin McCarthy, scholars such as the historian Freeman.

But Redpath, Pond, and their procession of lions (or dancing bears) had been able to succeed only because the taste and the basic organization for such ventures were already in existence. To return to the 1830s, when the idea first becomes feasible: at that time Emerson (himself a lifelong lecturer in New England and beyond) was trying to persuade Thomas Carlyle to visit America. "If you cared to read literary lecturers," he told Carlyle in 1834, "our people have vast curiosity & the apparatus is very easy to set agoing." In New England, he explained, "the Lyceum, as we call it, is already a great institution. Beside the more elaborate courses of lectures in the cities, every country town has its weekly evening meeting, called a Lyceum, and . . . if a man speak well he shall find this a well rewarded work." In Boston, the center of the lecturing business, there was a choice of two or three lecturers a night in winter. Lecturers usually got twenty dollars a lecture, but Carlyle could hope for more, and by the late 1830s he was being assured (and not only by Emerson) that he could "make a fortune in six months." He was indeed tempted to make the journey in the hope of gaining a thousand pounds, on which he could retire to some quiet and remote cottage "and sit silent there for ten years to come, or forever and a day perhaps!" After much shilly-shallying, Carlyle decided against going, though as late as 1860 and 1870 hopes and rumors recurred that he might do so; but this correspondence represents, I think, the first serious attempt to attract to America a major British author as a lecturer.[19]

Meanwhile, some minor ones were already arriving. The traveler, journalist, and politician James Silk Buckingham, unseated from Parliament in the 1837 election, toured America for the next three years, lecturing on the Holy Land (which he knew well) and on various philanthropic issues; he reckoned that two million Americans heard or read his discourses. But he, like the Scottish phrenologist George Combe who was lecturing here at the same period, was not trying to make a quick fortune. Rather, both of them wanted to see the country, study its institutions and meet its people, and write a book about their experiences. Lecturing was not their purpose in coming here, but a convenient way of subsidizing a lengthy visit and extensive travel. Soon after this, however, the first substantial fortune was made here by a British lecturer when the popularizer of science, Dr. Dionysius Lardner, caught up in matrimonial complications that made it prudent for him to leave England, lectured and published in America and Cuba with profits (it was said) of forty thousand pounds in five years. Later in the 1840s came the first, apparently, of the touring author-recitalists who were to become an important feature of the lecture circuit; the great names, of course, are Dickens and Mark Twain (who acknowledged Dickens as the significant pioneer), and others such as Wilkie Collins and Conan Doyle offered such readings from their works instead of formal lectures. The pioneer in the 1840s was the minor poet, novelist, and composer Samuel Lover—an Irishman, like Lardner—who successfully toured the United States and Canada for two years with a selection from his songs and stories entitled *Irish Evenings* and received a charmingly macabre tribute from one fan: "Sir, you are admired and respected in this country, and you may rely upon it, if you die here, we should give you a beautiful monument."[20]

Nevertheless, lecturing was not yet the obvious way for a visiting notability to pay his way around America, let alone make a fortune. Dickens, never slow to appreciate ways of making honest money, visited America in 1842, but he financed the trip in the way indicated five years earlier by his Tony Weller when advising Mr. Pickwick to escape from Mrs. Bardell's clutches by decamping across the Atlantic—"and then let him come back and write a book about the 'Merrikins as'll pay his expenses and more, if he blows 'em up enough."[21] Dickens was contracted to supply his publishers with a book about America before he left England (though his prejudices were pro-American at that time). A quarter of a century later he returned, but as a platform performer and to his incomparably greater financial advantage. Other British authors visiting America up to the 1840s wrote books about it, but seem not to have lectured: Basil Hall, Captain Marryat, and Harriet Martineau, for example.

Dickens in 1842 found the American passion for lectures a matter for quizzical amusement rather than respect or exploitation. Particularly in the culturally influential New England states, the Puritan tradition was opposed to such "innocent and rational amusements" as the theater, and "the only means of excitement excepted" from these denunciations were (he remarked) the church, chapel, and lecture room. Or, as his Martin Chuzzlewit hears, in the American episode based on this visit, "Devotions and lectures are our balls and concerts. The ladies go to these places of resort, as an escape from monotony; look at each other's clothes; and come home again"—and these ladies tell Martin how their week passes, from courses on "The Philosophy of Crime" on Mondays and "Government" on Tuesdays to "The Philosophy of Vegetables" on Fridays."[22] Trollope saw the phenomenon in similar terms twenty years later: "Ladies come in large numbers . . . lecturing is the favourite diversion of the steady-minded Bostonian," who could no more do without lectures than Parisians without theaters.[23] Another English observer in 1870, explaining how incomparably more common, and better rewarded, lecturing was here than in Britain, remarked that every New England town of more than five thousand inhabitants had its weekly lectures "as regularly as their market-days and their pork and beans on a Sunday." Ladies, he noted, were prominent among lecturers, as well as providing a large part of the audience.[24] One is reminded here of Verena Tarrant, the young lady given to lecturing in Henry James's *The Bostonians*, set in the 1870s: also of old Miss Birdseye, in the same novel, who "looked as if she had spent her life on platforms, in audiences, in conventions" and in whose "faded face there was a kind of reflection of ugly lecture-lamps; with its habit of an upward angle, it seemed turned towards a public speaker, with an effort of respiration in the thick air in which social reforms are usually discussed."[25]

The popularity of lectures was certainly due partly to the lack of alternative recreations and social occasions, and visiting Englishmen were struck by the general absence, or poor quality and unpopularity, of theaters and the paucity (by English standards) of other amusements. New England seemed to them particularly dismal in this respect, but in the Midwest Mrs. Trollope reported, in 1832: "I never saw any people who appeared to live so much without amusement as the Cincinnatians. Billiards are forbidden by law, so are cards. . . . They have no balls, excepting, I think, six during the Christmas holidays. They have no concerts. They have no dinner parties. They have a theatre, which is, in fact, the only public amusement of this triste little town; but . . . it is very poorly attended. Ladies are rarely seen there, and by far the greater proportion of females deem it an offense against religion to witness the representation of a play."[26]

It is noteworthy that Major Pond attributes the later decline in the lecture business to the growing acceptability of theatrical and musical entertainments, with Gilbert and Sullivan representing a significant breakthrough: "The curtain went up where previously it had been forbidden." The late nineteenth century growth of magazines and of magazine-like Sunday newspapers, he said, provided much of the education and entertainment that had previously been obtained at the Lyceums.[27] The lecture habit should not, however, be dismissed as primarily an occasion for ladies to parade and compare bonnets, an uplifting if dismal substitute for theater-going, or (in Anthony Trollope's words) as, at best, "a respectable killing of an evening which might otherwise have been killed less respectably."[28] The persistence of the lecture habit, if on a reduced scale, into our own day when there is an abundance of entertainment, suggests that it has deeper and more respectable roots, too. Dickens might find those earnest Boston ladies ludicrous, and many British observers criticized the single-lecture system as encouraging a butterfly superficiality, pretensions to knowledge without the substance of it; to quote Trollope again, "It is attractive, that idea of being studious without any of the labour of study; but I fear it is illusive." Nevertheless many were impressed, even moved, by ordinary Americans' zest for such studies. "Poet" Bunn in 1853, for instance: "It is a matter of wonderment . . . to witness the youthful workmen, the over-tired artisan, the worn-out factory-girl . . . rushing . . . after the toil of the day is over, into the hot atmosphere of a crowded lecture-room."[29] Sir Charles

Lyell, a few years earlier, found it admirable, but less a matter for wonderment: Massachusetts had a good popular education system, so it was not surprising, he wrote, that crowds of "labourers and mechanics, mingled with those of higher station" went nightly through the snow "to listen with deep interest to lectures on natural theology, zoology, geology, the writings of Shakespeare, the beauties of [Milton] . . . , treated in an elevated style by men who would be heard with pleasure by the most refined audiences in London."[30]

Many visiting British lecturers, the beneficiaries of this passion for lectures, could regard it also as culturally very encouraging, especially as it was already widely agreed that what America was today, Europe would be tomorrow. Evidently, democracy and culture were not incompatible; indeed, more democracy (in respect of a wider diffusion of education in Britain, along American lines) might mean cultural improvement. Even Matthew Arnold, who had been warning Britain against Americanization long before he visited the country, and who disliked much that he saw during his visit, here found something to respect. Before he sailed, he had been told that over there "all the railway porters and guards have read my books!" His letters from America contain no confirmation or contradiction of this surprising statement, but at least he could report: "The young master of the hotel asked to present his steward to me last night, as a recompense to him for his beautiful arrangements of palms, fruit and flowers in the great hall. The German boys who wait in the hair-cutting room and the clerks at the photographer's express their delight at seeing 'a great English poet', and ask me to write in their autograph books, which they always have ready."[31] Just before, in 1882, young Oscar Wilde had been stamping the same trail and finding even more spectacular evidences of his fame; he needed, he said, to employ three secretaries in New York. "One writes my autographs all day for my admirers, the other receives the flowers that are left really every ten minutes. A third whose hair resembles mine is obliged to send off locks of his own hair to the myriad maidens of the city, and so is rapidly becoming bald."[32] One doubts the literal truth of Wilde's account, as also one doubts whether all those admirers

14

had read the one book he had then published (*Poems*, 1881, hastily reprinted in Boston, 1882), but one must forgive these itinerant lecturers for not drawing too severe a line between genuine intellectual appreciation and a nine-days'-wonder ballyhoo. The significant fact remains that, as Arnold put it, "the people, far lower down than with us, live with something of the life and enjoyments of the cultivated classes."[33]

This homage to culture was apparent at the official level, too. American presidents throughout this period were remarkably assiduous in attending lectures by notabilities touring through Washington and receiving them personally at the White House. To give just one example: in 1857–58 Charles Mackay—a poet now totally forgotten except for the banal opening lines of two poems that appear in dictionaries of quotations: "There's a good time coming" and "Cheer, boys, cheer"—toured North America. In Washington, he was received more than once by President Buchanan and, having given one lecture on "Poetry and Song," he was petitioned to give the other two in his repertoire, the signatories including Jefferson Davis, William Henry Seward, Alexander Hamilton Stephens, John Jordan Crittenden, and thirty other leading politicians. Similarly, when lecturing in Montreal, he had not only an audience of sixteen hundred, but also a public supper after it with the band of the 73rd Regiment playing a serenade.[34] Dozens of other such lecturers received similar flattering attention. Samuel Lover, another very minor author, found his auditorium at Washington so full of senators that it looked, he said, like an adjourned meeting of Congress.[35] American presidents were then less burdened with the cares of office, and their reception of all these lecturers was doubtless a confused and undiscriminating gesture towards culture; but it contrasts not only with the later general indifference of the White House to unprofitable men of mind, but also with the hardy Philistinism, then and since, of Buckingham Palace. Dickens, vexed by Queen Victoria's summoning to audience the celebrated dwarf "General" Tom Thumb, published in 1844 a scathing piece of sarcasm about the chances of getting there through mere intellectual or artistic distinction. He himself succeeded a mere twenty-six years later, but Her

Majesty had not meanwhile done much to reciprocate the presidential attentions to visiting British sages by inviting, say, Emerson or Hawthorne to the Palace (though Longfellow, indeed, was summoned to Windsor in 1868). Similarly, young Oscar Wilde, touring the United States in 1882, went to stay with Jefferson Davis, but one can hardly imagine Mr. Gladstone inviting, for instance, James Whitcomb Riley for a weekend at Hawarden. Altogether the transatlantic comparison was much to America's credit, just as the admiration and envy of British authors were excited by the American authorities' nod of recognition to their intellectual luminaries at that time by appointing them to ambassadorships, consulships, and other such comfortably honorific posts; the British Foreign Office was conspicuously disinclined to do likewise. Another comparison relevant to this topic is between the two nations' universities. In the later decades of the century, American campuses welcomed many of these British lecturers, who very rarely received such invitations from British ones. And similarly the generosity of American plutocrats and of college alumni to their universities had and has few parallels in Britain: another kind of homage to education.

Hospitality at the presidential or state-governor level was agreeably ego-boosting for these touring lecturers, as were the public dinners in Boston or New York, with flattering speeches in the visitor's honor, which greeted many of them at the beginning of their tour—though the tour might then continue (as it did for Thackeray) with such superabundance of feastings that he called it "one unbroken indigestion."[36] But, from day to day, hospitality of a comfortable domestic kind was very welcome too: what Leslie Stephen called the "specially American talent . . . of making guests feel themselves at home."[37] Wilkie Collins can speak for many of his brethren about the kindliness of their reception: "The prominent people in each place visit me, drive me out, dine me, and do all they can to make me feel myself among friends. The enthusiasm and the kindness are really and truly beyond description. I should be the most ungrateful man living if I had any other than the highest opinion of the American people. I find them to be the most enthusiastic, the most cordial, and the most sincere people I have ever met with in my life. When an American says, 'Come and see me', he *means* it. This is wonderful to an Englishman."[38] Some Englishmen, however, preferred to remain very English, Matthew Arnold being a prime example of this; as a Detroit journalist remarked, he was so stiff and cold that one wanted to poke him in the ribs and say "Hello Matt! Won't you have suthin'?"[39]— a moment which, had it occurred, one would have much enjoyed witnessing. Arnold, indeed, broke almost every rule in the book. He *read* his lectures, which American audiences hated; he was inaudible anyway; he seemed supercilious and patronizing; he rushed off to the seclusion of his hotel instead of glad-handing and hobnobbing with the local committee; he chose Boston as the place to dilate upon the shortcomings of Emerson. No wonder that his tour was an incomplete success and that he received the splendidly-worded warning: "Denver is not yet ripe for Mr. Arnold."[40] Even Princeton proved slightly underripe; its students, having gathered that their visitor's father had been Headmaster of Rugby School, used the question time to ask him about rugby football.

He had his tribulations, and that some of his animadversions on American civilization were justified is suggested by the hilarious account of his lecture to the Jersey City Aesthetic Club, which Lionel Trilling extracts from the local newspaper:

> After Mrs. Smith, the president, had opened the meeting with an address, the Meigs Sisters, quartet, sang "God Save the King," Miss Henrietta Markstein rendered a piano solo—"Old Black Joe" with variations—and "not a sound or movement in the audience until the last note had died away." Then Arnold was introduced as the "most distinguished aesthetician of the age." Mr. Arnold delivered his lecture. Mrs. Studwell sang "The Star-Spangled Banner," the audience joining; Chief Justice Shea of New York was introduced and made a neat speech in which he referred to meeting Mr. Arnold in Oxford. Mrs. Studwell sang "Within a Mile of Edinburgh Town." Mr. Arnold left. The Meigs Sisters sang "Little Jack Horner;" Miss Markstein played "Pretty Girl Milking Cow" and "The Girl I Left Behind Me" (both with variations). Mr. Lincoln did imitations of Mr. Irving and Miss Terry, showing how each would play the

Tragedy of Cock Robin. "There were present during the afternoon many people who stand high in the New York world of letters, art and music."[41]

Evidently, even with a lecturer as illustrious as Arnold, the intellectual severity of the occasion was sometimes relieved by less exacting fare, and "the most distinguished aesthetician of the age" may be forgiven for feeling quizzical about what standards and preferences were prevailing. Other local practices struck visiting lecturers oddly. Justin McCarthy, touring in 1886 to advocate Irish Home Rule, was warned in one town that a bouquet from his lady admirers would be presented to him after the lecture by "the prettiest little girl in the place" and, his chairman added confidentially, "I think you had better give her a kiss; it would look graceful." McCarthy took the idea in his stride, expecting some charming little ten-year-old, but balked when the bouquet-bearer turned out to be a very handsome girl of twice that age.[42]

Such incidental embarrassments aside, most itinerant lecturers reveled in the friendliness and adulation they received. Even an old has-been like Martin Tupper, whose reputation as a poet had long since waned in Britain and was well past its peak in America by 1876, enjoyed this brief and not very spectacular reassurance that he was liked and wanted. He lived a dozen years longer, but this (writes his biographer) was his last experience of large-scale publicity.[43] At the other end of life, Oscar Wilde—only twenty-seven when he toured America in 1882—could gleefully report, within days of his arrival: "I am torn to bits by Society. Immense receptions, wonderful dinners, crowds wait for my carriage. . . . I have a sort of triumphal progress, live like a young sybarite, travel like a young god." The entertainment he received, even out in the Far West, was delicious, including such exotic items as a banquet down a silver mine, where (he wrote) "The amazement of the miners when they saw that art and appetite could go hand in hand knew no bounds; when I lit a long cigar they cheered till the silver fell in dust from the roof on our plates; and when I quaffed a cocktail without flinching, they unanimously pronounced me in their grand simple way 'a bully boy with no glass eye'."[44] No wonder that on his return home he found Europe cold and hard after these intoxicating adventures—despite his famous quip, on hearing that Rossetti had given some importunate hanger-on enough money to go to America, "Of course, if one had enough money to go to America one would not go." Wilde inevitably had a witticism for, or about, many moments on his tour, beginning with his splendid words to the Customs officer at New York ("I have nothing to declare—except my genius"), and including such unexpected jokes—who would have attributed this chestnut to Oscar?—as the notice he found (or so he said) in those silver miners' dancing-saloon: "Please do not shoot the pianist: he is doing his best."[45] Though he received, in big Eastern towns, the thousand dollar fee, he spent lavishly and did not bring much money home: but, like many of his compatriots on this trail, he was rewarded too by the excitement and the adulation. It was something, he said, to see one's name placarded in enormous letters: "printed it is true in those primary colours against which I pass my life protesting, but still it is fame, and anything is better than virtuous obscurity, even one's own name in alternate colours of Albert blue and magenta and six feet high. ... I feel I have not lived in vain."[46]

When Oscar Wilde got back to England, he made further money out of his tour by lecturing about the United States; Matthew Arnold did likewise. Samuel Lover, that early author-recitalist, devised a new entertainment, *Paddy's Portfolio*: a "mirthful, rambling" program of "anecdote and commentary" based on what was "novel and diverting in his American experiences" that kept him going in Britain for two years.[47] Others on their return home wrote books about it all. One such book by a well-known cleric of the day, Dean Hole, began: "Why should they, who have the opportunity, make a tour in the United States of America?"[48] I shall return to the answer he gives, but must allude first to reasons which, in his clerical innocence or delicacy, he failed to mention: money, "solid pudding" as well as praise (empty or otherwise), hospitality, and other benefits that Dean Hole deemed unmentionable. Charles Kingsley, for instance, went to America, as his latest biographer avers, "for the same reason as any other transatlantic lecturer goes—for the money." His wife dispatched him, indeed, because the house needed repairing and decorating; and decorated and repaired it soon was, with his Dearest Fanny duly sending grateful letters, though the illustrious lecturer survived only a few months to enjoy the results of his fatal labors.[49] Many of these lecturers were, of course, using a visit to the New World as a means of redressing their bank balances in the Old: or, to be more just, many who were eminent enough to get invitations were also old enough to be worrying about how their wives, daughters, and spinster sisters would fare if they dropped dead. Thackeray is a good example of a lecturer driven to it by concern for his womenfolk, and, as an unusually intelligent and self-critical man, he displays with clarity and candor the mixed feelings, the triumph and guilt, of many of his fellows. "Aren't you bored," he keeps interjecting in his letters home, "by my perpetual talk about dollars?" Like others on the circuit, he alternated between triumphant computation of the piles of "dirty greenbacks," and recurrent self-disgust about "this ignoble dollar-hunting" (as he called it), and a gentlemanly insistence that of course he was not doing it out of personal greed. Like others on tour incessantly repeating a lecture or short series of lectures, he became "so sick of them, that I am likely to stop any day and think them perfect rubbish by this time. I must however try to make another 1000£ with them before I stop." Much the same on his second tour: "Every week makes the girls about 500$ richer. . . . I hold out my hat perseveringly, and am determined to go on resolutely singing my dreary old song. . . . A few months boredom may well be borne for the sake of 2 such good girls as mine. . . . So let us trudge on till the Summer comes, and the bag is pretty full."[50] And pretty full it got, though never quite as overflowing as he had hoped. Like Dickens and other authors in this business, he found that he could make more money by lecturing than by writing and that the real money was to be made in America. Totting up his literary earnings a few years before his death, Thackeray found that nearly a third had come from his few intensive spells of lecturing, and well over a half of this from America. Similarly, about one-fifth of the large fortune that Dickens left when he died, after thirty-four years as the world's leading author, came from his four-and-one-half months' tour of the United States.

In this, as in all ways, Dickens was indeed "The Inimitable." His tour was so popular that no advertising costs proved necessary, and his best box-office take ($3,456 for his final performance in Boston) was only a thousand dollars less than the American theatrical box-office record set by Irving in Boston twenty years later—but Irving had his company, playing *Faust*, to pay, whereas one of the advantages of lecturing, or reading, was that the soloist took as near to the total box-office as could be negotiated. Dickens had originally hoped for ten thousand pounds in America; he brought home nearly twenty thousand, and with better management could have made it forty thousand.[51] Lesser men hoped for one thousand, with a long holiday, all expenses paid, thrown in. Their frequent complaint was that their agent had booked them in to a lower league (financially) than they deserved: Matthew Arnold, for instance, found he was committed to too many $150 lectures, and, like many others, he concluded that: "The business . . . will not have brought the profit which some people had expected, but it . . . has shown me how a really large profit may be made if I come again."[52] Another lecturer precontracted at the $150 rate was told, after his first lecture, that it was a bad mistake: the novelist and fantasist George MacDonald lectured so eloquently that his agent, Redpath, protested, "See here, Mr. MacDonald, why didn't you *say* you could do that sort of thing? We'd have got 300 dollars for you. Guess the Lyceums all over the United States'll think they've *done* Redpath and Fall, sure. You make me sick! Yes, *Sir*." Flattering, if exasperating; but MacDonald with his wife and daughter had an enjoyable eight-month tour.[53]

This holiday aspect, as well as the cash and the glory, was indeed an important attraction. Lecturers could see the famous east coast cities from Boston down to Baltimore (occasion for the expected tribute to the beauty of its young women, and no one failed to make it). Other beauties and wonders could be seen: Niagara and, as travel facilities improved, the Rockies and the Yosemite; and the adventurous could get to San Francisco, New Orleans, and northward into Canada. For many of these British visitors there were friendships to renew, also, or literary pilgrimages to be made, particularly in Boston, where or near to which lived so many of the American authors increasingly known and admired in Britain. Many of these celebrities were untiringly generous in entertaining the stream of British callers. Longfellow, of course, was particularly sought after, and, as his brother says, "His courtesy and his kindness were often subjected to a heavy strain." One would guess so, when his journal for 9 October 1879 reads, "This forenoon fourteen callers; thirteen of them English."[54] He was indeed generously hospitable, and so were—perhaps the most important of the Boston households for these British visitors—the publisher James T. Fields and his enchanting wife Annie. They are mentioned with affection and gratitude by many British lecturers and by such local residents as young Henry James, who had the opportunity to meet the great international lions in Mrs. Fields's famous Charles Street drawing room.

Besides the financial, the social, and the picturesque, there were the political reasons for wanting to visit America—Dean Hole's reasons, to which I said I would return. People should tour the United States, if they had the chance, he wrote, "because they will see such results of political and industrial progress as have never been achieved, according to all the records of history, in the same period of time. . . . They will find an organisation of government, designed by statesmen of consummate wisdom, vast information, and laborious thought." And so on, though, he sagely added, the success of this complex scheme of government was, to date, "far from complete."[55] That was in 1895; and when, in the Ur-version of this essay, I quoted these words at Bowdoin College in 1972 a few days after the election of Richard Nixon—no great favorite on the campuses—I did detect a little titter here, tactfully deaf a foreigner though I tried to be. Who now believes in schemes of government "designed by statesmen of infinite wisdom"? But there was then great curiosity about, often great hope in, this enormous, exciting, and radically new nation. "Here is the future," as Thackeray wrote home from Boston. The hopes were sometimes excessive and led to inevitable disappointment: "This is not the Republic of my dreams," Dickens reported after his first American tour.[56] Still, America compelled the imagination and attracted far more British visitors who, by lecturing, could make more of an uncostly tour of it than the great British dominions overseas (India, Australia, Canada, South Africa) ever did.

"The people who are not pleased with America," wrote one of these lecturers, Edmund Gosse, in 1884, "must be those whose sympathies are fossilized or whose eyes have no power of observation." His days were "crowded with every species of excitement and entertainment." The people, he reported, "are bluff and good-natured, civil if you are civil to them, as sharp as needles to detect and defy pretension. Come with a simple civility and an obvious desire to be pleased, and you will be surprised at the good time you will have." A note of condescension to the bluff natives seems evident, but Gosse continues with confidence in his winning ways: "We have enjoyed . . . the greatest social success that any Englishman of letters has enjoyed since Thackeray lectured in Boston. Old Dr. Wendell Holmes . . . said that he had never known a stranger make such a conquest as I have made. He wrote me, 'we are all a little in love with you'."[57] Whitman, it will be recalled, wasn't: "Gosse, Matthew Arnold—such fellows!" But Gosse's official biographer, describing his visit to Whitman, dwells upon his winning ways: Gosse had an "unrivalled aptitude for situations, . . . was a born medium. His eagerness was contagious, his sympathy compelling, and his gift for letting fall the right word at the right moment instantaneously effective." If effective, his charm was more instantaneous than permanent. More likely, he was self-deceived from the start. How then, finally, did these British lecturers strike their American audiences?

Here I must be tentative, for I have studied the British end— the lecturers' letters, memoirs, and biographies—much more than American newspapers and other such records. Another essay indeed could be devoted to the reception end of this "traffic in brains," but an American should write it. Louis B. Wright, quoted above, judged that these lecturers "did much to unsweeten Anglo-American relations" through their condescension. The publisher George Haven Putnam (certainly no Anglophobe) said of the historian Freeman, lecturing in America in 1881, that "he could not get over the impression, shared by more than one English lecturer, that his audience was made up, if not of youngsters, at least of hearers whose mental capacities were still immature."[58] He was inaudible, too, like Matthew Arnold: and Arnold displayed another characteristic, or vice, of the English tradition (as some Americans at least saw it)—its amateurishness. As Howells wrote, Arnold was "the heir of the false theory and bad manners of the English school. The tradition of that school has apparently been that almost any person of glib and lively expression is competent to write of almost any branch of polite literature." *Touché*, Arnold should have acknowledged (whether or not this is an apt description of "the English school"), for had he not, a year before visiting America, published an essay, "A Word about America," concerning which he wrote in a letter: "One has to trust a great deal to one's 'flair', but I think my 'flair' served me here pretty well"?[59] Another face of English amateurishness appears in Charles Kingsley, touring in 1874, and annoyed when Americans asked him about his writings. "We never talk shop in England," he replied.[60]

Such traits could be exasperating but also could be part of the charm: that air of effortless superiority that the public schools instill into their pupils, that relative abstinence from academic jargon and dislike of specialism that still sometimes distinguishes British intellectuals from American. Inaudibility was carrying amateurishness too far, but again there was a contrast with native speakers. Anthony Trollope remarked on "that wonderful fluency which is peculiarly the gift of an American"; another English observer acknowledged that "The average of speaking ... in America, both in Congress and elsewhere, is far higher than it is in England. Rhetoric and elocution are parts of American education." (Here, at least, Kingsley could happily claim to be a professional: "They are finding out," he reported, "that I can speak, which no Englishman of late has been able to do; and I was expected to mumble and hesitate like the rest."[61]) The inaudibility or mediocre platform manner of some British visitors was no commendation, and the prospects of those piles of dollars attracted across the Atlantic some notabilities who were inexperienced or untalented as speakers—and, if they failed, at least it would not be in front of their friends. "He has left his reputation safely at home when he left England," wrote one of Thackeray's American critics. "He can afford to damage it or lose it altogether in America, in consideration of the handsome profits he can make here." And Thackeray summed up other such press notices as alleging that he was importing "an inferior article—glass beads as it were for the natives."[62] Unfair as this was about Thackeray, it certainly applied to some of his compatriots. But even the lack of experience, the lack of that American education in rhetoric and elocution, could provide at least an attractive change for American audiences. It is striking how many reports on British lecturers remarked on their not using any gestures; similarly, Dickens's recitals struck many reviewers as gentlemanly, restrained, quiet. Huxley, who did lecture at Johns Hopkins, engaged in no histrionics (noted a reporter) and made no points to elicit applause, which broke out only two or three times during his lecture.[63]

It made a change, evidently. I recall that, on my first day ever in America, I was ordering a meal and, having ordered quite enough, was urged by the waitress to "Go on talking; your accent is so lovely." Americans visiting England must have found our waitresses similarly bewitched by their exotic accents. For people on each side of the Atlantic, visitors from the other have the attractiveness of "sameness with difference": a common language, much in common in intellectual and social traditions, but also that different accent (whether lingustic, or features of platform manner, or, more subtle and interesting, matters of intellectual style and approach). Both sides had their virtues, both their vices: the arrogance, condescension, and amateurishness that some British displayed in America, the bumptiousness and impenetrable jargon that British visitors sometimes detected in American speakers. Similar remarks can be heard today when reminiscences of lectures endured shift from the polite to the candid. What, however, was and is incomparable is the hospitality and the organization that existed and exists for such intellectual visiting on the other side of the Atlantic.

This essay is a revised version of a lecture originally given at Bowdoin College (the Annie Talbot Cole Lecture, 1972). A few phrases are borrowed from the author's *Reading Aloud: A Victorian Métier* (Lincoln: The Tennyson Society, 1972).

1. Charles Lyell, *Travels in North America*, 2 vols. (London, 1845), 1:111.

2. Anthony Trollope, *North America* (London; 1862), 1:345-46. A few years after this, Trollope warned his American friend Kate Field, very popular there as a lecturer, that she should not expect much financial reward from lecturing in England: £10 was the average fee paid, and he had lately been earning £10 or £15 for a lecture (*Letters*, ed. Bradford A. Booth [Oxford, 1951], p. 261). Another English commentator in the 1860s, however, noted that it was only in "the last few years" that Britain had witnessed a "rush for the lecture-room . . . even bordering on mania. . . . The lecture amusement . . . is now almost a necessity in modern civilisation": it was a phenomenon "in the highest degree novel and unique" ("Lectures and Lecturing", *Meliora*, 12 vols. [1860], 2:198-99).

3. Charles Mackay, *Life and Liberty in America*, 2 vols. (London, 1859), 1:67, and *Through the Long Day*, 2 vols. (London, 1887), 2:142; Oscar Wilde, *A Woman of No Importance* (1894), act 2.

4. *Letters and Private Papers*, ed. Gordon N. Ray, 4 vols. (London, 1945-46), 3:166, 130.

5. Ibid, 3:620.

6. James Silk Buckingham, *America, Historical, Statistical, and Descriptive* (London, 1841), 3:373.

7. *Letters and Private Papers*, 3:652, 545n, and facing p. 88.

8. Horace Traubel, *With Walt Whitman in Camden* (New York, 1915), 2:497. Cf. his "Our Eminent Visitors: Past, Present and Future" (*November Boughs*, 1888).

9. Louis B. Wright, *Culture on the Moving Frontier* (Bloomington, 1955), pp. 235-36.

10. John Lambert, *Travels through Canada and the United States 1806-8*, 3d ed., 2 vols. (London, 1816), 2:95-96, cited in Jane Louise Mesick, *The English Traveller in America 1785-1835* (New York, 1922), p. 238.

11. William Bayle Bernard, *Life of Samuel Lover*, 2 vols. (London, 1874), 1:246.

12. Bellew's letter cited in *Letters and Memoirs of Sir William Hardman*, ed. S. M. Ellis (London, 1925), p. 262.

13. *Correspondence of Arthur Hugh Clough*, ed. Frederick L. Mulhauser, 2 vols. (Oxford, 1957), 1:316.

14. Ibid, 2:349, 362; Gordon N. Ray, *Thackeray: The Age of Wisdom* (London, 1958), p. 220.

15. Robert C. Burt, "A Dealer in Brains: Major J. B. Pond and his Association with Great Men," *Pearson's Magazine* 5(1898):80-81.

16. Major J. B. Pond, *Eccentricities of Genius: Memories of Famous Men and Women of the Platform and Stage* (London: 1901), p. 369.

17. Ibid., 3:531.

18. *Works*, ed E. T. Cook and Alexander Wedderburn, 39 vols. (London, 1903-1912), 27:170; Joanna Richardson, *The Pre-eminent Victorian: a Study of Tennyson* (1962), p. 141, referring to an earlier such invitation.

19. *The Correspondence of Emerson and Carlyle*, ed. Joseph Slater (New York and London, 1964), pp. 110, 143, 171, 122, 222n, 279, 530, 571-73.

20. Bernard, *Samuel Lover*, 1:318.

21. Charles Dickens, *Pickwick Papers* (London, 1837), ch. 45.

22. Charles Dickens, *American Notes* (London, 1842), ch. 3; Charles Dickens, *Martin Chuzzlewit* (London, 1844), ch. 17. In 1844, Dickens urged his friend, the actor Macready, not to undertake any lecturing in America. If he did so, he would reduce himself to the level of the second-raters then dominating this market "in that low, coarse, and mean Nation. . . . Lecture you, and you fall into the roll of Lardners, Vandenhoffs, Eltons, Knowleses, Buckinghams.—You are off your pedestal, have flung away your glass slipper, and changed your triumphal coach into a seedy old pumpkin" (*Letters*, vol. 4, ed. Kathleen Tillotson, Pilgrim Edition [London, 1977], pp. 10-11).

23. Trollope, *North America*, p. 346.

24. G. M. T[owle], "Our American Letter", *Athenaeum*, 18 June 1870, p. 806; cf. Towle's *American Society*, 2 vols. (London, 1870), 2:271-74, on lyceums and lectures.

25. Henry James, *The Bostonians* (1886), ch. 3.

26. Mrs. [F. E.] Trollope, *Domestic Manners of the Americans* (London, 1832), 1:99.

27. Pond, *Eccentricities of Genius*, pp. 543, 548.

28. Trollope, *North America*, pp. 346, 347.

29. Max Berger, *The English Traveller in America 1836-1860* (New York, 1943), citing Alfred Bunn, *Old England and New England* (London, 1853), p. 30.

30. Sir Charles Lyell, *A Second Visit to the United States of North America* [in 1845-46], 2d ed., 2 vols. (London, 1850), 1:198.

31. *Letters of Matthew Arnold 1848-1888*, ed. George W. E. Russell, 2 vols. (London, 1895), 2:220, 225-26.

32. *Letters of Oscar Wilde*, ed. Rupert Hart-Davis (London, 1962), p. 86.

33. Ibid., p. 226.

34. Charles Mackay, *Forty Years' Recollections*, 2 vols. (London, 1877), 2:380-81, 408-10.

35. Bernard, *Samuel Lover*, 1:273-74.

36. Eyre Crowe, *With Thackeray in America* (London, 1893), p. 21.

37. F. W. Maitland, *Life and Letters of Leslie Stephen* (London, 1906), p. 209.

38. Letter of 2 January 1874, in R. C. Lehmann, *Memories of Half a Century* (London, 1908), p. 65.

39. Quoted by Lionel Trilling, *Matthew Arnold* (London, 1949), p. 396.

40. *Letters of Matthew Arnold*, 2:255. See also E. P. Lawrence, "An Apostle's Progress: Matthew Arnold in America", *Philological Quarterly* 10 (1931):62–79, and John Henry Raleigh, *Matthew Arnold and American Culture* (Berkeley and Los Angeles, 1957), pp. 61–74, from which the Princeton story is taken (p. 73).

41. Trilling, *Matthew Arnold*, p. 394.

42. Justin McCarthy, *Reminiscences*, 2 vols. (London, 1899), 2:17–18.

43. Derek Hudson, *Martin Tupper: his Rise and Fall* (London, 1949), p. 280.

44. *Letters of Oscar Wilde*, pp. 94, 112.

45. Hesketh Pearson, *Life of Oscar Wilde* (London, 1946), pp. 59, 73.

46. *Letters of Oscar Wilde*, p. 117.

47. Bernard, *Samuel Lover*, 1:320.

48. S. Reynolds Hole, *A Little Tour in America* (London and New York, 1895), p. 1.

49. Susan Chitty, *The Beast and the Monk: a Life of Charles Kingsley* (London, 1974), ch. 9.

50. *Letters and Private Papers*, 3:531, 580, 218, 569–70.

51. See the Introduction to my edition of *Dickens: the Public Readings* (Oxford, 1975), p. xxix.

52. *Letters of Matthew Arnold*, 2:237, 263.

53. Greville MacDonald, *George MacDonald and his Wife* (London, 1924), pp. 414, 425.

54. *Final Memorials of Henry Wadsworth Longfellow*, ed. Samuel Longfellow (London, 1887), 3:290.

55. Hole, *A Little Tour*, pp. 1–2.

56. Thackeray, *Letters and Private Papers*, 3, 181; *Letters of Charles Dickens*, ed. Walter Dexter, 3 vols. (Bloomsbury, 1938), 1:413.

57. Evan Charteris, *Life and Letters of Sir Edmund Gosse* (London, 1931), pp. 167–69, 172.

58. George Haven Putnam, *Memories of a Publisher 1865–1915* (New York and London, 1915), pp. 262–63.

59. William Dean Howells, in *Harper's Monthly Magazine* 77 (1888):314, quoted by Raleigh, *Matthew Arnold and American Culture*, p. 66; Arnold, *Letters*, 2:200.

60. Annie Fields' diary, March 1874, quoted by Arthur A. Adrian, "Charles Kingsley visits Boston," *Huntington Library Quarterly* 20 (1956): 95.

61. *North America*, 1:347; Goldwin Smith, *Reminiscences* (New York, 1910), p. 405; Chitty, *The Beast and the Monk*, p. 286. The *New York Daily Tribune* critic was, however, less impressed with Kingsley: He "launches out with a voice that sounds like the wail of miserable sinners in his own Abbey service. For an hour and a half this mournful cry keeps on, with

scarcely a change of note, with hardly a dying fall, and with such wide mouthed rolling vowels and outlandish accent that many a time what he is saying might as well be Greek for all that can be made of it" (quoted by Chitty, *The Beast and the Monk*). He continued nevertheless to attract audiences of up to four thousand (Chitty, *The Beast and the Monk*, p. 288).

62. *Letters and Private Papers*, 3:545n, 652.

63. *New York Herald*, 19 September 1876, quoted by William Pierce Randel, "Huxley in America," *Proceedings of the American Philosophical Society* 114 (1970):93.

II

ALEXANDER WELSH

Writing and Copying in the Age of Steam

THE PRESENT ESSAY ASSUMES WRITING AND COPYING TO BE analogous activities, but the second is also the multiple extension of the first. No doubt writing itself is copying, whether of speech, as Socrates insisted in the *Phaedrus,* or of bits of information such as might be assembled in a tally—an imitation of an imitation one way or the other.[1] Socrates' thoughts will be touched on below, but his historical situation should also be recalled. It would have been strange for him to philosophize or teach by means of writing. "The Athenians of those spacious days did not write books."[2] In Plato's generation they evidently did write books, but for our purposes it makes little difference whether the Socratic dialogues were imitated or invented by Plato. The disparagement of writing and copying in the dialogues is at once deeply ingrained in our culture and inappropriate to the industrial and information revolutions of the last two centuries.

The nineteenth century marks a distinctly new era in this respect. Though literacy is as old as recorded history, and printing—the principal means of attaining multiple copies of writing—is an invention of the fifteenth century, as social phenomena both developments must be studied as part of the history of the nineteenth century. Literacy is extremely difficult to measure since neither the number of books nor the number of pupils in school are sure indicators. But it is certain that at the beginning of the nineteenth century, few persons in the most advanced industrial nation of Europe could read and write and that by the end of the century few could not. The rate of literacy came unstuck in the last decades of the eighteenth century. Until then, in Richard D. Altick's estimate, literacy remained about where it had stood in the reign of Elizabeth I.[3] Political ferment seems to have provided the new impetus, but until literature was mass produced there was no such thing as a reading public. The Fourdrinier machine for making paper and the powered rotary press were necessary to the many-sided contribution of literacy to the modern social state. The decades indicated by Altick coincide with the "take-off," according to W. W. Rostow, of the first modern economy in the years from 1783 to 1802.[4] Increased literacy created a demand for print, and print stimulated literacy in turn. For better or worse, the age of information commenced about two hundred years ago.[5]

Writing and copying have not solely to do with information or the capacity of storing and communicating knowledge. They also have a social and ritual function, as many sacred books and political manifestos attest. Yet when Claude Lévi-Strauss, arguing from an experience among the Nambikwara but within the tradition of Plato and Rousseau, claims that the social functions of writing outweigh the intellectual, a nostalgic prejudice defeats common sense.[6] Lévi-Strauss carefully restricts his dismissal of writing to civilization before the rise of science, but his acknowledgment of what happened next is extraordinarily grudging. "During the neolithic age," he writes, "mankind made gigantic strides without the help of writing; with writing, the historic civilizations of the West stagnated for a long time. It would no doubt be difficult to imagine the expansion of science in the nineteenth and twentieth centuries without writing. But, although a necessary precondition, it is certainly not enough to explain the expansion." The truth is that science partly helped produce literacy. Scrubbed free of political exaggeration and bias in favor of the primitive, Lévi-Strauss's position is acceptable if one adds that in modern industrial society intellectual forces are no longer separable from social forces. The political hypothesis that writing "seems to have favoured the exploitation of human beings rather than their enlightenment" must be very broadly conceived to deserve any credence at all.[7] If some feat of world-historical statistics could prove the statement correct, it would still strike someone who had learned to read in order to study Tom Paine's *The Rights of Man*, or who had fought the great fight in early Victorian times for repeal of the so-called taxes on knowledge, as an exceedingly cruel irony. But by carefully hedging on the rise of science, Lévi-Strauss need not commit himself on the age of steam.

By attacking writing in the *Phaedrus* dialogue, Socrates identified two arguments in its favor. He contended that writing weakened the memory; but of course that is because writing provides a record independent of individual or collective memory. And he protested that written words knock about in the world, loosed from the writer; but of course words free of special intent, inflection, or reservations on the part of the speaker have enhanced value as information. In *Tristes Tropiques* Lévi-Strauss takes due note of the first argument and, by implication, the second also. These are functions of writing that have always been understood—so much so that they would hardly be noticed if not attacked in this way. In the late eighteenth century, the arguments were rehearsed in the context of English common law, since by then attempts were being made to rationalize the law of evidence, and the question repeatedly arose as to the weight of written evidence. "Evidence" had primarily meant testimony, but the evolution of the jury, the authority of inductive science, and the increasing dependence on commercial paper widened the scope of juridical proof. Hence in his treatise on evidence, Jeremy Bentham included a chapter "Of Writing, Considered as a Security for the Trustworthiness of Testimony," which went over some of the familiar ground. Under the headings of *distinctness, recollection, permanence*, and *existence* (the case in which a witness is physically unable to appear in court), Bentham enumerated four advantages of writing, and he ventured the following historical point:

> Causes of a certain degree of simplicity—and happily the great majority of causes are within this desirable degree,—may, supposing probity on the part of the judicatory, be tolerably well decided without

writing: because decision may follow upon evidence before the memory of it in the breast of the judge is become incorrect or incomplete. In a cause involved in a certain degree of complication, the use of writing is in a manner necessary to good judicature. But civilization must have stopped far short of its present advanced stage, if complicated causes had not been susceptible of just decision as well as simple ones.

Bentham being Bentham, he also enumerates ways in which writing can negate truth and justice. Writing is as capable of indistinctness as of distinctness; the recollection that it assures cannot be tested by cross-examination; and for related reasons its capacity for deception can be even greater than that of *viva voce* testimony. In this mode Bentham is very Platonic; and when he expands on the subject of how writing can thwart the collateral ends of justice, by "factitious delay, vexation, and expense," his mode is openly satirical. In this attack on "excrementitious matter . . . wrought up to the highest possible pitch of voluminousness, indistinctness, and unintelligibility," he demonstrates a skill in writing comparable to Dickens's upon themes appropriate to *Bleak House*:

> Office upon office, profession upon profession, have been established for the manufacturing, warehousing, and vending of this intellectual poison. In the capacity of suitors, the whole body of the people (able or unable to bear the charge) are compelled to pay, on one occasion or another, for everything that was done, or suffered or pretended to be done, in relation to it: for writing it, for copying it, for abridging it, for looking at it, for employing others to look at it, for employing others to understand it, or to pretend to understand it: interpreting and expounding imaginary laws, laws that no man ever made.[8]

From consideration of writing, Bentham slips rather naturally to copying and the sheer accumulation of written words. Tape recorders have since blurred this distinction between spoken and written words, but one of the vices of writing's virtues (and the same now applies to voice recording) is accumulation beyond the advantages for use.

My purpose is to ponder especially this matter of copying, the multiplication of writing. One can see that the thrust of Bentham's entire program for reform of the common law was in a broad sense Platonic. He wished to bring practices into direct relation with rational principles, to derive laws from truths and not from series of imitations of imitations. The spirit of Victorian reform and the modern faith in legislation are in many ways a monument to Bentham's writing. Nevertheless, the times demanded and created a new and un-Platonic ideal of copying. Let me fix on the older ideal by referring to one earlier treatise on evidence and also by referring very briefly to Coleridge, to recall one romantic view of the question. Then I shall appeal to Charles Babbage to explain what I believe to be the attitude essential to the industrial and information revolutions.

Bentham's *Rationale of Judicial Evidence* was the first substantial treatise on evidence in English law and the one most faithfully devoted to first principles. But the rules of evidence had been gathering force since the seventeenth century, and one short treatise, Gilbert's *Law of Evidence*, was frequently cited in the later eighteenth century. In it the interest in written evidence is pretty much confined to public records. Since such records cannot be brought into court, a copy of the record is allowed to be the best evidence.

> But a Copy of a Copy, is no Evidence, for the Rule demands the best Evidence, that the Nature of the Thing admits, and a Copy of a Copy can't be the best Evidence, for the farther off a Thing lies from the first Original Truth, so much the weaker must the Evidence be, and therefore they must give a true Copy in Evidence, which is to reduce it to its first and best Certainty: Besides, where you will give the Copy of a Copy in Evidence, there must be a Chasm or Gap in your Evidence; for if you have the first Copy, and by Oath or otherwise prove that a true Copy, then the second Copy is altogether idle and insignificant: If you have only the second Copy, then it cannot appear that the first was a true Copy, because it is not there to be sworn to, and by consequence it is not proved in Court, and there is no Evidence, and consequently the Transcript of that which is in itself not Evidence, cannot be Evidence.[9]

The public record itself, a philosopher might add, is but a record of the fact in question, and a true copy, duly sworn to, also a copy of a copy. The hovering of Gilbert's logic in one place expresses the need to stay as close as possible to "the first Original Truth." The "true Copy" is only the best evidence and not the same with the truth, which is troublesomely unavailable in His Majesty's court except by such approximations. The rule of evidence that Gilbert is setting forth is thus a lesson in frustration. One could not, say, build a house with such a rule.

The Coleridgian view of copying at first seems contrary to this demand for the best evidence, since Coleridge places so much stress on the role of the imagination in the process. One might instance a number of texts, but for its brevity consider this extract from the *Biographia Literaria*: "The formation of a copy is not solved by the mere pre-existence of an original; the copyist of Raphael's Transfiguration must repeat more or less perfectly the process of Raphael. It would be easy to explain a thought from the image on the retina, and that from the geometry of light, if this very light did not present the very same difficulty. We might as well rationally chant the Brahmin creed of the tortoise that supported the bear, that supported the elephant, that supported the world, to the tune of 'This is the house that Jack built'."[10] The skilled copyist of Raphael would seem to be a very different person, with an entirely different task, from the sworn witness or law copyist. The copyist of Raphael really has to lay on the paint by the same process as that of the master; if anything, the task is more difficult in that the copyist is not the master. But the way in which Coleridge swiftly generalizes the problem shows that this is not the issue. He is concerned with perception, with what he calls in this context "co-adequate forces in the percepient [*sic*]" and in the notorious epitome at the end of chapter 13 of the same work, "the primary imagination." Copying presupposes an act of perception, and perception itself presupposes "co-adequate forces." Copying depends on underlying correspondences or else it never could take place: "the formation of a copy is not solved by the mere pre-existence of an original." Coleridge's articulation of the problem is immediately Kantian and ultimately Platonic also. His thought is far more ambitious than that of Gilbert's *Law of Evidence* but is troubled by the same general problem of the relation of the copy to the original. If the entire universe is implied in every copy of an original, that may be philosophically satisfying, but it is not tidy and practical. One might build a house like the house that Jack built, but not an entire housing development.

Hindsight suggests that there must be a less troubled notion of copying than these, and one that we take for granted today—not because the desirability of the best evidence or the value of the romantic theory of perception are in doubt, but because mass production is now so commonplace in our experience. For a positively enthusiastic view of copying, we can look to one of the earliest and most insightful treatises on mass production, Babbage's *On the Economy of Machinery and Manufactures*. The observations recorded in this book are of such an immediate practical sort and its organization so cheerfully lax that it does not at first reading seem very profound. The treatment of the division of labor, for example, is more imposing in Adam Smith. Babbage lacked the analytical ability of Bentham, the critical thrust of Coleridge, or the political consciousness of Marx; and many of the practical developments that stirred his enthusiasm seem elementary today. But as we can better appreciate after the rediscovery of Babbage's calculating machines, his combination of professional mathematics and industrial curiosity was a very happy one. The longest chapter of *On the Economy of Machinery and Manufactures*, which is perhaps Babbage's most revealing work, is called "Of Copying." The chapter is hardly more than a survey, and the best way to characterize it is to reproduce here the contents, omitting only the section numbers.

CHAPTER XI.
OF COPYING

Division of subject.—*Of Printing from Cavities.* Copper-plate Printing. Engraving on Steel. Music Printing. Calico Printing from Cylinders. Stencilling. Printing Red Cotton Handkerchiefs.—*Printing from Surface.* Printing from Wooden Blocks. From movable Type. From Stereotype. Lettering Books. Calico Printing. Oil-cloth Printing. Letter Copying. Printing on China. Lithographic Printing. Reprinting old Works by Lithography. Lithographic Printing in Colours. Register Printing. —*Copying by Casting.* Iron and Metals. Casts of Vegetable Productions in Bronze. Casts in Plaster. Casting in Wax. Imitations of Plants, of the Human Body. —*Copying by Moulding.* Bricks, Tiles, Cornice of Church of St. Stefano. Embossed China. Glass Seals. Square Glass Bottles with Names. Wooden Snuff-boxes. Horn Knife Handles. Umbrella Handles. Tobacco-pipe making. Embossing on Calico; on Leather. Swaging. Engraving by Pressure on Steel. Bank Notes, Forgery. Gold and Silver Mouldings. Ornamental Papers. —*Copying by Stamping.* Coins and Medals. Military Ornaments. Buttons and Nail Heads. Clichée. —*Copying by Punching.* Boiler-plates. Tinned Iron. Buhl-work. Cards for Guns. Gilt Paper Ornaments. Steel Chains. —*Copying with Elongations.* Wire Draw-

ing. Brass Tube Drawing. Leaden Pipes. Iron Rolling. Vermicelli. —
Copying with altered Dimensions. Pentagraph. Turning. Rose Engine
Turning. Copying Dies by Lathes. Shoe Lasts. Copying Busts. Screw-
cutting. Printing from Copper Plates with altered Dimensions. En-
graving from Medals. Veils made by Caterpillars. Weight of various
Fabrics. Copying through six Stages in Printing this volume.[11]

Though the list of processes tempts one to read it as a satiric
catalogue, it is nothing of the kind. The odd juxtapositions,
such as that of rolled iron and vermicelli, result from Babbage's ability to generalize over method, and the occasional
digressions stem from the same alert observation that fuels
these generalizations. The great importance of the chapter is
nothing less than the discovery, which Babbage does not
present as a discovery, that production is inherently a process
of copying. Production has always relied on copying, but
through the introduction of machinery it has become copying. And Babbage does not restrict his vision to machinery as
such, but rather to the machine-like organization of labor as a
whole, not excluding the gathering of materials for production and the distribution of goods. If good wool can be
acquired cheaply, the object becomes to repeat the acquisition; if the coat can be sold profitably, the object is to find
more customers like the first. The processes of manufacturing
are only the most obvious acts of copying. That Babbage is
unperturbed by the secondary status of copies in the world of
things is seen from the two sentences that he devotes to
originals at the beginning of the chapter "Of Copying":
"Almost unlimited pains are, in some instances, bestowed on
the original, from which a series of copies is to be produced;
and the larger the number of these copies, the more care and
pains can the manufacturer afford to lavish upon the original.
It may thus happen, that the instrument or tool actually
producing the work, shall cost five or even ten thousand times
the price of each individual specimen of its power" (p. 69).
Clearly to this vision the original is worth both more and less
than the copy. The sole end of the original is the copy.

The second thing to notice in Babbage's chapter "Of Copying" is the unprivileged status of the printed word. The most
common form of manufacturing readable text, of copying
writing, is merely one subcategory of *"Printing from Sur-*

face." Since all explanations in this chapter "are restricted to the shortest possible detail which is consistent with a due regard to making the subject intelligible" (p. 69), what he has to say about this subcategory can be given in its entirety:

> *Printing from movable Types.*—This is the most important in its influence of all the arts of copying. It possesses a singular peculiarity, in the immense subdivision of the parts that form the pattern. After that pattern has furnished thousands of copies, the same individual elements may be arranged again and again in other forms, and thus supply multitudes of originals, from each of which thousands of their copied impressions may flow. It also possesses this advantage, that wood-cuts may be used along with the letter-press, and impressions taken from both at the same operation. [P. 74]

This is fair enough, since Babbage acknowledges that letter-press is the most influential case of copying and takes cognizance of "a singular peculiarity" of language. At the same time there is no hint, as the above table of contents also makes clear, of any sacral or political privilege in language, writing, or the printed word. The interest of the brief description lies in the sharp perception of "multitudes of originals" awaiting the mere rearrangement of a minimal number of "individual elements" in the pattern. It is perceptions of this kind that reveal Babbage thinking in advance of his time.

That printing in the most ordinary sense should be tucked away in a bulky survey "Of Copying," should not lead one to suppose that Babbage was unconcerned about writing. To the contrary, he exhibits what I take to be the normal insistence of any scientist, reporter, or author of books on the importance of writing. He is not worried that writing is an imitation of an imitation, since he is fascinated by imitation in any case. Nor is he worried that writing may be a power play in the game of enslaving peoples. He was perhaps too young at this time to realize, with Bentham, that there could be too much of a good thing. The importance he places on writing is precisely that which Socrates, Lévi-Strauss, and Bentham admit in the process of qualifying it—the use of writing as a substitute for memory and means of communication. He states, "The remark—that *it is important to commit to writing all information as soon as possible after it is received, especially when numbers are concerned,*—applies to almost all inquiries"

(p. 114). He then specifically advises preparing a question-naire, or what he calls a "skeleton," for conducting inquiries such as his own. He draws up a sample list of questions and suggests that such a form be printed, with spaces for the investigator's notes.

Babbage is untroubled about writing and copying but quite aware of the part they play in his own work, as this allusion to the method of conducting inquiries shows. Twice in *On the Economy of Machinery and Manufactures* he makes bold use of his book as an object of inquiry itself. He devotes several pages to "an analytical statement of the expense of the volume now in the reader's hands," which affords an illustration of the breakdown of costs in manufacturing and incidentally exposes "the nature and extent of the taxes upon literature" (pp. 205-10). He likewise uses his book at the end of the chapter "Of Copying," as the contents promises, to illustrate at least six stages "of repeated copying of which these very pages are the subject." These stages are (1) the printing of the pages from stereotype plates, (2) the casting of the plates from plaster of paris molds, (3) the casting of the molds from movable types set up by the compositor, (4) the casting of the types from copper matrices, (5) the shaping of the matrices by steel punches, and (6) the partial shaping of the punches by other steel punches. Between the descriptions of the third and fourth steps—that is, between copies of text and of types—Babbage very sensibly calls attention to the writer's contribu-tion to the production, in a bracketed paragraph that reads as follows: "[It is here that the union of the intellectual and the mechanical departments takes place. The mysteries, however, of an author's copying, form no part of our inquiry, although it may be fairly remarked, that, in numerous instances, the mental far eclipses the mechanical copyist.]" (pp. 112-13). The "mysteries" are referred to a little ironically. "Numerous instances" hedges the philosophical question, certainly, and suggests a mild satire on unoriginal authors rather than the impossibility of any origin.

The honest bracketing and protective irony cannot disguise the dismissal of a large question. On the other hand, the dismissal is very practical, and Babbage's admiration for copying and his close observation of the progressive division of labor in manufacturing led to his important insight into mental processes and how they might be enhanced. His chapter "On the Division of Mental Labour" describes the construction of logarithmic tables in France by an arrangement consciously adopted from Adam Smith's famous account of pin manufacturing in *The Wealth of Nations*. It is this spirited extension of copying that almost certainly inspired Babbage's design of calculating machines. Just as he had observed British manufacturers progressively replacing human labor in the phases of production that invited the use of machinery, he would have a machine perform certain mental calculations. His designs were limited by strictly mechanical operation and by the use of the decimal number system, and their conception was bound by the state of manufacturing arts and the sources of energy then available. As Babbage wrote admiringly of the pressroom of the London *Times* in that day, "The hand of man is now too slow for the demands of his curiosity, but the power of steam comes to his assistance" (p. 272). By the time the power of steam and thrust of gears became too slow for the demands of curiosity, an electronic technology and more sophisticated mathematics would be available, to be borrowed in much the same spirit for the design of computers.

Babbage did not worry the question of the relation of the copy to its original except as a practical problem of producing more and better copies cheaply. He tended to check such problems by double entry bookkeeping, whereas the Platonic concern with copying is epistemological and ontological. The latter is most movingly evident in the *Cratylus*, in which dialogue Socrates disputes the view that names are merely conventional in order to support both the authority of language and the presumption of objective reality. The argument is not very persuasive, because of the mistaken demands it places on etymologies and because of the circularity with which it taxes inferior copies to infer reality. Socrates has finally to admit that knowledge cannot be derived from names. His quandary moves him to shift the discussion from representation to reality. "Which is likely to be the nobler and clearer way; to learn of the image whether the image and the truth of which the image is the expression have been rightly conceived, or to learn of the truth whether the truth and the image of it have been duly executed?" The nobler and clearer way is to learn directly of the truth, but that way is unfortunately "beyond you and me" because the truth is known only from copies—and the dialogue ends in exhortation and questioning of existence.[12] This is the quandary that Babbage apparently elides when he brackets "the mysteries . . . of an author's copying." Nowhere in *On the Economy of Machinery and Manufacturers*, however, does he confuse a copy with its original. He knows the differences between a punch and the impression made by the punch, between a stereotype plate and the printed page, between handwriting and types in a row. His reflections focus repeatedly on these differences. But he differs from the historical Socrates in a heightened awareness that copies produced from the same original *are* alike. The system of mass production depends upon this likeness, which Babbage greets with wonder and respect. "Nothing is more remarkable, and yet less unexpected, than the perfect identity of things manufactured by the same tool" (p. 66). This is a remark not so likely to have been made by Socrates. Athenians of those spacious days did not experience vast amounts of copying of this kind; instances of such were familiar to them, but for the most part the making of two things just alike in the fifth century B.C. took far greater pains than making them unlike. The reverse situation has prevailed since the commencement of the age of steam. It became easier and then necessary to make most things just alike. It would be surprising if this likeness among copies (Babbage calls it "perfect identity," but of course it is not that) did not erode the consciousness of the difference between the copies and the original. In an industrial economy, the likeness of products becomes more obvious than their authority, and the perfected copy is the goal of production.

Babbage's untroubled contemplation of copying should not be taken to mean the end of the matter. Farther down the track were troubles to which he gave too little thought, troubles inherent in the industrial and information revolutions. The

41

most obvious is that of industrial waste, the smoke and tailings of the age of steam and the still more toxic results of latter-day invention. Furthermore, though many desirable products of man's ingenuity are consumed or exported, knowledge apparently accumulates without stint. Babbage, a key influence in the early nineteenth-century statistical movement as well as a precursor in modern information technology, did not reckon with the exponential growth of knowledge and the requirements of storage and retrieval of information that it posed. Nor did he foresee that the division of intellectual labor would increase to the point of incomprehension of the whole by any one person or profession. It is safe to say that no one of his generation worried greatly about either problem, both of which were wistfully remarked at the end of the century in a chapter of *The Education of Henry Adams* entitled "The Law of Acceleration."[13] Though Babbage had some acquaintance with politics, he did not reckon with the force of monopolies or the tasks of democratic regulation posed by industrial advances. There is some guarded mention of labor combinations in *On the Economy of Machinery and Manufactures* but no consideration of the alienation of labor that is pretty well implicit throughout its pages. Not even Marx reckoned with the alienation of a culture fed with information, knowledge that can and must be stored and communicated as impersonally as possible. But that reflection turns us back to Plato. Even though the modern consumer prefers a good copy to a bad for his money and may be ignorant of the relation of the copy to the original (the consumer who wants an automobile and not a lemon, say, and not an hydraulic press from Fisher Body, either), there still lingers a yearning and respect for authority (frequently exploited by advertising). The writer who is grateful to an editor for improving his expression and to the printers for constructing a fine book, who never sought or requested the return of his original manuscript, may still be upset when a reader, and especially a reviewer, misunderstands his or her thought.

It was a bad day for Socrates when "goods" in England came primarily to mean property shipped by railways. That Socrates partially lost an argument to history should not diminish his stature as a teacher, however, and a teacher who did not publish. He had an impressive way, after talking his way into a question with great skill, of narrating his way out. He sensed that originality was less effective at the end of a dialogue than at the beginning and sometimes settled the argument by means of a myth or fable that dressed uncertainty in old clothes. I can think of no better procedure to copy here, taking similar care to invent nothing and to write everything exactly as it was written.

Such a fable of writing and copying was told in Victorian times of Mr. Dick and King Charles. It was after the ruin of Aunt Betsy Trotwood that the interesting part of the story took place, and one Traddles was the principal mover. "'You see,' said Mr. Dick, wistfully, 'if I could exert myself, Mr. Traddles—if I could beat a drum—or blow anything!'" The kindly and highly practical Traddles, not put off by Mr. Dick's manner, suggested that he might "copy writings"—law writings, like those that Bentham challenged and Dickens satirized elsewhere. Mr. Dick was doubtful, and David Copperfield, who was standing by, "explained to Traddles that there was a difficulty in keeping King Charles the First out of Mr. Dick's manuscripts." Traddles persisted, pointing out that such writings as could be copied for a fee were "already drawn up and finished," and as a result of this conversation Mr. Dick found gainful employment the next day:

> On a table by the window in Buckingham Street, we set out the work Traddles procured for him—which was to make, I forget how many copies of a legal document about some right of way—and on another table we spread the last unfinished original of the great Memorial. Our instructions to Mr. Dick were that he should copy exactly what he had before him, without the least departure from the original; and that when he felt it necessary to make the slightest allusion to King Charles the First, he should fly to the Memorial. We exhorted him to be resolute in this, and left my aunt to observe him. My aunt reported to us, afterwards, that, at first, he was like a man playing the kettle-drums, and constantly divided his attentions between the two; but that, finding this confuse and fatigue him, and having his copy there, plainly before his eyes, he soon sat at it in an orderly business-like manner, and postponed the Memorial to a more convenient time.[14]

Here is writing about writing again, and copying of copying, in the form of a fable. I swear the above to be a true copy of Nina Burgis's copy of the 1850 copy of *David Copperfield*, but that is not evidence. The similarity of the names in the fable to that of Charles Dickens, the famous novelist, has frequently been noted by other witnesses. When Mr. Dick first appears in the novel, the Memorial is already a great trouble to him, but he has a large kite consisting of more manuscript, which he frequently publishes by sending it aloft. The textual notes to chapters 13 and 14 in the Clarendon Edition reveal that in the manuscript Mr. Dick was at first Mr. Robert and the allusion to King Charles' head something about a bull in a china shop. The author apparently did not set out to use his own names but revised his way toward a subjective and objective association with Mr. Dick and his obsession: David Copperfield senses his aunt's kindness through her kind treatment of Mr. Dick, whose real name, Richard Babley, must never be mentioned because of the way his family abused him; at the same time the simple-minded Mr. Dick becomes David's first truly affectionate friend. Similar fanciful associations with the author play over the three characters at Buckingham Street, but it is Mr. Dick's peculiar madness that presents a challenge to interpretation. His "great Memorial" is both a petition, an appeal to someone in authority to save him from his obsession about his identity—his identification with King Charles the First—and the autobiographical fiction that exercises this obsession. The moral, if this is an allegory, features and favors the discipline of copying, presented as the antithesis of the dangerous obsession. Before settling down "in an orderly business-like manner," Mr. Dick has had to confront squarely these other close associates of the author—Traddles, who himself first made his way as a law copyist, and David Copperfield, whose first act of businesslike responsibility is to take up shorthand reporting, as Dickens had.

The fable is also about production in general. Work that is strictly to be copied is "already drawn up and finished," whereas the Memorial is an "unfinished original." Somewhere along this scale of completion, between the conditions of language and work that are given and the possibilities of language and work that are open, production takes place. The hard question that tries Socrates also, whether a copy can validate the original when the original authorizes the copy, is like the "constantly divided" attention of Mr. Dick. The note on the episode in Dickens's number plans reads simply, "Mr. Dick useful / *Kettle Drums*" (Appendix C, p. 767). Thus playing the kettle drums is a memorable image of writing and copying from the philosophical point of view, but the plot and moral of the fable are expressed by "Mr. Dick useful"—he who wished he could "beat a drum—or blow anything!" The disciplining of Mr. Dick is both indirect autobiography and relatively straightforward Victorian celebration of writing and copying.

1. Plato, *Phaedrus*, 274-79. That Platonic idealism reduces all discourse to an imitation of an imitation is explicit in *The Republic*, bk. 10.

2. A. E. Taylor, *Socrates* (1933; rpt. New York, 1953), p. 12.

3. Richard D. Altick, *The English Common Reader: A Social History of the Mass Reading Public, 1800-1900* (1957; rpt. Chicago, 1963), p. 30.

4. W. W. Rostow, *The Stages of Economic Growth: A Non-Communist Manifesto* (Cambridge, 1960), p. 38.

5. That Plato was fending against "information" is brought out by Alvin W. Gouldner, *Enter Plato: Classical Greece and the Origins of Social Theory* (New York, 1965), pp. 270-71.

6. Jacques Derrida dissects the chapter in *Tristes Tropiques* called "The Writing Lesson" in *Of Grammatology*, trans. Gayatri Chakravorty Spivak (Baltimore, 1976), pp. 101-40.

7. Claude Lévi-Strauss, *Tristes Tropiques*, trans. John and Doreen Weightman (New York, 1974), pp. 296-300.

8. Jeremy Bentham, *Rationale of Judicial Evidence*, ed. John Stuart Mill, 5 vols. (London, 1827), 1:429-44. The papers edited by Mill for these volumes were written between 1802 and 1812.

9. Sir Geoffrey Gilbert, *The Law of Evidence*, 2d ed. (London, 1760), p. 9. Gilbert died in 1726; this work was first published posthumously in 1754.

10. Samuel Taylor Coleridge, *Biographia Literaria*, ed. J. Shawcross, 2 vols. (London, 1907), 1:92.

11. Charles Babbage, *On the Economy of Machinery and Manufactures*, 4th ed. (1835; rpt. New York, 1971), pp. xvi-xvii. The first edition was published in 1832. Subsequent page numbers will be included in the text.

12. *Cratylus*, 439-40, in *The Dialogues of Plato*, trans. B. Jowett, 2 vols. (New York, 1937), 1:229.

13. Henry Adams, *The Education of Henry Adams: An Autobiography* (1918; rpt. New York, 1928), pp. 489-98.

14. Charles Dickens, *David Copperfield*, ed. Nina Burgis (Oxford, 1981), ch. 36, p. 451.

III

ROBERT A. COLBY

"Rational Amusement": Fiction vs. Useful Knowledge in the Nineteenth Century

"A GREATER PROPORTION OF THE TEACHING OF THE DAY THAN any of us have yet acknowledged" is derived from the reading of novels, affirmed Anthony Trollope in 1879 in the course of reviewing new collected editions of Thackeray and Dickens for the *Nineteenth Century*.[1] Trollope inherited a long tradition that regarded fiction as "pleasurable instruction in reference to character, emotion, action," to translate the ancient geographer Strabo. Long before church and chapel appropriated the novel to spread their various gospels, classical romances like the *Ethiopica* and *The Golden Ass* were conceived by their authors (as many classical scholars believe) to propagate the worship respectively of the Sun and of the goddess Isis, later to be imitated by the New Testament Apocrypha, this time as a means of disseminating the ideal of Christian asceticism. Medieval anthologies like the *Gesta Romanorum* and *The Golden Legend*, blends of pseudo-history and myth, were clearly intended as aids to faith as well as demonstrations of holy living and holy dying. In its long history, fiction has of course served a variety of secular humanistic functions as well. Medieval tragic romances (among which Chaucer's *Troilus and Criseyde* has proved the most enduring) offered consolation to star-crossed lovers. Works of fiction were among the earliest of conduct books, like that most popular of chivalric romances *Amadis de Gaul*, whose hero served its age as a model of the Christian gentleman. *Euphues* and *Arcadia* furnished pattern figures for their era. Meanwhile, the Renaissance novellas of the continent educated their aristocratic and bourgeois readers to current social issues, one instrument of what has been called "a vogue for ethical propaganda." The more plebian fiction of the sixteenth and seventeenth centuries, like *Lazarillo De Tormes* and its analogues on the continent, and Thomas Deloney's novels in England, with their knights of labor replacing knights errant, offered guidance to the upwardly mobile.[2]

With the eighteenth century, especially through the popularity of Samuel Richardson, the exemplary influence of fiction came to be recognized—an influence put forward with special urgency by promulgators of the novel during the nineteenth century. As we move into the period of revolutions, such writers as Bage, Godwin, and Holcroft—like Frances Trollope, Dickens, Collins, and Reade after them—seized upon the novel as a medium for polemics. Sir Walter Besant, one of the most popular of late Victorian novelists, apparently was aware of this heritage when he observed in his *The Art of Fiction* (1884): "The world has always been taught what little morality it possesses by way of story, fable, apologue, parable, and allegory."[3] The usefulness of fiction had been amply demonstrated by the nineteenth century, but the great age of the novel inaugurated by Sir Walter Scott saw an expansion of the reading public that not only enhanced the prosperity of novelists but raised their sense of calling. Along with popularity the novel now sought prestige. The nineteenth century novel consequently played a part in the democratization of culture characteristic of the age.

By coincidence the first large-scale survey of the novel, John Colin Dunlop's *History of Prose Fiction*—beginning with Xenophon the Ephesian and ending with Mrs. Radcliffe—was published in 1814, the year when *Waverley* came out. A landmark not so much of scholarship as of the recognition of the coming of age of the novel, Dunlop's history stresses that fiction "occupies an important place in the progress of society" and hence is worthy of the notice of the philosopher and scholar, for "by contemplating the fables of a people we have a successive delineation of their prevalent modes of thinking, a picture of their feelings and tastes and habits." Moreover, Dunlop thought of his history as "providing a collection of facts concerning the philosophy of mind, which we study not in an abstract and introspective method, but in a manner certain and experimental."[4] A Glasgow-born officer of the law and product of the Scottish Enlightenment, Dunlop conceived of the novel not as an art form but as a by-product of civilization, as well as ancillary to the then infant science of "human nature," the subject of David Hume's famous philosophical treatise, and as such a kind of laboratory in which ideas about mankind are tested. A few years earlier, Hugh Murray, a countryman of Dunlop's and also a student of cultural history, observed in his treatise *The Morality of Fiction* (1805): "In all stages of human society from the time at least of its emerging from absolute barbarism, no disposition seems more general than the delight taken in works of fiction." As proponent of the classical *utile dulci* principle, Murray went on to conclude that "it appears improbable that so universal an inclination should be altogether of a vicious and hurtful nature, as that there should not be some useful purpose which it is destined to serve." Like Dunlop, Murray thought fiction capable of advancing the knowledge of human nature, and furthermore put forward three kinds of instructional functions for works of fiction that anticipate some of the didactic tasks assumed by nineteenth-century novelists "with a purpose": (1) communicating knowledge of ordinary life and manners—the "biography of private life," that Murray felt supplied the deficiency of history, preoccupied as it tended to be with public events and extraordinary people; (2) proving the truth of some philosophical opinion, or the obligation of some moral principle—the aim of so-called "reasoning fictions"; (3) exhibition of examples of conduct superior to those that are met with in ordinary life.[5] Murray provides no specific examples of these functions in practice, but among novelists listed in the conspectus of literature that makes up the second part of his treatise are: Fanny Burney, whose *Evelina* certainly can be described as a "biography of private life"; Johnson, whose *Rasselas* belongs in the category of "reasoning fictions" along with Godwin's titles, also listed; and Samuel Richardson, whose Sir Charles Grandison had been a subject of debate among novelists and critics, considered a paragon worthy of imitation among some, too good to be true among others.

Such claims for fiction did not of course protect it against attack by clergymen and educators at this time any more than they had in the past. Imaginative writing was on the defensive at least as far back as Lucian's *True History*, which burlesques the alleged authenticity of fabulous travel narratives like *Of the Incredible Things in Thule*. During the time of the late Roman Empire, Julian the Apostate is said to have scorned the fictitious romances circulating round his court. Photius, Patriarch of Constantinople during the ninth century and compiler of the *Bibliotheca Graeca*, praised with one stroke of his quill in commending the *Babylonica* of Iamblichus the Syrian for its "soft and flowing language," and damned with the next by regretting that its author had not turned to "serious subjects" rather than to "puerile fictions." To medieval authorities any writing was suspect that did not serve as a "handmaid of philosophy" or "vassal of theology" (as Chaucer was aware).

Novelists of the generation of Maria Edgeworth, Jane Austen, and Sir Walter Scott had to face the traditional rivalry of "serious" literature and the opposition of religious authorities, which in their time took the form of evangelical revulsion against any kind of "useless" recreation. But more importantly they confronted a growing concern over the reading of the "rising generation," generally assumed from the advent of Richardson to be the main audience for novels.[6] Hugh Murray, for example, in his "Advice to Readers" that accompanies his *The Morality of Fiction* states that the age at which exemplary works of fiction can be perused to greatest advantage is "that which immediately precedes and follows the entrance upon active life, the stage of life when habits are formed that tend to be fixed through life." Such also was the assumption behind the contemporaneous pamphlet by the Reverend Edward Mangin entitled *An Essay on Light Reading As It May Be Supposed To Influence Moral Conduct And*

Literary Taste (1808). To Mangin there was no doubt that the
principal readers of novels and romances ("light literature" as
opposed to "useful arts" and "elegant studies") were the sons
and daughters of tradesmen ("the very life blood of the
realm"). Like many an educator of the previous generation as
well as of his own, he feared for the effect of this reading on
pliant minds, making them obsessed with love and filling
them with false ideas of affluence that ill prepared them for
the actualities of married life. Dismissed as "fit manuals for
the rake and courtesan," along with the works of Mrs. Behn,
are *Tom Jones, Roderick Random, The Sorrows of Werther,*
and *Anna St. Ives.* However, the Reverend Mangin does
concede, if grudgingly, that "proper" fiction can provide
guidance in right living—among his chosen instances being
the novels of Samuel Richardson (which he later edited) and
The Vicar of Wakefield, presumably because of their warnings
to the unwary and their upholding of the values of the
hearthside.[7]

A number of Mangin's contemporaries, performing the
literary equivalent of fighting fire with fire, wrote novels
against novels. The great prototype of the antinovel, or
counter-romance, was of course *Don Quixote*; and included in
Mrs. Barbauld's *British Novelists* (1810) is an eighteenth-
century imitation, *The Female Quixote,* by Charlotte Lennox,
a member of the circle of Dr. Johnson who is thought to have
collaborated on this satire in which the mind of the heroine is
temporarily deranged by reading the romances of Mme. de
Scudéry. The later *Anti-Delphine* (1806), possibly inspired by
the *Anti-Pamela* that followed on the heels of Richardson's
first novel, was an attempt by Medora Gordon Byron to stamp
out the vogue for Mme. de Staël and other French writers of
love stories. The most readable of Maria Edgeworth's *Moral
Tales* is a parody entitled "Angelina; ou l'Amie Inconnue"
whose heroine is purged of a surfeit of the literature of sensibility. Without doubt, the masterpiece of this contragenre is
Eaton Stannard Barrett's *The Heroine; or the Adventures of
the Fair Romance Reader*—read certainly by Jane Austen and
possibly by Scott, remembered in later years by Anthony
Trollope and praised in his lecture "On English Prose Fiction

as a Rational Amusement"—which parodies vi
popular fictional genre of the day: epistolary r
romances, novels of sensibility, picaresque tales
of passages from Mrs. Ann Radcliffe, Regina .
the Misses Cuthbertson, "Monk" Lewis, and Lady Mοɪɢ
among many others.[8]

In treatises, in critiques, and in antinovels, fiction was excoriated for a variety of transgressions against sense, reason, and morality. Novels of sensibility were denounced for playing on the sentimental propensities and allowing too free an outlet to the emotions; gothic romances were condemned for making readers "impatient with the sober facts of history" and deflecting the mind from serious study; love stories (like the *Nouvelle Heloise*) were thought to make vice attractive and virtue dull, and to blunt the moral sense. Domestic novels for their part were blamed for all manner of social ills: for arousing too high expectations in young maidens for potential husbands (e.g., *Pamela*); for making young wives dissatisfied with their marriages (e.g., *Amelia*); for making unmarried women discontented with their appointed lot (e.g., *The Spinster's Journal*, By a Modern Antique); for producing recalcitrant and disobedient children, negligent parents, and divided households (an objection that came to be raised against *Clarissa*, among the earliest and most familiar family novels). Outside the domestic fold, novelists were accused of making workers discontented with their situations, even indisposed toward labor, owing to the mental apathy induced by reading novels.[9]

Lord Brougham, who was to make a strong impact on education for the working classes, ruled out works of imagination by implication in the curriculum outlined in his pamphlet *Practical Observations on the Education of the People* (1825), calling for "a judicious selection from the best authors upon ethics, politics, and history . . . Also elementary treatises on mathematics and natural history." The first resolution of the Society for the Diffusion of Useful Knowledge that was launched the next year under Brougham's direction at a "meeting of Gentlemen" convened at Furnivall Inn stipulated "Elementary Works upon the various branches of Knowledge written in a plain manner, containing the fundamental doctrines with their most useful applications to the purposes of life and the explanation of Natural and Moral Appearances."[10]

As a preliminary step toward inaugurating the SDUK, Lord Brougham sent out an inquiry in 1826 to mechanics' institutes, literary societies, and other reading associations throughout Great Britain, requesting inventories of the contents of their libraries as well as their collecting policies. A sampling of replies offers a spectrum of attitudes toward fiction on the part of upwardly mobile working men and their mentors from the decade before Victoria came to the throne. The catalogs provided by most of the institutions—quite possibly because many of the books listed in them were donated by patrons—tend to lean heavily in the directions that the SDUK was to move in: applied science (introductions to mechanics and architecture), social sciences as they were then constituted (principally law, commerce, geography, history, and antiquities). The humanities were represented mainly by a few treatises on the various branches of philosophy. Poetry, drama, and fiction, while in evidence, were subordinate to, sometimes subsumed under, "useful" studies. An extreme of rigor is represented by the Shropshire Mechanics Institute whose brochure explicitly proscribed "Works of fiction, of Religious Controversy, or of Political Tendency." Somewhat more liberal is the Dunbar Mechanics Institution which declared a predilection for travels, biography, and religious and moral books, along with "scientific instruction, or useful practical information," while making clear that "frivolous, irreligious, and polemical works will be . . . zealously rejected and carefully excluded." Although left unsaid, fiction is presumably to be categorized under the "frivolous."[11]

Other institutions seem to have attempted some *modus vivendi* between the useful and ornamental (or "elegant") reading. The Hackney Literary and Mechanics Institution, for example, announced in its First Year Report that it purchased books "not only on Mechanics but several on Literature in general," thus living up to its name, if in a perfunctory way. The literature section of its catalog stays pretty much on the safe side with such staples as *Don Quixote* and Shakespeare's plays. The only other dramatist represented is George Lillo, whose *The London Merchant: or the History of George Barnwell*, representing the downfall of an apprentice, had an all too obvious cautionary significance for this audience (which Wopsle and Pumblechook later try to impress on young Pip). The poetry selection clearly leans toward the didactic: Pope, Prior, "Beauties of the Poets" (selected by Mr. C. Cary). The fiction collection seems to have been confined to Aikin's *Evenings at Home* and educational works like Fenelon's *Télémaque*. It is probably no coincidence that this much translated didactic adventure story was the book, according to Samuel Smiles, that awakened Jeremy Bentham as a boy to the principles of "utility".

The fullest of the surviving catalogs in the SDUK records, that submitted by the Holbeck Book Society (actually appended to the response of the Leeds Mechanics' Institution), displays wider latitude than most, with Maria Edgeworth's collection of tales entitled *The Parent's Assistant* admitted under Grammar, *The Pilgrim's Progress* under Theology and Ecclesiastical History, while under Natural Philosophy are found semifictional popularizations like the Reverend J. Joyce's *Dialogues on Chemistry*. Although some shelf space was allotted to works of fiction by this society, it is significant that each title is related to some area of the literature of knowledge represented in the collection: e.g., education (Mrs. Trimmer's *Tales*, Maria Edgeworth's *Moral Tales* and *Popular Tales*, Mrs. Hamilton's *The Cottagers of Glenburnie*, Hannah More's *Stories and Tales*); theology (Johnson's *Rasselas*, Godwin's *St. Leon*, a Rosicrucian tale); history (Mme. de Genlis' *Belisarius*, Jeanne Pierre de Florian's *The History of Numa Pompilius*; and travel (*Robinson Crusoe*, *Humphry Clinker*). In general the "light" reading recommended by the mechanics' institutes and literary societies queried by Lord Brougham could be characterized by the phrase employed in the catalog of the Kilmarnock Philosophical Institution—"Rational Recreations," coming close to Trollope's famous defense of fiction as "Rational Amusement."

Trollope's very words are anticipated in a letter submitted

by Sir Benjamin Heywood, one of the founders of the Manchester Mechanics' Institute, to Thomas Coates, Secretary of the SDUK, in 1838, betraying an emergent dissatisfaction with the ironclad publication policies of Lord Brougham's colleagues: "The apathy on the part of the Mechanics must be overcome by a tempting bait, and it is this—making the Mechanics Institutions places of rational amusement which ought to be a great object now."[12] Heywood's letter points up a conflict that had erupted in the SDUK between that society's avowed mission to provide reading for mental improvement and a need expressed by some of its members for recreational reading. Long before this occasion, Charles Knight, Director of Publications for the SDUK, had written to Coates from Manchester, while on a survey tour under its auspices, that the two biographies on their list were in greater demand than their scientific treatises.[13] Consequently, Knight pushed vigorously for a Library of Entertaining Knowledge to supplement (not supplant) the Library of Useful Knowledge. Knight's idea of "entertaining" knowledge was hardly frivolous, but even his rather sober plan for a series to embrace, besides biography, history of peoples, natural history, arts and antiquities met with opposition. "I was sorry to find that it was your intention to diffuse *amusing* publications . . . for the avowed purpose of meeting the wishes of those of your Correspondents who think the treatises are too scientific," fumed an irate bookseller in a letter to Lord Brougham. "If you are to find amusement for those Gentlemen, pray form a society for the diffusion of funny knowledge. And let those Gentlemen have all the fun to themselves. . . . I do hope and trust that you . . . will not condescend to cater for such *Lazy Drones* or incurable blockheads."[14] Nevertheless, the series was established in 1829, headed off by George Lillie Craik's collection of exemplary biographies *The Pursuit of Knowledge under Difficulties* (prototype of such autodidact fiction as *Alton Locke* and *John Halifax, Gentleman*) and Charles Knight's three volumes, *The History of Quadrupeds*. The list went on to Jardine's *Criminal Trials* (real-life "Newgate Novels") and such presumably diverting fare as a treatise on the Elgin Marbles by Sir Henry Ellis, the director of the British

Museum, and T. Keithley's *Secret Societies of the Middle Ages.* A so-called "Minor Series" that would have represented the one bow of the SDUK in the direction of *belles lettres*— with such titles as Defoe's *Journal of the Plague Year* and *Robinson Crusoe,* Mrs. Barbauld's Selections from the *Rambler, Tatler, Idler,* and *Spectator,* along with *Paradise Lost*—was projected, but for reasons that remain obscure never materialized.[15]

Actually Lord Brougham himself recognized the educative potential of fiction, as indicated by his encouragement of Harriet Martineau, the one fiction writer who published under the sponsorship of the SDUK. He regretted that the Society had not published her *Illustrations of Political Economy* which he read and admired, writing to his friend McVey Napier, the editor of the *Edinburgh Review*: "She is as prolific as Scott and reasons as well as A. Smith, she has the best feelings and generally the most correct principles of any of our people."[16] Subsequently, he suggested that she undertake an analogous series centered on the Poor Laws, to spur reforms currently in progress by a Government Commission (part of the background of *Oliver Twist*). Despite this entrée, Miss Martineau's dealings with Brougham's Sub-Committee on Publications over the tales issued collectively as *Poor Laws and Paupers Illustrated* are themselves illustrative of that body's uneasiness with "entertaining" knowledge.

Miss Martineau's letters to the Sub-Committee openly appeal to their passion for fact, conscientiously pointing out the "useful applications" of her tales. She explicitly sets forth the "Groundwork" of the four stories (each based on one of the leading queries raised by the Poor Law Commissioners in their investigations). She clarifies her intention to exhibit examples of maladministration contrasted with the beneficent effects of enlightened capitalism, assuring these gentlemen that "all my representations of parochial abuses & pauper encroachments" can be backed up by unimpeachable authorities. Nevertheless, as is evident from other letters, Miss Martineau's foundations in fact were undermined by Lord Brougham's monitors. Various readers of her manuscript questioned the soundness both of her religious principles and of her economic theories, her knowledge of parish elections, even the accuracy of such picturesque details as Methodists employing divining rods in Cornwall, about which she claimed first-hand knowledge. She was forced to remove a "sneer" at the clergy as too flippant and to cut down the description of a ball in one of the tales (considered space wasting) as well as some love matter regarded as "not much to the purpose." One change she refused to make was the deletion of an incident of infanticide, which she argued was essential to the moral force of her story. One member of the Sub-Committee preferred straightforward lectures on Political Economy offered to the Board by J. H. McCulloch. If Miss Martineau's tales are to be published, continued this referee, they "ought to be carefully revised, or the Society will be lending itself occasionally to the propagation of Bentham's or Utilitarian notions; and there are various loose passages about Religion, and the observance of the Laws, which I think would be improper, in the hands of Youth at least." The outcome appears to have been a compromise, the tales being published in 1833 under the imprint of Miss Martineau's first publisher Charles Fox, though "Under the Superintendence of the Society for the Diffusion of Useful Knowledge." In her preface to the first of them ("The Parish"), the author assures her readers: "As any utility which may be contemplated from the following tale must be impaired by the supposition that the woes and vices it displays are the offspring of an uncontrolled imagination, I beg to state that all is strictly true." She proceeds to invoke the authority of Poor Laws Commissioners Reports as well as the personal testimony of the administrators.[17]

Miss Martineau tried to meet one pervasive objection to fiction—the utilitarian—by utilizing it to "illustrate" social ills with a zeal for documentation that would have made her a social scientist in our day, a zeal moreover carried on by fellow novelists like Frances Trollope, who interviewed workers and labor organizers for *Michael Armstrong the Factory Boy*; Mrs. Gaskell, whose *Mary Barton* grew out of her living among and visiting with her husband's parishioners; Charlotte Brontë, who read back issues of Leeds newspapers to get her facts straight for *Shirley*; and Dickens, who studied reports on the Preston strike and made a field trip to that town for *Hard Times*. Reacting to the recurrent attack on the novel in general by intellectuals as shallow, one of Miss Martineau's contemporaries, Letitia Elizabeth Landon, promoted it as an adjunct to the March of Mind. A character in her *Romance and Reality* (1830) remarks: "Who that reflects at all can deny that the novel is the Aaron's rod that is rapidly swallowing all the rest? It has supplied the place of drama. . . . Have we a theory, it is developed by means of a character; an opinion it is set forth in a chapter, not a scene." The epigraph to a later reprint of *Romance and Reality* in Bentley's Standard Novels reads: "Pictures of life and manners, and stories of adventure, are more eagerly received by the many than graver productions."; but in the novel itself, Miss Landon's spokesman Edward Lorraine, caught by an elder relaxing over "trashy novels," places his favorite reading matter on a lofty shelf with "graver productions," as not merely "a pleasant hour's amusement," but by now "the very highest effort—the popular vehicle for thought, feeling, and observation—the one used by our first-rate writers." His chosen instances are Disraeli's *Vivian Grey* and Bulwer's *Pelham* which in particular have "enlarged the boundaries and pour fresh life into the novel. . . . There had been fashionable novels, and of real life so called; but they wanted either knowledge, or talent to give that knowledge likeness," to which his companion adds: "I know no writer [besides Bulwer] who has united so much philosophy with so much imagination."[18] Indeed, Bulwer invited such an identification, contending in the "Dedicatory Epistle" to his historical romance *Devereux* (1829) that he had composed it as well as its predecessor, *The Disowned*, while "in the midst of metaphysical studies and investigations" and was at one time contemplating a book on philosophy. It is clear that the society novel was aspiring to become something more than "the amber which served to preserve the ephemeral modes and caprices of the passing day . . . a valuable addition to our lighter literature," in the words of one observer of the passing parade in Mrs. Gore's *Women as They Are* (1830).

Much later George Eliot, recollecting this period, was to

refer, in "Janet's Repentance," to "the light vehicles of weighty morals" published by the evangelical authoress Eliza Pratt. George Eliot was aware that the novel as it grew in popularity had to justify itself to clergymen as well as to educators and social reformers. If to humanitarians and social activists fiction tended to remove us too much from the real world and its problems, and if to the philosophical it deflected us from serious ideas, to the religious it diverted us from the City of God. One extremist denounced novels for deluding men with "romantic notions of the perfectibility of human nature" in opposition to the doctrine of original sin and for attributing man's fortunes to luck or fate instead of to God's judgment.[19] Mrs. Sarah Ellis (better known for *Daughters of England, Mothers of England*) cited among the abuses of the novel, in "An Apology for Fiction" that introduces her *Pictures of Private Life* (1833), the tendency of authors to make the moral virtues arise "solely from an amiable heart, without the assistance of religion, or the control of good principle."[20] The stories that follow were intended to correct this abuse with their case studies of households lacking proper religious instruction and their demonstration that secular learning alone is insufficient to support life. Like a medieval "vassal of theology," Mrs. Ellis reconciles herself to writing fiction, "the most humble means of moral instruction," on the ground that "it finds itself to the dense multitude who close their eyes upon the introduction of purer light."

Many others sought the way to the "dense multitude," as is verified by a review essay in *Fraser's Magazine* toward the end of the decade, that discusses, among other works, Newman's *Loss and Gain*, Elizabeth Harris's *From Oxford to Rome* (to which Newman's novel is a reply), Lady Georgina Fullerton's *Ellen Middleton* and *Grantley Manor*, Elizabeth Sewell's *Amy Herbert* and *Margaret Percival*, the Reverend Sewell's *Hawkstone*, as well as the anonymous *Rest in the Church* and *Steepleton; or High Church and Low Church: being the Present Tendencies of Parties Exhibited in the History of Frank Faithful*. This reviewer had basis for his observation that "for all who might wish to acquire the current controversial small-talk without the labour of reading grave works of theology," the press was providing "abundant instruction in the shape of novels and storybooks illustrating the doctrines and the practices of the newly risen 'ism,'" and that moreover these are to be added to "the materials which must be mastered by the future Church historian who would qualify himself for describing the workings of the late controversies on the mind of our generation."[21] Somewhat later, Charlotte Yonge, one of the most respected religious novelists of the Victorian period, distinguished between a "religious tale" laden with controversy and forcing its moral and "a tale constructed on a strong basis of religious principle which attempts to give a picture of life as it really is seen by Christian eyes."[22] Edward Maitland had no hesitation in calling his fictitious spiritual autobiography, *The Pilgrim and the Shrine*, a "new Aid to Faith."[23] Toward the end of the century, Walter Pater could categorically pronounce: "Who will deny that to trace the influence of religion upon human character is one of the legitimate functions of the novel?" in his review of Mrs. Humphry Ward's *Robert Elsmere*, undoubtedly with his own soon-to-appear *Marius the Epicurean* in mind.[24]

It is evident that the novel was quite *discutable* long before Henry James, and that nineteenth-century readers were expected to chew and digest them, not swallow them like puddings. Actually, quite a burden was placed upon the shoulders of "puerile fictions" owing to the strong influence attributed to reading. Assumptions as to the impressionableness of readers, which made some educators fearful for the effect of the novel, eventually redounded to its favor. Even so vehement an attacker of novels as the Reverend Andrew Reed, author of a once controversial pseudobiography, *No Fiction* (1820), indirectly justified them by quoting Dr. Johnson on his title page as to the effectiveness of "familiar histories" that may be turned to "greater use than the solemnities of professed morality, and convey the knowledge of vice and virtue with more efficacy than axioms and definitions." "Familiar history" is certainly one direction that the nineteenth century novel took, frequently adopting the guise of biography and autobiography. Hugh Murray, a supporter of fiction, as has been noticed, thought that the most important instructional function it served, of the three he proposed, was as an "exhibition of examples of conduct." He attributed the effectiveness of fiction as moral exemplum to man's natural imitative faculty: "So strong is the propensity to imitation, that it will take place even in regard to persons whom he views with a great deal of indifference, provided that they be continually before his eyes." Going back to theories of Locke and Lord Kames, Murray asserts the superior force of concrete impression over abstract idea, a principle that was to become a commonplace to apologists for fiction, as crystallized in the motto that Harriet Martineau attached to her *Illustrations of Political Economy*: "Example before precept."

As for the distrust of imagination—if, as moralists warned, images could inflame passions, it was demonstrated on the positive side that they could bring light to the mind, enhancing the power of the novel, along with poetry, as an educational instrument. Unlike the romancer of old or the contemporary purveyor of Gothicism, the modern novelist of real life, it was argued by its defenders, uses his imagination not to conjure up never-never lands but to vivify the world around us. Even the emotional susceptibilities of readers, which some educators feared were played on to excess by novelists, could be channeled to arouse sympathy for humanitarian causes, as was recognized by such writers as Charlotte Elizabeth Tonna, Frances Trollope, and of course Dickens. Moreover, the growing custom of family reading, with novels written expressly to be read aloud by parents to children, as well as representing all ages in their casts of characters, guaranteed their being adaptable to young ears. The status attained by the novel at mid-century, as well as the prospect held out for it, are both suggested by a reviewer in *Fraser's Magazine* who wrote, "The novel, if it would take the place in literature which seems marked for it, must become the fearless though unformal censor of the age and hold society in check by mercilessly exposing the errors, weaknesses, absurdities, excesses, and even crimes, which disfigure and disturb it." Moreover, continued this writer, the novelist should "compel the reader to reflect on the tendencies of the period in which we live, and ask himself towards what goal it is that events are now precipitating society."[25] This was written in 1848 but could have described Trollope's *The Way We Live Now*—published twenty-five years later.

"The influence of fiction is unbounded. Even the minds of well-informed people are often more stored with characters from acknowledged fiction than from history, or biography, or the real life around them," says Sir Arthur Helps's spokesman Mr. Milverton in *Friends in Council*,[26] attesting to the omnipresence as well as prestige of fiction ten years after Queen Victoria's coronation. "We have become a novel-reading people from the Prime Minister down to the last appointed scullery maid. . . . Poetry also we read and history, biography and the social and political news of the day. But all our other reading put together hardly amounts to what we read in novels," declared Anthony Trollope in 1870.[27] However, in this same lecture Trollope makes clear that the "Rational Amusement," while widespread in its reach, was still suspect in some quarters as wasteful of time if not downright pernicious. Although the Society for the Diffusion of Useful Knowledge had closed its doors in 1846, it continued to cast its shadow over novelists, at least the serious ones concerned with "the useful applications to the purposes of life" of their work. In this connection it is significant that apologists for fiction tended to promote it not for what it was uniquely able to do but for accomplishing better what competing nonfiction attempted. In various ways the worlds of fact and fiction impinged upon one another in readers' minds. The tendency of institutional libraries to select fiction that was ancillary to theology, philosophy, history, and travel has been noted. With the emergence of the literary reviews, readers became accustomed to seeing fiction interspersed among articles on politics, religion, and topics of the day. Sometimes novelists, notably Lever, Thackeray, Trollope, and Dickens, reflected in their stories issues under discussion elsewhere in the journals they edited or contributed to. The most famous of the circulating library proprietors proclaimed in a characteristic advertisement: "This Library comprises all the BEST WORKS OF THE PRESENT SEASON and nearly every readable book of the past thirty years. The preference is given to works of

History, Biography, Religion, Philosophy, Travel and Adventure: the best works of fiction are also freely added."[28] While Mudie betrayed a certain condescension toward what was undoubtedly the most profitable of his wares, his notice that reached the weekly and monthly magazine reading public had the dual effect of elevating "the best works of fiction" into the company of what Matthew Arnold referred to as the best that is known and thought in the world and of placing fiction in rivalry with the prose of ideas.

Among Mudie's categories travel and adventure in particular have lent coloration to fiction from its beginnings (e.g., the Homeric epics, *Of the Incredible Things in Thule*). Sometimes, as with Lucian, Rabelais, and Swift, travel fiction was intended to parody the tall tales of travelers' supposedly true narratives. In the Victorian period, however, it served the educational function of opening up foreign lands and providing vicarious travel for the homebound reader, as Thackeray recognized in his essay "On Some French Fashionable Novels," in which he sees the society novel as an inexpensive substitute for the Grand Tour: "On the wings of a novel from the next circulating library [the reader] sends his imagination a-gadding, and gains acquaintance with people and manners whom he could not hope otherwise to know."[29] Thackeray donned the wings himself, drawing freely on his own travels in his peripatetic and cosmopolitan novels. Travel propels many a *bildungsroman* of his age, e.g., Bulwer's *The Caxtons* and *My Novel*, George Henry Lewes's *Ranthorpe*, James Hannay's *Singleton Fontenoy*, and Charlotte Brontë's *Villette*. The sore tried continental venturers of Charles Lever's *The Dodd Family Abroad* (an imitation of *Humphry Clinker*) may have made some less affluent or leisured readers relieved that they stayed home.

Thackeray suggested that although travel books often are confined to the surface of life, the novelist is in a position to make us more intimately acquainted with "the inward ways, thoughts, and customs" of foreign people. Something like this argument was put forward to establish the advantage of the novelist over another rival, the historian. Scott of course, with his prefaces detailing his sources, precise documentation, and factual digressions, attempted from the outset a *modus vivendi* with the historical scholar.[30] His contemporary and countryman John Galt went to the extreme of characterizing his *Annals of the Parish* (1821) as "a kind of treatise on the history of society in the west of Scotland during the reign of George III." Works of fiction continued long afterwards to be camouflaged variously as annals, chronicles, histories, and narratives. However, a rather neat division of the province of Clio was suggested at the time when Scott made his debut as a novelist by John Dunlop, who pointed out in his *The History of Prose Fiction*: "History treats of man, as it were in the mass, and the individuals whom it paints are regarded merely or principally in a public light, without taking into consideration their private feelings, tastes, or habits."[31] The concentration on "familiar" history as against public history, on the fortunes of individuals and families, rather than courts, armies, and states, came to be the hallmark of the historical novelist. This emphasis is pointed up in typical titles by one of the most popular historical romancers of the age, Harrison Ainsworth: *Cardinal Pole, or the Days of Philip and Mary*; *Boscobel, or the Royal Oak, A Tale of the Year 1651*; *Guy Fawkes, or the Gunpowder Treason*; and *Beau Nash, or Bath in the Eighteenth Century*, as well as of the prolific G. P. R. James: *Henry of Guise, or The States of Blois*; *The Huguenot, A Tale of French Protestants*; *Henry Smeaton, A Jacobite Story of the Reign of George the First*.[32]

"I wonder shall History ever pull off her periwig and cease to be court-ridden? Shall we see something of France and England besides Versailles and Windsor?" asks Henry Esmond at the beginning of his reminiscences. "Why shall History go on kneeling to the end of time? I am for having her rise up off her knees, and take a natural posture: not to be for ever performing cringes and congees like a Court-chamberlain. . . . In a word, I would have History familiar rather than heroic." In his anti-Carlylean *The Cloister and the Hearth*, Charles Reade purports to be resurrecting "obscure heroes, philosophers, and martyrs" buried in dusty annals: "The general reader cannot feel them, they are presented so curtly and coldly; they are not like breathing stories appealing to his heart. . . . Thus records of prime truths remain a dead letter to plain folk; the writers have left so much to the imagination, and imagination is a rare gift. Here, then, the writer of fiction may be of use to the public—as an interpreter." Possessed by the spirit of history, George Eliot speculates in *Romola*: "There is knowledge . . . to be had in the streets below, on the beloved *marmi* in front of the churches, and under the sheltering Loggie, where surely our citizens have still their gossip, and debates, their bitter and merry jests as of old. For are not the well-remembered buildings all there? The changes have not been so great in those uncounted years. I will go down and hear,—I will tread the familiar pavement, and hear once again the speech of Florentines." Harrison Ainsworth really brought the idea of "familiar history" home in his address to young people in an issue of *Ainsworth's Magazine* where he informed them that his tales were intended "to exhibit many of those pictures of manners and social habit in bygone time, by which the happy instrument of introducing every young reader to his own great-grandfather."[33] Occasionally, a novelist may seem to have overstepped his province, like Bulwer who not only claimed to consult original authorities for his romances but even presumed to correct Sismondi and Gibbon in *Rienzi*. If now and then a historian like Francis Palgrave denounced the historical novel as "melodrama set to the sound of kettledrums and trumpets,"[34] Thackeray, for one example, was respected enough to be invited by Adam Black to contribute the article on the Age of Anne to the *Encyclopedia Britannica* on the basis of *Henry Esmond*, and that "teeming parent of romance" G. P. R. James for a time occupied the post of Historiographer Royal.

In his lecture "On English Prose Fiction as a Rational Amusement," Trollope complains that attacks on novels come not only from "grave and thoughtful" writers but from clergymen in their pulpits as well. Indeed, during the mid-Victorian period, the preacher was the primary rival of the novelist, published sermons accounting for at least half of the product of the English presses. It is understandable, therefore, why Trollope emphasized his own function as lay preacher. In fact, Trollope, like Richardson in his time, thought that the novelist was taking the place of the preacher in society. Unlike Richardson, however, he did not feel that the clergy were derelict in their duty but that they lacked the novelist's power to sway multitudes. "Teaching to be efficacious must be popular," he later wrote. "I am inclined to think that the lessons inculcated by the novelists go deeper than most others."[35] Dinah Mulock Craik, whose exemplary *John Halifax, Gentleman* enjoyed great popular success, testified: "It were idle to reason how the thing has come about; but, undeniably, the modern novel is one of the most important moral agents of the community. The essayist may write for his hundreds; the preacher preach to his thousands; but the novelist counts his audience by millions. His power is three-fold—over heart, reason, and fancy."[36] Alfred Austin (later to become Poet Laureate) proclaimed not only proudly but defiantly in one of his novels: "The old teachers are largely dispossessed of their authority. The pulpit no longer has the monopoly of instruction. You have ousted the preachers, and you are standing aloft in their stead." And he throws out a challenge to novelists: "Have a care that you preach the right sermons!"[37] That self-styled "week-day preacher" Thackeray, referring to himself in chapter 8 of *Vanity Fair* as "the moralist holding forth on the cover" (alluding of course to the wrapper on the monthly parts depicting a clown addressing a heterogeneous audience from a barrel top), can be taken as emblematical. Edward Maitland, son of an evangelical minister, rebel from the orthodoxy of his childhood, went so far as to affirm in *The Pilgrim and the Shrine*: "The highest teaching of our age is not to be found in sermons, for Humanity has outlived Dogma, Faith has survived Belief."[38] All of these and other writers could have given to their novels the title of one of Miss Mulock's nonfiction books, *Sermons Out of Church*. Whatever their differences in belief, there was a consensus among them that the novelist was better equipped than the cloistered clergyman to apply religion to real life situations.[39]

In the secular realm, the conjunction of fiction with topical journalism was evident at least as early as Harriet Martineau's *Illustrations of Political Economy*. This alliance was taken for granted by the philosopher Thomas Hill Green who, though he had some misgivings about the intellectual weight of the novel, observed in his Chancellor's Prize Essay presented at Balliol College in 1862, "The Value and Influence of Works of Fiction in Modern Times," that by calling attention to human suffering in advance even of the daily newspaper, the novelist "becomes an agent of social reform."[40] Green singles out for special mention Thackeray, who in *The Newcomes* "told the miseries of the marriage market before the *Times* took them up," but he also cites Kingsley and Scott, as well as Fielding and Defoe before them. In the mid-1860s a writer for the *Saturday Review*, addressing himself to "The Uses of Fiction," recalled that John Stuart Mill thirty years back had written that the two most direct ways to influence society were as a member of Parliament or as the editor of a London newspaper. By now, in the opinion of this writer, the novelist had outdistanced both journalists and statesmen when it came to reaching the hearts as well as the minds of the public, because novels are more widely read, especially by women; they can be "bolted" and still leave an impression on the mind, unlike articles and speeches that demand intense concentration; they can be read over a more extended period of time; their concrete imagery makes them more vivid, hence easier to commit to memory than the prose of ideas (this last is a harking back to the arguments of Hugh Murray and other early apologists).[41]

With the late Victorian period, a stepped-up journalism furnished a new and lucrative medium for fiction writers—Tillotson's Fiction Bureau, although it is associated with popular novelists like M. E. Braddon, Rhoda Broughton, and Marie Corelli, also provided an outlet for Stevenson and Hardy—but at the same time vied for the leisure of the beneficiaries of Forster's Education Bill and other busy readers with limited attention spans. Among novelists, Sir Walter Besant expressed concern over this source of competition in his article "The Value of Fiction" contributed to *Belgravia* in the early seventies. By this time the tabloid was undercutting the so-called "sensation" novelists whose stock-in-trade was precisely that purveyed by *Lloyd's Weekly Newspaper* and the

Illustrated Police News: fraud, murder, and sex. In protecting the province of the novelist from the incursion of the Fleet Street hack, Besant elevated even Mrs. Wood, Mrs. Braddon (the editor of the journal to which he was contributing), and company to the level of moral teachers. Even their most sordid subject matter, Besant argued, is invested with "the dramatic touch, the stroke of genius which makes the actors alive, and not mere puppets"; furthermore, the novelist probes the motives behind crime and sin whereas the news sheets tend to produce mere circumstantial accounts of the nefarious incidents they report "without the concomitant circumstances which explain or mitigate the guilt, and which may warn the reader."[42]

The warning to the reader represents the cautionary aspect of what is probably the longest standing didactic role of fiction, the exemplary biography, with a tradition extending as far back at least as the Greek *erotika pathemata* centering on virtuous lovers who pass successfully through a series of ordeals (including assaults on their virginity) before they are rewarded at the altar. In the nineteenth century, when life tended to be conceived as a continuation school of morality, fiction became ancillary to ethical treatises like *Aids to Development, or Mental and Moral Instruction, Hints towards the Formation of Character, Shades of Character, Improvement of the Mind, Education of the Feelings,* and *The Discipline of Life.* A prototypical work for Victorian biography and fiction alike was George Lillie Craik's *The Pursuit of Knowledge under Difficulties,* a popular collection of life histories first published, as has been noted, under the auspices of the SDUK. This edifying work has been likened by Richard D. Altick to the saints' legends of medieval Europe, "a vehicle of consolation, guidance and inspiration, though couched in secular and primarily materialistic terms."[43] Although Craik tends to give short shrift here to writers of fiction, his life histories conceived as models of achievement, his stress on self-education, on the efficacy of struggle—mental as well as physical—in the molding of character, on contact with the living world, on the humanizing of knowledge, and, above all, on moral culture, anticipate the form and

content of many Victorian novels. One of the more icono-
clastic of them, to be sure, mocks Craik in an aside to the
reader in his most famous novel: "The pursuit of fashion
under difficulties would be a fine theme for any very great
person who had the wit, the leisure, and the knowledge of the
English language necessary for the compiling of such a
history" (*Vanity Fair*, chapter 37). An early reader who took
Craik seriously was Samuel Smiles, eventually author of *the*
inspirational best-seller of the century, *Self-Help* (1859), expressly modeled on Craik's work of anecdotal portraiture but
addressed more to "the ordinary business and pursuits of
common life" as "illustrated by examples of conduct and
character drawn from reading, observation, and experience."[44]
Although, like Craik, Smiles tended to elevate life above literature, he did remark in his later book *Character* (1871),
echoing Carlyle: "What are all the novels that find such a
multitude of readers, but so many fictitious biographies?
What are all the dramas that people crowd to see, but so much
acted biography?" In fact, believing so firmly in the school of
experience, Smiles was surprised "that the highest genius
should be employed on the fictitious biography, and so much
commonplace ability on the real."[45]

Smiles inadvertently seems to have accounted for why the
authors of *Jane Eyre, An Autobiography*; *The Personal
History of David Copperfield, the Younger, of Blunderstone
Rookery (Which He Never Meant To Be Published On Any
Account)*; *The History of Pendennis. His Fortunes and His
Misfortunes, His Friends and His Greatest Enemy*; or *The
Ordeal of Richard Feverel. A History of Father and Son* had
little to fear from the competition of "real" biographers.
"Examples, which neither man nor woman will follow when
set before them in a more peremptory manner, sometimes
make an imperceptible impression conveyed unobtrusively,"
declared a forgotten novelist of this period. "Precepts un-
heeded in dogmatic form may be acknowledged when presenting themselves in agreeable society, and illustrated by what
dramatists call a 'striking situation.'"[46] As Harriet Martineau
provided *Illustrations of Political Economy*, many a nineteenth-century novelist, it is clear, saw his function as furnish-

ing "Illustrations of Character." Unlike Samuel Smiles, who believed that "the authentic picture of any human being's life and experience ought to possess an interest greatly beyond that which is fictitious, inasmuch as it has the charm of reality," Walter Besant, the staunchest of late Victorian upholders of "the Value of Fiction" as well as of authors' rights, argued that the novel offers both fuller characterization and greater candor than the biography. Whereas the biographer "describes his man as he thinks he wishes to be considered," suppressing undesirable traits, the novelist, Besant points out, is freer to follow his character to "its legitimate consequences" precisely because it is of his own creation.[47] Besant was writing of course in the pre-Stracheyan days when biographers were hampered by the *nil nisi bonum* code.[48]

"I like to do my best for the diffusion of useless knowledge," quips a character in a novel of the late 1860s, a lonely woman who has invited two young girls from her neighborhood to partake of her library of hundreds of novels, as an inducement to stay with her as house guests and divide her desolation. This widely, but by her own admission not wisely, read lady (Mrs. Troubridge by name) adds: "Not that I consider novel reading really useless . . . I only contrast it with what is called useful knowledge, which I hated at school."[49] Mrs. Troubridge's unnamed schoolmaster sounds like a disciple of Lord Brougham. By the time she had grown up, the novelist was abroad, as she was aware, and the best along with the worst were dedicated to making their product useful. Before Oscar Wilde came forward to proclaim the utter uselessness of the arts, novelists served their growing public as, among other things, teachers of history, popular philosophers, political commentators, social critics, lay analysts, vocational counselors, and above all as guides to character and conduct.

1. "Novel Reading," *Nineteenth Century* (1879; rpt. George L. Barnett, ed., *Nineteenth-Century Novelists on the Novel* [New York, 1971], p. 214).

2. For historical background I have found the following sources especially useful: John Colin Dunlop, *History of Prose Fiction* (London, 1814); T. M. Warren, *A History of the Novel Previous to the Seventeenth Century* (1895; rpt. New York, 1969); Arthur Heiserman, *The Novel before the Novel* (Chicago, 1977); Robert J. Clements and Joseph Gibaldi, eds., *Anatomy of*

the Novella (New York, 1977); Walter Davis, *Idea and Act in Elizabethan Fiction* (Princeton, N. J., 1969); Rowland Prothero (Lord Ernle), *The Light Reading of Our Ancestors* (1927; rpt. New York, 1970).

3. Sir Walter Besant, *The Art of Fiction* (Boston, 1884), p. 9. Originally delivered as a lecture at the Royal Institution, London, 25 April 1884.

4. Dunlop, *History of Prose Fiction*.

5. Hugh Murray, *The Morality of Fiction* (Edinburgh, 1805), Introduction, pp. 5–7. Murray attempted to put his theories into practice with indifferent results in his two novels *The Swiss Emigrants* (1804), whose hero exemplifies the ideal of altruism against a background of the Revolution of 1798, and *Corasmin* (1814), centered on a disillusioned statesman who chooses early retirement rather than compromise his principles.

6. E.g., this anathema by the Quaker polemical writer John Kendall: "The hurt which attends the reading of these books [novels] is like to be great, to the youth in particular . . . when it appears that they are intended merely for the purpose of amusement, and rather to banish serious thought and reflections, than to strengthen them in us; it gives room to fear great harm will come from this method of spending our precious time; much the same as by seeing and hearing the action and speeches of the stage" (John Kendall, *Remarks on the Prevailing Custom of Attending Stage Entertainments; Also On The Present Taste For Reading Romances And Novels*, 3d ed. [London, 1801], p. 14).

The only kinds of novels that Kendall made allowance for were those "exhibiting Christian characters," as did an increasing number from the early nineteenth century on.

7. (London, 1808), p. 13, pp. 31–46.

8. For a discussion of these and other antinovels, see my *Fiction with a Purpose: Major and Minor Nineteenth-Century Novels* (Bloomington, 1967), pp. 42–52.

9. For example, Scott refers to strictures by others on novel reading as conducive to "an indisposition to real history and useful literature" in his chapter on Fielding in *Lives of the Novelists*, and in chapter 3 of *Waverley* is himself critical of his hero's "desultory" reading of romances and memoirs that inadequately trains him for "concentrating the powers of his mind for earnest investigation"; Jane Austen pokes fun in *Love and Freindship* at naïve ideas of love and courtship in the novels of her time; in *Practical Education* Maria Edgeworth remarks that the novel-reading habit makes young girls mistake "plain William and Thomas for my Beverley" (2, 51); Clara Reeve, among others, complained that some novels had the effect of making young people look down upon their guardians (*The Progress of Romance*, 2, 78–79). In a late eighteenth century American pamphlet, *Observations on Novel-Reading In An Essay Written By A Member Of The Belles-Lettres Society Of Dickinson College At Carlisle, Pennsylvania In The Year 1789* (Philadelphia, 1792), it is alleged that young men who read novels are loath to enter trades and professions, becoming so imbued with a false sense of their gentility. For a useful overview of attacks on fiction in the late eighteenth and early nineteenth centuries, see John Tinnon Taylor, *Early Opposition to the English Novel* (New York, 1943), ch. 3. None of the

denouncers of fiction went so far as the anonymous author of *Observations on Novel-Reading* (see above), which concluded with a proposal that Congress impose a tax on publishers, importers, or sellers of novels.

10. Quoted in Monica Grobel, "The Society for the Diffusion of Useful Knowledge, 1826–1846, and Its Relation to Adult Education in the First Half of the Nineteenth Century" (M.A. thesis, University College, London, 1932), p. 18.

11. The content of this and the next two paragraphs is summarized from the *Replies from Mechanics' Institutes to a Series of Questions (on the General Conduct of their Libraries and the Use of Books), sent out by Lord Brougham* (SDUK Papers, Watson Library, University College, London).

12. Benjamin Heywood to Thomas Coates, 12 May 1838 (SDUK Reports, Manual Mech. B).

13. 5 June 1829, from Manchester (SDUK General Committee Minutes I, 27 July 1829).

14. William Bate of Coggeshall to Henry Brougham, 22 May 1828 (SDUK Letters, 1828).

15. SDUK papers . . . Minor Series, 1827.

16. Lord Brougham to McVey Napier, 17 November 1832, quoted in Grobel, "Society for the Diffusion of Useful Knowledge," p. 260; additional detail is found in Vera Wheatley, *The Life and Work of Harriet Martineau* (Fair Lawn, N. J., 1957), p. 85.

17. Summarized from SDUK Correspondence (Martineau).

18. (London, 1831), ch. 17 (Edward Lorraine to Mr. Morland).

19. Francis Barnett, *The Hero of No Fiction* (Boston, 1823), Introduction.

20. Sarah Ellis, First series (London, 1833), p. iii.

21. "Religious Stories," *Fraser's Magazine*, August 1848, p. 150. Abundant confirmation is supplied by the 121 titles in the reprint series *Novels of Faith and Doubt*, ed. Robert Lee Wolff (New York: Garland, 1977) classified under such rubrics as: Catholicism, Anti-Catholicism, Tractarianism, Broad Church, and Evangelicalism.

22. "Children's Literature of the Last Century," *Macmillan's Magazine* 20 (1869): 310; quoted in Elizabeth Jay, *The Religion of the Heart: Anglican Evangelicalism and the Nineteenth-Century Novel* (Oxford, 1979), p. 3.

23. Edward Maitland, *The Pilgrim and the Shrine* (London, 1868), Preface.

24. Walter Pater, " 'Robert Elsmere,' " *Essays from 'The Guardian'* (London, 1901), pp. 56–57.

25. "Recent Novels," *Fraser's Magazine*, July 1848, p. 33. The novels reviewed are *Rose, Blanche, and Violet*, by George Henry Lewes; *The Half-Sisters*, by Geraldine Jewsbury; and *Leonora*, by Mrs. Marsh.

26. Sir Arthur Helps, *Friends in Council*, First Series (London, 1847), 1:203 ("Fiction").

27. "On English Prose Fiction as a Rational Amusement," *Four Lectures*, ed. Morris L. Parrish (London, 1938), p. 108. First delivered in Edinburgh, 28 January 1870.

28. This particular advertisement is quoted from the *Saturday Review*, 20 July 1861, but it recurs with variations throughout the periodical press.

29. William Makepeace Thackeray, "On Some French Fashionable Novels," *Paris Sketch Book, Works* (Biographical Edition), 5:83.

30. An American educator, addressing the members of the New York Mercantile Society early in the 1830s, referred to the common authorial phrase "founded on fact" as "a sort of deceptive epithet to cheat those who wish to become acquainted with history, and have not the courage to sit down and study it." Remarking on "the cormorant appetite" for Scott's romances, he predicated that "even our own wonderful history must be illustrated by tales and stories," as it came to be by Scott's American imitators, notably Cooper, Bird, Cooke, and Kennedy. This lecturer generally approved of the trend, even praising Mrs. Radcliffe for having "brought into her work a spirit of Italian history, which was full of romance and taste" (Samuel L. Knapp, *Advice in the Pursuits of Literature* [New York, 1832], pp. 16, 165).

31. Dunlop, *History of Prose Fiction*, Introduction, p. 3.

32. Sir James Stephen, professor of modern history at Cambridge (father of Leslie and James Fitzjames Stephen and grandfather of Virginia Woolf), remarked, in the course of a lecture to members of The Young Men's Christian Association in Exeter Hall in 1853, with a combination of awe and dismay on "the hundred and odd volumes" strewn about the stalls of W. H. Smith & Sons railway libraries ("the Smithery") "in which the history of France may be read in the shape of so many consecutive novels" (*On Desultory and Systematic Reading* [London, 1854], p. 8).

33. "To Our Readers," *Ainsworth's Magazine*, July 1842, pp. i–ii.

34. Quoted in James C. Simmons, *The Novelist as Historian: A Study of the Early Victorian Historical Fiction, 1828-1850* (The Hague: Mouton, 1974), p. 225. Another eminent historian of the time, John Richard Green, once dubbed the novel "history without documents—nothing to prove it."

35. Barnett, "Novel Reading," p. 201.

36. "To Novelists—and A Novelist [George Eliot]," *The Unkind Word, and Other Stories* (Leipzig, 1869), pp. 296-97.

37. *Jessie's Expiation* (1867), 1:87.

38. *The Pilgrim and the Shrine* 3:392-93.

39. Their conviction seems to have been supported by the findings of a survey conducted by the Free Libraries of Birmingham, Darlington, Portsmouth, and Liverpool of the reading interests of their patrons in the late 1880s. As reported by the *Pall Mall Gazette*: "It may be noticed as an illustration of the saying that novelists have usurped the functions of preachers, that in nearly all the public libraries, prose fiction is in most demand, religion the least" ("What Books Are Read Most" in *"The Best Hundred Books" By The Best Judges, Pall Mall Gazette* Extra, no. 24, American Edition [Boston, 1890], p. 25).

40. *The Value and Influence of Works of Fiction in Modern Times*, ed. Fred Newton Scott (Ann Arbor, 1911), pp. 68-69. As a "creator of public sentiment," Green continues, the novelist removes "barriers of ignorance

and apathy" and becomes thereby a molder of public opinion. Green is thought to be the prototype of Mr. Grey in *Robert Elsmere*.

41. *Saturday Review*, 15 September 1866, p. 323. The writer refers to Mills's essay "Civilization," which originally appeared in the *Westminster Review*, April 1836.

42. *Belgravia* 16 (1871/72): 48-51.

43. *The English Common Reader* (Chicago, 1957), p. 242.

44. *The Autobiography of Samuel Smiles*, ed. Thomas Mackay (New York, 1905), p. 222.

45. Samuel Smiles, *Character* (1871) ch. 10. In *Self-Help* he is ambivalent toward the novel, on the one hand discouraging overindulgence in it as "a sort of intellectual dram drinking," on the other upholding it at its best as "a high intellectual pleasure" (chapter 11). Smiles himself, according to his *Autobiography*, was an avid reader of fiction.

46. Charles Clarke, *Myra Gray; or, Sown in Tears, Reaped in Joy* (1870), 1, ch. 2.

47. That a rapid change of attitude towards biography ensued within the following decade can be illustrated by the following passages: A book of advice on reading published in the 1880s warns the reader of biography that "the biographer is commonly, though less commonly than once, a eulogist. He praises the virtues, and with a light touch passes over the defects, of his subjects" (Charles F. Thwing, *The Reading of Books: Its Pleasures, Profits, and Perils* [Boston, 1883], p. 13). Yet by 1897 a librarian, addressing the International Library Conference in London, could remark that as a result of standards of exactitude set by advances in the sciences, "We today find the candor once rare in biography steadily growing common" (George Iles, *The Appraisal of Literature* [New York, 1897], p. 3). His examples are Hare's *Story of My Life*, and Purcell's *Life of Cardinal Manning*.

48. Smiles, "The Value of Fiction," *Character*, p. 51. The quotation from Smiles is from *Character*, chapter 10. Besant's point is made from another angle in a contemporaneous novel where it is observed that many worthy men refrain from writing autobiographies "from the laudable and conscientious dread of overstepping in their delineations the bounds of imperishable verity and incurring thereby a taint of moral guilt." They turn instead to fiction which offers "an allowable space over which the mind may expatiate with full license, and if keeping within the limits of good taste and probabilities, may present many useful lessons to the world" (Grace Webster, *A Skeleton Novel; or The Undercurrents of Society* [1866], ch. 26, opening paragraph).

This may help account for the preponderance of feigned autobiographies by writers who were not inherently novelists, e.g., Frederic Denison Maurice's *Eustace Conway*, William Edmonstoune Aytoun's *Norman Sinclair*, William Delafield Arnold's *Oakfield*, James Hannay's *Singleton Fontenoy*, Edward Maitland's *The Pilgrim and the Shrine*, and John Henry Newman's *Loss and Gain*.

49. Catherine Ellen Spence, *The Author's Daughter* (1868), ch. 14 ("Novels and Real Life").

IV

DONALD J. GRAY

Macaulay's *Lays of Ancient Rome* and the Publication of Nineteenth-Century British Poetry

MY FIRST INTENTION FOR THIS ESSAY WAS TO WRITE A preliminary summary of research I have been doing in the business of publishing poetry in nineteenth-century England. But when I compressed the data I have gathered so far they flattened to a conclusion that can be stated in a sentence: nineteenth-century British writers and publishers seldom prospered from poetry, and few writers ever made a living from it. One of the vivid exceptions is Macaulay, whose *Lays of Ancient Rome* sold well in the first few years after its publication in 1842, and then began a remarkable publishing history that by the end of the century made it one of the most popular books of the Victorian period. I decided that it is appropriate in this tribute to Richard Altick, who showed me the excitement and significance of studying nineteenth-century publishing history, to write about one of the grand events in that history and to consider some of its implications, rather than to sample the more frequent failures and modest successes of nineteenth-century British poets and their publishers.

I

To measure the remarkable success of the *Lays*, I will begin with two points about the publication of books of poetry in nineteeth-century England. The first is that few writers made their livings principally from poetry. In 1962 Richard Altick published an essay on "The Sociology of Authorship" in which he categorized the social origins, educations, and extraliterary occupations of 1,100 British writers who worked between 1800 and 1935.[1] Of these writers 849 were included in the 1800–1900 volume of the then-current edition of the *Cambridge Bibliography of English Literature* (1941). Professor Altick found biographical information about 737 of these nineteenth-century writers. He was more interested in, and more sure about, the class or caste from which they came and where they went to school than he was in how they made their livings. He listed occupations other than literature, but including journalism, for 350 of 737 nineteenth-century writers, and then threw in a "dozen or so" bankers and businessmen and 24 writers who worked as artisans or common laborers. I adapt one of Altick's tables (p. 401); the computation of the percentage of writers in each occupation is mine, using the number 386–98 as the total of writers with extraliterary occupations. See table 1.

Richard Altick's essay characteristically helps to direct the study it stimulates. When I became interested in the occupations of nineteenth-century British poets, I used his essay as a ground from which to start and against which to put what I found. I began with the names of 218 writers whose poetry appears in one of the first nine volumes of Alfred H. Miles' edition of *Poets and Poetry of the Nineteenth Century* (London: Routledge, 1891, 1905) and who are listed in the 1941

TABLE 1

EXTRALITERARY OCCUPATIONS OF NINETEENTH-CENTURY BRITISH WRITERS

Occupation	Number	Percentage
Practicing journalists	84	21.7–21.1
Clergymen	83	21.5–20.8
Practicing solicitors or barristers	17	4.4–4.2
Government office, civil or diplomatic service	61	15.8–15.3
Artists, architects, musicians, actors	42	10.8–10.5
Teachers, professors	46	11.9–11.5
Practicing physicians	17	4.4–4.2
Bankers and businessmen	12–24	3.1–6.2
Artisans and laborers	24	6.2–6.0

edition of CBEL.[2] Poets who got into both Miles and the CBEL, I figured, had attained and at least until recently preserved a certain presence in their literature and its history. (Only three poets included in volumes 1-9 of Miles are not listed in the 1941 CBEL.) Four of the 218 writers—Thomas Carlyle, Jane Welsh Carlyle, Ruskin, and Macaulay—are included in CBEL but not in the sections on poetry, not even in cross-reference. I could find nothing about the occupations of seven other writers. Of the remaining 207 writers, 119 practiced occupations Altick characterized as extraliterary. In the following table, I have somewhat refined Altick's categories. Again, the percentages of poets and of writers in general who worked in each occupation are percentages not of the total number of writers about whom Altick and I collected information, but of the number of poets (119) and writers in general (386-398) whose principal occupations were extraliterary. See table 2. Presuming that the 339 to 351 writers for whom Altick did not find an extraliterary occupation all lived either from literature or from a private income, I made one final comparison. When the whole is the total number of nineteenth-century writers included in Altick's census and mine, then about the same proportions of poets and writers in general pursued no principal occupation outside literature. See table 3.

"In the nature of the case," Altick wrote in his essay, "no clear-cut answers are possible" about the principal occupa-

TABLE 2

EXTRALITERARY OCCUPATIONS OF NINETEENTH-CENTURY BRITISH POETS

Occupation	Number	Percentage
Literary and intellectual journalism	23	27.7
Political and general journalism	10	
Clergymen	11	9.2
Practicing solicitors or barristers	7	5.8
Government office, civil or diplomatic service	30	25.2
Artists, architects, musicians, actors	8	6.7
Teachers, professors	13	10.9
Practicing physicians	3	2.5
Bankers and businessmen	7	5.8
Clerks, artisans, laborers	7	5.8

Donald Gray

TABLE 3

SOURCE OF INCOME FOR NINETEENTH-CENTURY POETS AND WRITERS
WITHOUT EXTRALITERARY OCCUPATIONS

Occupation	19TH-CENTURY POETS (207)		19TH-CENTURY WRITERS (737)	
	Number	Percentage	Number	Percentage
Literature, principally poetry	14			
Literature, principally other forms	36	42.5	339–351	45.9–47.6
Private income (including patronage, pensions, marriage)	38			

tions of many nineteenth-century writers (p. 400). I am uneasy about perhaps twenty of my decisions,[3] but for my present purposes the categories are steady enough. It is interesting, for example, that compared to all nineteenth-century British writers proportionately fewer poets were clergymen (the inclusion of volumes 10 and 11 of Miles' anthology would have adjusted this difference) and that proportionately more of them worked as journalists and in government employment. But that intriguing matter for speculation must await further study and refinement. The point here is that only a third of the poets whose principal occupation was literature chose or eventually managed to live principally from the publication of poetry. To put it another way, nineteenth-century British society supported only fourteen poets full-time. Even among that number only a few earned their livings from poetry throughout their careers: Felicia Hemans, L. E. Landon, perhaps William Watson, who in his last difficult years in the present century claimed that in the 1890s he made £500 a year from his poems.[4] Byron can be included in this number because he could have lived on the sales of copyrights for his poems, although not in his lordly manner, had he chosen not to give away those of his first successful volumes. Wordsworth, Tennyson, and Robert Browning all required the support of family and friends until in mid-career or later their volumes of poems began to sell uncommonly well. Swinburne also lived on an income from his family, and like Yeats he worked as a literary journalist as well. Others in this small group of writers who lived principally by poetry did not fare well: John Davidson's career was a struggle, and Edwin Atherstone and P. J. Bailey (and Watson), after early success, required assistance from pension funds before the end of their long lives. Finally, I include in this category John Clare and David Gray, whose attempts to live as poets in London were disastrous, fatal to Gray, and the effective end of Clare's working life.

The reason for these difficulties and delayed successes is the second point I want to make about the business of publishing poetry in nineteenth-century England. It was not a big business; but it had its triumphs, retold in every pertinent biography and history of publishing. Scott's publisher sold 15,000 copies of *The Lay of the Last Minstrel* within five years of its publication, 28,000 copies of *Marmion* within four years, and 25,000 copies of *The Lady of the Lake* within eight months. Thomas Moore's *Lalla Rookh* was in its seventh edition a year after its publication in 1817, and in the 1840s and 1850s Longmans was still publishing over 30,000 copies of the poem. Murray sold 10,000 copies of Byron's *The Corsair* to booksellers in a single day. Half a century later the first printing of Tennyson's *Enoch Arden* was 40,000 copies.[5] Especially after the 1820s, when poetry became less popular, the business of its publication also had its slumps and disappointments. Frank Arthur Mumby writes that in the 1830s "the second John Murray, the Prince of Publishers, . . . now made it a rule to decline all original works" of poetry.[6] In the 1870s two different publishers, Strahan and Henry King, signed contracts with Tennyson guaranteeing him an annual income of £5000; both publishers lost money on the contracts (Martin, p. 549). Lesser poets took their own losses. One poet recalls how in 1878 he went £45 into debt to subsidize the publication of his first book of poems (with beveled edges: "it seemed the great secret of success was beveled edges"), and received in return one scornful review and a shipment of unbound sheets with a message from the publisher that "at the present moment the finest poetry was 'a drug on the market'."[7]

Donald Gray

The usual course of business, however, is better seen in a
sample of seventy-four titles, including *Lalla Rookh* and
Macaulay's *Lays*, published by Longmans between 1800 and
1900. All except *Lalla Rookh*, for whose copyright the publisher paid Moore £3000 for "a poem the length of *Rokeby*"
(*Letters of Thomas Moore*, 1:343) even before the poem was
finished, were published on commission or an agreement to
divide profits (usually half and half) between publisher and
author. The usual first printing of these books, even of those
that turned out to be successful, was between 500 and 1000
copies. About two-thirds of these seventy-four titles—fifty
titles, including eight whose first printings were 2000 or
more—did not go into a second printing. About two-thirds
earned a profit.

		Profit	*Loss*
First printing 500–1,000	43	24	19
First printing 1,500–3,000	8	4	4
Multiple printings	23	23	0
	74	51	23

The profit on these volumes was usually between £25 and £50,
and the loss between £30 and £60. Most of the dozen or so titles
that were more than usually successful were moderately so. A
one-volume collection of Amelia Opie's poems, for example,
went through six editions (1000–1500 copies in each edition)
between 1802 and 1811, earning profits (to be divided) of £120
to £170 on each edition. On only four of these seventy-four
titles did author and publisher do exceptionally well. A one-
volume edition of Southey's poems earned over £1070 from the
publication of 5500 copies between 1844 and 1853. Thomas
Campbell's *Gertrude of Wyoming* (1809), published on commission, sold out its first printing of 3000 in the year of its
publication, and then took *Gertrude of Wyoming and Other
Poems* through six editions of 2000 each between 1810 and
1819. (Campbell's earnings from the two volumes were nearly
£2000, and Longmans made about £240.) James Montgomery's *The Wanderer in Switzerland*, published by Longmans
after a first edition had been brought out by a provincial
bookseller, sold about 10,000 copies by the end of the 1820s,

79

and Montgomery's *The World Before the Flood* (1813) sold about as many copies during the same years. Author and publisher split profits of about £800 on the first title and over £1700 on the second.

II

By 1842 Macaulay of course did not need to live on the income earned from his poetry. Even before the extraordinary sales of the first volumes of his *History of England from the Accession of James II* (1849) began to make him wealthy, an inheritance, the money he had saved from his £10,000 annual salary as a member of the Supreme Council in India, and his connection with the *Edinburgh Review* allowed him, as he wrote in 1841, to "consider myself as one of the richest men of my acquaintance. For I can well afford to spend a thousand a year: and I can enjoy every comfort on eight hundred."[8] The *Lays of Ancient Rome* assisted but did not provide such comfort. But before Macaulay's death in 1859, Longmans had published 30,500 copies of the original edition of the poems, and another 6000 copies of an illustrated edition inaugurated in 1847. These two volumes together showed a profit of £5088 19s. 6d. on Longmans' books by June 1860. Macaulay's half share worked out to about £150 annually in the seventeen years before his death, an income that could have respectably sustained a settled, middle-aged London bachelor of a poetic turn, although not in the Albany.

After 1860 the sales of the *Lays* were yet more striking. By 1912 Longmans had published more than 293,000 copies in seven different editions at prices ranging from six pence to a guinea, as well as including the poems in editions of Macaulay's collected works and in a volume with some of his essays. By the end of the first decade of the twentieth century, Longmans' editions of the *Lays* had earned a profit of over £17,000, of which Macaulay and his heirs (after 1866 the profits were divided three-fourths to the author and one-fourth to the publisher) received nearly £11,000 and the publisher over £6000. Other publishers put out their editions of the *Lays* after the copyright expired in 1884. Before the end of the century, fifteen cheap editions are listed in the *English*

Catalogue of Books, most of them priced between a shilling and 3s. 6d. and three selling at threepence or sixpence. When he revised his life of his uncle in 1908, George Otto Trevelyan had even better ground than he did in 1876 when he wrote "that, taking the world as a whole, there is probably never a moment when [the *Lays*] are out of the hands of the compositor. The market for them in their native country is so steady, and apparently so inexhaustible, that it perceptibly falls and rises with the general prosperity of the nation; and it is hardly too much to assert that the demand for Macaulay varies with the demand for coal."[9]

The book that generated all these big numbers is short, rather slight, and a little playful. Its conceit—which Macaulay, who enjoyed and collected the penny street ballads of his own time, took seriously—is that Roman historians drew on the popular ballads of an oral tradition for some of the matter of their histories. In a general preface to the *Lays*, Macaulay cites Niebuhr as an authority for this idea, documents it in his usual way with instances drawn from his reading about the cultures of Europe, Africa, South America, and the Sandwich Islands, and offers his poems as a fanciful reversal of the process of writing and reading history, a transformation of "some portions of early Roman history back into the poetry out of which they were made."[10] Macaulay plays out the game by inventing for each poem a situation and a teller, one of the "ancient minstrels who know only what a Roman citizen, born three or four hundred years before the Christian era, may be supposed to have known" (p. 36). The longest of the four poems in the volume is only about 600 lines; one poem is incomplete, masquerading as a fragment. In his letters Macaulay makes the point that the *Lays* were conceived as a recreation while he was in India, and he consistently calls them "trifles" (in one letter he promotes them to "scholar-like and not inelegant trifles," *Letters,* 4:44) and their volume "a little book." He forbade Longmans from puffing the book, and he reminded the editor of the *Edinburgh Review* that no review of any of his books was to be commissioned. The publisher believed these depreciations; Longmans started the book off with a normal printing of 750 copies. And

Macaulay's diffidence is genuine. He already had the subject and plan of his *History* in view. As he moved toward it, he wrote a friend, "I shall certainly leave this volume as the ostrich leaves her eggs in the sand" (*Letters*, 4:58–59).

Why was the *Lays* so surprisingly popular? In the latter decades of the century, its sales were undoubtedly kept up by the status of the book as a school classic. But that status enlarges rather than compromises the terms of its popularity. Sixty years after its publication, the *Lays* was one of those securely canonized books that educated people want to read and, for reasons having to do with the maintenance of an *ethos* as well with the education of taste, want those under their authority to read as well. There are two relatively uncomplicated reasons for the success of Macaulay's poems. Their verse and the movement of their stories are quick and energetic, and the moral design of the whole book is clear and sharply resolved. There is another, more complicated reason for their popularity. In their vigorous sound and certain resolutions they are different from the kind of poetry usually esteemed by mid- and late-Victorian literary critics, if not always enjoyed by Victorian readers. In the hopeful, happy endings of their stories, they are even different from many nineteenth-century popular poems that are like them in the simple energies of craft. The idea of the world enacted in the *Lays*, of how things are likely to go in it and the character of the human acts and qualities that will make them go better or worse, is also different from that Macaulay set out in his essays and the *History*. These differences make the success of the book an interesting event in Victorian social as well as literary history. They suggest that the *Lays* pleased readers who knew that experience was not and had never been so simple and satisfying, but who put the book among everything else they knew and let themselves enjoy the improbably whole successes of possibilities they nonetheless hoped to be real, and of virtues they believed to be really effective.

Whether or not they liked them, almost all Macaulay's nineteenth-century reviewers, biographers, and commentators drew on a stock of closely associated words to describe the characteristics of his verse: vigorous, energetic, manly ("to use an epithet which always comes up in speaking of him," Leslie Stephen wrote), bold, animated, unflagging.[11] The feel of his poetic line was described by several writers as metallic, its sound compared more than once to a trumpet, its motion summed up in a sentence by John Wilson in his *Blackwood's* review: "We do dearly love to see a poem of action go over the ground."[12] "Horatius" and "The Battle of the Lake Regillus," the first two poems in the volume, are almost entirely poems of action. Each is organized by the rhythm of a battle, from its fearful prelude through its bloody fights to its peaceful sortings-out at the end. Macaulay is good at building up to the battle.

> Hard by the Lake Regillus
>   Our camp was pitched at night:
> Eastward a mile the Latines lay,
>   Under the Porcian height.
> Far over hill and valley
>   Their mighty host was spread;
> And with their thousand watch-fires
>   The midnight sky was red.
>   ("The Battle of the Lake Regillus," stanza 9)

He is even better when the storm breaks.

> He reeled, and on Herminius
>   He leaned one breathing-space;
> Then, like a wild cat mad with wounds,
>   Sprang right at Astur's face.
> Through teeth, and skull, and helmet,
>   So fierce a thrust he sped,
> The good sword stood a hand-breadth out
>   Behind the Tuscan's head.
>   ("Horatius," stanza 45)

And Macaulay is good too at bringing the rattle and satisfying excess of these violent episodes to a comforting final chord. The teller of "Horatius" sings his ballad 120 years after the battle, and he ends by describing how the story is told on winter nights in lonely cottages,

> When the oldest cask is opened,
>   And the largest lamp is lit,
> When the chestnuts glow in the embers,
>   And the kid turns on the spit; . . .
> When the girls are weaving baskets,
>   And the lads are shaping bows. . . .
>   (stanza 69)

"The Battle of the Lake Regillus" begins in the domesticity secured by war ("Now on the place of slaughter / Are cots and sheepfolds seen": stanza 3), and the poem ends in a great public ceremony in which pious citizens of the now flourishing state thank the gods who according to legend intervened in the battle.

The other two poems of the *Lays* are not really poems of action. "Virginia," the pretended fragment, tells the story of the murder by the plebian Virginius of his beautiful young daughter rather than surrender her to the lust of the wicked aristocrat Appius Claudius Crassus. Much of the poem is given to political harangues, by the teller and by a character in the tale, against the oppressions of the aristocracy. Most of "The Prophecy of Capys," the last poem of the collection, is a prediction to Romulus of the vast empire, from the Nile to "the dusky forest / Of Byrsa's thousand masts" (31), that will grow from the city he will found. These latter poems share with the battle poems a directness and clarity not of action but of moral design. The sides are always clearly drawn. In the battle poems the city is defended against invaders, among whom in both poems is "false Sextus," a traitor and a coward at whose appearance women spit and "No child but screamed out curses, / And shook its little fist" ("Horatius," 25). In "Virginia" the enemy is internal, the lustful Appius Claudius and the inequitable political condition he represents. On the other side are the innocent Virginia, her honest, loving father, and the righteously indignant plebians. In "The Prophecy of Capys" the threat is both internal and external. Macaulay sets the poem in a celebration of the victory of the Roman legions over a Greek army in the Pyrrhic war. The war began, Macaulay writes in the preface to the poem, when the arrogant Greeks of Tarentum mocked the ambassador of Rome for his poor Greek and allowed a buffoon to insult him "with gestures of the grossest indecency" and to bespatter "the senatorial gown with filth" (Macaulay, *Lays*, p. 169). The poem itself describes Romulus and Remus returning after their defeat of Amulius, the great-uncle who usurped their power and tried to kill them as children. There are brave men and bloody deeds on both sides. Romulus and Remus walk into the poem bearing the severed heads of Amulius and one of his ministers, and the oppressed plebians riot after Virginius murders his daughter.

> One stone hit Apius in the mouth, and one beneath
>   the ear;
> And ere he reached Mount Palatine, he swooned with
>   pain and fear. . . .
> And when his stout retainers had brought him to his door,
> His face and neck were all one cake of filth and clotted
>   gore.
>
> ("Virginia," *Lays*, p. 164)

But Macaulay makes sure that his readers do not mistake the rectitude of the violence his heroes (and obviously Macaulay himself) enjoy. Not only are Appius Claudius and Amulius justly punished. The consequences of the violence against them are unambiguously good. "Virginia" is supposed by Macaulay to be sung after an election in which the plebians have again turned back attempts to defeat their most effective tribunes and return the state to the years of unmoderated aristocratic power. The result of lust, murder, and riot in this poem is political reform and progress, just as the issue of Romulus' slaying of Amulius is the empire prophesied by both Capys and the minstrel of his prophecy to the victors over usurping great-uncles and arrogant Greeks.

There is a right side, in short, and it wins, both in the stories of the *Lays* and in the history in which they are set. Macaulay's most artful use of the historical identity of his stories is his habit of piling victory on victory. Unlike Scott, he does not often remind his readers that the brave culture he celebrates has itself been defeated and gone to dust. Only in the preface to "Horatius" are we reminded that after the city was saved and the song was made, Rome fell to the Gauls. Even if we don't know that Rome subsequently regained and enormously expanded its power, the stories and situations of the following three poems in the collection will educate us in the success of early Roman history. For the poems of the *Lays* are arranged chronologically to run from the defensive victories of Horatius at the bridge and Lake Regillus to the political triumph of the plebians to the passing of imperial dominance from the Greeks to the Romans. Then, at the moment when his readers might begin to reflect on the historical fate of empires, Macaulay takes Roman history out of ordinary time. "The Prophecy of Capys" arrests it at the moment it begins to unfold into the rise that will require its decline, and the poem returns its readers to the vigorously simple beginnings of Roman history in the legend of Romulus and Remus. The careful selection from the whole rhythm of history leaves the readers of the *Lays* in a comforting loop of success, cheered by the company of clear-minded men of direct action who turn danger into the origins of security, prosperity, political stability, and dominion.

The difference between the *Lays* and most other nineteenth-century British poetry, then, is that in its plots and resolutions, as well as its sound, it is a poetry without overtones and shadows, a poetry without many metrical turns and syntactical surprises, without complexity of narrative and character, pretty much without irony. These deficiencies distinguish Macaulay's poems from some other long narrative poems of the same kind that his contemporaries thought to be more estimable: Scott's *Marmion*, with its dark, flawed, rightfully defeated but compelling central character; Tennyson's "Morte d'Arthur" and "The Passing of Arthur"; Arnold's "Sohrab and Rustum"; Rossetti's "The White Ship," the story of the drowning of the son of Henry I at the moment Henry had secured his lands in France for the Prince; the plangent tales Morris's fleeing adventurers tell one another as they look for a refuge from time in *The Earthly Paradise*. Macaulay's poems also come out differently from some other short, popular poems which, like his, engage principally by the memorably straightforward drive of their verse and the clarity of their situations and stories. I am thinking of poems like some of the ballads, in Scott's *Minstrelsy of the Scottish Border* ("Sir Patrick Spens," "Lord Randal," "Proud Margaret"), Charles Wolfe's "The Burial of Sir John Moore," Hemans's "Casabianca" ("The boy stood on the burning deck"), W. E. Aytoun's *Lays of the Scottish Cavaliers*, Frances Hasting Doyle's "The Return of the Guards" and "A Private of the Buffs" (poems about the casualties of military engagements in the Crimea and China); Tennyson's "The Charge of the Light

Brigade," and at the end of the century some of Kipling's *Barrack Room Ballads* and Henry Newbolt's ballads of brave admirals and seamen. It is remarkable how often at the end (in the case of Sir John Moore and his mourners, at the beginning) of these poems their central characters are lorn, defeated, or dead. Some, like Virginius and his daughter, are sacrifices to a cause that may flourish without them. Most, however, are victims like Sir Patrick Spens and the Light Brigade of a world too dangerous or devious for their simple strengths, or like Aytoun's cavaliers of a history that turned against them, or like Gunga Din and the boy on the burning deck of a loyal gallantry that seems to be its own reward.

It is easy to understand why some nineteenth-century commentators thought Macaulay a classic of the Philistines, their very Prince, in Leslie Stephen's phrase (p. 570). In the *Lays*, even more sharply than in his essays and *History*, Macaulay saw a progress in history. He measured progress by material achievements—firesides and cottages after the battles, the civic shows of piety and power, the geographical boundaries of empire—and such triumphs of the orderly middle way as the political emergence of the plebians in Rome and the consolidation of Roman authority over the turbulent feudal contentions of the tribes and cities of pre-Roman Italy. Despite his admiration of Greek literature and his opinion that it is superior to that of the Romans, Macaulay in the *Lays* is much more Roman than Greek. His Romans are plain, practical, plebian, men of availing action who even when their motives are personal (Virginius' honor, the vengeance of Romulus and Remus) serve the progress of stability and justice in the state. In the preface to "The Prophecy of Capys," Macaulay writes that when Pyrrhus brought sophisticated Greek tactics and arms, elephants and all, against the Romans, he found "a people who, far inferior to the Athenians and Corinthians in the fine arts, in the speculative sciences, in all the refinements of life, were the best soldiers on the face of the earth" (p. 171). Greek culture is discounted all through the *Lays* as it is in that sentence, with its emphasis finally on the qualities that win. It was the "victory of the foreign taste," Macaulay writes in the general preface, that caused later

Romans to neglect "the rude lays which had delighted their fathers" (pp. 25-26), and he pretends that a "slight tincture of Greek learning and of Greek superstition" (p. 80) has stained even the early song of "The Battle of the Lake Regillus," making it indeed less rude and rousing than its predecessor "Horatius." Because, as I have noted, Macaulay does not allow history to take Rome to a decadence like that of the overrefined, arrogant Greeks of Tarentum, his Romans remain always at once ancient and young, heroes of the actual victories of military and political contest rather than of the moral victories of sensibility and the less palpable advances of art and thought.

In his review of the *Lays* in 1842, John Wilson used the Philistine character of its verse, movement, and theme to mount one of the last skirmishes of his own long war against the now middle-aged Young Poets who "potter, potter, potter all about their own dear, sweet, consumptive, passionate, small, infantile selves" (p. 804). But the war was already lost. By the end of the century a taste for the *Lays* had become so common, in two meanings of the word, that George Saintsbury could patronize it when he defended the poems as "coin for general circulation": "hundreds and thousands of immature and 'prentice tastes have been educated to the enjoyment of better things by them; thousands and tens of thousands of tastes, respectable at least, have found in them the kind of poetry which they can like, and beyond which they are not fitted to go."[13] It is a version of the fate that Macaulay imagined in the *Lays* for the ballads he pretended to imitate. The triumph of a sensibility that aspired to Arnold's spacious and speculative Hellenism had pushed Macaulay's rude trifles down to a respectable vulgarity. It would be fair to leave them there. The *Lays* must have been popular in large part because, as Arnold wrote of all Macaulay's writing, it hit "the nascent taste for things of the mind" of many readers and satisfied them "with fine writing about the object of one's study [and] with having it praised or blamed in accordance with one's own likes or dislikes."[14] One of the offices of popular literature is to flatter and reassure. Among the many practical-minded Victorians moving through literacy towards affluence there must have been many who were pleased to discover in the *Lays* that there was something classical about their views and progress and who must have been glad for the chance to rest in their opinions for a space in a respectable literature that did not trouble and perplex.

But there is one final point to be made about the popularity of the *Lays*. Its author, and I would argue that some of its readers, knew their own experience to be less simple than the version they enjoyed in these stories of success. I suggest that they brought their knowledge of complexity to the book, and took its lessons back with them when they turned again to engage the intricate and compromised ways in which the world really ran. Consider Macaulay's own idea of history and progress. As Jane Millgate writes in her excellent book, Macaulay did possess an imagination that "habitually translates linear sequence into forward motion and transforms change into progress."[15] But he also found seasons within these sequences, alternating swings toward anarchy or repression through which the moderating agents and institutions of progress had to tack their way.[16] He also saw cycles beyond the sequences of progress, whole histories turning finally to decline; one of the most popular images he gave his contemporaries was that (in his essay on von Ranke) of the New Zealander come from the regions to which progress has moved to contemplate the ruins of London. Joseph Hamburger remarks that "despite his reputation as a believer in progress," Macaulay in the 1840s "was quite gloomy about the immediate future" (p. 133). He was disturbed then by the possibility of civil riot conducted not by plebians but by Chartists and others who were worked up by democratic and socialist rhetoric, just as later he was distressed by the violence both of the Indian Mutiny and the surge of his own wish that it be strongly repressed and punished. In and out of the *Lays*, Macaulay wrote about such episodes of crisis in which the order and safety of the state is at risk. In the *Lays* he relieves his gloom by putting force in the hands of leaders who use it to make, finally, a kind of plebian republic or enlightened oligarchy. Out of the *Lays* Macaulay, like many of his contemporaries, feared the resolution of crisis by force. The heroes of the essays and the *History* are not warriors but negotiators and conciliators who steered the state safely around violence, men like William III in his accommodation to Parliament, and Halifax, "the Trimmer of Trimmers," and Whigs in general in their role as mediators between the repressive Tories and the leveling radicals.

Yet Macaulay in his writing and political career did not meet his own heroic standard. John Clive judges Macaulay's considerable achievements in India to have come short of their possibilities because "a capacity for conciliation had not been among the chief qualities he brought to his tasks."[17] Clive quotes a dispatch from Auckland, the Governor-General of India, regretting "the exaggeration with which, when provoked to controversy, [Macaulay] states his own views and opinions" (p. 340). The complaint was common. Macaulay, after all, learned to write in the robustly polemical school of the political journalism of the 1820s. His gift of vivid statement and taste for dramatic scene made it difficult for him in politics and in his writing not to choose sides and try to carry all before him. Like Thucydides, whom he thought to be the greatest of historians, Macaulay wrote, as Hamburger puts it, "to recognize great historical acts of civil prudence and so to identify models for statesmen in his own time" (p. 165). He was not sufficiently prudent to be one of those statesmen, and it can be said that he also injured the purpose of his writing by being too partisan in his advocacy of mediation.

My point is that as the *Lays* stands to Macaulay, and Macaulay to the complex political and historical situations in which he lived and about which he wrote, so does his popular book of poems stand to their nineteenth-century readers. The *History* is not as complicated as history iself, and the *Lays* is less complicated still. Macaulay knew at least the second of these statements. He conceived and wrote the *Lays* when the trouble of his exile and frustration in India, the death of one sister and the marriage of another, and the uncertainty of his career after he returned to England sent him to the solace of reading: "What a blessing it is to love books as I love them,—

90

to be able to converse with the dead and to live amidst the unreal" (*Letters*, 3:129). But when he wrote the *Lays*, he did not close himself entirely within the unreal. He took some of what he was—his plebian identity and sympathies, his ambition, his energy, combativeness, and wish to win, and put it on a field to engage some of what he knew the world to be. The *Lays* is a scrimmage rather than the game. Better, the book is like a drill in which without real opposition Macaulay runs through the tactics and talents for which he wishes success. Sometimes he indulges himself in fantasies of force that he knew to be really dangerous. Always, however, he promotes virtues he thinks to be really important as he drives his stories of civic-minded, practical heroes to happy endings he thinks to be possible, however difficult and diluted their actual achievement may be.

I suggest that the pleasure of at least some of the adult nineteenth-century readers of the *Lays* was like that Macaulay found in writing them. He and these readers knew that it would not, in the event, ever be so simple. Yet they also thought they knew, and wanted their children to learn, what was at issue in the contest and the qualities required for success in it. Not all popular books work in the way I am guessing that the *Lays* worked for Macaulay and some readers. Some books, like the trivial romances Macaulay enjoyed, act out wholly implausible wish and dream. Some, like the popular nineteenth-century poems which the *Lays* resemble in its verse, let us think of ourselves as weighty and serious by letting us feel how sad things can be. The *Lays* enact a plausible wish. If it confirms its readers' ideas about themselves and the world, that confirmation is the means by which the book is brought to play among the actual forces and chances of their experience. It is a recreation in which Victorian Romans could establish their sensible way with satisfying force and nearly unambiguous result. It is also a kind of ritual in which, in this successful poem by a successful and esteemed writer, they could practice and recall the worth and consequence of qualities they must remember to use in more confusing contests of which the issue is not as certain.

1. *Bulletin of the New York Public Library* 66 (1962): 398-404.

2. I chose the 1941 edition of *CBEL* partly because Richard Altick used it, and partly because it contains references to about fifty poets, most of them late-century writers, who have been dropped from the *New CBEL*. I used only the first nine volumes of Miles' anthology because volume 10 is given to humorous verse and volumes 11 and 12 to "Sacred Poetry." The writing of some poets appears both in one of these volumes and in earlier volumes. Most of the writers of humorous verse who did not get into one of the earlier volumes in the anthology were journalists, dramatists, or whimsical school-masters and dons; most of the writers of the sacred verse in volumes 11 and 12 were clergymen. Their inclusion would have markedly increased the number of writers of verse who worked in occupations other than literature, and I think that my point about the occupations of poets can be made more solidly if these occasional poets are not included in my calculations. I want to thank Susannah Gray for her most useful assistance in collecting information about the occupations of nineteenth-century poets.

3. For example: Theodore Watts-Dunton kept up his practice as a solicitor until 1900, long after he had joined the staff of a literary weekly and taken over the stewardship of Swinburne's allowance from his family. Elizabeth Barrett Browning probably could have exploited her popularity in the 1830s and 1840s to live principally from literature if not from poetry, had not her circumstances made that unnecessary. Southey, Moore, and Campbell were all known principally as poets—or at least that was how they first became known—but all of them made a significant part of their earned incomes as editors and literary journalists for most of their lives. I categorized Watts-Dunton as a literary journalist (which would have pleased him), Elizabeth Barrett Browning as living on private income, Moore as living by other forms of literature, and Southey and Campbell as literary journalists.

4. James G. Nelson, *Sir William Watson* (New York, 1966), p. 162.

5. Edgar Johnson, *Sir Walter Scott: The Great Unknown*, 2 vols. (New York, 1970), 1:225, 279, 335; *The Letters of Thomas Moore*, ed. Wilfred S. Dowden, 2 vols. (Oxford, 1964), 1:443; Leslie A. Marchand, *Byron: A Biography*, 2 vols. (New York, 1957), 1:433; Robert Bernard Martin, *Tennyson: The Unquiet Heart* (Oxford, 1980), p. 452.

I have learned the information about the printings of *Lalla Rookh* from *The Archives of the House of Longman 1794-1914*, Alison Ingram, comp., published on microfilm by Chadwyck-Healey and Somerset House. These records are also the source of the information about other books of poetry published by Longmans, including the *Lays*. I have not included reel and frame numbers of the microfilms of the *Archives*. References may be found in the *Index of Authors and Titles and Guide to the Archives of the House of Longman 1794-1914* (Bishops Stortford, 1975).

6. *Publishing and Bookselling*, rev. ed. (London, 1948), p. 232. In the fifth edition of this book, revised by Mumby and with additional chapters by Ian Norrie (London, 1974), Mumby drops this anecdote and adds one of Thomas Longman IV refusing the manuscript of poems by a woman in the 1840s: "It is no good bringing me poetry; nobody wants poetry now. Bring me a cookery book, and we might come to terms" (p. 206).

Donald Gray

7. W. J. Dawson, *The Autobiography of a Mind* (London, 1925), pp. 85, 87.

8. *The Letters of Thomas Babington Macaulay*, ed. Thomas Pinney, 4 vols. (Cambridge, 1975-77), 4:12.

9. *The Life and Letters of Lord Macaulay*, 2 vols. (London, 1976), 2:125.

10. Thomas B. Macaulay, *Lays of Ancient Rome* (London, 1842), p. 36.

11. Stephen's remark is in his essay in *Cornhill* 33 (1976): 581; the essay was reprinted in the third volume of *Hours in a Library* (1879). Representative nineteenth-century reviews of the *Lays* and essays on Macaulay are: H. H. Milman's review in the *Quarterly Review* 71 (1842): 453-77; the reviews in the *Athenaeum* 5 November 1842, p. 942, and in *Fraser's* 27 (1843), 59-75; R. H. Horne's essay in *The New Spirit of the Age* (1844), 2:33-50; John Morley's essay in *Fortnightly Review* 25 (1876): 494-513; and the introductory comments in Miles' anthology (vol. 3) and in volume 4 of T. H. Ward's edition of *The English Poets* (London, 1885).

12. *Blackwood's* 52 (1842): 812.

13. *A History of Nineteenth Century Literature* (London, 1896), p. 227.

14. "A French Critic on Milton," in *The Complete Prose Works of Matthew Arnold*, ed. R. H. Super, 11 vols. (Ann Arbor, 1960-77), 8:170. Arnold published this essay in the *Quarterly Review* in 1877.

15. *Macaulay* (London, 1973), p. 48.

16. See Joseph Hamburger's analysis of Macaulay's opinions in *Macaulay and the Whig Tradition* (Chicago, 1976), especially chapters 1 and 2.

17. *Macaulay: The Shaping of a Historian* (New York, 1973), p. 166.

V

U. C. KNOEPFLMACHER

Genre and the Integration of Gender: From Wordsworth to George Eliot to Virgina Woolf

ALL CREATIVE ARTISTS, TENNYSON ONCE OBSERVED, POSSESS AN imagination that is necessarily hermaphroditic. Still, the poet whose passive Marianas, Ladies of Shalott, and Elaines act as surrogates for his own threatened creativity seems to have regarded the full-scale fusion of Hermes and Aphrodite, brother and sister selves, as a desirable but sadly unattainable psychic ideal. In the Victorian era, when gender stereotyping was at its height, men as much as women vacillated between tendencies too rigidly labeled as "feminine" or "masculine." This vacillation produced rich but one-sided myths.[1] For, as Fliess and Freud, those scrutinizers of a late-Victorian psyche, noted with almost voyeuristic relish, an excessive suppression of the traits of the opposite sex resulted in a wide array of inhibitions and neuroses.[2]

The full integration of male and female selves, however, preoccupied another major Victorian writer, George Eliot. Unlike Tennyson, and very much like her favorite Wordsworth, the novelist resorted to a myth rooted in her own psychology. Among Wordsworth's many attractions for George Eliot was his expression of the need to recover what he identified as the feminine component of his imagination. That the novelist who wrote *The Mill on the Floss* in 1860 and the "Brother and Sister" sonnets in 1867 was drawn to

94

U. C. Knoepflmacher

Wordsworth's repeated celebrations of his sister Dorothy no longer requires documentation. George Eliot's life-long eagerness to find specimens of harmonious brother-sister relations, after all, even led her to exculpate a Byron whose work she intensely disliked, yet whose love for Augusta Leigh made him, she felt, "deeply pitiable, like all of us sinners."[3] Conversely, that same obsession made her unduly harsh to Branwell Brontë, whom she dismissed as "this drunken brutal son and brother."[4]

Although the Wordsworthian myth of a childhood paradise of undifferentiated gender held a steadfast appeal for George Eliot throughout her career, she also gave this ontogenetic myth much wider cultural or phylogenetic applications. Margaret Homans has perceptively suggested how, in her revisions of Wordsworth, George Eliot sought to find "a paradigm more suitable than that of the silent sister" in order to accommodate the "limits" of gender that she, as a woman and a realist, could not find in Wordsworth's visionary poetry.[5] Yet it could be argued that, artistically at least, George Eliot in fact expanded limits that Wordsworth had introduced in his later poetry. For she moved, in her own career, in a direction contrary to that which Wordsworth had taken after *The Prelude*. I have previously noted that *The Excursion* can be seen as a direct progenitor of *Scenes of Clerical Life* and *Adam Bede*.[6] If so, however, the link needs to be qualified. For, with *The Excursion*, Wordsworth had actually moved away from the feminine sensitivity he had once regarded as "the nurse,/ The guide, the guardian" of his being.[7] As a narrative poet, he yielded to masculine history, to the temporal reality he had earlier tried to counter in his antinarrative lyrics and ballads.

George Eliot, on the other hand, increasingly eschewed the role of chronicler when, after *Adam Bede*, her male pseudonym was pierced and her identity as a woman had become known. Although, like Wordsworth, she moved from pastoral to epic, to broader and more ambitious constructs encompassing ever-wider segments of human history, she also came to regard historical growth as a threat to a mythic memory that she continued to endow, as the early but not the later Wordsworth had done, with female properties and female

95

characteristics. And the preservation of a myth of female origin led her, as it would lead Virginia Woolf, to introduce ahistorical dimensions into her historical narratives. The division between George Eliot the realist, a writer interested in cause and effect, verisimilitude, analysis, and explanation, and George Eliot the creator of romances, a writer interested in dream, premonition, visionary or empathetic divination, the fluidity of myth and archetype, has been carefully studied by critics such as Barbara Hardy, George Levine, U. C. Knoepflmacher, Gillian Beer, and John P. McGowan.[8] What has not been sufficiently noted, however, either by these critics or by those who, like Sandra Gilbert and Susan Gubar, have explored the proto-feminist dimensions of her fiction,[9] is the direct correlation between the novelist's attempts to fuse contrary genres and her attempts to harmonize the gender divisions she so persistently sought to reconcile. The split between history and romance signified for George Eliot, as it had signified for Wordsworth and would signify for Woolf, a psychic split between male and female aspects that her powerful hermaphroditic imagination tried to overcome.

In her handling of these divisions, then, George Eliot must be located at the exact midpoint of a continuum that runs from Wordsworth to Woolf, from Romantic to modernist resolutions of the clash between incomplete male and female psychic halves. Just as all three authors tried to go beyond these offsetting halves by triangulating them into a higher fused self, so is the organization of this essay deliberately and self-consciously triangular; in joining a male poet with two female novelists, I deliberately want to break down some of the dualisms to which we all too often succumb. We must not be seduced by the notions that the analysis of poetry has to be kept apart from that of prose fiction, that women writers living in a male-dominated culture are best examined as the exclusive cross-fertilizing members of a creative sisterhood, that the labels of "Romantic" and "Victorian" or those which presumably set apart "Victorian" from "modernist" are irrevocably fixed. Like George Eliot's efforts, my own are synthetic: the novelist with the male pseudonym is flanked by a literary father and a literary daughter. Though each redefines his or her literary predecessor, all three share common concerns.

The materials I examine are necessarily selective. I begin with a look at some early poems by Wordsworth, written before the poet of *The Excursion* would give primacy to history and to a masculine historical self. I shall then take a close look at the opening paragraphs of chapter twelve of *The Mill on the Floss*, with their opposition of two kinds of narratives and two kinds of narrators, in order to make some generalizations about that novel as a pivotal work that allowed George Eliot to move in new directions. After some brief remarks about current trends in George Eliot's criticism, I shall conclude by showing how Woolf, though retaining a fictive concern with gender distinctions in *To The Lighthouse*, subverted, or at least reformulated, both Wordworth's and George Eliot's myths of unity.

I

George Eliot deliberately evokes "Tintern Abbey" when, at the end of *The Mill on the Floss*, she has Tom Tulliver stare into his sister's flashing eyes. Looking into "the shooting lights / Of thy wild eyes," Wordsworth's speaker welcomed a glimpse of what he once possessed before his painful fall into male self-consciousness: "Oh! yet a little while / May I behold in thee what I was once, / My dear, dear Sister" (ll. 118–21). Tom Tulliver, on the other hand, finds no such confirming reflections of a former self: Maggie's eyes all too belatedly produce "a new revelation to his spirit, of the depths in life, that had lain beyond his vision which he had fancied so keen and clear."[10] The bifurcation that Wordsworth resignedly accepts in his 1798 poem can, in George Eliot's 1860 novel, be overcome only through a violent fusion-through-death.

Yet Wordsworth had resisted this bifurcation in those shorter lyrics celebrating Dorothy which he wrote between 1798 and 1802, before his marriage to Mary Hutchinson and the masculine self-assertions which ensued. In poems such as "To a Butterfly," "The Sparrow's Nest," "Nutting," "To My Sister," as well as in the better-known Lucy poems, Wordsworth identified Dorothy with his own intense desire of

97

arresting or reversing a process of separation that he equated with the loss of a much coveted, presocial, Edenic oneness. The opening words in "To a Butterfly" ("Stay near me—do not take thy flight!/A little longer stay in sight") are not just addressed to the insect whom Wordsworth mock-heroically magnifies as the "historian of my infancy," but also to his onetime female companion, "my sister Emmeline," herself an emblem of that undivided infancy. Again, in "The Sparrow's Nest," those "bright blue eggs together laid" that boy and girl jointly discover come to signify, as will that legendary figure with the ovarian name, Ogg son of Beorl, a primordial oneness that precedes gender distinctions. In each case, little Emmeline is credited with an intuitive capacity for divination similar to that which George Eliot will attribute to female figures such as Dinah Morris or to feminized male seers such as Latimer or Philip Wakem. In each poem, the female child thus proves her superiority both to her older boy-companion as well as to the remembering male adult.

In "To a Butterfly," the boy's response to the insect associated with the human psyche markedly differs from that of his younger sister:

> A very hunter did I rush
> Upon the prey;—with leaps and bounds
> I followed from brake to bush;
> But she, God love her! feared to brush
> The dust from off its wings.
>
> (ll. 14–18)

That the intended contrast here is not just between female restraint and male aggressiveness but also between a higher and a lower imagination is evident from Dorothy Words-worth's own gloss to these lines. In her journal entry for 14 March 1802, she noted that William "used to kill all the white [butterflies] when he went to school because they were french-men."[11] A schoolboy's immersion into military history results in the fanciful transformation of unoffending butterflies into hostile opponents. Here, as in "Nutting" or in "Lucy Gray," Wordsworth deliberately subverts a destructive masculine fancy. And, by depreciating that lesser fancy, the ironic male speaker subordinates himself to the superior sororal imagina-tion of an Emmeline (or of that "dearest Maiden" invoked at the end of "Nutting"). Wordsworth thus anticipates in his self-mockery as a "hunter" the characteristics that George Eliot will attribute to Tom Tulliver in *The Mill on the Floss*. He allows what Tom will fail to allow when, in order to impress Maggie with his superior prowess, he disastrously tries to impersonate the Duke of Wellington, yet only manages to maim himself with Mr. Poulter's huge sword. It is Philip Wakem, masculine yet also highly feminine, who, only a few pages earlier, had recognized his own incompleteness when, after looking, Wordsworth-like, into Maggie's eyes, "he wished *he* had a little sister" (p. 158).

Neither Wordsworth nor George Eliot ever banished their regressive wishfulness for complementarity and gender fusion: just as the adult Wordsworth celebrated the infant Emmeline or the little girl "untouched by solemn thought" who walks besides the speaker in the 1802 sonnet, so did the novelist continue to fantasize her reincarnation as a half-submissive "little sister" should "another childhood world" become her "share."[12] Even in *Middlemarch*, the novel that Woolf deemed suitable for grownups, the successful heterosexual relations between Mary and Fred, and Dorothea and Will, are rendered imagistically in terms of the hand-holding girl and boy we first see in the novel's "Prelude," when little Teresa and her brother Rodrigo "toddle" out from Avila.

Still, both Wordsworth and George Eliot realized the need for finding other modes of resolution for their intense desire to counter the split they so acutely felt. After "To My Sister," a poem of greater sophistication than "The Sparrow's Nest" or "To a Butterfly," Wordsworth gradually accommodated the world of history that he, like George Eliot, persistently identified with a male modality. After her half-hearted expiation for breaking with the patriarchal world of Robert Evans she had so painstakingly reconstructed in *Adam Bede*, George Eliot began to move in exactly the opposite direction. She no longer yielded to the pressures of the "hard, unaccommodating" actuality presented in *Adam Bede*, that novel with an epigraph from *The Excursion*. Instead of killing Hetty Sorrel or of forcing Dinah Morris to submit to an Adam's masculinist values, she began to find ways to inundate a male reality with mythic moments or "unhistoric acts" that she, like Wordsworth, identified with female figures or with feminized males.

As an effort to superimpose the atemporality of myth on a time-bound world, Wordsworth's "To My Sister" holds a special relevance for what George Eliot would attempt, through the myth of Ogg, in *The Mill on the Floss*. "To My Sister" significantly differs from "To a Butterfly," "The Sparrow's Nest," and "Nutting" in that the speaker no longer strains to return through recollection to what George Eliot's remembering narrator calls, in her own sonnet-sequence, the "primal passionate store" of childhood.[13] The poem is set in the present, not in the past; and it relies on exhortation, rather than on memory. Instead of returning to time-mutilated bowers or lost Edens, the speaker urges an adult sister to join him and a little boy on an imaginative journey. Forward-looking, rather than regressive, the poem thus expresses a protracted wish: "One moment now may give us more / Than years of toiling reason" (ll.25-26). That moment, mythical and epiphanic, resembles, as we shall see, the wishful trans-formation that occurs in *The Mill on the Floss* when woman, ferryman, and child are also lifted above years of toiling reason. It resembles that "one supreme moment" in which Tom and Maggie supposedly gain in death the childhood unity their growing up had sundered. And it resembles, too, to anticipate the final portion of this essay, that moment in which Mr. Ramsay springs, "like a young man" again, on to the rock of the lighthouse, to the amazement of his daughter and son.

In "To My Sister," the speaker insists that the ordinary sequentiality of time can, if not totally annulled, be displaced, flooded with new meaning: "We from to-day, my Friend, will date / The opening of the year" (ll. 19-20). On a special day, linear time (of which novels and verse narratives must partake much more than such short lyric outbursts) can be dissolved altogether. Speech itself, words in sequence, become incon-sequential: "Some silent laws our hearts will make" (l. 29). The same kind of mute communion so briefly experienced by a Tom whose "lips were silent" and a Maggie who "could make no answer" here results not in an expedition that leads to death or to a lighthouse that has become an emblem for the specter of Mrs. Ramsay. Instead, the speaker of "To My Sister" simply asks Dorothy to indulge what Mr. Ramsay will refuse his wife and little son. As an imaginative unit of trinitarian wholeness, William, Dorothy, and little Edward, the pre-pubescent child who acts as an emblem of their former childhood oneness, become cyclical figures. The poem itself is cyclical. Just as *The Mill on the Floss* will begin and end with a biblical epigraph that enfolds a sequential narrative, so do the concluding lines of "To My Sister" echo and remodulate earlier ones.

The tentative resolution of "To My Sister," however, is as far as Wordsworth can venture in trying to recover the female components of an imagination threatened by the rigid divisions that sunder the masculine from the feminine in a world of growth and socialization. In his later career, Wordsworth continued to pay fulsome tributes to Dorothy. Yet for the pastoralist who now turned to the epic mode, his dear, dear Sister began to recede in importance.[14] *The Excursion* may open with the legendary Margaret whose name three Tulliver women come to bear; but "The Ruined Cottage" was, of course, composed long before the completed 1814 poem. Despite his empathy with Margaret, the speaker of *The Excursion* prefers to look to male models, the Wanderer and the Pastor, and to a male anti-self, the Solitary, for his self-definition. Even in *The Prelude*, that hoarded relic of his earlier imagination, Wordsworth's repeated tributes to the sister whose name George Eliot was to assign to the heroine of *Middlemarch*, though sincere and profoundly moving, are of a different cast. His sister gift-of-God is now at best a worthy helpmeet, like Mary Wordsworth or Mary Garth (or the discarded Mary Burge of *Adam Bede*). Like Dorothea, the exquisite mate of Will Ladislaw, Dorothy, the sister-mate of Will Wordsworth's youthful imagination, becomes a found-ress of nothing. Still, like Dorothea Brooke, she will survive as a literary archetype to aid future imaginations—especially, the imaginations of women novelists interested in the sororal archetype.

II

Rhetorically, the opening paragraphs of chapter 12 of *The Mill on the Floss* act as a foil to the novel's first chapter, "Outside Dorlcote Mill." In that first chapter the novelist-dreamer who began by describing the linear flow of the "broadening Floss" had become arrested and drawn into a more quiescent, moist, "softening," pastoral scene. In Wordsworthian fashion, the narrator who stands on a stone bridge spans an adult present with a childhood past; and, like the early Wordsworth, too, the narrator identifies that past with the figure of a little girl. As "rapt" as the child, the narrator tries to screen out, as the girl apparently does, the dry activities of "the world beyond" (p. 8). Yet the narrator has promises to keep. She cannot lose herself in a Wordsworthian moment of lyrical ecstasy. She is a novelist and not a poet, and, as such, she must tell a story that requires sequential unfolding. She thus reproves herself for her reverie and sets out on her appointed task to inform her readers "what Mr. and Mrs. Tulliver were talking about, as they sat by the bright fire in the left-hand parlour, on that very afternoon I have been dreaming about" (pp. 8–9).

The first four paragraphs of chapter twelve, "Mr and Mrs Glegg at Home," each longer than the preceding one, move in a direction that reverses that of the five paragraphs that make up the first chapter. Lured by the domestic title, we expect an uninterrupted resumption of the plot that has been unfolding ever since we overheard what Mr. and Mrs. Tulliver were talking about in their own home. Yet, instead of being introduced to the Gleggs at home, we are conducted on a broadening excursion through time and space.

The first paragraph, itself an elongated single sentence, insists that in order to see the Gleggs at home we must become reacquainted with the same "red-fluted roofs" and "black ships" first mentioned in the book's opening sentences. As the sentence progresses, its tone becomes increasingly mocking. Addressed as "my refined readers," we are made uncomfortable by the narrator's insistence that we confront a larger world from which we, like Maggie in the previous chapter, had expected to be sheltered. We do not enter a domestic enclosure but observe a wider socioeconomic panorama in which products from "the far north" are exchanged for "precious inland products." The shift in setting is disconcerting. For the "refined readers" who associate "inland products" such as wool and cheese with "the medium of the best classic pastorals" will again find their expectations thwarted. The novelist is about to shift media, as well, by moving away from the eclogue (p. 103).

The soothing natural images that start the long and complex sentence that opens the second paragraph (p. 104) seem, on the surface, still auspiciously pastoral; so, too, ostensibly does the quotation from Wordsworth's *The Excursion* that takes up half of the short sentence ("It is a town 'familar with forgotten years.'") Yet if the old, old town carries "traces of its long growth and history like a milennial tree," that tree proves to be severely scarred. The linear succession of cruel and rapacious invaders suggests a continuity of strife. As we soon discover, defeated Roman legions turn their back on the civil order they had once tried to impose with their swords; greedy Vikings look with "fierce eager eyes at the fatness of the land"; male ghosts, a lustful "Saxon hero-king" and a "dreadful heathen Dane, who was stabbed in the midst of his warriors," carry little of the aura of male heroism with which Carlyle invested his Norsemen in the first lecture of "On Heroes, Hero-Worship, and the Heroic in History." Quite to the contrary, history is a nightmare from which the narrator would like to, but cannot, awake. Eager to soften that nightmare, the narrator tries to find some palpable relic which, like Shepperton Church or the Hall Farm in George Eliot's earlier fictions, might offer a partial reassurance by its very solidity. The narrator thus welcomes the fusion of a Norman "old hall" with a later Gothic structure, and asks the reader to show "loving pardon" at the crass "inconsistencies" of such "widely-sundered generations." Still, historical progress yields few such "loving" tokens. The old town's evolution only reveals its instinct for survival, the hard masculine ethos that Tom will later learn there under the tutelage of Mr. Deane. Even the allusion to *The Excursion* turns out, on closer inspection, to have been a decidedly hard touchstone, a reference to that "tall crag" or mountain peak by which the poet's male tutor, the Wanderer, learns the measure of austere and granitic truths, "the history of many a winter storm" (I. 278).

Unable to find refuge in a pastoral world, unwilling to yield to the crushing forward momentum of history, the narrator reaches out for still another "medium" in the chapter's third paragraph (pp. 104–105). He (for I am convinced that the speaker of chapter 12 is a *he* and not the feminine presence of the book's opening chapter) reverses the onward progress he has followed by retreating into an era perhaps "older than this old hall." From that era, the narrator seizes, not just another shard of masonry, but a fluid legend, a timeless myth. Self-consciously, he thus turns to a totally different sort of "history" than that alluded to in the previous paragraph. He chooses one of several versions, he jocularly explains, because it is the briefest. And he professes to believe in it even "if it should not be wholly true." Like Lockwood in *Wuthering Heights*, this male narrator thus relinquishes his narrative authority to another storyteller. The civilized voice of a self-conscious rationalist and antiquarian collector of manuscripts becomes submerged, drowned out by a fabulist's simpler and more archaic speech rhythms. Like the speaker in the novel's opening who lost herself in a moist female Eden, away from "the drier world above," and like the Wordsworth who conducted his sister to "the banks of this delightful stream" ("Tintern Abbey," 1. 150), this "private hagiographer" invites us to cross over into the undifferentiated world of myth. Indeed, the myth this anonymous and genderless new speaker proffers is itself a myth of crossing, a myth of return to primitive kernels of truth that must be rescued from the ossified layerings of history, the sedimentations that followed each overspill of the angry floods.

The myth of St. Ogg recounted in the remainder of the chapter's third paragraph represents George Eliot's efforts to render in narrative and cultural terms what had been presented as a wishful lyrical moment in "To My Sister." The trio of man, woman, and child are set apart from the ordinary men who rudely question the ragged female stranger. By opposing these questioners, Ogg detaches himself from the order of reality that had dominated in the previous paragraph, and, by so doing, also manages to detach himself from the questioning male narrator and that narrator's limited notions of truth. Ogg defies the current of history and thereby furthers a magical transformation in which a mournful and seemingly powerless female figure assumes her full potency and beauty. The ferryman not only contributes to her translation but also is himself translated. As someone who successfully bridges alternate realities, he assumes the identity the female narrator had lost in the book's opening chapter when a bridge turned into a domestic armchair and an Eve "in love with moistness" changed into a male historian.

The female narrator of chapter one recognized the seeds of her own creative powers in the nameless little girl she glimpsed by the water's darkening edge. The vanished male narrator of chapter twelve allows himself to be momentarily displaced by the luminous female radiance who sheds light on the water. Like Wordsworth's Dorothy or Keats's Cynthia, like Jane Eyre, like the magical women in Victorian fairytales,[15] the radiant figure in the prow is twice identified with the moon, that Romantic emblem of a higher imagination. Invested with her powers, Ogg can henceforth "save the lives of men and beasts." The Raphael Madonnas whose "blond faces and somewhat stupid expression" the narrator had ridiculed in chapter two (p. 13) now undergo a transmutation similar to that which Anna Jameson effected when, in her *Legends of the Madonna*, she chose "to change the scene" and contemplate the Virgin, not as "the glorious empress of heaven," but as "the mere woman, acting and suffering, loving, living, dying, fulfilling the highest destinies in the humblest state."[16]

"Ogg son of Beorl" is not the first male figure whom George Eliot feminizes as a worshiper of an earthly madonna. But the Amos Barton who belatedly worships Milly, the Seth Bede who becomes content as uncle to Dinah's children, even the Philip who mourns at Maggie's grave are all constrained by the harsh patriarchal world of male history. Ogg, on the

105

other hand, is allowed to enter a metaphoric, ahistorical, matriarchal world of myth such as the one into which Romola will be transported when she glides away from Florence, the city of history, or Daniel Deronda, when he finds Mirah on the banks of the Thames. As a female male or a male nurturer, he is chosen, as Silas Marner will be in George Eliot's next novel, as the agent for a novelist divided between male and female modalities, male and female narrators, masculine Dodsons and feminine Tullivers, a masculine pseudonym and a female name. He helps keep in suspension the polarities that George Eliot has so frantically tried to bring into psychic harmony. His own ovarian name is, as I already have suggested, highly significant. In a novel that mocks Mrs. Tulliver as an ineffectual hen, that shows the infertility and obsession with death of Mrs. Pullet, that, later, in this same chapter, shows the equally infertile Mrs. Glegg to be much harder than her tender, garden-nurturing husband, Ogg's naming is hardly coincidental.[17] In still another gender reversal, he is, in effect, the egg fertilized by a woman. Once in Raveloe, Silas Marner will be stirred by maternal memories suppressed during his sojourn in Lantern Yard. In St. Ogg's, however, the inhabitants forget the matriarchal origins that have led to Ogg's canonization and to their town's name; they therefore also unlearn what Silas must be forced to remember—the "loving" matriarchal origins through which they might aspire a secular salvation and "save the lives of men and beasts."

Thus drawn into a myth of female origins, female power, and female renovation and fusion, the reader is invited to forget the harsh world of history. But not for long. We are jolted out of our reverie in the next paragraph. History resumes its forward movement. The self-conscious male narrator hastily returns. All he purports to see in the legend of Ogg is the factual evidence for an early appearance of the intermittent floods: "This legend, one sees, reflects from a far-off time the visitation of the floods, which, even when they left human life untouched, were widely fatal to the helpless cattle" (p. 105). No symbolist, no explicator of metaphoric meanings, the narrator chooses to underplay the legend's moral. The floods may have spared human lives, but as the history-obsessed narrator now shows us, "the town knew worse troubles" than such natural disasters: a new succession of warriors who kill in the name of religious justification and historical right returns us to the earlier cycles of slaughter.

The ruthless process which the myth of St. Ogg has momentarily arrested reasserts itself with a vengeance. In the succeeding years, we discover, the town became "a continual fighting place, where first Puritans thanked God for the blood of the Loyalists, and then Loyalists thanked God for the blood of the Puritans" (p. 105). Not Ogg the believer, but those hard-hearted men who declared a needy woman to be foolish are the perpetuators of history. A single "aged person" can still remember how "a rude multitude had been swayed" by John Wesley, the mild preacher whom Dinah Morris had so vividly recalled in *Adam Bede* (p. 106). Yet life in St. Ogg's remains mundane, historical, uninundated and unfertilized by the spontaneous overflow of a mythic imagination. Only with this sobering realization in mind are George Eliot's "refined readers" finally allowed to enter the domicile of the Gleggs.

III

In "The Turn of George Eliot's Realism," John P. McGowan contrasts the modes of *The Mill on the Floss* and *Middlemarch* to suggest that in the former novel George Eliot herself too stubbornly clings, as the inhabitants of St. Ogg's do, to a hard and infractable notion of reality. Maggie's creator, he argues, thus blames her heroine for her very own dilemma when she upbraids Maggie for divorcing imagination from the real. By way of contrast, McGowan shows that in *Middlemarch* George Eliot achieves a fluid new realism by altering her notions of what a "referent" is. She now recognizes the metaphoric texture of all human aspirations and allows that such a metaphoric process can be as veracious as factual knowledge. Arguing against J. Hillis Miller's readings of *Middlemarch*[18] and endorsing my own contention that the rhythms of that novel blend fact and ficticity,[19] McGowan insists that in her greatest novel George Eliot does not deconstruct an unknowable sociohistorical reality, but is primarily interested, instead, in "how socially held meanings are created." She displays, he holds, "a new interest in visionary or metaphoric language, the direct means by which new meanings are introduced."[20]

Though in full agreement with McGowan on *Middlemarch*, I would quibble with his treatment of *The Mill on the Floss*, fully aware of the inadequacies of my own previous discussions of that novel (which McGowan rightly faults).[21] Where exactly, at what point in her development, did George Eliot's realism "turn"? Can we really dismiss *The Mill on the Floss* so easily? And, if, as agreed, the turn of George Eliot's realism achieved its highpoint in *Middlemarch*, what precisely brought that turn about? To the first question, McGowan gives essentially the same answer I offered in *George Eliot's Early Novels*: it is in *Silas Marner* that George Eliot first harmonizes the conflicting orders of reality at war in *The Mill*. On the second question, McGowan proves to be harsher to *The Mill* than Barbara Hardy, George Levine, or myself. On the third question, McGowan is as silent as I was in *George Eliot's Early Novels*.

The preceding analysis of the shifts in mode in the first and twelfth chapters of *The Mill* calls into question McGowan's notions about the essentially fixed, nonmetaphoric "realism" of *The Mill*. It suggests a closer contiguity between *The Mill* and *Silas Marner*, that legendary fable which interposed itself as George Eliot wanted to move from *The Mill* to *Romola*. And it suggests that George Eliot's increasing experimentation with alternating narrative modes, interpenetrating genres, double plots, and conflicting orders of perception directly stemmed from her needs to integrate the discordant male and female elements at war within her own creative psyche.

Silas Marner can be read as a sequel to the one-paragraph myth of St. Ogg analyzed in the previous section. Silas unwillingly enacts what Ogg has done willingly. Subject to the same cataleptic dreaminess that besets both Maggie and the narrator of chapter one of *The Mill*, the asexual Silas is ejected from Lantern Yard by a rival suitor who exploits his passivity. Although, in Raveloe, he continues to be victimized by a rapacious male, his passivity now becomes an asset. The male narrator of *The Mill* can at best find a temporary refuge in the dream-like legend of Ogg, woman, and child; Silas, ferried back into a matriarchal world, can, with Dolly Winthrop's help, become fully feminized as a male mother to Eppie. Told by a narrator as genderless or double-gendered as the narrator of *Middlemarch* will be, the fable that George Eliot claimed only William Wordsworth (besides Lewes) would have appreciated brings together the trio of woman, feminized man, and small child. The novel thus provides a step-by-step enactment of what is merely adumbrated by Ogg, woman, and child in *The Mill*. If the flood that claims Maggie and Tom is necessary to remind their survivors that there is a higher reality than that represented by Ogg's harsh countrymen and their descendants throughout history, the draining of the Stone-pit reveals the skeleton of a phallic male: still clutching his brother's gold-handled "hunting-whip" and Silas's hoard, Dunstan is found, "wedged between two great stones." "Do you think he drowned himself?" asks Nancy. "No, he fell in," replies her husband.[22]

Without delving further into the relations between *The Mill on the Floss* and *Silas Marner*, I would submit that, despite McGowan's contention, George Eliot had already in the former novel begun her repudiation of the old realism evident in the *Scenes* and in *Adam Bede*, fictions told by a distinctly male narrator. The visionary world that George Eliot identified with a predominantly female sensibility is asserted in *The Mill*. Indeed, the book's conclusion—though flawed, as readers keep insisting—stems from the author's compelling need to assert the primacy of symbolic myth. Maggie has become the radiant female figure in Ogg's boat; Tom, who "could ask no question" (p. 455), has become an Ogg who was "blessed in that thou didst not question" (p. 105). The reiteration is obviously deliberate. And so is the description of Maggie's superhuman "energies" when she rows against the tide in what suddenly becomes "a story of almost miraculous divinely-protected effort" (p. 455). The emblem of the child, too, reappears to signify the reconciliation of female and male polarities: in drowning their separate adult identities, the gender-divided brother and sister can return to an undifferentiated childhood. To demand, as I once did, that Maggie and Tom take their place in the adult world they have inherited is to subvert a closure that, George Eliot feels, can only be represented in the mythic terms of romance. Brother and sister must acquire a legendary or emblematic status for those who remain behind in a world of time—narrator and reader, Stephen and Lucy, and the lonely Philip Wakem.

Read in this fashion, the ending of *The Mill on the Floss* becomes far more palatable, certainly more important, than most of us have allowed over the years. It is a Wordsworthian moment lifted out from the temporal world with its hurling, fragmenting, dead, and "wooden machinery." It belongs to the metaphoric world of romantic realism to which George Eliot would now turn with renewed zest, a world closer to that of a Charlotte Brontë whose metaphoric excesses she had previously eyed with considerable suspicion. Brontë, too, had striven to harmonize male and female energies through the maiming of Rochester or by drowning M. Emmanuel. Yet George Eliot fundamentally differs from Charlotte Brontë, as even Gilbert and Gubar somewhat reluctantly admit when they separate the bulk of her work from that of their Gothic satanists. If George Eliot, too, occasionally turned male sadism on the male, she nonetheless remains primarily interested in inwardly harmonizing female tendencies with the male tendencies that she, like other women novelists, had introjected. Like those other daughters of domineering fathers—Fanny Burney, Maria Edgeworth, Mary Wollstonecraft Shelley, the Brontës, and Virginia Woolf—she resorted to acts of exorcism that involve more than a gallery of overtly and covertly angry female characters, the victims of male history. If Professors Gilbert and Gubar allow that George Eliot *is* Latimer[23] (whose name becomes transposed in that kinder, but still sterile self-projection called Nancy Lammeter in *Silas Marner*), why not allow that she also "is," as she herself signified, a Casaubon or a Lydgate? Latimer, after all, was created because the novelist was unsatisfied with the excessive suppression of her female side in *Adam Bede*. Her turn from realistic pastoralism in *Adam* to supernatural horror story in "The Lifted Veil," like her many other shifts in media both from fiction to fiction as well as within a single work of fiction, must be read in terms of gender divisions such as those I have briefly tried to sketch.

IV

I began this essay with Wordsworth as a reminder that male poets see themselves as possessing an imagination composed of interacting male and female elements. I want to conclude with Woolf to remind ourselves that women novelists within an ever-more discernible "female tradition" are, for all their sympathy and acute understanding of their precursors, constantly forced into revising and redefining the fictional tropes they inherit from their precursors. Just as it was unnecessary to document George Eliot's Wordsworthianism, so does it seem unnecessary to document the Eliotism of Virginia Stephen, the daughter of a man who misread both Wordsworth and George Eliot.[24]

It is in *To the Lighthouse*, a novel embedded with allusions to Wordsworth and George Eliot, that Woolf shows herself to be every bit as self-conscious of her literary, as well as of her biological, parentage. Given her need to achieve distance, it is surprising neither that many of these allusions should be faintly ironic nor that the irony should be primarily directed at Mr. and Mrs. Ramsay, the incarnations of Leslie and Julia Stephen. William Bankes nostalgically recalls Mr. Ramsay as a fallen Wordsworthian Solitary, once capable of striding on a Westmorland road with a "natural air," yet betraying his impending socialization when, showing "his sympathy with humble things," he stopped before a "hen, straddling her wings out in protection of a covey of little chicks, upon which Ramsay, stopping his stick . . . said, 'Pretty—pretty.' "[25] And Mrs. Ramsay, too, though no hen-like Mrs. Tulliver, but an earthly Madonna who out-radiates the "picture of Queen Victoria" against which she stands "quite motionless" (p. 25), becomes an illustration of the pitfalls of that Wordsworthian sympathy which George Eliot had tried to strip of all residues of romantic egotism: "She praised herself in praising the light, without vanity, for she was stern, she was searching, she was beautiful like that light. It was odd, she thought, how if one was alone, one leant to inanimate things; trees, streams, flowers; felt they expressed one; felt they became one" (p. 97).

When Minta Doyle remembers how "frightened" she had first been by Mr. Ramsay's "really clever" talk about George Eliot, "for she had left the third volume of *Middlemarch* in the train and she never knew what happened in the end" (p. 148), Woolf does more than merely expose the flaws of both Minta and Mr. Ramsay. As her 1919 essay on George Eliot hints, that last third of *Middlemarch*, with Dorothea Brooke's "seeking wisdom and finding one scarcely knows what in marriage with Ladislaw," strikes Woolf as an inadequate compensation for the cherished recreation of a world of "fields and farms" in the earlier novels.[26] Instead of pastoralism and humor, there remain only those "great emotional scenes" that clearly embarrass Woolf and the talkativeness of dialogues which, since no longer in Midlands dialect, she finds to be "tediously slack."[27] Woolf protests that George Eliot "allows her heroines to talk too much . . . She lacks the unerring taste which chooses one sentence and compresses the heart of the scene within that. 'Whom are you going to dance with?' asked Mr. Knightley, at the Westons' ball. 'With you, if you will ask me,' said Emma; and she has said enough. Mrs. Casaubon would have talked for an hour and we should have looked out of the window."[28]

If Minta Doyle has, like Virginia's stepbrother George Duckworth, never finished reading *Middlemarch*, Woolf has. And in *To the Lighthouse* she sets out, among other things, to rewrite that unfinished third of a novel she respects, for all her strictures, as "magnificent." The figure of Mrs. Ramsay reenacts the dilemma of Dorothea Casaubon, and, by extension, the dilemma, too, of Julia Stephen and of Mary Ann Evans Lewes Cross, the loving "Mutter" of Lewes's children, the presiding presence at those Priory gatherings: "Nothing seemed to have merged. They all sat separate. And the whole effort of merging and flowing and creating rested on her" (p. 126). The figure of Mr. Ramsay reenacts the dilemma of the Reverend Edward Casaubon, and, by extension again, the dilemma of a Leslie Stephen over-eager to disengage the "unfeminine" habits of mind of a masculine George Eliot, and, hence, also of George Eliot herself—a George Eliot forced, but unwilling, to assign into two separate pigeonholes what Woolf calls in her 1919 essay, "the ordinary tasks of womanhood" and "wider service of their kind,"[29] and that amassed learning and overwhelming mastery of dry facts that she falsely continued to identify with a purely masculine domain. Oppressed by the motions of the historical flux, Mr. Ramsay, who can so eloquently and heroically discourse on Locke, Hume, Berkeley, "and the causes of the French Revolution," becomes as "timid in life" as the timid Mr. Casaubon (p. 70).

Read in this fashion, *To the Lighthouse* emerges as a critical homage to Woolf's antecedents—antecedents she both embraces yet feels compelled to reject. And her rejection becomes most manifest in her refusal to provide a mythical fusion for the gender distinctions she so insistently retains. Like Wordsworth and George Eliot, Woolf abhors a world of flux and severance, a reality that destroys sisters and brothers, a Prue as well as an Andrew Ramsay. But she also resists the fusions desired by an androgynous imagination. This resistance is particularly evident through Woolf's evocations of Wordworth and George Eliot. Walking by the shore with Paul Rayley and Minta Doyle, Andrew and Nancy feel a momentary oneness; sharing the boat with their father and the Macalisters, James and Cam briefly join in a silent alliance. But Woolf relentlessly sunders that fusion with the sharp wedge of gender division.

Nancy and Andrew are not the children who played by "that immortal sea / Which brought us hither"; we may see them "sport upon the shore, / And hear the mighty waters rolling evermore," but we derive no intimations of either immortality or oneness.[30] United at first in their antagonism towards the adult Paul and a Minta who still exhibits, in Andrew's opinion, "sensible," unfeminine habits, brother and sister soon stray apart. Once alone, Nancy crouches Eve-like over the surface of pools she imaginatively wants to possess as her "own," while Andrew wanders off to a craggy promontory. Like the dreamy Maggie Tulliver hypnotized by the mill's churning water or the little sister who, in "Brother and Sister" sonnets, converts the brown canal into a floating "dream-world," Nancy yields to a reverie which shuts out the world beyond: "Brooding, she changed the pool into the sea, and made the minnows into sharks and whales, and cast vast clouds over this tiny world by holding her hand against the sun, and so brought darkness and desolation, like God himself, to millions of ignorant and innocent creatures, and then took her hand away suddenly and let the sun stream down" (pp. 114–15). But this Eve-like aspiration to godhead is short-lived. From an Infinite I Am Nancy returns to her finite ego. It is Andrew who shouts that the sea is about to rush in, just as Tom interrupts Maggie's, and "boyish Will" interrupts his little sister's, watery reveries.

What is more, both children now witness Paul and Minta embracing, "kissing probably." Outraged, indignant, yet "in dead silence," Nancy and Andrew feel more apart than before: "Indeed, they were rather sharp with each other. She might have called him when she saw the crayfish or whatever it was, Andrew grumbled. However, they both felt, it's not our fault. They had not wanted this horrid nuisance to happen. All the same it irritated Andrew that Nancy should be a woman, and Nancy that Andrew should be a man, and they tied their shoes very neatly and drew the bows rather tight" (p. 116).

Like the scene in *The Mill on the Floss* in which Maggie, stung by Tom, pushes Lucy into the mud, this brief episode depicts a mock-heroic version of the Fall. But whereas George Eliot, like Wordsworth, still tries to recover a childhood paradise, Woolf regards the severance of miniature Eves and Adams as an emblem of an alienating reality in which the prime fluidity is that of time. Her narrator, correspondingly, can have no fixed identity or fixed gender but must flit from consciousness to consciousness. To try to envelop, as Nancy so briefly did, an entire cosmos is a Miltonic impossibility. As Lily Briscoe later observes while speculating about Mr. Carmichael's attachment to Andrew, "this was one way of knowing people, she thought: to know the outline, not the detail" (p. 289).

In "Time Passes" Woolf again revises literary precedent. She deliberately evokes *The Excursion* by depicting a female abode which, like Margaret's ruined cottage or Maggie's Dorlcote Mill, is about to succumb to the unmending ravages of nature. And she rescues it from corruption: "Then the roof would have fallen; briars and hemlock would have blotted out path, step, and window; would have grown, unequally but lustily over the mound, until some trespasser, losing his way, could have told only by a red-hot poker among the nettles or a scrap of china in the hemlock that here once some one had lived; there had been a house" (pp. 208-9). But no trespassing Wanderer and Poet, Lucy and Stephen, or solitary Philip are allowed to extract thoughts that lie too deep for tears. The catharsis is spread out, and it carefully avoids that emotionalism that Woolf so distrusted in her predecessors.

First the snorting Mrs. McNab, then a Lily Briscoe who must keep at bay the ghost of Mrs. Ramsay as well as the flesh-and-blood Mr. Ramsay who finds such unexpected comfort in his boots, and, finally, the pilgrimage to the Lighthouse subvert a Wordsworthian or Eliotic closure. An epiphany occurs. But it is acknowledged as impermanent: "But what did it matter? she asked herself, taking up her brush again" (p. 310). And in the boat, though it reaches its goal, the fusion is similarly qualified. Cam, peeling her "hard-boiled egg," is no radiant Madonna, but remains at odds with brother and father and Mr. Macalister and the Macalister boy who, in defiance of all Wordsworthian notions of childhood, mutilates a fish and throws it back into the water. Nor is Mr. Ramsay idealized. Though executing at last his dead wife's wish, though as unquestioning now as Ogg son of Beorl had been, he is not a feminized male out of some ancient legend: "He was shabby," Cam notes, "and simple, eating bread and cheese; and yet he was leading them on a great expedition where, for all she knew, they would be drowned" (p. 305). Yet no such apotheosis occurs. Unlike Tom and Maggie—and unlike Virginia Woolf herself—Cam does not drown.

1. See, for instance, Nina Auerbach, *Woman and the Demon: The Life of a Victorian Myth* (Cambridge, Mass., 1982).

2. Alfred Adler, *Cooperation Between the Sexes: Writings on Women, Love, and Marriage, Sexuality and Its Disorders*, ed. and trans. Heinz L.

Ansbacher and Rowena R. Ansbacher (Garden City, N.Y.; 1978), pp. 32–35. It remained for Adler, whose theories on sexuality challenged Freud's, to remove "psychological hermaphroditism" from "any direct dependence on biological" disorders (p. 285).

3. *The George Eliot Letters*, ed. Gordon S. Haight, 9 vols. (New Haven, Conn., 1954–78), 5:54.

4. Ibid., 2:320

5. Margaret Homans, "Eliot, Wordsworth, and the Scenes of the Sisters' Instruction," *Critical Inquiry* 8 (Winter 1981):234.

6. "A Nineteenth-Century Touchstone: Chapter XV of *Biographia Literaria*," in *Nineteenth-Century Literary Perspectives: Essays in Honor of Lionel Stevenson*, ed. Clyde de L. Ryals (Durham, North Carolina, 1974), p. 5.

7. "Lines Composed a Few Miles Above Tintern Abbey," lines 109–10. These and future references (to be given in the text) are taken from *Wordsworth: Poetical Works*, ed. Ernest De Selincourt (London, 1966).

8. Of particular relevance to section two of this essay are Hardy's and Levine's discussions of *The Mill on the Floss* in "The Mill on the Floss" in *Critical Essays on George Eliot*, ed. Barbara Hardy (New York, 1970), pp. 42–58, and "Intelligence as Deception: *The Mill on the Floss*," *PMLA* 80 (September 1965): 402–9; John P. McGowan's discussion of *The Mill* and *Middlemarch* in "The Turn of George Eliot's Realism," *NCF* 35 (September 1980): 171–92; Gillian Beer's and my own discussions of *Middlemarch* in "Myth and the Single Consciousness" and "Fusing Fact and Fiction," both in *The Particular Web: Essays on 'Middlemarch,'* ed. Ian Adam (Toronto, 1975), pp. 91–115 and 43–72; and, finally, George Levine's discussion of *Middlemarch* and *Daniel Deronda* in "George Eliot's Hypothesis of Reality," *NCF* 35 (June 1980): 1–28.

9. *The Madwoman in the Attic: The Woman Writer and the Nineteenth-Century Literary Imagination* (New Haven, Conn., 1979), pp. 443–535.

10. *The Mill on the Floss*, ed. Gordon S. Haight, Riverside Edition (Boston, 1961), p. 455. Future references to this edition will be given in the text itself.

11. *Journals of Dorothy Wordsworth*, ed. Mary Moorman (London, 1971), p. 101.

12. "Brother and Sister," *The Legend of Jubal and Other Poems* (Boston, 1874), sonnet 11, ll. 13–14, p. 203.

13. Though Wordsworth assigned "To a Butterfly" and "The Sparrow's Nest" to "Poems Referring to the Period of Childhood," he placed "To My Sister" in the category he called "Poems of Sentiment and Reflection." Like "Nutting," however, it could just as well have been included among "Poems of the Imagination."

14. As Judith Schelly observes in her unpublished doctoral dissertation on the brother-sister relation as a metaphor (Berkeley, 1981), a subtle change in outlook already takes place earlier in the 1800 *Poems on the Naming of Places*: in "Emma's Dell," Dorothy merely acts as a passive recipient of the dell's name, without presiding over it as, say, Maggie will preside over the "Red Deeps." The fresh and clear "Rivulet" that comes to meet the male

116

U. C. Knoepflmacher

speaker is itself masculine, "delighting in its strength /... with a young man's speed" (I. 2-3). It thus is unlike the active, "wild," moon-bathed, mist-drenched Dorothy whom Wordsworth had only two years before associated with the "fair river" Wye; and it is unlike, too, the "little" Ripple that flows with such "lively current into the Floss," a rivulet whose "dark, changing wavelets" retroactively remind the reader of the young Maggie Tulliver (*The Mill*, p. 7).

15. See, for instance, George MacDonald's Princess Daylight or Nycteris in "The Day Boy and the Night Girl." The rejuvenation of a withered old woman dates back, or course, to Chaucer's "Wife of Bath's Tale," a story I have linked to George Eliot's myth-making in "Unveiling Men: Power and Masculinity in George Eliot's Fiction," *Men by Women*, ed. Janet Todd, *Women & Literature*, Vol. 2, n.s. (New York, 1981), pp. 130-36.

16. *Legends of the Madonna As Represented in the Fine Arts* (London, 1885), p. 134.

17. Cf. Charlotte Yonge, "Names from Teuton Mythology," *History of Christian Names* (London, 1884): "The root of the name Oegir is, in fact, *og* or *uok*, the same as our awe. Thence come many words, such as . . . the verb *eggan*, to incite, still common in the North; while we have *to egg on*" (p. 323). Also known as Agir or Ygg, Oegir was a Jotun or giant originally called Hier, a demigod of the sea or "wave" known to raise storms and drown sailors (p. 322). By calling the mythical ferryman "Ogg," George Eliot seems to have wanted to conflate the destructive Pagan figure of Norse mythology with the Christian chivalric figure of "Ogier le Danois," known in Italian romances as Oggieri or Oggero. Charlotte Yonge (whose etymological *History* first appeared in 1863, three years after the publication of *The Mill*) notes that "this Oggier was without doubt a contribution from the stores of Norman tradition; for Holger, or Olger, Danske is the grandest national hero of Denmark" (p. 402). Yonge speculates that Oggier, too, originally had been a god or "mythical king" from the "sacred island" of Heligoland; his "name itself," she therefore concludes, connotes "*holy*, our very word holy—the *halig* of the Anglo-Saxons, the *hellig* of the North, the *heilig* of Germany, and these words sprang from those denoting health; as the Latin *salve*, hail, *salvus*, safe, and *salvation*, safety, are all related to soundness" (p. 403).

18. "Narrative and History," *ELH* 41 (1974): 455-73; and "Optic and Semiotic in *Middlemarch*," in *The Worlds of Victorian Fiction*, ed. Jerome H. Buckley, Harvard English Studies 6 (Cambridge, Mass., 1975), pp. 125-45.

19. See note 8, above.

20. McGowan, "George Eliot's Realism" (see note 8, above), 189.

21. Ibid., 180.

22. *Silas Marner*, ed. Jerome Thale (New York, 1962), chap. 18, pp. 201-2.

23. Gilbert and Gubar, *The Madwoman in the Attic*, p. 447.

24. See Elaine Showalter, "The Greening of Sister George," *NCF* 35 (December 1980), 292, 295-97, 310-11, for a valuable discussion of the ways in which Woolf corrected the male prejudices (including Stephen's own) that had clouded George Eliot's reputation by 1919, the centennial of her birth.

25. *To the Lighthouse* (New York, 1955), pp. 35–35; future references to this edition are given in the text itself.

26. "George Eliot," *Women and Writing,* ed. Michele Barrett (New York, 1979), pp. 157, 156. Woolf wrote two further essays on George Eliot in the *Daily Herald* of 9 March 1921 and in the *Nation and Athenaeum* of 30 October 1926.

27. Ibid., p. 158.

28. Ibid., p. 159.

29. Ibid., p. 159.

30. "Ode: Intimation of Immortality," ll. 167-68, 170-71.

VI

JOHN CLUBBE

Carlyle as Epic Historian

Carlyle in the whole make-up of his genius is utterly unclassical.

J. A. K. Thomson[1]

"'What!' I exclaimed, 'is the Revolution of France a less important event than the siege of Troy? Is Napoleon a less interesting character than Achilles? For me remains the Revolutionary Epick.'"

Disraeli[2]

CARLYLE MAINTAINED AN INTEREST IN HISTORY ALL HIS LIFE. The past fascinated him from his school days; early and late, history constituted his favorite reading; and the contemporary events he lived through and read about during his long life he understood as living history. Carlyle was longer a historian than he was an essayist, a poet, a journalist, a translator, a lecturer, or a novelist. When he contemplated writing his first book in 1822, he thought to undertake a history of the English Commonwealth. His last, published in 1875, is a history of the early Norwegian kings. Only as a commentator on public affairs and as a letter-writer was Carlyle active longer, and in both these activities he remains very much a historian: a historian not of the past, however, but of the present. Yet *The French Revolution*, Carlyle's first major historical work and the first book to which he affixed his name, was not published until 1837, fifteen years and more after his earliest essays had appeared in print. Why did Carlyle take so long to determine his true vocation? Why did he not write history before the mid-1830s? Why after this time did he write little else but history? In good part the answers to these questions lie in a work of literature Carlyle read in the winter of 1834 while still at his moorland farm, Craigenputtoch. That work is Homer's *Iliad*. By transforming Carlyle's vision of what history could become, the *Iliad* released his energies in ways not before possible. Carlyle's reading of it in 1834 had a decisive, and still largely unrecognized, importance upon his later works, several of which—*The French Revolution* and *Frederick the Great*—he consciously intended as modern epics. In others—*Past and Present* and *Latter-Day Pamphlets*—he attempted to redefine the nature of epic. Before 1834 Carlyle had little to say about the epic; after that year, every major book he wrote reflects his awareness of it.

I

The first fruit and finest bloom of Carlyle's epic vision, a work written in the full glow of his newfound enthusiasm for Homeric epic, is *The French Revolution*. Froude considered it the "most powerful" of all Carlyle's books "and the only one which has the character of a work of art." [3] This last observation, if somewhat overstated, retains an essential truth. *The French Revolution* is more a work of art than of history, and though its historical value is by no means negligible, it is more as literature than as history that it merits our attention today. It is a literary artifice that is, arguably, as dense in meaning, as tightly-written, as rich in allusion, as Joyce's *Ulysses*—and as consciously in the epic mode. To come to terms with it demands something of the same energy and imaginative effort that we expend on Joyce's masterpiece.

The French Revolution awed Carlyle's contemporaries. They considered it his major work. And, more often than one might surmise from reading the few twentieth-century discussions that the book has received, they considered it an epic. John Stuart Mill set the tone for subsequent criticism when he hailed it as "an epic poem; and notwithstanding, or even in consequence of this, the truest of histories." For Henry David

Thoreau, *The French Revolution* was "a poem, at length got translated into prose; an Iliad"; for Alton Locke, in Kingsley's novel of that name, only *Paradise Lost* had "quickened and exalted [his] poetical view of man and his history" more than had *The French Revolution*, "that great prose poem, the single epic of modern days"; for Francis Espinasse, at the end of the century, it was a "great prose epic."[4] Among the novelists the book's impact was enormous. Thackeray wrote that it "possesses genius, if any book ever did"; Meredith thought it "perfect" and written by a "seer"; and Dickens, several of whose novels reveal a heavy indebtedness to it, wrote to Carlyle in 1851 that he was "reading that wonderful book . . . again for the 500th time." Even a late Victorian like Edward Ponderevo in Wells's *Tono-Bungay* can still exclaim, "Lord! what a book that French Revolution of his is!"[5] Nor did Carlyle's contemporaries fail to compare him explicitly to Homer. Trollope ironically apostrophized him as "our dear old English Homer—Homer in prose." And for James Russell Lowell, Carlyle, "with the gift of song, . . . would have been the greatest of epic poets since Homer."[6] With such tributes did the Victorians acknowledge Carlyle's achievement as a writer of epic—an achievement that twentieth-century students of the period have virtually ignored.

Brian Wilkie begins his influential *Romantic Poets and Epic Tradition* (1965) by observing that literary historians commonly assume "that the epic, moribund in the late eighteenth century, was dead by the beginning of the nineteenth."[7] Wilkie would not make this statement today. Since he wrote, several studies in addition to his own have appeared that chart the epic impulse in the Romantic poets. These studies argue for the renewed vitality of the epic in the hands of Blake and Wordsworth, of Byron, Shelley, and Keats.[8] But the effort to explore the epic tradition in the nineteenth century has largely stopped with the Romantics.

Only a few scholars in the past twenty years have investigated the epic impulse among the Victorians. In 1964 John Loofboorow explored *Henry Esmond*'s affinities to epic tradition, both classical and English; in 1968 George Levine analyzed Macaulay's *History of England* from the perspective of epic; and, also in 1968, Albert LaValley discussed *The French Revolution* as an epic within a tradition of the modern that includes Blake and Nietzsche.[9] Although LaValley's pioneering discussion remains the most comprehensive analysis of *The French Revolution's* epic qualities, his study is based on an incomplete and, in my view, limited notion of the epic. It does not ask why Carlyle should turn suddenly and without previous indication to the epic as a model; nor does it seem aware that Carlyle maintains, though with important modifications, the epic mode in his subsequent works. Of twentieth-century scholars before LaValley, only B. H. Lehman had taken cognizance of "the epic temper" of Carlyle's mind.[10] Since LaValley, Jules Seigel has argued for the kinship of *Latter-Day Pamphlets*, and Morse Peckham for that of *Frederick the Great*, to epic tradition.[11]

In this essay I wish to prepare the grounds for considering Carlyle as an epic historian on a firmer basis than before. To make as convincing a case for the overwhelming impact of Homer on Carlyle, and Carlyle's subsequent absorption in the epic, I will discuss in some detail his reading of the *Iliad* in 1834, a reading that led Carlyle consciously to mold his major works after 1834 upon the epic. When we realize this, we may begin to reconsider the later Carlyle not simply as an increasingly shrill prophet of England's woes or of Prussia's greatness but as a historian and literary artist working in the epic mode.

The epic fascinated the Victorians to a degree that seems largely to have escaped modern critical awareness. Writers in nineteenth-century journals often spoke of the novel as assuming the dominant position in the literary firmament once held by epic poetry. Carlyle prefigures this attitude in his 1832 essay "Biography," where in the same sentence he laments "the wholly dead modern Epic" and expresses hope for the "partially living modern Novel."[12] But in 1832 Carlyle had not yet come to grips with Homer; nor had the epic died a premature death. Rather, the epic as an ideal lived on in the Victorian consciousness. "Literary traditions now unnoticed," John Loofboorow has written, "were still so familiar to nineteenth-century readers that critics took their identification for granted" (p. 107). Modern readers tend to walk right by the many epic signposts in the literature of the age.[13]

We are still far from understanding the degree and extent to which the epic impulse becomes a dynamic factor in Victorian literature. It gives vitality to novels as diverse as Thackeray's *Esmond*, Kingsley's *Westward Ho!*, and Eliot's *Middlemarch*; it permeates Arnold's *Sohrab and Rustum* and *Balder Dead*; it animates Elizabeth Barrett Browning to capture in *Aurora Leigh* her own "full-veined, heaving, double-breasted Age" (Book 5); it appears, as a diminished thing, in poems by Tennyson, Browning, and Clough; it gives artistic coherence to Darwin's *Origin of Species*; and it provides the underpinning for the great histories of Macaulay and Froude.[14] At times, I admit, these writers consciously react against epic tradition more than they follow it. Tennyson, for example, in "Morte d'Arthur" has the poet Everard Hall refer to the epic as a literary "Mastodon" and ask why a modern author should "take the style of those heroic times." The "twelve books" of his epic poem on King Arthur, Hall says, "were faint Homeric echoes." But Tennyson himself, though wary of Homer as a model, succumbed to the lure of epic. His own twelve-book *Idylls of the King* may well be, as Richard Jenkyns has recently argued, a "full-dress epic."[15] Others, like Thackeray, adopted an ironic stance toward epic tradition. Of all the major Victorians, no one responded more fully to the challenge of Homeric epic than did Carlyle or adopted epic modes so often or used them in so many major works.

II

In 1866, looking back upon his life, Carlyle observed that in regard to classical literature he "knew nothing . . . for years after leaving College;—little about it still tho' always rather learning." Then he mentions his reading of the *Iliad* in Greek: "Homer in *original* (read with difficulty), after *Wolf's* broad flash of light thrown into it."[16] This statement encapsulates two crucial, intimately related experiences: Carlyle's study of Homer in Greek, a study that began in earnest only in January 1834; and his reading, several months later, of Friedrich August Wolf's *Prolegomena ad Homerum*.

123

The organic filaments that led to Carlyle's decision to undertake a careful reading of Homer in the original stretched far into the past. Unlike most schoolboys south of the Tweed, he did not follow a course of study in the classical languages. Though he learned the Greek alphabet at Annan School, he never gained the easy familiarity with the Greek classics that, for example, Macaulay or Arnold or Froude received from their schooling. Newly arrived at the University of Edinburgh, he took during the spring semester of 1810 the beginning Greek class under Professor George Dunbar. He had received good grounding in Latin at Annan School and always remained a fair Latinist. But Greek was another matter. "I know almost nothing about [Homer]," he wrote a college friend in 1816, "having never read any thing but Pope's translation, and not above a single book of the original—& that several years ago. Indeed I know very little of the Greek at any rate." [17] But despite his lack of knowledge of Greek and his limited awareness of Homer through Pope's translation (which he disliked), there lurked throughout the years to come a sense that Homer's greatness was genuine, if only partially understood by him at this time. His comments on Homeric epic after 1816, whether in praise or dispraise, often appear perfunctory. In 1820 he opined that Homer had "had his day," and even as late as 1832 he rated him "a partially *hollow* and false singer" (*CL* 1:232; *Works* 28:50). Yet by the later 1820s he usually ranked Homer with Shakespeare (e.g., *Works* 26:245; 28:47). At times, Carlyle expressed contempt for contemporary epics, at one point lumping together "iron-mailed Epics" with "our innumerable host of rose-coloured Novels" (*Works* 26:271). By 1834, although he had dipped into Homer on a number of occasions, he had not come to grips with him. Doing so, he sensed, could only come about through reading him in the original. By himself he could not cope sufficiently with the Greek to get through more than a few dozen lines. During these years he also vaguely felt that the time to tackle Homer in Greek had not yet come.

Carlyle's sixth sense is his awareness of time in his own existence. He knew that he could pace his life, that things came to him if he had the patience to wait for them. It is not a question of his procrastinating, nor of scholars looking over his life with an awareness of how things turned out, or even of their seeing the inevitable in the accidental. Rather, Carlyle was aware from early maturity that his development would be slow and uncertain, that his "apprenticeship" would seemingly never end; yet he knew too that eventually he would find his way and write the great work he felt was within him. Although not always aware of what he was doing or why, he had an inner sense that often whispered to him, "Patience! Patience! It has to be so. All will yet work out for you." When late in 1833 he decided to devote a block of time in the coming year to reading the *Iliad* in Greek, he had pondered doing so for more than a decade.

The early 1830s marked a difficult period for Carlyle. During the winter and spring of 1830–31, he wrote *Sartor Resartus* in a sustained burst of energy. At the end of July 1831 he went to London to market it, but without success. Spending the winter in London, he wrote there "Characteristics" and a major essay on Boswell's *Life of Johnson*. Despite the fervid admiration of a few, he remained relatively unknown. Upon his return to Craigenputtoch in April 1832, he set down a long study of Diderot and another of his hero Goethe, who had died that year. Then nothing. Commissions to write new articles no longer came in, no journal would take the work he had completed. The *Edinburgh Review* had closed its doors to him several years before. Other journals to which he had contributed gradually followed suit. Carlyle's income, which came from periodical writing, virtually ceased. In August 1833 *Sartor*, which a reluctant James Fraser had agreed to take in installments, began to appear in *Fraser's Magazine*. It offended all but a very few readers. By early 1834 Carlyle had not put pen to paper for remunerative writing for over a year. He brooded over his inactivity. He also brooded over a subject for a book. A biography of John Knox or a study of the French Revolution seemed the likeliest possibilities. But he took no steps to begin either. Any book he undertook had also to be a work of literary art, and he had not found a model that offered him a satisfactory imaginative framework.

As the years at Craigenputtoch went by, Carlyle felt increasingly dissatisfied with the loneliness of his life there and with the uncertainty of his future prospects. At an age when most men are settled he seemed more than ever at an impasse. What should he be doing with himself? "I feel in general that I am at the end of an epoch," he writes Mill in October 1833. "All barriers seem *overthrown* in my inward world" (*CL* 7:24). He continued to bide his time. Everything worthwhile that ever emerged out of Carlyle had been long pondered. "What a blessing that I can sit here," he says in this same letter, "not *forced* to speak, for months yet; till the Inward have grown clear" (*CL* 7:25). In late 1833 Carlyle's subsequent turn to historical epic was, on the surface, neither predictable nor inevitable. The "Inward" might not for a while, or ever, have "grown clear."

In October 1833 Carlyle "determined, by way of practicing myself in Narrative, to write a small historico-poetico Piece on the famous *Diamond Necklace*" (*CL* 7:21). Doing so would serve as a trial run for what might possibly become a major work, or a major mode of expression, or both. Writing "The Diamond Necklace" in November and December demonstrated to Carlyle that he indeed had a gift for sustained narrative. Interestingly enough, he does not mention the epic in this work, nor is there influence of the epic in it. It is the last piece he completed before he began *The French Revolution* in September 1834. After writing "The Diamond Necklace," Carlyle knew that he could handle narrative history; he had not yet realized that it could be epic history.

In January 1834 Carlyle felt he stood at a crossroads in his life. The month previous he had turned thirty-nine. On January 21, the day before he began to read the *Iliad* in Greek, he wrote to Sarah Austin: "As for myself, I think I have arrived at a kind of pause in my History, so singular is the course of things without me and within me. I have written very little for a year; less than for any of the last seven. I stand as if earnestly looking out, in the most labyrinthic country, till I catch the right track again" (*CL* 7:83). Drifting, uncertain what he should be doing, of what lay ahead, in this mood he began to read Homer.

III

"I have been purposing to read . . . (Homer's *Iliad*) for the last thirteen years," Carlyle wrote on 28 January 1834, "and never could fairly set upon it, *for want of company*" (*CL* 7:87). Now he had "company" in William Glen, a young man whom he had met in London in 1831, intelligent, precocious, unstable mentally, but who, most usefully, knew Greek. After Glen came to Scotland late in 1833, Carlyle determined to "set him to read Homer with me" (*CL* 7:5). Not until January 22 did he and Glen actually begin. Fifteen years before, in 1819, Carlyle had commenced the study of German by exchanging lessons in French for lessons in German with a university friend, Robert Jardine, who was more proficient in German than he. Now he began a similar arrangement, this time exchanging lessons in geometry for lessons in Greek. For the next three months, his evenings at Craigenputtoch fell into a regular pattern. At five, "otherwise a quite worthless hour" for him, he prepared his daily reading in the *Iliad* (*CL* 7:89, 106). Glen arrived at seven, and for an hour they worked on geometrical propositions together. The next hour they spent going over the Greek that Carlyle had parsed. He and Glen usually got through no more than fifty lines an evening, though once or twice they managed a hundred.

Within a week of the commencement of the nightly study sessions Carlyle found himself completely absorbed in the *Iliad*. In his eagerness he winged ahead by reading Johann Heinrich Voss's translation into German hexameters, a translation he termed "the best . . . I ever in my life looked into." [18] This is high praise indeed from Carlyle, a translator himself and one who often spoke caustically of translations by others. Thus, behind the excited labor of struggling through his fifty to a hundred lines a night, there stood the reinforcing integrity of Voss's translation, which assured him that he understood what he read in Greek and, by allowing him to move along more quickly, spurred him to continue that reading.

Carlyle's Journal and his letters of this time testify to the mounting excitement he felt as he forged ahead in the Greek.

"Began *Homer* two weeks ago," he recorded on February 9: "nearly through the first book now—like it very considerably. Simplicity, sincerity, the singleness (not quite the word) and massive repose as of an ancient picture."[19] Three days later he had finished the *Iliad*'s first book. "Pleasantest most purely poetical reading I have had for long. Simplicity (not multiplicity), almost vacuity, yet sincerity, and the richest toned artless music" (ibid., pp. 405-6). To Mill he confessed, on February 22, a month to the day that he had begun, that he liked "the old fellow real[ly] *amazingly*; he does more good than I can express; creates a whole Portici"—a gallery of characters—"under my Kilmarnock Bonnet" (*CL* 7:102). By February 25 Carlyle had nearly finished the second book. "Nothing I have read for long years so interests and nourishes me: I am quite surprised at the interest I take in it. All the *Antiquity* I have ever known become *alive* in my head: there is a whole Gallery of Apelleses and Phidiases that I not only look upon but *make*" (*CL* 7:107).

As spring approached Carlyle's enthusiasm remained unabated. By March 24 he was "nearly thro' the 4*th* Book, and my delight is still great" (*CL* 7:124). A month later, he informed Leigh Hunt, "I am writing *nothing*; reading, above all things, my old *Homer* and Prolegomena enough; the old Song itself with a most Singular delight" (*CL* 7:132-133). On the same day he told Mill: "But the reading worth all other readings continues to be my *Homer*. Glorious old Book, which one would save, next after the Bible, from a universal conflagration of Books! I will talk to you about this till your head ring with it, as my own does" (*CL* 7:135). And on April 28, just before he left Craigenputtoch to seek lodgings in London, he realized that "here ends for the present my intercourse with *Homer*: I have read several Books of his Rhapsody as with spectacles, and diligently surveyed all the rest" (*CL* 7:138).

Carlyle had averaged about two books a month since he had begun on January 22. Thus he had read about six books of the original "with spectacles," from the initial clash between Achilles and Agamemnon to the moving leave-taking of Hector and Andromache on the walls of Troy. The remaining eighteen books Carlyle had "diligently surveyed" in Voss's German translation. Two years afterward Carlyle writes of this experience, "the German Homer I shall never forget" (*CL* 8:292). Of Voss's translation Sir John L. Myres has written: "His rendering is sometimes faulty, often as uncouth as Chapman's, but his heart was in his work, and he achieved for Germany very much the same result as the great Elizabethan translators in England two centuries earlier; he naturalized Homer and made him a national classic only second to Luther's rendering of the Bible."[20] The resonance of Voss's version of the *Iliad*, to which Schiller and Goethe had earlier testified, had as sustained an impact upon Carlyle's imagination as had his reading of the original in Greek. For Carlyle, Voss's rendering was "not only the best of that old Singer, but the best ever executed of any Singer, under such circumstances: a really effectual work, which one rejoices to look into, true, genuine to the heart in every line" (*CL* 7:137–138). In London, occupied with finding a house and settling in, Carlyle had to put aside his intensive study of Homer. But he left the *Iliad*, he said, "with increased knowledge, and love it better than any other Book, I think, except the Bible alone. It is not the richest intrinsically perhaps, but the richest-oldest" (*CL* 7:138).

IV

It is difficult to exaggerate the extraordinary nature of Carlyle's expressions of enthusiasm for Homer. Here he is, nearly forty, moved to wonder and admiration and to a sustained pitch of excitement by a work of literature. Carlyle's exhilaration before the *Iliad* we may compare to Keats's sense of discovery upon reading Chapman's translation of the *Odyssey*. Not since Carlyle had struggled through Goethe's *Wilhelm Meisters Lehrjahre* fifteen years before had he expressed such enthusiasm over a literary work. When he first came upon the *Lehrjahre*, he felt "that, since the age of 15, he had read no such deep, clear, great, and widely illuminative Book:—that here, credibly and probably, *was* a man who could 'reveal' to him many highest things."[21]

Reading the *Iliad* was for Carlyle an experience of at least equal intensity and significance as reading the *Lehrjahre*. His indwelling in epic, particularly Homeric epic, after 1834 affected the manner in which he conceived the world. As his German study had altered his style and deepened his thought, so his wrestling with the *Iliad* gave to his understanding of literature and of society, past and present, an epic cast. His immersion in epic also accentuated the irritation he felt with all of modern life that fell short of the heroic. Whereas earlier the German reading had led to translations and to essays about German authors, the *Iliad* stimulated Carlyle's *own* creativity. As much as had the *Lehrjahre*, it opened up for him a new heaven and a new earth. Both experiences, we must remember, involved Carlyle's grappling with a difficult work in translation, one which to read he had to learn a new language. Both experiences also placed him in the role of an outsider viewing an alien culture. All his life Carlyle thought of himself as one apart from, even in opposition to, the society that swirled around him. Being an outsider gave him strength as a personality and as a thinker.[22] A Scot, isolated at Craigenputtoch, soon to be an *emigré* in London, he relished the strange, compelling new world he found in Homer. (Reading the *Iliad* in both Greek and German made it, in effect, doubly strange, doubly compelling.) In the early 1830s, Carlyle groped to fuse together various elements of a literary and prophetic vision still largely inchoate. Homer catalyzed them into fusion. Carlyle's task became henceforth to convey the meaning of the Homeric world in modern terms and to use the epic to present a vision of historical process. "I saw that the French Revolution and German literature were the cardinal phenomena of the century," Carlyle told Espinasse later in life.[23] He had made his countrymen aware of the significance of German literature; now, with the *Iliad* ringing in his ears, he could contemplate doing the same for the Revolution. Whereas his reading in German had led to his decade-long missionary activity for things German and to *Sartor*, his reading of the *Iliad* launched him on his own epic, *The French Revolution*, sustained him through the writing of that book, and left its stamp on virtually every major work he wrote afterwards.

After Homer, Carlyle never experienced another literary catalyst of like intensity. What stimulated him in the future were usually public events—the 1848 revolutions, for example. Such stimuli, real and invigorating as they certainly were, yet gave Carlyle no controlling vision, no organizing principle by which he might construct a coherent literary work. But the epic did give to Carlyle just such a standard against which he could attempt to recreate past societies as well as urge upon his own a consciousness of its history and its potential. In *Past and Present* he finds in epic an underlying model for English society; in *Cromwell* he tries, with only limited success, to encompass Puritan England into what he called a "Cromwelliad"; in the *Latter-Day Pamphlets* his vision, despairing before the gloomy present of an ever more democratic England, lapses into mock-epic; in *Frederick* he reaffirms through an immense act of will something of his belief in epic, for Prussia if perhaps no longer for England. Again and again Carlyle seeks to recapture or transform the expansive epic vision that had been so triumphantly his while writing *The French Revolution*. More than a historian, Carlyle is an artist, and a very great one, but without an organizing structure, a shaping model, he increasingly botched the problem of form, always the weakest point in his literary endeavors and the one he most agonized over. *Cromwell* and *Frederick*, important in their day as pioneering revaluations, lack the artistic integrity of *The French Revolution* and, in a different way, of *Past and Present*.

Reading the *Iliad* in 1834 thus constitutes a watershed experience for Carlyle. It signals a division between his earlier and his later work, a division that scholars who halt their investigations with the year 1834—for instance, Charles Frederick Harrold, Hill Shine, Carlisle Moore, G. B. Tennyson, and Jacques Cabau—rightly emphasize. The outward sign of this division is the move from Craigenputtoch to London in May 1834. It led to a change in habitat, in mode of life, and, eventually, in the public's attitude toward Carlyle's work. But Carlyle's overwhelming response to Homer, although it took place at the same time, has passed virtually unnoticed. Homer's name has almost never been coupled with

Carlyle's. When one thinks of literary influences on him, one thinks of Goethe, Schiller, and Jean Paul in Germany; Milton and Shakespeare in England; Dante in Italy; possibly Voltaire and Rousseau in France; and everywhere the rhythms, stories, and prophetic urgency of the Bible. But Homer—and Homer in Greek and German? Hardly. Yet, except for Goethe, no figure of the past influenced Carlyle in more fundamental ways than did Homer. The understanding of epic that he gained through close study of the *Iliad* exerted incalculable influence in determining his mode of utterance after the mid-1830s. Like the immersion in German fifteen years before, the reading in Homer effected a fundamental change in his conception of literature. The epic became for Carlyle the paramount literary form, the form to which the historian who viewed himself as a poet and prophet to his age should aspire. The *Iliad* also led Carlyle to think of the epic as a paradigm for society, how it had evolved, how it functioned. Without knowing at the time the import that his reading in Homer would have for him, Carlyle had arrived at the literary perspective that would dominate his subsequent career as a writer.

V

In determining Carlyle's understanding of Homer, one man stands out preeminently: Friedrich August Wolf. When in April 1834 Carlyle reports with joy that he is reading "my old *Homer* and Prolegomena" and when in 1866 he still recalled the "broad flash of light" that Wolf had cast on the *Iliad*, he refers in both instances to the German philologist's *Prolegomena ad Homerum*, a book that immediately upon its appearance in 1795 had marked an epoch in Homeric studies. In this work Wolf argued that the *Iliad* consisted of a number of disparate ballads sung by bards over the centuries; that, at a late date, these ballads were joined together, written down, and revised by master compilers and editors; and that, as a consequence, no single person could be designated as the *Iliad*'s author. Wolf's theory that the epic originated in disparate songs made "Homer" comprehensible to Carlyle. Before he read Wolf, he had thought of Homer as an individual who described events "two centuries" before his birth (e.g., *Works* 26:271; 28:45-46). Now he concluded, with Wolf, that the *Iliad* "was not the work of one man" (*L* p. 19).

Interest in Homer revived in England during the later eighteenth century. "While Homeric fire and invention had never been questioned," Douglas Bush has observed, "Homeric judgment and decorum had been, and here too the defects of irregularity and 'naiveté' became the glory of an inspired child of nature."[24] With their interest in ballads and primitive societies, the Romantics viewed Homer as "spontaneous, natural, gloriously imperfect and unpredictable."[25] English opinion had at first been mixed in its response to Wolf's theory; privately, Coleridge had expressed his approbation.[26] But by Victorian times the situation had altered. The question of Homeric unity became intimately related to that of the authority of the Bible as the authentic voice of God. Doubting the unity of the one implied doubting the veracity of the other: "Existing fears [were] that legitimization of a critical approach to Homer would encourage a similar approach to the Bible."[27] The Wolfians, few in number, were often radicals or agnostics. Among those who adopted, with qualifications, the German's views were George Grote, the influential historian of Greece, and George Eliot. Macaulay remained ambivalent. Lockhart, De Quincey, Gladstone, Froude, and Matthew Arnold were strongly opposed; for them, "the unity of Homer was a matter of faith, of believing what one could not prove."[28] Carlyle's adoption of Wolf's theory that the *Iliad* was not by a unitary, historical Homer but, instead, had emerged from a group of ballads subsequently put together places him in the distinct minority of English opinion.

Wolf the man Carlyle learned about through the sketch of him in K. A. Varnhagen von Ense's *Memoirs*. Varnhagen had become acquainted with Wolf in 1806 when he was a student and Wolf a professor at Halle. His sketch of Wolf made real to Carlyle the theorist whose "broad flash of light" had so powerfully illumined Homeric epic. Varnhagen describes Wolf in these words: "Friedrich August Wolf stood out as a king among scholars, surrounded as he was by such intellectual prestige and the power and awesomeness of his presence. His large but not overpowering build, his remarkable serenity, and a manner that had the effect of dominating what was around him: all contributed to the general awareness of his brilliance and dignity, even though these would have been evident anyway. He readily joined in as an equal with his colleagues and liked—just as Frederick the Great used to do— to shed the prerogatives of his position and share in the free exchange of wit and humor, and thereby to play the role of a beloved and respected leader." [29] Carlyle, in his 1838 essay on Varnhagen's writings, recreates the author of the *Prolegomena* as "Homeric Wolf, with his biting wit, with his grim earnestness and inextinguishable Homeric laugh, the irascible great-hearted man" (*Works* 29:93). Wolf becomes both a hero stepping forth from Homer's pages and, as so often in Carlyle's descriptions of the great men he admired, something of a self-portrait. Wolf's having a heroic personality no doubt increased the attractiveness his ideas had for Carlyle. If Carlyle could have learned something about Homer, he would surely have included him among his heroes, but instead, by a process of substitution, Wolf becomes "Homeric" because he had replaced the individual Homer with an impersonal, composite Homer and thus explained, in one bold stroke, how the *Iliad* had come into being.

Once Carlyle had adopted Wolf's theory, he held to it with the tenacity to which he held to most of his own opinions. It became for him the key that unlocked Homeric and other epics and, in time, the key by which he interpreted the evolution of human history. In the 1838 *Lectures*, he develops an analogy between the composition of the *Iliad* and the composition of the Robin Hood ballads that directly follows Wolf's views (*L* 19–20). In *Past and Present* he elaborates upon this analogy: "The great *Iliad* in *Greece*, and the small *Robin Hood's Garland* in *England*, are each, as I understand, the well-edited 'Select Beauties' of an immeasurable waste imbroglio of Heroic Ballads in their respective centuries and countries." [30] Many individuals took part in the long creative process necessary for both works, not only earlier bards, some talented and some not, but also numerous other semi-inarticulate individuals. Only at a late stage did conscious literary artists enter upon the scene. Carlyle's speaking of the "beating of the studious Poetic brain" indicates his awareness that no *Iliad* can come into existence without such artists. All these individuals labored "before the Wrath of a Divine Achilles, the Prowess of a Will Scarlet . . . , could be adequately sung" (ibid.). In the *Latter-Day Pamphlets*, Carlyle reaffirms the Wolfian theory, claiming that "Homer's *Iliad*, if you examine [it], is no Fiction but a Ballad *History*" (*Works* 20:322).[31] By "*History*" Carlyle implies that the *Iliad* is a true and essentially accurate portrayal of the events it chronicles. Nor does he stand alone among Victorians in regarding "Homer" as Greece's first historian. According to Frank Turner, "every significant Victorian commentator believed that in describing and criticizing Homeric characters, religion, or society, he was dealing with events that had actually occurred or with a society that had actually existed" (p. 136). For Carlyle, then, Homer was a historian as well as an artist in the epic mode. Homer "does not seem to believe his story to be a fiction," Carlyle writes in the 1838 *Lectures*; "he has no doubt of its truth" (*L* 21). Convinced of the reality behind the depictions in Homeric epic, he sought in his own epic ventures to capture the actuality of later societies.

In addition to unlocking the *Iliad* and other epic endeavors for Carlyle, Wolf's theory also had important repercussions for his understanding of religious writings and of human history. The liturgy, Carlyle thought, arose in the same way as the *Iliad*. "Before the incompletest *Liturgy* could be compiled," he writes in *Past and Present*, there had to be "thousand thousand articulate, semi-articulate, earnest-stammering *Prayers* ascending up to Heaven." Like the *Iliad* and the Robin Hood ballads, the liturgy "was what we can call the . . . 'Select Beauties' well-edited . . . from that wide waste imbroglio of Prayers already extant and accumulated, good and bad" (*P & P* 132). As the *Iliad* had emerged over the centuries from innumerable songs sifted, selected, and finally "well-edited," so too had the liturgy developed from "the old Prayer-Collections of the first centuries" (*P & P* 234). Carlyle even goes one step further: not only did the *Iliad*, the *Robin Hood's*

Garland, and the liturgy thus arise but also, "it is the way with human things" (*P & P* 132).

Wolf's ballad theory gradually became for Carlyle the closest equivalent that he would allow to a theory of historical evolution. One reason why Carlyle later shied away from the Darwinian hypothesis is that it implied no principle of selection other than brute strength or cunning. With Wolf he felt more secure, for the German argued that at some point there had to be an active (even a literary) consciousness, sifting and editing, presumably even shaping our own awareness of "human things." Wolf's theory, in addition to enabling Carlyle to grasp how major literary and religious writings of the past had come into being, also gave him a key to understanding the development of human history. Thanks to the original stimulus of the *Prolegomena,* by the time Carlyle published *Past and Present* in 1843 he had enlarged his conception of epic to include in it the cumulative progress of a nation.

VI

Carlyle's epic intent may be more readily granted in the large-scale histories than in *Past and Present* and *Latter-Day Pamphlets,* which focus on contemporary events. Yet as much as the histories these works are determined by Carlyle's vision of epic. I will concentrate on *Past and Present,* for to my knowledge it has never been considered in connection with Carlyle's ideas on epic. Although Grace Calder and John Holloway long ago established the book's literary artistry, most students of Victoria's reign prefer to view it primarily as a social tract. Critics who value its diagnosis of society's ills often wonder whether it has a coherent literary structure or even any structure at all.[32] My concern here will not be to assess the book on its merits, current or past, as an analysis of the English situation in 1842, either by discussing the validity of Carlyle's social pronouncements or of the remedies he suggests, but to argue that even when writing about a contemporary subject Carlyle thinks in literary terms. Like *The French Revolution, Past and Present* builds upon epic modes and epic tradition. But in the six years that separate the

136

two works Carlyle has redefined, or rather extended, what he means by epic.[33]

When Emerson observed that *Past and Present* was an "Iliad of English woes," he did not mean the phrase as a mere rhetorical flourish.[34] Rather, he designated the book as Carlyle's epic of modern England or, more precisely, as his epic on the "woes" that prevented the English from fulfilling their national destiny. In his very first sentence, Carlyle describes the paradox of an England "full of wealth" yet "dying of inanition." Her repressive laws, social injustices, uncontrolled industries, have created a depressive, not a healthful, environment. In Carlyle's terms, the Actual no longer attempts to realize the Ideal.

In his essay on Burns (1828), Carlyle had insisted that for the poet "the Ideal world is not remote from the Actual" (*Works* 26:272). A poet is a poet because he can discern the Ideal "under" and "within" our everyday existence. The Ideal exists both in man and in society. It can only be realized, Carlyle writes in a climactic passage in "The Everlasting Yea" of *Sartor*, "in this poor, miserable, hampered, despicable Actual" (*SR* 196). For man to grasp that in his own life he can approach the Ideal through the Actual, that the Ideal lies in himself, liberates him. A few years later, in an 1833 letter to Mill, Carlyle wonders "*How* Ideals do and *ought to* adjust themselves with the Actual." John Knox and the Scottish Kirk impressed him as "a *genuine* Ideal" that lasted for a century-and-a-half. Attractive as he found contemplation of the Ideal, Carlyle often expresses a growing preference "for the Actual . . . , for what *has realized* itself." "Is not all Poetry," he asks, "the essence of Reality (could one but get at such essence), and true History the only possible Epic?" (*CL* 7:24). Understandably, the French Revolution at this time began to exercise a potent hold over his imagination. In the important second chapter entitled "Realised Ideals," Carlyle explores more fully the relation of the Actual to the Ideal. "Realised Ideals" are the symbols, "divine or divine-seeming," that man has attained in the past (*FR* 1:10). In societal terms they are chiefly two: Church and State (the latter, in Carlyle's analysis, the concern of kings). This chapter surveys the reign of Louis XV, only to conclude that it is one "of those decadent ages in which no Ideal either grows or blossoms" (*FR* 1:12). The Church has lapsed into skepticism; the King, no longer the "Acknowledged Strongest," shifts his position with every turn of events. What such cessation of the Ideal bodes we learn in *Heroes and Hero-Worship.* "Ideals can never be completely embodied in practice," he writes there; but "if they be not approximated at all, the whole matter goes to wreck" (*H* 226).

By the time Carlyle wrote *Past and Present,* the epic had become for him more than a major literary form of the past or the proper embodiment for the poetic history of the future. Even before he had read Homer in Greek and German, Carlyle conceived of the epic as a means of delineating the Actual. By realizing the Actual, a people might realize its epic potential. Already in an 1832 essay entitled "Corn-Law Rhymes," he speaks of Ebenezer Elliott's "The Village Patriarch" as, "in its nature and unconscious tendency, Epic." It is epic because "a whole world lies shadowed in it." Elliott's poem narrates the troubles of a heroic miller, Enoch Wray, brought to ruin, as are all about him, by the Corn Laws. "No Ilion had he destroyed; yet somewhat had he built up." For Carlyle, his story contains "rudiments of an Epic . . . and of the true Epic of our Time,—were the genius but arrived that could sing it! Not 'Arms and the man,'" he concludes; "'Tools and the Man,' that were now our Epic." The echo of the *Aeneid's* first line is deliberate. The tools can be Enoch Wray's "Hammer and Plummet" or the "Pen" Carlyle uses to write. Either can make Chaos recede "some little handbreadth" (*Works* 28:161-62). In *Past and Present,* written a decade after "Corn-Law Rhymes," Carlyle's working definition of this new epic for modern times, what he calls there "an infinitely wider kind of Epic" (*P & P* 248), gradually emerges.

In Carlyle's view the true epic theme has become the birth of the modern world. That birth occurred in the convulsion of the French Revolution. Of equal interest for him now is the condition of the complex, newly-industrialized society that had come into existence in England as a result of the Revolution. *Past and Present* analyzes the current status of that society, what Carlyle terms "our National Existence" (*P*

& P 184). In the chapter entitled "The English," he makes explicit what he means by "National Existence": it consists of a dynamic industrial society, technological superiority, overseas empires. England's skill in mastering the complexities of modern life makes its national life an epic not less, but greater, than the *Iliad*. Carlyle lauds the "depth of practical sense" that lies in the silent English people, a people unable to articulate, unwilling to theorize. "They can do great acts, but not describe them. Like the old Romans, ... *their* Epic Poem is written on the Earth's surface" (*P & P* 159.) Over the centuries "the hands of forgotten brave men" have cut thistles, drained marshes, contrived "wise" schemes, done valiant deeds, in effect, "have made it a World for us" (*P & P* 134). Thus, Carlyle extends the meaning of epic from the literary to the practical, from Homer's poem in hexameters to man's dominion over the earth. If "the spoken Word, the written Poem, is said to be an epitome of the man," he asks; "how much more the done Work?" (*P & P* 160). England's "Epic, unsung in words, is written in huge characters on the face of this Planet,—sea moles, cotton-trades, railways, fleets and cities, Indian Empires, Americas, New-Hollands; legible throughout the Solar System!" (*P & P* 162).

Such an achievement, in which the Actual realizes itself, is epic and greater than any literary epic. Carlyle takes the conventional notion of an epic as a work of a particular magnitude and, by extension, insists that it embodies a magnitude of a different kind, namely, the heroic achievement of a people. The correlation between epic and people is acute. When a people are inactive, no epic is possible. But when they begin to achieve the potential lying in them, then their epic— a societal rather than a literary epic—will fulfill itself. "Great honour to him whose Epic is a melodious hexameter Iliad," Carlyle writes in a culminating passage of the chapter "The English." "But still greater honour, if his Epic be a mighty Empire slowly built together, a mighty series of Heroic Deeds,—a mighty Conquest over Chaos; *which* Epic the 'Eternal Melodies' have, and must have, informed and dwelt in, as *it* sung itself! There is no mistaking that latter Epic. Deeds are greater than Words (*P & P* 162). In Carlyle's view the creators

139

of a nation deserve even more credit than the poet of the *Iliad*. He hymns the collective spirit that over the centuries, from Hengst and Horsa to the potentially heroic captains of industry, has made present-day England the most advanced of western nations. With all his reservations about the consequences of that achievement—most obviously, the present economic crisis—and his uncertainty about the future, Carlyle yet took enormous pride in the triumph of English civilization on so many fronts. England held within itself the seeds that might enable it to fulfill its national destiny. The Actual, as embodied in present hopes, could yet lead to a still greater epic in the future.

"The proper Epic of this world is not now 'Arms and the Man,'" Carlyle writes in the chapter "Reward"; "no, it is now 'Tools and the Man'; that, henceforth to all time, is now our Epic" (*P & P* 208). What does he mean by this? He obviously echoes "Corn-Law Rhymes," where he had stated that "Tools" were "Arms" with which man does "battle against UNREASON without or within" (*Works* 28:162). Carlyle's minatory language in this 1832 essay, no less than his growing belief in the value of deeds over words, suggests that he will look to action for salvation rather than to literature or even to a religion based on believable formulas. His subsequent attempts at epic history celebrate, not Goethe or Knox or Luther, but the French Revolution, Cromwell, and Frederick the Great. In his essay on Mirabeau, Carlyle had translated Napoleon's "la carrière ouverte aux talens" oddly but revealingly as "the tools to him that can handle them" (*Works* 28:409–10). The new epic that Carlyle advocates for the English in *Past and Present* no longer requires the weapons necessary for survival in the Homeric poems and in the *Aeneid*, but asks instead that they master the "tools" wherewith to shape their own destinies, that they use them in the larger struggle, the combat against the centrifugal forces of modern society, in short, that with them they make, in Carlyle's terms, "cosmos" out of "chaos."

Men, Carlyle believed, did not reach their present level of civilization except through the hard work of conquering the chaotic elements that lay around them and in their own beings. They did not live in the past, nor can they contemplate existence in the future, except by denying "Hypocrisy, Injustice, or any form of Unreason." Once they again realize the overriding importance of labor in all its useful forms, labor that leads to the never-completed conquest of chaos, "their acted History will then again be a Heroism; their written History, what it once was, an Epic" (*P & P* 240). Thus, before historians can set down the epic of the future, it has to be lived, and lived meritoriously. The realization of this modern epic demands heroic endeavor from those who are active and strong, willing to work and to strive. In their collective achievement, they can create a new epic. At the end of *Past and Present*, Carlyle denies the possibility of traditional epic for his own day. Even if the older values of earlier epic could be resurrected, the heroic achievements of the future would dwarf them. These achievements will not take place "on Ilion's or Latium's plains" or in military victories, Carlyle concludes, but in triumph "over demons of Discord, Idleness, Injustice, Unreason, and Chaos come again" (*P & P* 293). For him the great theme of epic, past and present and future, remains the heroic struggle of the forces of order against the chaos that is always coming. In *Past and Present* Carlyle believes in the epic potential of England and of the English people. Englishmen using their God-given endowment, their "tools," can realize the Actual and in so doing create the stuff of modern epic.

By the late 1840s, when Carlyle's mind was churning with the political and social subjects that found expression in *Latter-Day Pamphlets*, his belief in an eventual victory, in England at least, over the demons of Discord and Unreason had waned. The failure of the 1848 revolutions abroad, the disintegrating situation in Ireland, finally the unexpected deaths of Charles Buller and of Robert Peel—the latter the one contemporary English leader he trusted—all contribute to the despairing vision of the *Pamphlets*. "I anticipate light *in* the Human Chaos," Carlyle had written in *Past and Present* (*P & P* 267). When that light failed for him, the despairing vision of the *Pamphlets* was inevitable. The epic of England becomes a mock-epic. With corruscating wit and devastating satire, Carlyle explodes in the *Pamphlets* the still essentially hopeful vision of *Past and Present*. But, though disillusioned, he continued to seek epic achievement in societies of the past. The societal epic, if perhaps no longer possible for England, had appeared in modern times in eighteenth-century Prussia. In his massive *History of Friedrich II. of Prussia, called Frederick the Great*, Carlyle rallied his forces for another attempt at epic history.[35] He would depict a heroic figure, "the *last* real *king* that we have had in Europe,"[36] forging a modern nation in a work that was in itself an epic. But Carlyle's age, his overlong struggle with a vast and elusive subject, and his doubts about Frederick himself conspired against him. His last major narrative describes in tremendous detail and at all-too-great length a man of dubious epic stature combatting with skill against the hostile forces deployed against him. He tells this story well but, as an epic, *Frederick* is a mixed achievement. But the work does reveal Carlyle still faithfully striving to maintain the vision of history as a modern epic that he had first glimpsed, thirty years before, reading Homer in Greek and German.

An earlier version of this essay was given in Tacoma, Washington, on 9 October 1981 before a joint meeting of the Research Society for Victorian Periodicals and the Victorian Studies Association of Western Canada. I wish to thank Professor Rosemary van Arsdel for providing me with the occasion that led to my putting down my initial thoughts on this very large subject.

1. J. A. K. Thomson, *The Classical Background of English Literature* (London, 1948), p. 246.

2. Preface to *The Revolutionary Epick* (London, 1834).

3. *Thomas Carlyle: A History of the First Forty Years of His Life, 1795-1835*, 2 vols. (London, 1882), 2:417.

4. John Stuart Mill, an unsigned review of *The French Revolution* in the *London and Westminster Review* 5 and 27 (July 1837): 17; Henry David Thoreau, "Thomas Carlyle and His Works" in *Graham's American Monthly Magazine of Literature and Art* 30 (April 1847): 239; Charles Kingsley, *Alton Locke* (London, 1850): ch. 9; Francis Espinasse, *Literary Recollections and Sketches* (London, 1893), p. 55. The Mill and Thoreau passages are included in *Thomas Carlyle: The Critical Heritage*, ed. Jules Paul Seigel (London, 1971), pp. 52, 290.

5. *The Works of William Makepeace Thackeray*, Biographical Edition,

John Clubbe

13 vols., ed. Anne Ritchie (London, 1898-1899), 13:249; Meredith, cited from *Carlyle and His Contemporaries*, ed. John Clubbe (Durham, N. C., 1976), pp. 262, 264; *The Letters of Charles Dickens*, ed. Walter Dexter, The Nonesuch Dickens, 3 vols. (Bloomsbury, 1938), 2:335; *Tono-Bungay*, 2.2.2.

6. Anthony Trollope, in Michael Sadleir, *Trollope: A Commentary* (London, 1933), p. 421; James Russell Lowell, in *My Study Windows* (Boston, 1887), p. 148.

7. Brian Wilkie, *Romantic Poets and Epic Tradition* (Madison, 1965), p. 3.

8. E.g., Thomas A. Vogler, *Preludes to Vision: The Epic Venture in Blake, Wordsworth, Keats, and Hart Crane* (Berkeley, Calif., 1971); Hermione de Almeida, *Byron and Joyce through Homer: Don Juan and Ulysses* (New York, 1981).

9. John Loofboorow, *Thackeray and the Form of Fiction* (Princeton, N. J., 1964); George Levine, *The Boundaries of Fiction: Carlyle, Macaulay, Newman* (Princeton, N. J., 1968); Albert LaValley, *Carlyle and the Idea of the Modern* (New Haven, Conn., 1968).

10. *Carlyle's Theory of the Hero* (Durham, N. C., 1928), pp. 168-70.

11. Both essays are in *Carlyle Past and Present*, ed. K. J. Fielding and Rodger L. Tarr (New York, 1976).

12. *Works of Thomas Carlyle*, ed. H. D. Traill, Centenary Edition, 30 volumes (London: 1896-99), 28:52. Hereafter cited in the text as *Works*. Except for the texts listed below, I quote Carlyle's writings parenthetically from this edition.

FR *The French Revolution*, ed. John Holland Rose, 3 vols. (London, 1902).

H *On Heroes, Hero-Worship, and the Heroic in History*, ed. Archibald MacMechan (Boston, 1901).

L *Lectures on the History of Literature*, ed. J. Reay Greene (New York, [1838] 1892).

P & P *Past and Present*, ed. Richard D. Altick, Riverside Edition, (Boston, 1965).

SR *Sartor Resartus*, ed. Charles Frederick Harrold (New York, 1937).

13. Loofboorow is one reader who does not. One who often does is E. M. W. Tillyard, whose *Epic Strain in the English Novel* (London, 1958) disappoints expectation. Except for a discussion of the epic qualities of three of Scott's Waverley novels, it virtually skips over nineteenth-century fiction.

14. For brief discussion of the relation of several of these works to epic tradition, see Richard Jenkyns, *The Victorians and Ancient Greece* (Cambridge, Mass., 1980), ch 2.

15. Jenkyns, *The Victorians and Ancient Greece*, p. 34.

16. *Two Reminiscences of Thomas Carlyle*, ed. John Clubbe (Durham, N. C., 1974), p. 32.

17. *The Collected Letters of Thomas and Jane Welsh Carlyle*, ed. Charles Richard Sanders, Kenneth J. Fielding, Ian M. Campbell, John Clubbe, and Janetta Taylor, 9 vols. to date (Durham, N. C., 1970-), 1:78. Hereafter abbreviated as *CL* and cited parenthetically in the text by volume and page

number. For the actual editions of Homer that Carlyle owned, see Hill Shine, *Carlyle's Early Reading to 1834* (Lexington, 1953), items 56, 3133, 3135. Shine summarizes Carlyle's reading in Homer to 1834 in his edition of *Carlyle's Unfinished History of German Literature* (Lexington, 1951), pp. 101-2.

18. *CL* 7:125. Carlyle first alludes to Voss's translation—"best of the whole and perhaps worth the whole"—in his letter to Henry Inglis of 30 January 1834, where he asks Inglis to procure him a copy of it (*CL* 7:92). He knew of Voss before 1834, however. In an 1831 essay, he praises "the German *Shakspeare, Homer, Calderon*" (*Works* 27:366). "*Homer*" here can refer only to Voss's version. In early 1834 Carlyle also dipped into Madame Dacier's French, and Samuel Clarke's English, translation of Homer, but it is to Voss that he keeps returning with increasing rapture.

19. Carlyle's journal, cited from James Anthony Froude, *Carlyle: First Forty Years*, 2:404-5.

20. *Homer and His Critics*, ed. Dorothea Gray (London, 1958), p. 72.

21. Clubbe, *Two Reminiscences*, p. 45. Cf. Carlyle, *Reminiscences*, ed. Charles Eliot Norton, 2 vols. (London, 1887), 2:115.

22. "Editor's Introduction," *Froude's Life of Carlyle*, ed. John Clubbe (Columbus, 1979), pp. 32-33.

23. Espinasse, *Literary Recollections*, p. 219. Cf. *P & P*, p. 234.

24. *Mythology and the Romantic Tradition in English Poetry* (Cambridge, Mass., 1937), p. 44.

25. Jenkyns, *The Victorians and Ancient Greece*, p. 197.

26. See *The Table Talk and Omniana of Samuel Taylor Coleridge*, ed. T. Ashe (London, 1896), pp. 74-75. According to H. N. Coleridge, Coleridge arrived at his position independently of Wolf.

27. Frank Turner, *The Greek Heritage of Victorian Britain* (New Haven, Conn., 1981), p. 145. On the Homeric controversy in Britain, less vehement than in Germany, see pp. 83-84, 138-47 of this book. Jenkyns's chapter on "Homer and the Homeric Ideal" nicely points out the high valuation accorded Homer by the Victorians, who often ranked him above Shakespeare. Neither he nor Turner, though both discuss Homer's importance for the Victorians, seems aware of the *Iliad*'s shaping influence on *The French Revolution* or on the later Carlyle.

28. Jenkyns, *The Victorians and Ancient Greece*, p. 207.

29. *Denkwürdigkeiten des eignen Lebens*, 3d ed., part 1 (Leipzig, 1871), p. 329. My translation of Varnhagen's labored prose is necessarily somewhat free. See also pp. 333-35, 339.

30. P. 133. Although the *Robin Hood's Garland* seems to have dropped out of current literary awareness, the British Library catalogue lists some two dozen editions between 1700 and 1815.

31. See also *Works*, 30:25 ("Shooting Niagara").

32. E.g., Peter Keating, "Backward or Forward? Carlyle's *Past and Present*," in *Thomas Carlyle 1981*, ed. Horst W. Drescher (Frankfurt am Main / Bern, 1983), p. 209.

33. I omit from consideration here several major aspects of epic influence

on *Past and Present*, e.g., that exerted by Carlyle's intensive reading in Norse saga and mythology. This reading, which occurred in the years after the completion of *The French Revolution*, strongly influences both *Heroes* and *Past and Present*. The Norse subjects remained of interest to Carlyle until the end.

34. *Dial* 4 (July 1843): 96. Also in Seigel, *Carlyle: The Critical Heritage*, p. 219.

35. Nor was it the last. Carlyle wrote *The Early Kings of Norway* (1875) to reawaken in the English a sense of their epic origins and to illustrate once more his main epic theme of the triumph of cosmos over chaos.

36. *Last Words of Thomas Carlyle* (London, 1892), p. 263. Carlyle to Varnhagen von Ense, 29 October 1851.

VII

GEORGE H. FORD

"A Great Poetical Boa-Constrictor," Alfred Tennyson: An Educated Victorian Mind

THE SOMEWHAT AMUSING CIRCUMSTANCES IN WHICH THE following essay was first put together deserve to be spelled out. At a conference held recently at the University of Richmond, I had been invited to offer a paper on some writer who would be representative of "An Educated Mind in the Victorian Era." The choice of writer was left entirely to me, and, as might be expected, there was a good deal of speculation, in advance of my presentation, which Victorian it would be.

During the extended period when I was exploring possible choices, I was reminded of a similar guessing game that had occurred in the mid-1950s during a series of lectures on modern poetry at the University of Cincinnati. One lecture had been advertised under the tantalizing title of "The Greatest Modern Poet," and many persons in the audience had been placing advance bets on the most likely choices. Would it be Yeats perhaps? Or Eliot? Or Frost? No, it was none of these, and no one, in fact, collected on any bets, for the poet chosen by the speaker turned out to be Edna St. Vincent Millay![1] The snorts of incredulity and consternation with which the audience greeted this announcement may readily be imagined.

At the Richmond conference, after I had decided Tennyson was to be my figure, I wondered: would my choice seem equally fatuous, or at least eccentric, to the members of my

146

audience? Happily, they did not seem unduly startled when the name was first announced, although fifty years ago such an audience would most certainly have regarded it as a joke. Even today the choice does call for some justification, for there are, indeed, many other Victorian candidates to consider, some of them seemingly more suitable: Newman, let us say, or Matthew Arnold, or Gladstone.

Each of these three persons was incontestably well qualified for the proposed role (all three, be it noted, were Oxford persons), and I spent some agreeable weeks reviewing the silver-veined prose of Newman and his celebration of the Imperial Intellect—a memorable phrase used by Dwight Culler as the title for his book on Newman. And after *The Idea of a University* there were the essays of Matthew Arnold, almost all of them concerned with education, directly or indirectly. Yet despite a sense of congeniality, neither of these writers seemed to offer avenues that have not hitherto been exhaustively explored by others. Moreover, both of them had written books about education, and it seemed to me that it would be more illuminating to focus on someone who was not formally what is called today an educator—Macaulay or George Eliot, for example. But in this latter category it was Gladstone who seemed most promising. Although as a person he has never, as it happens, been congenial to me, there is no doubt about his being suitable. Educated via the orthodox route from Eton to Oxford, Gladstone came to acquire a breadth of learning that is still dazzling to read about. In 1875, for example, a year in which, as it happens, he was leader of the opposition in Parliament rather than Prime Minister, Gladstone was chairing a meeting of a learned society in London. After a paper read by Fitzjames Stephen had so astonished the audience that there was a stunned silence, Gladstone summed up the situation with a quotation that he scribbled on a note and passed to a friend: "Then did the whole assembly fall into deep silence, marvelling at the words of Diomede, tamer of horses."[2] It is difficult to imagine a political figure today who could dash off an apt quotation from the *Iliad*, and it is impossible to imagine any of them who would cite these lines, as Gladstone did, in Greek!

My justification for not settling upon this remarkable Victorian mind comes from an unexpected quarter, which is from Gladstone himself, for Gladstone regarded Tennyson as the archetypal figure of the Victorian age, "flesh of its flesh," as he said, "and bone of its bone." Here is his comment (it is from a review of 1859):

> Mr. Tennyson is too intimately and essentially the poet of the nineteenth century to separate himself from its leading characteristics, the progress of physical science and a vast commercial, mechanical, and industrial development. . . . He cannot . . . lose its sympathies, for while he elevates as well as adorns [his century], he is flesh of its flesh and bone of its bone. We fondly believe it is his business to do much toward the solution of that problem, so fearful from its magnitude, how to harmonise this new draught of external power and activity with the old and more mellow wine of faith, self-devotion, loyalty, reverence, and discipline.[3]

What Gladstone's tribute stresses is that it was Tennyson's task to link the two cultures. The nature of that task will be explored later in this essay. Meanwhile we can ask a large general question as a preliminary enquiry: How well was Tennyson's mind equipped for such tasks? One clear answer to this question was provided in 1946 by W. H. Auden's celebrated evaluation. For Auden, Tennyson was "the stupidest of poets."[4] A short reply by Paul Turner, appearing in 1949, argues, in effect, that Auden's remark was the stupidest of remarks.[5] More recently, James Kincaid accounted for Auden's remark more indulgently by concluding that it had been written when Auden was "half asleep."[6]

My own response to Auden's verdict is limited to pointing out that almost all of Tennyson's *contemporaries* regarded him as the reverse of stupid. Here, for example, is Edward FitzGerald. When he came to know Tennyson, FitzGerald reports, he felt "a sense of depression at times from the overshadowing of a so much more lofty intellect than my own—*I could not be mistaken in the universality of his mind.*"[7] "He had a powerful brain for Physics as for the Idea."[8] According to Thackeray, Tennyson was the wisest man he knew.[9] A tutor from Oxford, who lived with the Tennysons when their sons were growing up, was astonished by the poet's learning, in particular by his command of languages, exemplified in his quoting Virgil and Sappho, his reading aloud from Goethe (admittedly with an English accent), and his reading of Cervantes and of Dante in the original.[10] In his thirties Tennyson passed an evening conversing with Jane Welsh Carlyle, an event she described in a lively letter: "for *three* mortal hours—talking like an angel— only exactly as if he were talking with a clever *man*—which— being a thing I am not used to . . .—strained me to a terrible pitch of intellectuality."[11] In old age he continued to impress his contemporaries. Montague Butler, Master of Trinity College, described Tennyson as "one of the foremost thinkers . . . of his day." In informal conversation, Butler reports, Tennyson would pass "rapidly and easily from the gravest matters of speculation . . . to some trifling incident of the moment."[12] And another Master, Benjamin Jowett of Balliol College, also commented on his talk. "In the commonest conversation," Jowett said, "he showed himself a man of genius. He had abundance of fire, never talked poorly, never for effect. As Socrates described Plato, 'Like no one whom I ever knew before.'"[13] And Jowett had further cause to be overawed by Tennyson's mind, for on a visit to Farringford he discovered that the Laureate had taken up the study of Hebrew. Jowett, himself a clergyman as well as a professor, had to admit to his host that he himself did not know Hebrew. Tennyson was shocked by Jowett's admission and scolded his guest roundly, saying: "What, you the priest of a religion and can't read your own sacred books!"[14] One wonders what Tennyson might have said to Auden!

In any event, the testimony of Tennyson's contemporaries gives us an awareness of his intellectual status in the later decades of his century. As his son, Hallam Tennyson, said: "During the last twenty-five years of his life, my father was probably, throughout the whole English-speaking race, the Englishman who was most widely known."[15] We could write this tribute off as mere filial piety, but it seems to have been an accurate observation. In 1900 a professor of Philosophy at Yale, Hershey Sneath, published a study entitled *The Mind of Tennyson* which asserted that Tennyson "was profoundly in touch with his age." "There were not many men who understood it better than he. He had his finger on its pulse, and his ear upon its breast, so that he heard its very heart-beat. He was acquainted with its problems, and he knew also the tremendous issues involved in the attitude of his age toward them."[16] Sneath's elaborate figure of the diagnostician may prompt a smile, but it is interesting to set it beside Matthew Arnold's tribute to Goethe as "Physician of the iron age." "He read each wound, each weakness clear;/ And struck his finger on the place,/ And said: *Thou ailest, here, and here!*"[17]

II

How did Tennyson's education help to condition him for this role, and what sort of education was it? To explore these issues calls for a review of the stages of his education, both formal and informal. "Informal" will refer to studies he made on his own, such as his learning Hebrew in his later years. "Formal" means, of course, his regular schooling, which in his case involved four years at a school, eight years of tutoring, and about three years at university.

From the age of seven to eleven, Tennyson was sent away from his Somersby home to a Grammar School in Louth in Lincolnshire. To characterize this establishment in short order we may resort to the hilarious account of Llanabba School in Evelyn Waugh's first novel, *Decline and Fall*. An employment agency, advertising a vacancy for a teaching position, classifies Llanabba as "School," and, in reply to enquiries from an applicant, explains that "Llanabba hasn't a very good name in the profession. We class schools, you see, into four grades: Leading School, First-rate School, Good School, and School. Frankly, School is pretty bad."

Louth Grammar School would have been ranked as "School," and the boy Tennyson hated it. He hated it first of all because of the bullying that went on. It is hard to think of Tennyson as a victim, for when he grew up he was a huge man, of great physical strength—"a guardsman spoiled by poetry" as Carlyle said of him. One of the most memorable pictures we have of him, when he grew up, is of his picking up the family pony and carrying it round the rectory lawn.[18] So it is hard to imagine him as a small child being beaten up by older boys. Not long after his enrollment at Louth, he was sitting on the school steps, crying with homesickness, when a seventeen year old boy came up and kicked him violently in the stomach. Seventy years later, Lord Tennyson was still talking bitterly about this childhood incident.[19] According to Thackeray and other nineteenth-century commentators, such bullying was not special but commonplace. In *Vanity Fair*, after describing the brutal beating of George Osborne by Cuff, the bully of Dr. Swishtail's Academy, Thackeray comments: "Don't be horrified, ladies, every boy at a public school has done it."

Even worse than the brutality of the school bullies at Louth would have been the brutality of the masters. The headmaster, according to Hallam Tennyson, was "a tempestuous, flogging master of the old stamp,"[20] the stamp to be memorialized later by Dickens' Mr. Squeers, or, better, his Mr. Creakle, about whom David Copperfield commented: "He had a delight in cutting at the boys, which was like the satisfaction of a craving appetite." Such punishments were not restricted to schools such as Creakle's; they were also generously meted out, of course, at famous old schools such as Winchester, where Anthony Trollope (according to his *Autobiography*) was "flogged oftener than any human being alive."

On this general topic of how English writers were affected by their treatment at school, there is a useful chapter in John Reed's book, *Old School Ties*, a chapter called "The Swindle of Education", that traces school experiences from Shelley to Graham Greene.[21] Reed also has much to say about the excessive emphasis on sports in schools, although in Tennyson's boyhood, sports were not yet a problem. His school days were also experienced before Thomas Arnold began initiating his reforms at Rugby in 1828, reforms of which the adult Tennyson seems to have approved, for he sent one of his own sons to Marlborough because of his admiration for its Rugby-trained headmaster, Granville Bradley. From his own school, however, Tennyson always affirmed that he had learned nothing, or, rather, nothing except the memory of three Latin words: "sonus desilientis aquae."[22] His other memory, he said, was "of an old wall covered with wild weeds opposite the

151

school windows." It is striking to compare this comment with Newman's memorable recollection of Oxford after his exile from his beloved college: "There used to be much snapdragon growing on the walls opposite my freshman's rooms there."

Finally, about his school days, mention should be made of his having been accompanied by two of his brothers during his stay at Louth, a circumstance that anticipates what happened to another literary family from the north of England whose children attended school together in Yorkshire, the Brontë sisters. The physical health of the Brontë sisters seems to have been affected for life by the deplorable conditions at their school. In Tennyson's case, it was his mental health rather than his physical health that was being affected by school experiences. The nightmare visions of his sadistic headmaster were so traumatic that his father decided to withdraw the boy from school, thus sparing him, during his adolescence, from what seems to have been a not uncommon horror story in the educational scene of early nineteenth-century England.

The second stage of Alfred Tennyson's education extended from age eleven to nineteen and can be passed over in briefer space. During the eight years before he went to university, he was educated at home by his father, Dr. George Tennyson, a learned scholar of Hebrew and Syrian languages, who taught his sons Greek and Latin, mathematics, and some sciences, and gave them access to his fine library.

Education at home may strike us as a peculiar arrangement, but it was not an unusual one in the nineteenth century, as the example of Browning illustrates, or, earlier, Jane Austen let us say. In the case of Tennyson, a psychological critic might speculate about the effects on an adolescent of being dependent upon his father not only for the usual paternal roles but also for spiritual guidance as his pastor, and intellectual guidance as his teacher.

For present purposes, what is of more consequence than psychology is the quality of the education imparted by the father. Young Alfred was not so striking a case of a Victorian prodigy as John Stuart Mill or Macaulay, but he did display early promise as well as assiduity. By the time he was six, he had been so drilled by his father that he could recite all the odes of Horace (and for the rest of his life, of course, Horace was one of the few classic writers whom he couldn't abide).[23] The same kind of drilling seems to have continued during his teens, but, in addition, he was encouraged to write poetry, with the result that when he entered as a freshman at Cambridge in 1828, he was already the author of a volume of poems. And an analysis of the literary allusions in this little volume shows that Alfred and his brothers were rather astonishingly well read. There are quotations from classical authors including Horace, Virgil, Lucretius, Tacitus, Pliny, Xenophon, Suetonius, Cicero, and from French authors (Racine and Rousseau), from the Bible of course, from English poets, Chapman, Shakespeare, Spenser, Milton, Scott, Moore, Byron, John Clare, and from assorted authors such as Hume, the Koran, Isaac Disraeli, and *The Mysteries of Udolpho*.[24]

What gives added impressiveness to this parade of early learning is that the Tennysons grew up in a Lincolnshire village where books were viewed as they might have been viewed by a mountaineer in nineteenth-century Kentucky. As someone said of the Tennyson family's neighbors, "They seemed to think that 'to hev owt to do wi books' was a sign of a weak intellect"[25]—a sentiment later to be echoed by Tennyson's Northern Farmer as he advises his son: "And boöks, what's boöks? thou knaws thebbe naither 'ere nor theer."

From the age of nineteen to twenty-two, Tennyson attended Cambridge. Unlike his two brothers, both of whom graduated, Alfred left without completing his degree, having been summoned home because of his father's illness. Despite the lack of a degree, Alfred was profoundly affected by his university experiences. If he, instead of Wordsworth, had written *The Prelude*, his account of the Growth of a Poet's Mind would probably have given much more weight to the importance of the exposure to Cambridge than Wordsworth did in his poem. This is not to say that Tennyson wasn't critical of some aspects of the university, but rather that what happened to him there had a lasting impact on the cast of his mind.

The exposure at Cambridge was of two kinds: the formal, institutional education on the one hand, and, on the other, the informal, out-of-the-classroom so to speak, education.

With regard to the formal variety it would be interesting to know what it was that Tennyson would have been expected to study at Cambridge. I was unsuccessful in tracking down the list of texts prescribed in 1829, but one can be relatively sure that they would have been very similar to the texts assigned forty years earlier when Wordsworth entered Cambridge, and about the texts prescribed for Wordsworth we fortunately know a good deal because of a useful book on the topic by Ben R. Schneider. The Cambridge freshman, as Schneider shows, would start off with a text from Xenophon, another from Horace, and a study of the Bible. "A bit of Latin, a bit of Greek, and a bit of Scripture would keep the freshmen busy during their first term; in the spring they could settle down to the serious business of Euclid."[26] Cambridge, as is well known, gave considerable attention—much more than Oxford—to mathematics. It was at Tennyson's college that the statue of Newton stood, later to be memorialized by Wordsworth in *The Prelude*:

> where the statue stood
> Of Newton with his prism and silent face,
> The marble index of a mind for ever
> Voyaging through strange seas of Thought, alone.

The mathematics to be studied when Tennyson was at Cambridge were classified by one of his tutors as "Permanent Mathematics," that is, mathematical problems that would have been understood by the Greeks and Romans: Euclidian geometry, hydrostatics, and astronomy.[27]

The same emphasis upon classical authority was likewise applicable in the study of literature, history, and philosophy. In 1845, one of Tennyson's tutors, William Whewell (later the Master of Trinity), published a book entitled *Of a Liberal Education . . . With Particular Reference to . . . the University of Cambridge* which explains why the only suitable texts for study must be classical texts in the original languages and why Shakespeare or Racine cannot substitute for Sophocles. As Whewell asserts:

> Hence we cannot, consistently with the meaning of a Liberal Education, substitute for the Classical Authors of Greece and Rome any other authors, for instance, eminent modern writers of our own or other countries. Even if the genius and skill shown in modern poems and orations were as great as that which appear in Homer or Virgil, Demosthenes or Cicero, the modern works could not supply the place of ancient ones in Education. No modern works can . . . [replace] the familiar models . . . which have been recognized as models for two thousand years.[28]

To encounter such a paragraph enables us to understand why a group of radical reformers founded the Modern Language Association in the late nineteenth century. On the other hand, we must view the argument of Tennyson's tutor from a historical perspective, for most educated persons, of Tennyson's generation, would agree with Whewell about classical texts. What Tennyson was to complain about was, as we shall see, how subjects were taught at the university rather than about what subjects were taught. John Ruskin is another eminent Victorian who would agree with Tennyson's tutor. "Novelty" said Ruskin "is the worst enemy of knowledge." The task of a university is "to teach what is securely known." One obvious corollary of such an argument is that research ought to be of no concern for a university. "Where investigation is necessary, teaching is impossible," Ruskin asserted. The student, he adds, "should see nothing or learn nothing 'but what the consent of the past has admitted to be true.'"[29] Newman's position is somewhat more complex, but, on the whole, he too believed that research should be the responsibility of a separate institute rather than of an Oxford-style college.

In view of this theory of education, it would seem likely that the Cambridge undergraduate could expect royal treatment from his instructors, and, for the past hundred years or more, such expectations seem indeed to have been met. In 1963, an American university president, Clark Kerr, remarked on this situation in a witty observation: "A university anywhere can aim no higher than to be as British as possible for the sake of the undergraduates, as German as possible for the sake of the graduates and research personnel, as American as possible for the sake of the public at large."[30] If British undergraduate teaching was regarded as the finest in 1963, we must recognize that in 1833 the reverse was true—at least if we can trust the comments of Tennyson and other undergraduates of his day. In their eyes, most professors and tutors at Cambridge were irresponsible. Professors put on shoddy performances in their lectures (and according to a letter of Thomas Arnold the same shoddiness also prevailed at Oxford),[31] and college tutors seemed to take a couldn't-care-less attitude towards their students.

I am painting this picture in bold colors, of course, for we do not have space for a detailed history of English education in the nineteenth century. Some historians contend that instruction at Cambridge was steadily improving during the period between when Wordsworth was a freshman and Tennyson was a freshman, but it seems more likely that the real changes occurred later, starting with a critical report on the universities appearing in 1852—one of those representative examples of how the Victorians set about changing and improving established institutions.[32] We do know that by the time E. M. Forster entered Cambridge in the 1890s, the teaching skills of the dons were seemingly miraculous. Forster's tribute to these skills, in his book on Lowes Dickinson, is a glowing appreciation:

> The tutors and resident fellows ... treated with rare dexterity the products that came up yearly from the public schools. They taught the perky boy that he was not everything, and the limp boy that he might be something. ... And they did everything with ease—one might almost say nonchalance—so that boys noticed nothing and received education, often for the first time in their lives. ... Body and spirit, ... work and play, architecture and scenery, laughter and seriousness, life and art—these pairs which are elsewhere contrasted were there fused into one. People and books reinforced one another, intelligence joined hands with affection, speculation became a passion, and discussion was made profound by love.[33]

A special reason for citing this passage is the emphasis Forster places on his key word, *love*, because the chief criticism Tennyson had to make of the Cambridge of the 1830s was the absence of love. In old age he commented to a friend about his undergraduate experiences: "There was no *love* in the system." As his friend explained, Tennyson was referring to the "lack of sympathy in his time between dons and undergraduates. This seemed to be a memory often present to his mind."[34]

It is noteworthy that Arthur Hallam used the same word in a letter written in 1829 but first published only recently. Writing to a friend about how "intensely" he hates Cambridge, Hallam later remarks: "I feel day by day that it is only in the pure atmosphere of Feeling (the word is not that which I need, but I have no better at the moment) I shall find ultimate peace of mind. What are thoughts and opinions? Cher ami, devices to grow cold! . . . The reasoning faculties are by nature sceptical: there is no *love* in them: and *what man can be happy beyond his love?*"[35] [Hallam's italics]

While Tennyson was still a student, this Cambridge lovelessness inspired him to write a sonnet called "Lines on Cambridge of 1830." It is a poem that sounds as if it might have been written on an American campus during the period 1969–73. The poet is here addressing his university directly:

> Therefore your Halls, your ancient Colleges
> Your portals statued with old kings and queens,
> Your gardens, myriad-volumed libraries,
> Wax-lighted chapels, and rich carven screens,
> Your doctors, and your proctors, and your deans,
> Shall not avail you, when the Day-beam sports
> New-risen o'er awakened Albion. No!
> Nor yet your solemn organ-pipes that blow
> Melodious thunders through your vacant courts
> At noon and eve, because your manner sorts
> Not with this age wherefrom ye stand apart,
> Because the lips of little children preach
> Against you, you that do profess to teach
> And teach us nothing, feeding not the heart.

In later years Tennyson disliked this poem because of its note of what he called "undergraduate irritability," and after visiting Cambridge in the 1870s, he felt his complaint of the 1830s was no longer applicable.[36] But for students of his own generation, his sonnet seems to have expressed their sense of dissatisfaction, and with them it was a favorite.[37] It is also worth noting that there is a similarity between the scenery of this sonnet and his better known early poem, "The Palace of Art," a poem that ingenious critics have sometimes interpreted as a veiled attack on the selfish isolation of university life.

If Tennyson found no love, no heart, in the Cambridge classrooms, he found an abundance of it in the sitting-rooms of the many friendly students with whom he became acquainted from 1829 onward, in particular, of course, the dazzlingly brilliant young man from Eton, Arthur Hallam. And with this group of his peers, Tennyson was to find both the affection and the intellectual stimulation that his university had failed to provide. With them, also, he was to find a cast of mind and a set of values as embodied in the informal society of the Apostles, of which most of Tennyson's friends were members. At meetings of this organization, papers and discussions were focused on such subjects as the poetry of Shelley, subjects not dealt with in the regular Cambridge curriculum. And, by the same token, classics and mathematics, "professionally considered," were excluded from Apostolic discussions.

This division between formal and informal education in a university setting may strike American readers as bizarre, but it still has its proponents in our century. Auden, for example, once remarked in an interview that although he enjoyed teaching at American universities, he found it disconcerting that American undergraduates keep imploring their professors to offer courses in contemporary literature. When he and Spender were at Oxford, they wanted their professors to talk about Milton and Shakespeare but not about T. S. Eliot. They wanted to talk about Eliot with their peers. Cambridge, one hundred years earlier, operated in the same way.

The subjects discussed among the Apostles were not restricted to Romantic poets such as Shelley, but covered a vast range of philosophical and political problems, the kinds of problems Tennyson was to air in parts of his *In Memoriam* such as: "Is an intelligible First Cause deducible from the phenomena of the Universe?"[38] In one section of his elegy, Tennyson records a revisit to Cambridge and Hallam's rooms: "Where once we held debate, a band/ Of youthful friends, on mind and art." Their debates he likens here to an archery contest, with Hallam, the "master-bowman" cleaving the mark while the other participants miss the target. Hallam's intellectual distinction seems beyond question, yet it would be fair to say that there were other outstanding archers in that company. As Robert Robson remarks, in an article on "Trinity College in the Age of Peel," "It was a brilliant generation, and knew it."[39] If in the Growth of a Poet's Mind Tennyson fared better at Cambridge than his predecessor, part of the reason was his good fortune in sharing in a confluence of other fine minds in the same time and place.

How much was Tennyson's mind actually affected by his exposure to this group of undergraduates? Some biographers argue that its role was minor, or, as Christopher Ricks says, "easy to exaggerate."[40] It is pointed out that he disliked writing papers and had to be classified as an "honorary member" of the Apostles, and that he was therefore something of a misfit.

It would be reasonable to say that Tennyson was not so overwhelmingly affected by the exposure as some of the others in his group. John Kemble, the Beowulf scholar, was one of these. In later life, looking back on how the Apostles affected him, he states: "To my *education* given in that Society, I feel that I owe every power I possess, and the rescuing myself from a ridiculous state of prejudice and prepossessions with which I came armed to Cambridge. From the 'Apostles' I, at least, first learned to think as a *free man*."[41] (Kemble's italics) Tennyson probably could not have offered such an unqualified testimonial. His career illustrates a generalization made by Arnold in his lecture at Cambridge on "Literature and Science." Arnold contended that Oxford had been "the centre of great movements," whereas Cambridge excelled in turning out great individuals, great men. Tennyson, in Arnold's terms, would be one of these great men and someone who was too strongly individualistic to be representative of a group. Nevertheless it seems incontestable that his mind was profoundly affected by the group of fellow students with whom he was linked, in particular by the Apostolic temper, a temper that marked these men for life.

One of the illuminating accounts of the Apostolic temper is provided by an observer who was himself not an Apostle or even a Cambridge student. This was Granville Bradley (1821–1903)—half-brother to the Shakespearian A. C. Bradley—who became Dean of Westminster late in life. Granville Bradley had attended Rugby and been exposed there to church controversies, and after Rugby he was at Oxford, with Matthew Arnold and Clough, where the passionate issues of Tractarianism were being fought out, and where there were also some hotly contested political issues, involving a radical elite, a story recounted in Christopher Kent's book on the mid-Victorians, *Brains and Numbers*.[42] After witnessing such controversies, Bradley was to be astonished when he encountered a number of the Apostles during a visit to London in 1842 (among them being Edmund Lushington, a professor of Greek, who was about to become Tennyson's brother-in-law). As Bradley described the meeting: "I shall never forget the impression made on me by coming in contact with men so striking in character and ability, and yet a circle so wholly . . . different from that which had gathered round Arnold at Rugby"[43] and (we might add) Newman at Oxford. "Tolerance, breadth of view, balanced judgment, and deep reverence for all that was noblest in human thought and achievement— these gave the keynote to their minds and energies. Partisanship, sectarian controversy, ecclesiastical disputes, seemed to belong to an alien world."[44]

It would be foolish to contend that Bradley's description of the Apostolic temper fits Tennyson like a glove; the Bard's comments on the Victorian scene, especially on religious issues, are too gruff to qualify him fully. What can be said, however, is that one of the distinctive traits of his thinking was an open mind—and not, as Auden would have it, an empty mind. And it was this quality that enabled him to live at peace with the natural sciences, a resolution that was one of the most remarkable accomplishments of the Victorian age.

III

The mention of science is a reminder that this account of Tennyson's education has so far been focused primarily upon his engagement to literature and has been overlooking natural science and religion, two areas of knowledge with which he and his contemporaries were strongly concerned. Both of these subjects he worked up himself, so to speak, rather than having them impressed upon him through academic disciplines. That is to say, Tennyson seems never to have taken a formal course in astronomy, yet he was a lifetime student of that science. As a boy in Somersby, he studied William Herschel and watched the stars with the naked eye. Later, he owned a telescope and also used to visit the observatory of Sir Norman Lockyer, one of several astonomers who have commended Tennyson's knowledge of the stellar universe and the accuracy of his observations. Lockyer recalled that the last time he saw the poet, in 1892, "He would talk of nothing but the possible ages of the sun and earth, and was eager to know to which estimates scientific opinion was then veering."[45]

The searching for answers about the age of our earth and of the universe goes back a long way in Tennyson's development. We have records of the schedule of studies he set up for himself after he left Cambridge and was living at home. Five out of seven afternoons of each week were scheduled for study of languages such as German and Italian, but most mornings, except Sunday, were devoted to studying the sciences. On Tuesday morning there was chemistry; on Wednesday, botany; Thursday was electricity; Friday: animal physiology; Saturday: mechanics.[46] Tennyson's program sounds like a course of studies which Milton might have undergone to prepare himself for writing *Paradise Lost*. Tennyson often felt, as FitzGerald said of him in 1847, that "everyday" science was unrolling "a greater Epic than the Iliad." This modern epic concerned "the history of the world, the great infinitudes of Space and Time!" And FitzGerald adds: "I never take up a book of Geology or Astronomy but this strikes me."[47]

The book of geology that first struck Tennyson was, of course, Charles Lyell's *Principles*, published at the time the young poet left Cambridge, a book that was later to leave its mark on *In Memoriam* and other poems. And geological theory was reinforced, in Tennyson's case, by paleontological observations. There is a delightful picture of him and one of his friends in 1854, when he was living on the Isle of Wight,

161

where the chalk cliffs supplied a treasure-trove of fossils. The daughter of his friend, a clergyman, has provided a sketch of her father and the poet at this date: "The two men roamed the country together, poetizing, botanizing, geologizing. The enthusiasm of science had begun to seize on all thinking humanity, and if botany was considered the only suitable science for ladies, geology had something like a boom among the privileged males. I can see my father now . . . armed with a hammer and girt with a capacious knapsack, setting forth joyous as a chamois-hunter, for a day's sport among the fossils of the Isle of Wight cliffs [and accompanied by] the tall, long-cloaked Bard."[48] This sketch readily evokes the early scenes of *The French Lieutenant's Woman* featuring Charles Smithson with his hammer out on the cliffs at Lyme Regis, although Charles's fossilizing takes place ten years later than Tennyson's.

About this same chalk cliff, Tennyson once commented: "The most wonderful thing about that cliff is to think it was all once alive."[49] Such a comment would have gladdened the heart of Thomas Henry Huxley, whose celebrated lecture "On a Piece of Chalk," is devoted to a demonstration of the same point Tennyson had made. Huxley keenly appreciated Tennyson's understanding of science, as was evident when he responded to the death of the poet by writing a poem in his honor; it was the only occasion on which Huxley had been moved to write verse in his later years. Earlier, in 1865, when Tennyson had been elected a member of the Royal Society, an unusual honor for someone not a professional scientist, Huxley exclaimed: "We scientific men claim him as having quite the mind of a man of science."[50]

Tennyson's open-mindedness extended also to biology, although he knew less of this science than of geology and astronomy. When Aldous Huxley grew disillusioned with the religion of his one-time master, D. H. Lawrence, he remarked (not quite accurately) that the trouble with Lawrence was that he had never looked through a microscope.[51] Tennyson, contrariwise, looked through microscopes many times. In 1833, after studying a slide, he remarked colorfully on "all the lions and tigers which lie perdus in a drop of spring water." Later he observed to his son how "strange" it is "that these wonders should draw some men to God and repel others. No more reason in one than in the other."[52]

Obviously, for most of his life, such wonders led Tennyson to God, or, in Clough's witty line in *Dipsychus*, to "something very like Him." Our account of Tennyson's education would be woefully incomplete if we overlook how much of his thinking was involved with religious issues. One phase of this involvement was with the Established Church itself, a complex relationship. When Alfred was sent to Cambridge, his grandfather assumed he would become a clergyman, like his father before him. And even though he elected to decline that role, he retained close contacts with the church. More than half of his Apostle friends became clergymen; one of them eventually became an archbishop, and three others became cathedral deans. And even if Tennyson might seem to persons such as Newman to be outside the orthodox establishment, he was nevertheless passionately interested in all religions. In fact, according to Jowett, Tennyson had at one time proposed to write a vast poem which would represent all the religions of the world, including "Oriental speculations," so as to bring out what Jowett called "the great historical aspect of religion."[53]

Were Tennyson's preoccupations with large scale religious issues representatively Victorian? On this point there is an amusing and helpful comment by Clough's eighteenth-century-minded uncle in the Prologue to *Dipsychus*. The uncle complains to his nephew that Thomas Arnold had ruined the minds of Clough's generation by what he calls an "over-excitation of the religious sense."[54] The avuncular diagnosis surely fits Tennyson as well as it fits Clough, and it was also applicable to most educated men and women of the Victorian age, including persons who had made what seemed to be a clean break with all religious establishments. Victorian scientists unblushingly talked a good deal about God—or something very like Him. I mean here ordinary scientists such as Huxley and Tyndall rather than zany eccentrics such as the zoologist and fundamentalist, Gosse, author of *Omphalos*. The over-excited "religious sense" is readily to be detected in discussions among the forty-two members of The Metaphysical Society, which Tennyson helped to found in 1869 on the model of the Apostles at Cambridge.[55]

This comment on religious issues leads back to our opening inquiry: were Tennyson's mind and temper representative of "the educated mind of the Victorian era"? In seeking an answer to such questions it is well to keep in mind the dangers of playing the game of "selective Victorianisms" as the historian, W. L. Burn, calls it.[56] What Burn showed was that if we select one kind of evidence, we can prove almost any thesis we want in characterizing that extraordinarily diverse period, the Victorian era. Conflicting accounts of the Victorian mind would not be difficult to contrive. Suppose, for example, we were to focus on such writers as Herbert Spencer, or Macaulay, or Samuel Smiles? We might decide that all Victorians think like a combination of Dickens's Mr. Gradgrind with his Facts, Facts, Facts, and his Mr. Bounderby with his bullying self-righteous assertiveness, as in his unwavering conviction that the whole object in life for the working classes is to feed on turtle soup and venison with a gold spoon.

As a poet, Tennyson sometimes creates characters who sound like Josiah Bounderby such as the speaker in "Locksley Hall: Sixty Years After." But behind the mask of monologue is a mind that is tentative, exploratory, curious, and what I have called open. Thackeray, after enjoying a talk with Tennyson, provided a vivid report on his kind of mind: "He reads all sorts of things, swallows them and digests them like a great poetical boa-constrictor, as he is."[57]

It is this quality that enabled Tennyson to come to terms with science. His may be an extreme case of adaptability, but on the whole, many Victorians adapted well. The Two Cultures, as Lord Snow was to style them, were already there in Victorian times, but their proponents at least listened to one another instead of shrieking at one another as F. R. Leavis shrieked at Snow in that unfortunate and ill-mannered controversy of the 1960s. To commend the Victorians on such issues is probably impolitic, but if we compare the hysterical tone and attitude of the late Dr. Leavis in our day, with the civilized tone and attitude of Arnold and Huxley in their memorable debate on literature and science, it is difficult not

George H. Ford

to praise the Victorians, or some of them at least, for an admirable supplemindedness, well-illustrated by Tennyson, a supplemindedness, that if he had thought about it a little more, even Auden might have found enviable.

1. The lecturer, Robert P. Tristram Coffin, appeared to be entirely serious in announcing his choice.

2. See Alan Willard Brown, *The Metaphysical Society* (New York, 1947), p. 107.

3. *Quarterly Review* (October 1859). Reprinted in *Tennyson: The Critical Heritage*, ed. John D. Jump (London, 1967), p. 248.

4. W. H. Auden, *Tennyson: An Introduction and Selection* (London, 1946), p. x.

5. See Paul Turner, "The Stupidest English Poet," *English Studies* 30 (1949): 1-12.

6. James R. Kincaid, *Tennyson's Major Poems* (New Haven, Conn., 1975), p. 14. See also Kincaid's comments on Tennyson's early poem, "Supposed Confession of a Second-Rate Sensitive Mind Not in Unity with Itself," which, he says, "is, in point of fact, the confessions of a first-rate sensitive mind expressing what is finally a terrible unity" (p. 18).

7. Hallam Tennyson, *Tennyson and his Friends* (London, 1912), p. 107. (Tennyson's italics).

8. Ibid., p. 145.

9. Ibid., p. 153.

10. Ibid., pp. 193-94; 275; and Hallam Tennyson, *Alfred Lord Tennyson: A Memoir* (London, 1897), 1:79.

11. *Jane Welsh Carlyle, Letters to her Family*, ed. Leonard Huxley (New York, 1924), p. 230.

12. Tennyson, *Tennyson and Friends*, p. 220. See also J. H. Buckley's *Tennyson* (Cambridge, Mass., 1961), p. 253.

13. Tennyson, *Tennyson and Friends*, p. 187. For an additional report, by an American visitor, on "the strength and brilliancy of his conversation," see *The Letters of Alfred Tennyson*, eds. Cecil Lang and Edgar Shannon (Cambridge, Mass., 1981), 1:192n.

14. See Brown, *The Metaphysical Society*, p. 18.

15. Tennyson, *Tennyson and Friends*, p. 485.

16. Hershey E. Sneath, *The Mind of Tennyson* (London, 1900), pp. 21-22.

17. The suggested comparisons acquire an extra dimension when Arnold's disparaging criticism of Tennyson's mind is recalled, a criticism representing an important minority report of the period. "Tennyson," he wrote, "is deficient in intellectual power." Quoted by Robert Bernard Martin, *Tennyson: The Unquiet Heart* (Oxford, 1980), p. 423.

18. See Tennyson, *Memoir*, 1:76.

19. Tennyson, *Tennyson and Friends*, p. 213.

20. Tennyson, *Memoir*, 1:6.

21. See John Reed, *Old School Ties* (Syracuse, N.Y., 1964). 45-93.

22. Tennyson, *Memoir*, 1:7.

23. Tennyson, *Memoir*, 1:16, and Tennyson, *Tennyson and Friends*, p. 265. Concerning his use of classical literatures in his poetry, see Theodore Redpath, "Tennyson and the Literature of Greece and Rome" in *Studies in Tennyson*, ed. Hallam Tennyson (Totowa, N.J., 1951), pp. 105-30.

24. Tennyson, *Tennyson and Friends*, pp. 34-35. It is interesting that almost all of the authors alluded to were part of Dr. Tennyson's library. See *Tennyson in Lincoln: A Catalogue*, comp. Nancie Campbell (Lincoln, 1971), pp. 1-24. For an interesting demonstration of Tennyson's close study of Goethe's *William Meister*, see Ian Kennedy's "Alfred Tennyson's *Bildungsgang*: Notes on his Early Reading," *PQ* (March, 1978): 82-103.

25. Tennyson, *Tennyson and Friends*, p. 32.

26. Ben Ross Schneider, *Wordsworth's Cambridge Education* (Cambridge, 1957), p. 9.

27. William Whewell, *Of a Liberal Education ... With Particular Reference to the University of Cambridge*, 2d ed. (London, 1850), p. 29.

28. Whewell, *Of a Liberal Education*, p. 24. See also a report on Cambridge in 1841 (ten years after Tennyson had been there) by an American visitor, Charles Astor Bristed, in his *Five Years in an English University* (New York, 1852), 1:347-51.

29. Quoted by Hilda Hagstotz, *The Educational Theories of John Ruskin* (Lincoln, Nebr., 1942), pp. 59-60.

30. Clark Kerr, *The Uses of the University* (New York, 1963), p. 18.

31. See Arthur Stanley, *Life of Thomas Arnold* (New York, 1846), pp. 240-41, and also Schneider, *Wordsworth's Cambridge Education*, pp. 27-28.

32. See M. L. Clarke, *Classical Education in Britain: 1500-1900* (Cambridge, 1959), ch. 8.

33. This quotation follows Lionel Trilling's inspired combination of passages in his *E. M. Forster* (Norfolk, Conn., 1943), pp. 28-29. The first three sentences are from Forster's *Longest Journey*, ch. 6; the other two are from his *Goldsworthy Lowes Dickinson* (New York, 1934), p. 35.

34. Tennyson, *Tennyson and Friends*, pp. 212-13. See also Tennyson, *Memoir*, 1:66-68.

35. *The Letters of Arthur Henry Hallam*, ed. Jack Kolb (Columbus, Ohio, 1981), p. 301. See also p. 232 and p. 343.

36. Tennyson, *Tennyson and Friends*, p. 68.

37. Tennyson, *Memoir*, 1:67.

38. Ibid., 1:44n.

39. In *Ideas and Institutions of Victorian England*, ed. Robert Robson (New York, 1967), p. 325.

40. Christopher Ricks, *Tennyson* (New York, 1972), p. 31; and Peter Allen, *The Cambridge Apostles* (Cambridge, 1978), pp. 134-35.

41. Quoted by Peter Allen, *Cambridge Apostles*, p. 8.

42. Christopher Kent, *Brains and Numbers . . . in Mid-Victorian England* (Toronto, 1978).

43. Tennyson, *Memoir*, 1:204.

44. Tennyson, *Tennyson and Friends*, p. 93. See also David Newsome, *Godliness and Good Learning* (London, 1961), pp. 11-12; and Martha Garland, *Cambridge Before Darwin* (Cambridge, 1980), pp. 83-86.

45. Tennyson, *Tennyson and Friends*, p. 287.

46. Tennyson, *Memoir*, 1:124; and see M. Millhauser, *Fire and Ice: The Influence of Science on Tennyson's Poetry* (Tennyson Society Monographs, number 4, Lincoln, 1971), 32 pp.

47. Tennyson, *Tennyson and Friends*, p. 136.

48. Ibid., p. 177.

49. Ibid., p. 137.

50. Quoted by Robert Martin, *Tennyson*, p. 462. Concerning the poem see Leonard Huxley, *Life and Letters of Thomas Henry Huxley* (New York, 1901), 2:359-60.

51. In chapter 26 of *Eyeless in Gaza* (1936), Huxley's spokesman, Anthony Beavis, asserts that Lawrence "had never looked through a microscope." Huxley apparently forgot that Lawrence studied botany at college, and that later, as a schoolteacher, he wanted to show his pupils how to use a microscope. See George Ford, "Jessie Chambers' Last Tape on D. H. Lawrence" (*Mosaic* [Spring, 1973]: p. 11).

52. Tennyson, *Memoir*, 1: 102.

53. Ibid., 2:464.

54. *The Poems of Arthur Hugh Clough*, ed. H. F. Lowry et al., (Oxford, 1951), p. 296.

55. An interesting contrast can be drawn between the Metaphysical Society, in which religious topics played such a prominent role, and an organization of the present day that also features a mixture of scientists and humanists: the International Society for the Study of Time. At one of the meetings of this Time-Society, held in Austria in 1979, learned papers were presented on the overall topic of "Beginnings and Endings." During the ten days of the conference (as was realized afterwards) the word *God* had only rarely been mentioned. See *The Study of Time IV: Papers from the Fourth Conference*, eds. J. T. Fraser et al., (New York, 1981).

56. W. L. Burn, *The Age of Equipoise* (New York, 1965), p. 8.

57. Gordon Ray, *Thackeray: The Uses of Adversity* (New York, 1955), p. 284.

VIII

JEROME BEATY

Jane Eyre at Gateshead: Mixed Signals in the Text and Context

THE GREATNESS OF *JANE EYRE* LIES IN ITS VIOLENT YOKING OF powerful opposing forces: the irresistible demands of the passional self and the immovable necessity of external restraints. No matter what the angle, if we look closely enough, we see something like this pattern. From a religious perspective, it is the story of Jane's progress from hubristic self-reliance to humble recognition of her dependency on God's mercy, guidance, and Providence. From a psychological or Freudian perspective, *Jane Eyre* as a novel is the story of the struggle between Jane's "it" and the "Above-I" which are eventually yoked by the "I" or self of the narrator.[1] From a political perspective, it is the story of a movement from an excessively violent rebellion against injustice and tyranny toward the willing and dignified submission to proper and limited authority, or "a fictionally transformed version of the tensions and alliances between the two social classes which dominated the Brontës' world: the industrial bourgeoisie, and the landed gentry or aristocracy."[2] From the more limited perspective of literary history, *Jane Eyre* conflates the themes and conventions of the "high" Romantic or Byronic with those of the "lower," domestic or Wordsworthian; by doing so it effects an "horizon change,"[3] a readjustment of expectations among novel readers that marks it as an important literary landmark.

Jane Eyre is frequently read, however, not as an early Victorian novel, one that has conflated two Romantic traditions into something new, but as a late, almost anachronistic high Romantic novel. Mistaking the tradition is understandable enough, for the high Romantic was the dominant tradition in the novel of its day, formed the literary canon and informed our literary histories; the low Romantic novel—domestic, religious, often female—was secondary in its own time and is all but forgotten in ours. Moreover, the narrative mode of *Jane Eyre* contributes to this misunderstanding: the voice of the mature Jane, a wife and mother, knowledgeable about life and love and man's dependency on God's Providence, intrudes only seldom and subtly upon the story of her younger days, so that we mainly perceive the events of the novel as did that younger, rebellious, proudly independent Jane. Yet the low Romantic tradition is distinctly there, not merely toward the end of the novel when the Providentialist world-view surfaces, not just in the form of the governess novels in antiphonal harmony with the Gothic in the Thornfield chapters, but from the very beginning. And from the beginning too there is, if we will notice, the cautionary voice of the older Jane, no matter how muted, alerting us to the fallacy of young Jane's perceptions of the nature of reality. So here in this essay I will look at the early chapters of the text of *Jane Eyre*, first in terms of the two traditions or their conventions, and then at those passages which here, early in the text, explicitly or implicitly qualify young Jane's callow views of herself and the world.

Jane Eyre. An Autobiography. Edited by Currer Bell. So reads the title page of the first edition. The first page of the manuscript (B.M. Add. Mss. #43, 474), however, reads simply, *"Jane Eyre. By Currer Bell."* There is no trace of an "editor" in the text—no preface, footnotes, afterword, or interpolation of any kind, no single word that is not "Jane's"—and the fiction of an editor is dropped from the title page of the second edition. The subtitle is retained, however, though it originated not with the author but with the

169

publisher: Charlotte Brontë agreed with the suggestion in a letter to Smith Elder on 12 September 1847.[5] It is as an autobiography that *Jane Eyre* was first read and reviewed, however, and it has been read so ever since.

Though the word "autobiography" had been in the language less than forty years when Charlotte Brontë's novel was published in 1847 (the Oxford English Dictionary records its first usage in 1809), by the 1830s Carlyle was referring to "these Autobiographical times of ours" (*Sartor Resartus*, 2, 2), and Harriet Martineau could say "of herself in 1831—'I had now plunged fairly into the spirit of my time—self-analysis . . .'" (*Autobiography*, iii, 3).[6] Self-analysis or introspection is the keynote both of autobiography and of the times: "Introspection as a 'note' of the thirties and forties has never been duly recognized; yet contemporaries regarded the 'diseased habit of analysis,' 'the ingenious invention of labyrinth meandering into the mazes of the mind,' or in nobler phrase, 'the dialogue of the mind with itself' as characteristic of the times" (Tillotson, p. 131). What Tillotson does not point out, however, is that the phrases from *Fraser's* in March 1848, *Blackwood's* in April 1846, and the "nobler" and more familiar phrase from Arnold's preface to his *Poems* of 1853 are all, in varying degrees, depreciative. So, too, it is the "coolest of the early reviews" of *Jane Eyre* that identifies it as belonging "to that school where minute anatomy of the mind predominates over incident; the last being made subordinate to description or the display of character."[7] Even a favorable review by A. W. Fonblanque in the *Examiner* for 27 November 1847, in urging that Currer Bell's fictional autobiography be compared only with works of its own kind, seems to imply that that kind is a lesser species: "Taken as a novel or history of events, the book is obviously defective; but as an analysis of a single mind, as an elucidation of its progress from childhood to full age, it may claim comparison with any work of the same species" (Allott, p. 77). The *Blackwood's* critic, John Eagles, writing not about *Jane Eyre* but about Anne Marsh-Caldwell's fictional spiritual autobiography *Mount Sorel* (1845)[8], like Fonblanque believes real novels are less internalized: "Such was not the mode adopted heretofore by more vigorous writers, who preferred exhibiting the passions by action, and a few simple touches, which come at once to the heart, without the necessity of unravelling the mismazes of their course."[9] He can remember "but one tale in which this style of descriptive searchings into the feelings is altogether justifiable—Godwin's *Caleb Williams*" (*Blackwood's*, p. 414). Fonblanque, too, places *Jane Eyre* squarely in the Godwin tradition: "It is not a book to be examined, page by page, with the fiction of Sir Walter Scott or Sir Edward Lytton or Mr. Dickens, from which (except in passages of character where the instant impression reminds us often of the power of the latter writer) it differs altogether. It should rather be placed by the side of the autobiographies of Godwin and his successors, and its comparative value may be then reckoned up, without fear or favour" (Allott, p. 77).

William Godwin's best-known fictional "autobiography," *Things as They Are, or, the Adventures of Caleb Williams* (1794), as it was first called, was published more than fifty years before the appearance of *Jane Eyre* and the phrases from the 1840s and 1850s identifying introspection as a "note" of the time. *St. Leon* (1799) and *Fleetwood* (1805), also "autobiographies," were both published before the word was introduced into the language. But *Deloraine*, his last novel, had appeared only in 1833, and *Caleb Williams* (#2), *St. Leon* (#5), and *Fleetwood* (#22) had all been reissued in the early 1830s in the long-lived Bentley's Standard Novel series and were still being advertised, as in the 17 July 1847 *Athenaeum* (#1029, p. 776), for example. Godwin was still at mid-century, then, very much a part of the literary landscape.

Author of the radical political treatise *Enquiry Concerning Political Justice* (1793), husband of the radical feminist Mary Wollstonecraft, father-in-law of Percy Bysshe Shelley, and grandfather, as it were, of Frankenstein, Godwin was an influential figure in the early revolutionary Romantic movement, eclipsed in his circle finally only by his son-in-law. In his autobiographies he characteristically pits the individual against society; in *Caleb Williams* the repressive power and injustice of privilege is so great it achieves almost supernatural or Gothic dimensions.

There were other influential novelists not thought of as "successors" of Godwin who had tried their hand at fictional autobiography between those of Godwin and *Jane Eyre*. One was no other than a writer of "real novels" mentioned by Fonblanque, Sir Edward Lytton. Though by 1847 the last dozen or so of his novels had all been in the third-person and many, like *The Last Days of Pompeii* (1834), histories of events in a rather literal sense, Lytton's first four novels had been in the first person: *Falkland* (1827), an epistolary novel; *Pelham* (1828); *The Disowned* (1829) and *Devereux* (1829). These early novels do not markedly resemble those of Godwin, but Godwin's influence is implicitly but significantly acknowledged by the names of his characters—though not the characters themselves—being echoed in Lytton: Falkland is the name of Caleb Williams' persecutor; Lytton's Falkland seduces a Lady Emily Mandeville, and Mandeville is the eponymous hero of another of Godwin's fictional autobiographies; a Tyrrel appears both in *Caleb Williams* and *Pelham*.

Why Lytton abandoned the first-person mode in the 1830s and turned to fictional histories of events may be inferred from his own criticism of *The Disowned* and *Devereux* in the dedicatory epistle prefaced to the 1836 edition of *Devereux*: "The external and dramatic colourings which belong to fiction are too often forsaken for the inward and subtle analysis of motives, characters, and actions."[10] This view of the novel clearly anticipates that of Fonblanque and Eagles, but Lytton blames his failure not on the genre but on his own metaphysical studies at the time. When Lytton tacks, however, we would be wise to look for a change in the popular and critical winds.[11]

Besides "meandering into the mazes of the mind," what characterizes introspective novels, according to Eagles, is "an unhealthy egotism; a Byronism of personal feelings" (*Blackwood's*, p. 413) and, despite Godwinian character names, it is Byron, not Godwin, who is Lytton's chief master. It is this that links him to his political opponent and friend, Benjamin Disraeli, for the two were "Byron's chief male disciples among Victorian novelists."[12] An "egotism; a Byronism of personal feelings" is evident from the very beginning of Disraeli's early

172

first-person novel, *Contarini Fleming: A Psychological Romance* (1832):

> When I turn over the pages of the metaphysician, I perceive a science that deals in words instead of facts. Arbitrary axioms lead to results that violate reason; imaginary principles establish systems that contradict the common sense of mankind. All is dogma, no part demonstration. Wearied, perplexed, doubtful, I throw down the volume in disgust.
>
> When I search into my own breast, and trace the development of my own intellect, and the formation of my own character, all is light and order. The luminous succeeds to the obscure, the certain to the doubtful, the intelligent to the illogical, the practical to the impossible, and I experience all that refined and ennobling satisfaction that we derive from the discovery of truth and the contemplation of nature.
>
> I have resolved, therefore, to write the history of my own life, because it is the subject of which I have the truest knowledge.[13]

In 1846 *Contarini Fleming* was reissued with a new subtitle, *A Psychological Autobiography*—making it one of the few novels before *Jane Eyre* to have "autobiography" in its title or subtitle[14]—and with a new preface, dated July 1845, that seems to anticipate Eagles' 1846 strictures and to justify its autobiographical form, as Eagles justified that of *Caleb Williams*:

> When the author meditated over the entireness of the subject, it appeared to him that the autobiographical form was a necessary condition of a successful fulfillment. It seemed the only instrument that could penetrate the innermost secrets of the brain and heart in a being, whose thought and passion were so much cherished in loneliness and revealed often only in solitude. In the earlier stages of the theme the self-discoverer seemed an indispensable agent. What narrative by a third person could sufficiently paint the melancholy and brooding childhood, the first indications of the predisposition, the growing consciousness of power, the reveries, the loneliness, the doubts, the moody misery, the ignorance of art, the failures, the despair? (*CF*, pp. ix–x)

Disraeli abandoned fictional autobiography after *Contarini*, and by the mid-forties had transmuted the fashionable and the Byronic into the political novel. *Coningsby* (1844), heralding the Young England Movement, was the first of the trilogy. It was rapidly followed by *Sybil* (1845), and not long thereafter by *Tancred* (1847). The new edition of *Contarini Fleming* thus appeared between the first and second of the trilogy and was timed to capitalize upon their success. Disraeli was at his zenith as a novelist and was on the eve of leadership of the Tory party, leaving written fiction for a time for the more consequential fiction of political power. In the year of *Jane Eyre*, Disraeli was a significant literary as well as political presence.

It is no wonder, however, that a reviewer seeking a precedent for *Jane Eyre: An Autobiography* would look past Lytton and Disraeli and back to Godwin. Disraeli's name in particular would seem strange linked to that of Currer Bell. Not as strange, however, as linking the names of the autobiographers: Contarini Fleming, eldest son of "Baron Fleming, a Saxon nobleman of ancient family" and the "daughter of the noble house of Contarini" in Venice; Jane Eyre, the plain, small girl, orphaned by the early deaths of her poor clerical father and disinherited mother. Nothing could be more different from the exotic cosmopolitanism of Disraeli's setting than the mundane provincialism of Brontë's. Nothing could be more different from the Byronic self-aggrandizement of Childe Contarini in a world that responds to his emotions and imagination than the shivering, shrinking, but resilient self of little Jane in her hostile, unresponsive world. Finally, nothing could be more different from the situations of the two autobiographers when we first meet them or the prose in which these two openings are couched. No one needs to be reminded of the opening of *Jane Eyre*—ten year-old Jane, an alien and unwelcome presence in the household of her deceased uncle's wife, having been banished from the fireside and the company of her aunt and three cousins is curled up in the curtained window seat in another room reading a book with pictures—nor of its prose, as raw and sombre as the weather on that English November day. *Contarini Fleming* opens with the still-young narrator, "Wandering in those deserts of Africa that border the Erythraean Sea" (*CF*, p. 1, the very first words of the novel), arriving at the "halls of the Pharoahs" and musing on the vanished past. "And I found that the history of my race was but one tale of rapid destruction or gradual decay" (*CF*, p. 2), he tells us.

> And in the anguish of my heart I lifted up my hands to the blue aether, and I said, "Is there no hope! What is knowledge, and what is truth? How shall I gain wisdom?"

174

> The wind arose, the bosom of the desert heaved, pillars of sand sprang from the earth and whirled across the plain; sounds more awful than thunder came rushing from the south; ... I knelt down and hid my face in the moveable and burning soil, and as the wind of the desert passed over me, methought it whispered, "Child of Nature, learn to unlearn!" (*CF*, p. 2)

It is after this "revelation" that Contarini discovers that truth lies within, rejects metaphysics and systems, and decides to write his autobiography.

Yet, if someone reading *Jane Eyre: An Autobiography* late in 1847, when it was first published, or soon thereafter, had recently read *Contarini Fleming: A Psychological Autobiograpy* or were reminded of that novel by its reissue, the opening action of the new novel might well recall the earlier, for these two autobiographies open with remarkably similar narrative incidents. Jane, we all remember, is discovered by her bullying cousin John, who strikes her, insults her, and throws a book at her; for the first time—for she has been mistreated before—she fights back and furiously, and for her pains is carried off by the servants and locked in the red-room. When, in the second chapter, Contarini actually begins his autobiography, his childhood self and situation are not unlike Jane's: "When I can first recall existence," he writes, "I remember myself a melancholy child" (*CF*, p. 4). His mother had died in childbirth and his father has remarried and sired two blond and wholly Saxon sons whom the dark Contarini dislikes. He feels alienated from his new family and the northern "rigid clime whither I had been brought to live" (*CF*, p. 5). In the first dramatized incident, which takes place when Contarini is about eight years old, one of his half-brothers calls him stupid and Contarini strikes him. "I was conducted to my room, and my door was locked on the outside" (*CF*, p. 6). Defiantly he bolts it on the inside, and all day long resists attempts by his family to get him to open the door. The servants finally break it down, but he gnashes his teeth and growls at them. His stepmother is forced to call his father, who enters the room. "I burst into a wild cry; I rushed to his arms. He pressed me to his bosom. He tried to kiss away the flooding tears that each embrace called forth more plenteously. For the first time in my life, I felt loved" (*CF*, p. 7).

175

There are, of course, significant differences between the scenes and between the use made of the scenes. Contarini, unlike Jane, is the older child, strikes the first blow, and, though locked in a room, is locked in his own room. It is he who prolongs the incarceration, refusing to come out when urged to do so. And his rebellion succeeds: for the first time he is assured of his father's love. Jane panics in the red-room, the room in which her uncle died, when it grows dark. She begs for release, but her aunt pushes her back into the room where she faints. Love-starved—"'You think I have no feelings, and that I can do without one bit of love or kindness; but I cannot live so . . . ,'" she later tells her aunt—Jane earns by rebellion not assurance of love, but further banishment; she loses even this poor substitute for a home.

Though there are these differences and though the incidents in themselves are not uncommon—isolating a child for fighting is not unheard of even today—that two fictions of the same subspecies, autobiography, open with such similar incidents might well have been, for the contemporary novel reader, noteworthy. What immediately follows makes it more so. There is no inherent reason why such a realistic and common scene would be followed by one in which there is at least the appearance of the supernatural, yet that is what happens in both *Jane Eyre* and *Contarini Fleming*, a coincidence that might strongly suggest an echo.

At the end of the first chapter, Jane is carried off to the red-room. While confined there in the darkening room Jane begins to think of death and ghosts:

> I lifted my head and tried to look boldly round the dark room: at this moment a light gleamed on the wall. Was it, I asked myself, a ray from the moon penetrating some aperture in the blind? No; moonlight was still and this stirred: while I gazed, it glided up to the ceiling and quivered over my head . . . [P]repared as my mind was for horror, shaken as my nerves were by agitation, I thought the swift-darting beam was a herald of some coming vision from another world. My heart beat thick, my head grew hot; a sound filled my ears, which I deemed the rushing of wings: something seemed near me; I was oppressed, suffocated. (*JE*, p. 15)

In *Contarini Fleming*, the young culprit has already been released from confinement, and the apparition is a separate, sequential incident. Still a child, Contarini falls in love with a young lady eight years or more older than he, his cousin Christiana, who has come to visit. Despite the expression of love he won from his father in the first episode, Contarini tells his cousin that no one loves him. She assures him that everyone does, that she herself does, "and she kissed me with a thousand kisses" (*CF*, p. 11). At a children's ball held just as Christiana's visit is coming to a close, however, she seems to be wholly absorbed by another partner, a boy two years older than Contarini. The despondent Contarini steals to his dark room:

> I had no light, but a dim moon just revealed my bed. I threw myself upon it, and wished to die.
> My forehead was burning hot, my feet were icy cold. My heart seemed in my throat. I felt quite sick. I could not speak; I could not weep; I could not think. Everything seemed blended in one terrible sensation of desolate and desolating wretchedness.
> Much time perhaps had not elapsed, although it seemed to me an age, but there was a sound in the room, light and gentle. I looked around; I thought that a shadowy form passed between me and the window. A feeling of terror crossed me. I nearly cried out. (*CF*, p 14)

The voice of the older Jane, Jane-the-narrator, rarely interrupts the action in the early scenes of the novel, but it does so here to explain away—conjecturally, at least—the "ghost": "I can now conjecture readily that this streak of light was, in all likelihood, a gleam from a lantern, carried by someone across the lawn" (*JE*, p. 15). Contarini's visitant too, is no ghost but Christiana come to fetch him back to the ball and to reassure him of her love. It is her visit rather than his father's expression of love that he calls "the first great incident of my life" (*CF*, p. 12).

In *Jane Eyre* the scene is causally connected to the earlier episode and to what immediately follows—her terror is interpreted by her aunt as temper; Jane interprets her aunt's response as cruelty; the child's frenzy and consequent illness make her aunt decide to send her away to school. The comparable scenes in *Contarini Fleming* are connected only by the theme of the boy's need for love, and the "apparition" is momentary and unmomentous. Nonetheless, the coincidence of opening scenes has become a coincidence of a suite of opening scenes; a point of resemblance, when there is another, becomes a line, and the reader who notes the similarity may well begin to expect a pattern. Though there will be no such pattern,[15] the conjuring up of the opening scenes of *Contarini* by the early chapters of *Jane Eyre* may reassure readers that they are in territory already familiar in the novel, but many will soon realize they are reading an autobiography of a kind quite different from those of Godwin's more Byronic successors.

Indeed, scenes analogous to the opening scenes of *Jane Eyre* and *Contarini Fleming* appear in several other novels of the period, novels that may be life-stories, "histories," or fictional biographies but not necessarily autobiographies in the narrow sense or even analyses of a single mind. One such, a new edition of which also, like *Contarini*, appeared in 1846, few readers could have missed: *Oliver Twist; or, The Parish Boy's Progress.* Neither an autobiography nor Byronic, this "history" or "progress" of a foundling by The Inimitable and Unclassifiable seems, in its sympathy for the underdog and antipathy for entrenched authority, Godwinian; though crime is overtly treated in a totally different fashion, even the Newgate aspects of *Oliver Twist* may recall *Caleb Williams*. In its faith in human innocence, its foundling theme and stereotypes (such as "the outcast waif and benevolent gentleman"),[16] *Oliver Twist* seems like the sentimental or "low" Romantic, and in its Bunyanesque subtitle and tendency toward moral as well as social allegory,[17] it is related to a still "lower" tradition, the religious, didactic, and domestic novel.

Oliver, like Jane but unlike Contarini, is poor and "diminuitive"; he is not only an orphan but a foundling, and he is locked up not once but twice in the early (though not the first) chapters of his "history." The first time, on his ninth birthday, he is confined with two other boys; the second time, like Contarini and Jane, for fighting. The second occasion is introduced by Dickens as an event of some significance, as the true beginning of Oliver's "progress," just as the similar incidents were the true beginnings of Jane's and Contarini's life-stories: "And now I come to a very important passage in Oliver's history; for I have to record an act: slight and

178

unimportant perhaps in appearance: but which indirectly produced a most material change in all his future prospects and proceedings."[18]

The ten-year-old Oliver (Jane was ten when we first met her, Contarini eight) has been apprenticed to an undertaker, and, like Jane, is the unwelcome intruder in the household. One day he and a fellow-worker, the charity-boy Noah Claypole, are awaiting dinner. Noah begins teasing the younger and smaller Oliver. He puts his feet on the tablecloth, pulls Oliver's hair and ears, taunts him. Like Jane on earlier occasions, Oliver endures the mistreatment. When Noah begins on the subject of Oliver's mother, however, the smaller boy warns him off; but Noah goes on:

> "A regular right-down bad un, Work'us ["Workhouse," Noah's name for Oliver]," replied Noah, coolly. "And it's a great deal better, Work'us, that she died when she did, or else she'd have been hard labouring in Bridewell, or transported, or hung: which is more likely than either, isn't it?"
> Crimson with fury, Oliver started up; overthrew the chair and table; seized Noah by the throat; shook him, in the violence of his rage, till his teeth chattered in his head; and, collecting his whole force into one heavy blow, felled him to the ground. (*OT*, vi, p. 32)

Noah screams that he will be murdered. Charlotte Sowerberry, the undertaker's daughter, and Mrs. Sowerberry come to his rescue. They finally "dragged Oliver, struggling and shouting, but nothing daunted, into the dust-cellar, and there locked him up" (*OT*, vi, p. 32), resisting "all the way" as Jane had done (*JE*, p. 9). He kicks violently in anger, as Jane screamed violently in panic, and they fear he will kick down the door. Noah, a clasp-knife held to his blackened eye, rushes off to bring the beadle. The beadle admonishes Mrs. Sowerberry. He tells her that this is what she gets for serving paupers meat and advises her to keep Oliver in the cellar a few days, feeding him nothing but gruel. Part of Oliver's bad conduct, he says, can be attributed to his having come from a bad family. At this point Oliver, believing his mother is being insulted again, recommences kicking.

When Sowerberry returns he releases Oliver, scolds him, shakes him and boxes his ears as Aunt Reed does to Jane when Jane challenges her (*JE*, p. 28). Oliver protests that Noah has brought his punishment on himself by insulting Oliver's mother.

> "Well, and what if he did, you little ungrateful wretch?" says Mrs. Sowerberry. "She deserved what he said, and worse."
> "She didn't," said Oliver.
> "She did," says Mrs. Sowerberry.
> "It's a lie," said Oliver.

Mrs. Sowerberry burst into a flood of tears (*OT*, vii, pp. 41–42).

Jane, too, brings her guardian to the verge of tears by accusing first Georgiana and then Aunt Reed herself of deceit: "'People think you a good woman, but you are bad; hard-hearted. *You* are deceitful'" (*JE*, p. 39). Her aunt looks frightened, drops her work, and twists "her face as if she would cry" (*JE*, p. 40).

It is as a consequence of her behavior leading to and during her incarceration that Jane is sent to Lowood Institution, a charity school. Oliver has already been confined in an institution, a workhouse, and indeed was born in a workhouse; after his punishment—he has been beaten by the undertaker and Bumble as well as having been locked away—he escapes Sowerberry, the undertaker to whom he has been apprenticed, and begins his odyssey. Jane is frightened by what she believes may be a ghost while confined to the red-room where her uncle died nine years before; Oliver has been confronted by the ghost-like earlier, the first night he is sent to his bed in the undertaker's workshop:

> Oliver, being left to himself in the undertaker's shop, set the lamp down on a workman's bench, and gazed timidly about him with a feeling of awe and dread. . . . An unfinished coffin on black tressels, which stood in the middle of the shop, looked so gloomy and deathlike that a cold tremble came over him, every time his eyes wandered in the direction of the dismal object: from which he almost expected to see some frightful form slowly rear its head, to drive him mad with terror. Against the wall, were ranged, in regular array, a long row of elm boards cut into the same shape: looking, in the dim light, like high-shouldered ghosts with their hands in their breeches-pockets. (*OT*, p. 25)

Oliver is too depressed by the loneliness, gloominess, and strangeness to be terrified; he falls asleep.[19]

Oliver, like a Godwin hero, is persecuted because he is a victim—an orphan, poor—as Jane is. Though Jane is not a foundling, she might be better off with fewer Reed relatives, and, like Oliver, her narrative-long quest may be seen as a search for a home, a hearth like the one she was banished from on the first page of the novel. Neither Contarini nor Oliver, different as they are, need to change or grow morally, though Contarini in particular must learn a good deal more about the world. Jane may well have seemed to the contemporary reader beginning the novel just such a protagonist, a blameless individual, pitted against a hostile world; many twentieth-century readers still see her so.

Brontë herself mentions in *Jane Eyre* another novel with an innocent and beleaguered heroine—*Pamela*. In the first chapter, Jane, in her windowseat, recalls, "the tales Bessie sometimes narrated . . . passages of love and adventure taken from old fairy tales and older ballads; or (as at a later period I discovered) from the pages of Pamela and Henry, Earl of Moreland" (*JE*, p. 5). The similarity of the central situations in the two novels—a virtuous young lady from a decent but not aristocratic family who is employed by a gentleman is subjected to sexual harassment—has led some reviewers and critics to see *Jane Eyre* as a latter-day *Pamela*.[20] Though in Richardson's novel, aristocratic exploitation and presumptions of privilege are criticized, class distinctions and the aristocracy as an institution or the institutions of the government are not attacked in anything like Godwinian or even Dickensian terms; the offense is primarily moral, as is the theme. *Pamela* is closer than are *Caleb Williams* or *Oliver Twist* (not to mention *Contarini Fleming*) to the "domestic" novel of the early nineteenth century.

So, too, is the other novel mentioned in the text of *Jane Eyre*, John Wesley's 1781, frequently reprinted abridgement of Henry Brooke's *The Fool of Quality* (1766-1770). In the opening chapter, as in *Jane Eyre* and *Contarini Fleming*, the young protagonist engages in a fight. Young Henry bloodies the nose of his older brother, Richard, for insulting their foster mother; Henry's real mother, who had set Richard on to test Henry, does not have him locked up but bans him from his home, saying she never wants to see him again. As a result he is raised by his simple foster parents and has a healthful, vigorous, unspoiled childhood, much unlike that of his pampered brother. He is a "fool" in that he is unsophisticated, innocent, "natural." His forthright honesty and virtue will win him back love and honor. This is clearly a sentimental tale in which man is naturally good, goodness is innocence, and the world is not so much hostile as corrupt and corrupting.

We have been moving, from *Contarini* and *Caleb Williams* through *Oliver Twist* to *Pamela* and *Henry, Earl of Moreland*, down from the high Romantic toward that kind of low Romantic novel with which many contemporary reviewers identified *Jane Eyre*. That kind in the early nineteenth century was called "the domestic novel," not a tag we would inevitably choose for *Jane Eyre*. But the *Atlas* on 23 October 1847 calls it "one of the most powerful domestic romances which have been published for many years" (Allott, p. 67), and *The People's Journal* for November agrees, upgrading it from romance to novel: "this is one of the most notable domestic novels which have issued from the press in this country for many years past" (Allott, p. 80). And there are others. Eugène Fourçade, in his highly favorable review in the *Revue des deux mondes* for 31 October 1848—a review approved of by Brontë herself—does not use the contemporary English) critical term but seems to be identifying *Jane Eyre* similarly. From his French perspective, he describes *Jane Eyre*—in a phrase reminiscent of the review of *Lady Chatterley's Lover* in *Field and Stream*—as "a novel of country life" (Allott, p. 102). "Domestic" seems to have meant British and familiar as opposed to foreign and exotic, of the present day or recent past as opposed to the historical, and, more significantly, of private life as opposed to the social or "fashionable."

One eighteenth-early-nineteenth-century tributary flowing into the main stream of the domestic novel was the moral didactic tale, often intended for children. One such tale was Barbara Hofland's long-popular *Ellen, the Teacher. A Tale for Youth* (1814), a novel that, Inga-Stina Ewbank points out,

Jerome Beaty

was available to the Brontës through the Keighly Mechanics' Institute Library. It is likely, Ewbank suggests, "that a story like *Ellen, the Teacher*, about a poor orphan girl who suffers miserably in a boarding school, eventually makes good as a governess and ultimately marries her cousin, . . . might have been one of the germs from which *Jane Eyre* grew."[21] Though the scene does not open the novel, and though the occasion is not fighting but a false accusation of lying at school (remember, Jane, too, is falsely accused of lying during her Lowood days), young Ellen Delville is also punished by being locked away in a room. Though no ghost appears or seems to appear while she is confined, she does faint during her punishment and does fall ill afterwards, just as Jane does. The physician called into treat Ellen's badly infected finger befriends her, and, like the apothecary Mr. Lloyd in *Jane Eyre*, seems the only sympathetic soul in the poor girl's hostile environment.

Though we are meant to be as sympathetic toward Ellen as we are toward the other young protagonists, childhood in Hofland's novel is not seen as a period of prelapsarian innocence or perfection with no future out in the world but corruption. Young Ellen is as fiery as young Jane, and, despite her protestations—"[I am] not passionate—I mean not *very* passionate; I never go into a rage"[22]—her mother insists at the very outset of the novel (her mother dies soon thereafter) that she must learn to control herself, for she gets excessively angry when there is little cause, and passion, she will learn, is inevitably followed by shame. The motherless Jane, as we will see, discovers for herself the same lesson. What I wish to emphasize here, however, is not necessarily the similarities between *Jane Eyre* and *Ellen* as product to source or influence, but that within the domestic tradition, particularly tales of youth and moral or religious tales, the young were part of the fallen world, were fallible, in need of moral or religious instruction, guidance and growth. Is Jane nearer to Oliver or Ellen?

The first-person narrative of domestic or private life in the English tradition derives in large measure from the anachronistically named spiritual autobiography. That tradition wends its way into fiction through Bunyan and Defoe[23] and

183

into a fictional autobiography such as Mrs. Sherwood's *Caroline Mordaunt; or, The Governess* (1835), didactic, religious, domestic, written by a female for a female audience.[24] The spiritual autobiographer, real or fictional, traces or witnesses to his or her own moral growth, conversion, or deliverance. What this means is that the protagonist in the early stages of the narrative must be, or have been, ignorant of God or His ways, if not sinful. The spiritual fictional autobiography of the governess Caroline Mordaunt bears some resemblance to *Jane Eyre*.

Most of the more obvious and significant similarities between Brontë's and Sherwood's novels lie on first reading outside our narrow focus on the opening chapters of *Jane Eyre*. Caroline, for example, "is brought back into religion by a pious little pupil who, like Jane Eyre's Helen Burns, dies in her arms"[25]; at the end she marries a clergyman whom she does not love at the time, as Jane is tempted to do. (It turns out well for Caroline Mordaunt, and for readers familiar with that novel St. John Rivers' proposal may have occasioned more suspense—and even hope—than it does for us.) The structural and thematic Providentialism that informs *Jane Eyre* is only gradually revealed. On first reading we begin to grow aware of divine guidance and intercession, if we do, not long before Jane does, unless we are so steeped in the tradition that such early problematic or casually dismissed episodes like that in the red-room serve as signals to alert us to what may be coming, or should be coming.

If in *Jane Eyre* we learn, in *Caroline Mordaunt* we are instructed. Mrs. Sherwood's autobiographer tells us what she has learned in the very first words of the novel:

> I am now arrived at that period of life, and, I thank God, to that state of mind, in which I can look back at the various adventures of my past years with no other feelings than those of gratitude to that Divine Providence which has rendered every apparent accident, and every difficulty which I have encountered in my passage down the stream of time, more or less subservient to my everlasting welfare. (CM, p. 203)

At least twice more in the first half of this rather short novel (it runs to a little over 100 pages in the edition I am using), the autobiographer, fearing that the "serious reader" may find her too caught up in the secular narrative, intervenes to assure us the religious bits will be coming: "I almost fear that my serious reader may be tired of . . . [my not] having evidenced [so far] the smallest regard for religion, . . . but I have much, very much to say of the various providences by which I was gradually brought to know myself, to esteem myself as the chief of sinners, and to comprehend in some degree what the Almighty has done and is still doing for me" (*CM*, p. 252).

The older Caroline Mordaunt is, in terms of the story of her own life, virtually an omniscient narrator, especially since now she has recognized the workings of Providence in her life. This reduces her younger self virtually to third-person status (and indeed Thackeray's fictional autobiographer in *Henry Esmond* will refer to his younger and unenlightened self as "he"). That Jane's elder self is so inobtrusive in telling the story of her earlier life masks for a time (and for some readers for the entire novel) the distance between the two in knowledge, behavior, and values (while at the same time this collapse between the narrative present and the narrator's past may account for the intensity of suspense in the novel).

The first-person narration of a life story may thus be used not merely to recount, reveal, or justify, but to instruct by exemplum, especially when the autobiographer has had to learn to change. The function of autobiography in Sarah Fielding's popular and influential children's book of the previous century[26]—a book which, not incidentally, has as its first narrative incident "An Account of a Fray, begun and carried on for the sake of an Apple. In which are shewn the sad Effects of Rage and Anger"— is to instruct the narrator as well as the audience. After the "fray" one of the students, Jenny Peace, recommends love not fighting, friendship not revenge, and then promises to tell something instructive about her life: "And after I have given you the Particulars of my Life, I must beg that every one of you will some Day or other, when you have reflected upon it, declare all that you can remember of your own; for, should you not be able to relate anything worth remembering as an Example, yet there is nothing more likely to amend the future Part of any one's Life, than the recollecting and confessing the Faults of the past" (Fielding, p. 23/121).

A novel in the autobiographical mode appearing in England in 1847, then, may be an apologia or an exemplum, egoistic and Byronic, or humbly Providential. A child in a novel who fights with other children and is locked away for punishment may be innocent victim or venial aggressor. Knowing some of the novels in the contemporary context thus informs expectations—not in telling what will happen next, but, on the contrary, in suggesting all the things that might happen next. Though some readers may have one or another of the possible developments of the plot and moral thrust of the novel in mind, most novel readers are likely to project several configurations, foregrounding first one, then the other. This is how suspense is created in fiction, and how richness of texture is created as well. Though "wrong guesses" are eventually discarded, they have been there in the novel, and insofar as they are signaled by the novel they are part of it. A novel with fewer or weaker false signals, though its plot and theme may be in other respects the same, is, in moral and narrative complexity, less compelling.

The rhythmic foregrounding and backgrounding of expectations is an important constituent of reading. The fighting, confinement, and ghostly appearance in *Jane Eyre* may, for the informed reader, immediately foreground Contarini and Oliver Twist. Contarini is sure to fade, as the novels diverge, but perhaps not entirely disappear; he has an extrasensory or supernatural experience involving the one he loves which the reader may recall when Jane hears Rochester's voice calling her across the miles. Oliver's presence will remain hovering over Jane a bit longer. She, too, is the victim of injustice, personal and institutional; her innocent little persecuted friend will die, just as Oliver's friend Dick dies. But as Oliver becomes a figure in a Newgate novel and Jane in a governess novel, his image will recede.[27] The quiet voice of Barbara Hofland in the opening chapters of *Jane Eyre* may become a bit stronger as Jane becomes a teacher like Ellen, fade during Jane's Gothic experiences at Thornfield, revive when, at Morton, Jane again becomes a teacher. The muted

Jerome Beaty

voice of Mrs. Sherwood's autobiographer will come through
more clearly when Jane becomes a governess and become loud
and clear as the workings of Providence in her life come to the
fore.

This is not to say that any one reader had or must have read
each and every one of the novels mentioned to bring the text to
life in all its complexity and potentiality (or that Charlotte
Brontë had to have read and had in mind these texts as she
wrote). Godwin, Disraeli, Dickens were, however, significant
presences on the literary scene. Barbara Hofland and Mrs.
Sherwood were significant presences on the domestic scene—
meaning both in the domestic novel and with early nineteenth-century mothers and children. Their novels or novels
like them—either those that fed into their works or those that
imitated or were influenced by them—were instrumental in
helping to define what the novel was or was expected to be in
the mid-forties.

There are traces of those expectations and themes defined by
the context, traces of the clash of the powerful opposing forces
that are to characterize and give meaning to the novel,
inscribed as well in the isolated text of the early chapters of
Jane Eyre, but they may be more difficult to perceive, retain,
and evaluate in a naive reading. The vulnerability of the little
child, the injustice of her mistreatment, the self-righteousness
and cruelty of her oppressors, and the natural tendency of
first-person narration to arouse sympathy, combine to put us
whole-heartedly on the side of the spunky rebel, Jane Eyre. So
strongly are we disposed in her favor by the action, character,
and narration here it is difficult to qualify our judgment of
her views or behavior. Yet in order to remain so partisan we
must resist the very words on the page, the older narrator's
own attempt to deconstruct the text as her younger self
dictates it, as it were; we must ignore the difference between
the Jane who rebels and she who tells us of that rebellion.

Though there is an inevitable separation between the older
narrator and her younger self—the vocabulary and the past
tense, if nothing else, define it—in the first chapter of *Jane
Eyre*, the narrator and subject are apparently as close to being

one as is possible. Though described in the narrator's words, almost everything that is seen, felt, or thought is the child's. The narrator does say, however, that the child's idea of the "death-white realms" described or depicted in Bewick's *History of British Birds* were "shadowy, like all the half-comprehended notions that float dim through children's brains, but strangely impressive," and that the pictures were "mysterious often to my undeveloped understanding and imperfect feelings."²⁸ And there is one somewhat ambiguous clause—"I don't very well know what I did with my hands"—which refers to both "now" and "then." Though we are thereby made aware that there is an older Jane telling the story, the two passages distancing the child have nothing to do with the action in the chapter or with the situation at the opening of the novel. Yet it is here in the first chapter that our sympathies for Jane are aroused, our antipathy to the Reeds established, our sense of justice outraged by John Reed's offensiveness and cruelty, and where Jane first rebels against her treatment. It may well be because the identity of narrator and young Jane is so firmly established here that it is so hard to shake later on.

Just past the middle of the second chapter, when Jane is in the red-room, however, the narrator draws back from the child. At first, it is only the child's failure to understand what no child could be expected to understand that is at issue: "What a consternation of soul was mine that dreary afternoon! How all my brain was in tumult, and all my heart in insurrection! Yet in what darkness, what dense ignorance, was the mental battle fought! I could not answer the ceaseless inward question—*Why* I thus suffered: now, at the instance of—I will not say how many years, I see it clearly." Then there follows, if not self-criticism (can one be criticized for one's nature, temperament, or appearance?), at least an attempt to understand from the vantage point of maturity the Reeds' response to her.

> I was a discord in Gateshead-hall: I was like nobody there: I had nothing in harmony with Mrs. Reed or her children, or her chosen vassalage. If they did not love me, in fact, as little did I love them. They were not bound to regard with affection a thing that could not

sympathize with one amongst them; a heterogeneous thing, opposed to them in temperament, in capacity, in propensities; a useless thing, incapable of serving their interests, or adding to their pleasure; a noxious thing, cherishing the germs of indignation at their treatment, of contempt of their judgment. I know, that had I been a sanguine, brilliant, careless, exacting, handsome, romping child—though equally dependent and friendless—Mrs. Reed would have endured my presence more complacently; her children would have entertained for me more of the cordiality of fellow-feeling; the servants would have been less prone to make me the scape-goat of the nursery.

There is a bit of the concealed boast here, of course: if Jane is different, she's different because she's superior. Yet there is something of implied self-criticism too: young Jane "cherishes" her indignation and contempt; and just as she does not love them any more than they her, so she had then no more fellow-feeling than they. Then, too, there is something in the passage, "had I been sanguine . . . romping," that may send us back to the opening paragraphs of the novel.

There Jane had been exiled from the hearth until she should make an effort to "acquire a more sociable and childlike disposition, a more attractive and sprightly manner,—something lighter, franker, more natural as it were." Is such a change beyond effort and will? Does Jane not confirm her aunt's criticism?

And then, in the light of the later passage of self-criticism, what do we make of Jane's response to her aunt's charge—the first words young Jane speaks in the novel—a response that on first reading surely seemed most natural and innocent?

> "What does Bessie say I have done?" I asked.
> "Jane, I don't like cavillers or questioners: besides, there is something truly forbidding in a child taking up her elders in that manner."

Is Jane's question a "cavil" or quibble? I confess I never thought so until I looked at the passage very carefully, led to do so, admittedly, by the contemporary moral and religious domestic novels I had been reading. Mrs. Reed has asked Jane to change her manner; she has not accused her of "wrong-doing": "What . . . have [I] done?" is thus not an appropriate question; it is a quibble. Unless we are prepared, despite the first-person narration that customarily enlists sympathy for and agreement with the narrator, to look at Jane's response

189

skeptically or objectively, we certainly will not question its appropriateness. If we carefully keep our distance—or one part of our judgment disengaged—from the mistreated and pitiable little orphan girl we may later think back to this passage and have some doubts.

The narrator, recounting the scene in the red-room, having seen her young self as a discord in Gateshead-hall, in the next paragraph again distances the child, seeing her through Mrs. Reed's eyes as an "uncongenial alien." This in turn prepares for a still more direct separation of narrator and child when, in the next paragraph, she interprets the light that glides from the wall to the ceiling of the red-room, terrorizing young Jane: "I can now conjecture readily that this streak of light was, in all likelihood, a gleam from a lantern, carried by some one across the lawn." Why "conjecture,"? and why "in all likelihood"? Why, in any case, both? To maintain the fiction of the limited perspective? To strengthen the authority of the child-witness somewhat by suggesting some doubt about the conclusion or conjecture of the narrator? To keep alive the possibility of the supernatural in the world of the novel? (Ironically, Jane at nineteen will prove more skeptical about the possibilities of a spirit world than Jane the thirty-five year-old narrator, and one major theme in the novel is discriminating materialism and that "realism" which accepts the supernatural, superstition and true religion.) We are impatient with the narrator's attempt to defend Mrs. Reed's cruel insistence that Jane stay in the red-room for another hour despite her terror—"I was a precocious actress in her eyes: she sincerely looked on me as a compound of virulent passions, mean spirit, and dangerous duplicity." This charity is too saintly for the Jane we know. But who is the older Jane? What are her values? We may come to know her and to approve them, but now we are, surely, on the side of the rebel. Still, a piece has been put on the table which, though it does not seem to have a place in the jigsaw of the novel now, will lie ready, should a matching piece appear as we read on.

The narrator does not seem able wholly to maintain her saintliness. Early in chapter 3, young Jane overhears Bessie admitting that "Missis was rather too hard," and the narrator, not quite able to forgive as she admits she ought, seems, by her own admission, not quite Christ-like enough: "No severe or prolonged bodily illness followed this incident of the red-room: it only gave my nerves a shock; of which I feel the reverberation to this day. Yes, Mrs. Reed, to you I owe some fearful pangs of mental suffering. But I ought to forgive you, for you knew not what you did: while rending my heart-strings, you thought you were only up-rooting my bad propensities." Later in the third chapter, after one or two small "corrections" of the child's view—the narrator says that she would probably find Mr. Lloyd's eyes shrewd, though young Jane did not; and that children cannot analyze their feelings—our whole-hearted identification with young Jane's feelings and values is shaken. Lloyd asks if she would like to go to poor relations on her father's side if they could be found. "I reflected. Poverty looks grim to grown people; still more so to children: they have not much idea of industrious, working, respectable poverty; they think of the word only as connected with ragged clothes, scanty food, fireless grates, rude manners and debasing vices: poverty for me was synonymous with degradation . . . ; no, I was not heroic enough to purchase liberty at the price of caste." So well-disposed are we to the small, spunky victim, we find this reasonable. She is a child, after all. We cannot expect heroism; this is not a romance, but a realistic novel. Nobody's perfect. Or do we say simply that she is a creature of her time and class? Still, distance has been put between the reader and the child, more so, perhaps, than by the narrator's superior moral position suggested earlier.

We are immediately thrust back on Jane's side as chapter 4 opens: she is suffering internal exile at Gateshead, she belts John in the nose when he tries to chastise her. When she shouts over the bannister to her aunt that her cousins are not fit to associate with her, and challenges her aunt to imagine what Uncle Reed would say if alive, most modern readers see spirit rather than sin in her actions. Victorians, whether novel readers or not, might have had more reservations, and, indeed, Jane herself feels wicked—"for I felt indeed only bad feelings surging in my breast."

Except for three brief passages, the narrator stays out of the action of chapter 4 until Jane is left alone toward the end. The second brief intervention is neutral, an attempt by the older Jane to reconstruct Bessie's appearance and nature from a more mature view. The first instance serves to put the reader closer to the child than the woman: "human beings must love something," the narrator tells us, but then professes not to understand how she could have doted on her shabby, faded doll. The last is the kind of distancing or criticism that engenders sympathy for the child—young Jane stands before the breakfast-room door, trembling before she answers her aunt's summons to enter: "What a miserable little poltroon had fear, engendered of unjust punishment, made of me in those days!"

All rebellious spirits are aroused on Jane's behalf as she responds to that black pillar, that pietistic Pharisee Mr. Brocklehurst—she'll avoid going to hell by staying healthy and not dying; yes, she likes the Bible, but selectively, and no, she does not like the Psalms—but I wonder whether there are not still, and were not more readers in mid-Victorian England who were at least shocked, perhaps offended. The narrator has discreetly withdrawn, we're on our own, our times and beliefs will answer more than the text itself in this passage. (We ought to note, however, that in her moment of desperation, when Bertha Rochester has been revealed, and Jane is about to flee Thornfield, pp. 374–75, it is in the words of Psalm 22 that she prays to God for help, and it is in the words adapted from Psalm 69 that the narrator seeks to describe her misery.) Even young Jane's mind is hidden from us during much of the dramatically rendered conversation between Brocklehurst and Mrs. Reed, during which our indignation is mounting as furiously as Jane's at the self-righteousness and hypocrisy of the two self-seeking, cruel adults. Left alone with her aunt, Jane cannot contain herself: "*Speak* I must." However wrong her conduct, deceitful it was not. It is Georgiana who lies, she tells the aunt, and, finally, "People think you a good woman, but you are bad; hard-hearted. *You* are deceitful!" Her growing vehemence frightens her aunt.

> "Deceit is not my fault!" I cried out in a savage, high voice.
> "But you are passionate, Jane, that you must allow: and now return to the nursery—there's a dear—and lie down a little."

Jerome Beaty

"I am not your dear; I cannot lie down: send me to school soon, Mrs. Reed, for I hate to live here."

We soar with her in her triumph, as unprepared as she for the backlash of those emotions that had been trained into her by her up-bringing. The language, the analysis, the generalizations are those of the narrator, but the emotions are those of the child, and they are as chastening as anything adult wisdom might have said:

> I was left there alone—winner of the field. It was the hardest battle I had fought, and the first victory I had gained . . . and I enjoyed my conqueror's solitude. First, I smiled to myself and felt elate; but this fierce pleasure subsided in me as fast as did the accelerated throb of my pulses. A child cannot quarrel with its elders, as I had done; cannot give its furious feelings uncontrolled play, as I had given mine; without experiencing afterwards the pang of remorse and the chill of reaction. A ridge of lighted heath, alive, glancing, devouring, would have been a meet emblem of my mind when I accused and menaced Mrs. Reed: the same ridge, black and blasted after the flames are dead, would have represented as meetly my subsequent condition, when half an hour's silence and reflection had shewn me the madness of my conduct, and the dreariness of my hated and hating position.
>
> Something of vengeance I had tasted for the first time; as aromatic wine it seemed on swallowing, warm and racy: its after-flavour, metallic and corroding, gave me a sensation as if I had been poisoned. Willingly would I now have gone and asked Mrs. Reed's pardon; but I knew, partly from experience and partly from instinct, that was the way to make her repulse me with double scorn, thereby re-exciting every turbulent impulse of my nature.

I quote this passage at length because it should give even the most Janian reader pause. (Indeed, the passage goes on for another long paragraph, Jane whispering over and over to herself, "'What shall I do—what shall I do?'") The next chapter, 5, opens with Jane prepared to leave Gateshead for Lowood Institution. The first stage of her life's journey is over. It has closed on a warning note: even a mistreated orphan may be too passionate in her rebellion, too vengeful, too self-assertive.

Jane Eyre reconciles with remarkable success the demands of self and the exigencies of otherness. It succeeds not only because it is intense and inclusive—it does not deny either the power of the passions or the rigors of restraint; it subsumes disparate psychological, social, religious, and even literary

193

perspectives—but because it has evolved the appropriate narrative strategies for doing so. By modulating the voice of the mature narrator, and letting us focus on the younger Jane, Brontë forces us first to *experience* Jane's growing awareness of the limits of the self and the nature of reality; understanding the *meaning* of the experience comes, if it comes, only after. It is possible by close reading of the early chapters of *Jane Eyre* to catch the mixed signals, the strategy of "cautionary anticipation,"[29] in the text, and so to be prepared for the authority of young Jane's values to be qualified by later developments in the novel. These anticipations are largely thematic and somewhat abstract, however, and Brontë's full narrative strategy is more inclusive, more concrete, more literary. Using the context and conventions of the fiction of her time, Brontë educates the expectations of the informed novel-reader not only intellectually but sensually. The precautionary signals come not only in verbal abstractions but in the shadowy yet human forms of Contarini Fleming and Ellen Delville, Oliver Twist and Caroline Mordaunt, and of other warm shades from the worlds of fiction.

1. I am here using the Freudian terminology as convincingly retranslated by Bruno Bettelheim in "Freud and the Soul," *The New Yorker*, 1 March 1982, pp. 52-93, esp. pp. 80-84: 'it' for 'id' and 'Above I' for 'superego.'

2. Terry Eagleton, *Myths of Power: A Marxist Study of the Brontës* (New York, 1975), p. 4. This passage actually refers to Charlotte Brontë's oeuvre as a whole, and underlies his reading of *Jane Eyre*. See, e.g., p. 32: "By the device of an ending, bourgeois initiative and genteel settlement, sober rationality and Romantic passion, spiritual equality and social distinction, the actively affirmative and the patiently deferential self can be merged with a mythical unity." As that passage suggests, Eagleton, too, sees the tension in areas other than the social, historical, or political though he insists "that the 'social' or 'historical' are never merely extra terms, to be blandly equated with others; they have, actually and methodologically, a radical priority of status" (p.2).

3. See Hans Robert Jauss, "Literary History as a Challenge to Literary Theory," in *New Directions in Literary History*, ed. Ralph Cohen (Baltimore, 1974), pp. 11-41.

4. See Jerome Beaty, "Jane Eyre and Genre," *Genre* 10 (Winter 1977): 619-54.

5. Arthur Pollard, "The Seton-Gordon Brontë Letters," *Brontë Society Transactions* 18 (1982): 100.

6. Quoted in Kathleen Tillotson, *Novels of the Eighteen-Forties* (London, 1954), pp. 131–32n.

7. Unsigned review in the *Spectator* for 6 November 1847, reprinted in part in *The Brontës: The Critical Heritage*, ed. Miriam Allott (London and Boston, 1974), p. 74; the description of the review is Allott's.

8. Allott, p. 95, identifies Aurilius, author of *Blackwood's* "Letter to Eusebius", as John Eagles.

The *Weekly Chronicle* reviewer of *Jane Eyre* was "tempted more than once to believe that Mrs. Marsh was veiling herself under an assumed editorship, for this autobiography partakes greatly of her simple, penetrating style, and, at times, of her love of nature; but a man's more vigorous hand is, we think, perceptible." "Opinions of the Press" reprinted from the third edition in Charlotte Brontë, *Jane Eyre*, ed. Jane Jack and Margaret Smith (Oxford, 1969), p. 631. Hereafter cited in text as *JE*.

9. "Letter to Eusebius," *Blackwood's Edinburgh Magazine* 59 (April 1846): 413.

10. Edward Bulwer Lytton, *Devereux* (Boston, 1891), p. vi.

11. Cp. Tillotson, p. 5: "When . . . a prolific and popular minor novelist changes his groove, as Lytton did with *The Caxtons* in 1849, he testifies to the establishment of a major change in subject matter." With that novel, too, in the wake of Brontë's success and *Copperfield's* appearing, from April, in monthly numbers, Lytton returns to first-person narration.

12. Donald D. Stone, *The Romantic Impulse in Victorian Fiction* (Cambridge, Mass., 1980), p. 197. The "most fervid worshipper of Byron among the great woman writers," according to Stone, is Charlotte Brontë.

13. Benjamin Disraeli, *Contarini Fleming* (London, 1927), vol 4, The Bradenham Edition of the Novels and Tales of Benjamin Disraeli, First Earl of Beaconsfield, 4. Hereafter cited in text as *CF*.

14. My search through Andrew Block, *The English Novel, 1740–1850* (London, 1963), has turned up only a handful. Most of the earlier ones seem to promise as much sociology or politics as narrative—John Galt, *The Member: An Autobiography* and *The Radical: An Autobiography*, both in 1832; William Pitt Scargill, *Autobiography of a Dissenting Minister*, *Autobiography of a Footman*, *Autobiography of an Irish Traveller*, 1834 and 1835, perhaps *Ferdinand Franck; an Autobiographical Sketch of the youthful days of a Musical Student*, 1826. There is then none until 1846 when *Contarini* was reissued and the anonymous *Margaret Russell: An Autobiography* was published by Longmans. *The Autobiography of Rose Allen*, "Edited by a Lady," 1847, seems to have been published (also by Longmans) virtually at the same moment or slightly after *Jane Eyre*: the catalogue of Smith Elder books in the first edition of *Jane Eyre* is dated "June, 1847" on the first leaf and "October, 1847" on the first page; the list of "New Works" in the Longmans, Brown, Green, and Longmans *Rose Allen* is dated "October, 1847."

15. There are several supernatural apparitions of extrasensory perceptions or visions in *Contarini Fleming* that may seem visual analogues to the "Jane! Jane! Jane!" episode in Brontë, and in both novels these have to do with lovers, but the relationship of the two novels beyond the coincidence of the opening suites is largely one of difference. Perhaps a reader might fancy that Brontë is saying, "Now, Ben, you've got it all wrong: *this* is the way life

195

really is, this is real Truth." I am not, however, attempting here to make out a case for influence, parody, or response—as will become increasingly evident.

16. Robert Colby, *Fiction With a Purpose* (Bloomington, Ind., 1967), p. 120. Colby's illuminating chapter, *"Oliver Twist*: The Fortunate Foundling," pp. 105-37, places the novel in its generic and contemporary context. Hereafter cited in text as Colby.

17. Colby, p. 119, calls it "a parable of society"; William T.Lankford's brilliant essay "'The Parish Boy's Progress': The Evolving Form of *Oliver Twist*," PMLA 93 (January 1978): 20-31, traces the metamorphosis of the realistic beginning into the moral allegory of the later portions of the novel.

18. Charles Dickens, *Oliver Twist*, ed. Kathleen Tillotson (Oxford, 1966), p. 35.

19. Florence Dry, *The Sources of "Jane Eyre"* (1940; rpt. n.p.: Folcroft Library, 1973), p. 6, conflates the passages from chs. 5 and 7 in *Oliver Twist* and thus heightens the similarity with *Jane Eyre*.

20. Elizabeth Rigby in the *Quarterly Review* for December 1848 (Allott, p. 106); Helen Shipton in the *Monthly Packet* for 1896; Janet Spens in "Charlotte Brontë," *Essays and Studies by Members of the English Association* 14 (1929): 53-70. Spens makes a lengthy case for Brontë's indebtedness to *Pamela*, which Kathleen Tillotson, p. 149n., finds convincing. *"Jane Eyre* and Genre" discusses and qualifies the relationship.

21. Inga-Stina Ewbank, *Their Proper Sphere* (Cambridge, Mass., 1966), p. 21.

22. Barbara Hofland, *Ellen the Teacher. A Tale for Youth* (London, 1819), p. 4.

23. See G. A. Starr, *Defoe and Spiritual Autobiography* (Princeton 1965).

24. "I beg my reader to understand that I had no idea whatever of religion at that period of my life. . . . She therefore (for I am chiefly addressing my own sex) . . ." Mrs. Sherwood, *Caroline Mordaunt; or, The Governess* in *The Works of Mrs. Sherwood* 13 (Boston, 1834-58): 219. Hereafter cited in text as *CM*.

25. Vineta Colby, *Yesterday's Woman: Domestic Realism in the English Novel* (Princeton, N.J., 1974), p. 165. This and other governess novels are discussed in *"Jane Eyre* and Genre."

26. Sarah Fielding, *The Governess; Or, Little Female Academy*, ed. Jill E. Grey (London, 1968), p. 103. Grey reprints in facsimile the 1749 text, in which this chapter begins on p. 5. Hereafter cited in text as Fielding, along with the original and facsimile edition page numbers.

27. When we remember Oliver's parents' story, however, what with bigamy and the West Indies and the like, there is a curious sense (or nonsense) in which Jane might have turned out to be Oliver's mother!

28. Where the passages cited in this portion of the essay are identified in the text by chapter and are in a narrow section of the text, I will not give Clarendon page numbers.

29. See Meier Sternberg, *Expositional Modes and the Temporal Ordering of Fiction* (Baltimore, 1978), esp. pp. 129-58.

IX

DAVID J. DeLAURA

Arnold and Goethe: The One on the Intellectual Throne

GOETHE PUZZLED AND DIVIDED THE ENGLISH INTELLECTUAL community throughout the nineteenth century. For some, he was "the impersonation of calm and dignified poetic wisdom"; for others, "the public symbol of all that is weak and trifling, cold and indifferent in human character."[1] Was he the "Old Heathen," as conservatives said, or "Jupiter, Apollo, all in one," as one enthusiast put it?[2] For the most thoughtful critics—including, as we shall see, Matthew Arnold—the division of opinion ran deep in the individual consciousness.

The cleavages in Victorian views of Goethe often become the fracture lines in English intellectual life, revealing the precise ethical and social weight of a number of broadly significant issues. More precisely, the debate over Goethe—much of it not easily recoverable until recently[3]—is the indispensable background for ideas that surface more clearly later in the century, especially those associated with Aestheticism. The attempt to plot the position of Arnold's early views of Goethe within this agitated sea of contemporary opinion shows that his views, though uniquely inflected, are far from being isolated or singular. Moreover the shifts and hesitations in Arnold's views, which as I shall argue follow the very pattern of his own career and aspirations, cannot be understood *except* in the light of these public struggles over Goethe.

The focus of this paper is a well-known passage, a crux, in Arnold's "The Scholar-Gipsy." Using a method that might be called "criticism by immersion," and showing that some of the best-known passages in Arnold's poetry are part of a large network of dialectically interrelated material, allow us freshly to grasp new connections among Arnold's poems, and the continuity of his views about Goethe, about poetry, and about himself. The central fact is the "phenomenon" of Goethe himself, the man and the creative artist, perceived as both a model and a danger, demanding interpretation and accommodation.

I

and amongst us one,
Who most has suffer'd, takes dejectedly
His seat upon the intellectual throne;
And all his store of sad experience he
Lays bare of wretched days;
Tells of his misery's birth and growth and signs,
And how the dying spark of hope was fed,
And how the breast was soothed, and how the head,
And all his hourly varied anodynes.

This for our wisest![4]

Goethe or Tennyson? A rather fitful debate has inclined slightly toward the latter.[5] Kenneth Allott deftly summarizes the evidence: "Tennyson became Poet Laureate in Nov. 1850; ll. 185–90 are an apt description of *In Memoriam* (1850); 'intellectual throne' (l. 184) is borrowed from Tennyson's 'The Palace of Art' (l. 216)."[6] I cannot find the evidence that "many contemporaries" saw Tennyson in the portrait, as Kathleen Tillotson claims,[7] but it is worth noting that Tennyson's elegy was indeed *blamed* in its own time for its mournfulness; as a clerical defender remarked in 1852, "To a coarser class of minds 'In Memoriam' appears too melancholy: one long monotone of grief."[8] Moreover, critics worried about who would occupy the "throne" of poetry; a reviewer of *The Princess* in 1849 rather churlishly noted that "Mr. Tennyson is not a great poet," and he cannot enter the "highest circle of the sons of song. . . . But he is the poet of the day; nor has any rival yet appeared who seems likely to

198

dethrone him. . . . He may sit in his place for many years. We will pay him due homage, with one exception. If he is a king, it is not in a generation of giants."[9] This is a grudging sort of kingship at best, and since Tennyson was far from being "our wisest" in Arnold's eyes too, those who argue for the Tennyson identification are sometimes forced to read the passage as a "devastating" irony directed at Tennyson.[10] I will later suggest that Tennyson's "intellectual throne" is indeed relevant, but the reference has little to do with *In Memoriam*.[11]

Several streams of converging evidence, in fact, point unmistakably to Goethe, though one should keep in mind that the anonymity is functional and intentional in a portrait meant to be in a sense "generic."[12] A main reason is that Arnold later *said* so: "He had Goethe in mind" when he wrote the lines "just after Mr. Arnold had read *Dichtung und Wahrheit*, and while he still felt the impression of its sadness."[13] Although plans for "The Scholar-Gipsy" may have been evolving from 1845, Allott believes the poem "almost certainly" dates from 1852–53, "and perhaps May-August 1853." And Arnold certainly knew the autobiography well. "I have been returning to Goethe's Life," he reports to his mother in May 1849, "and think higher of him than ever. His thorough sincerity—writing about nothing that he had not experienced—is in modern literature almost unrivalled."[14] One hears an echo perhaps of the "sad experience" (l. 185) in the poem. Yet another telling bit of evidence helps us focus on Goethe. When R. H. Hutton in 1871 identified John Henry Newman as the subject of the portrait, Arnold hastened to assure Newman: "What is said in those lines is not what I should have said if I had been speaking of you . . . I had quite another personage in mind."[15] Moreover, Arnold's Preface to the *Poems* of 1853, dated October 1 and written therefore almost simultaneously with the poem, associates Goethe's *Faust* with the "doubts" and "discouragement" of characteristically "modern" literature.[16]

James Simpson asserts that the lines "are not a very appropriate description of *Dichtung und Wahrheit* since Goethe's days were not conspicuously 'wretched.'" He concedes, however, that if one allows for a degree of poetic overstatement, one can easily reconcile the lines with Goethe's autobiography, which does, after all, recount a history of some unhappy love affairs.[17] But even he does not examine *Dichtung und Wahrheit*—and the supporting evidence there, extending well beyond "unhappy love affairs," becomes unexpectedly appropriate. The quarry Arnold drew from was Books 13 and 14, which are Goethe's account of the German *Sturm und Drang* movement in the 1770s and his relationship to it. And that source colors not only the portrait of the figure on the throne, but the rhetoric and dialectic of the larger background devoted to "us," the troubled young in mid-Victorian England. The One—Goethe, in effect—becomes a special case, an example of at least partial regeneration against a broad backdrop of spiritual and emotional malaise.[18]

Goethe offers a classic account of his own participation in a widespread mood of "disgust which men, without being driven by necessity, feel for life." (And one thinks of Yeats shaping and reshaping his version of the "tragic generation," for *his* own special purposes.) In this gloomy mood, "the greatest evil, the heaviest disease" is that of regarding life itself as "a disgusting burden." This widespread and suicidal "weariness of life" involved the paradoxical coexistence of "young boiling blood" and "an imagination easily to be paralyzed by single objects." This mood of agitation/paralysis was darkened further by the enthusiasm for the "earnest melancholy" of English literature—the works of Milton, Goldsmith, Gray, Young, Ossian—with their mingled moods of "elegiac melancholy" and "heavy oppressive despair." Hamlet's melancholy "soliloquies were spectres which haunted all the young minds." In this mood of "gloomy wantonness," he says, "tortured by unsatisfied passions," denied a field of "important actions," and facing a "dull, spiritless" bourgeois life, he and others like him were attracted to the idea of suicide as a form of free choice, a kind of *acte gratuite*, and "thus miserably enough [we] helped ourselves through the disgusts and weariness of the days."

Goethe then describes his own experience of this dangerous and slightly absurd state of mind and how he freed himself from it. In a fascinating literary-psychological maneuver for which he was assailed then and later on moral grounds, *Werther* (1774) was at once the chief fount of the tide of "Wertherish" emotion that swept over Europe and the instrument of its author's deliberately induced abreaction or catharsis. As one of those "whose life is embittered by want of action," he explains, "I . . . best knew the pain I suffered . . . [and] the exertion it cost me to free myself"; and in this hopeless state, he reflected at length "on the various kinds of death which we might choose." "I had freed myself from that stormy element, upon which, through my own fault and that of others, . . . I had been driven about in the most violent manner. I felt as if after a general confession, once more happy and free, and justified in beginning a new life. The old household remedy [i.e., composition] had been of excellent service to me on this occasion. But while I felt myself eased and enlightened by having turned reality into poetry, my friends were led astray by my work."

Thus Goethe's own "lawless disposition," his "life and action so aimless and purposeless," created, he admits, that suddenly fashionable "self-torture," even in the absence of "outward grievances," that "disturbed the very best minds." The most talented felt a moral obligation to subject even "transient pain" to "this painful work of self-contemplation"; "strange" lives developed from this combination of avoidance of action and the "vague notions arising from this half-self-knowledge." This new cult of "empirical psychology," practiced by "idlers and dabblers . . . mining into their own souls," unable entirely to approve or disapprove the new cultivation of "inner disquiet," led to "an eternal and unappeasable" conflict. *This* was "the universal tendency of the time, which was said to have been let loose by Werther."

Arnold seems clearly to have found Goethe's famous passages an apposite model for his treatment of his own age and, within that context, of Goethe's ambiguous example. The subject implicit in Arnold is explicit in Goethe: the intellectual young, undergoing characteristic phases of the modern experience itself. Arnold's hesitating and faltering contemporaries (l. 178)—among whom he numbers himself—are, to be sure, rather more passive, even neurasthenic, than Goethe's equally alienated idlers and dabblers: for Arnold makes much (ll. 142, 150) of the repeated shocks and changes that wear out life, tire one's wits, and spend one's fire. Moreover Arnold's emphasis on "languid doubt," "light half-believers of our casual creeds," and "our mental strife" (ll. 164, 172, 222)—all of this suggests a later, more Victorian phase of modern culture. But much else in Goethe's account seems to have shaped Arnold's bleak depiction of the debilitated modern condition. Goethe's aimless, purposeless life suggests Arnold on the sick hurry and divided aims, the failure to achieve "*one* aim" in life (ll. 204, 152). Goethe's emphasis on diseased consciousness, weariness of life, and an emphatic, almost Baudelairian disgust anticipate Arnold's "sick fatigue," "the infection of our mental strife," "this strange disease of modern life" (ll. 164, 222, 203). And Goethe's "heavy oppressive despair" and the death of hope, as well as the fashionable preoccupation with ending one's life, seem a source of Arnold's "despair" and the desire to end "the long unhappy dream" of life (ll. 195, 192).

The unhealthy neglect of *action* in Goethe's contemporaries is also plainly applicable to Arnold's languid and fluctuating moderns—and one thinks of Arnold's contemporaneous rejection, in the Preface of 1853, of dramatic situations in which "the suffering finds no vent in action" as well as of the "doubts" of Hamlet and the "discouragement" of Goethe's own Faust (*CPW*, 1:1-2). And although Goethe's young men indulge more blamably in painful self-contemplation and inward disquiet, their emotional states (gloomy, melancholy, wretched, sad, vexatious) obviously occupy some of the same ground covered by Arnold's favored terms: suffer, dejection, sad, wretched, pine. Most direct and obvious, I think, are the parallels between Arnold's picture of the suffering, hopeless "one," with his "varied anodynes," and Goethe's account of the pain he suffered, his decreasing hope and increasing sadness, the exertion it cost him to recover, and how thoughts of suicide "helped" him and others through the weary days.

We can perhaps best catch the relationship of Arnold's version of the Werther-period to its original in Goethe's autobiography by glancing at Carlyle's well-known mediatorship of the same topic.[19] If Arnold presents the young intellectual as the exhausted and numbed victim of the "strange disease of modern life," Carlyle moves to the opposite extreme, equally far from Goethe's complex account, pushing the feverish *Sturm und Drang* even further toward overwrought melodrama. He tends to portray the "Kraftmänner, or Powermen," the "race of Sentimentalists," as "a loud, haggard, tumultuous class"—and to neglect their counterbalancing sentimental and "tearful" qualities. Carlyle's power-men are in bitter agony, blackness, despair, desperation, a dark and wayward mood; they struggle blindly; they rage and lament and wail bitterly. One cause of this distortion is that Carlyle assimilates Goethe's account of *his* contemporaries to the later example of the more "spasmodic" Byron—strong, wild, and gloomy: his is "the mad fire of a volcano." This special purpose leads him, tendentiously, to describe *Werther* in terms that misrepresent our impression of that polite and sentimental young man: the book is, Carlyle insists, "the voice of the world's despair: passionate, uncontrollable."

One important consequence of Arnold's attempt to adapt to his own age Goethe's (and to some extent Carlyle's) analysis of the *Sturm und Drang*,[20] is the less than convincing or authentic tone of the culture-analysis in "The Scholar-Gipsy." For Arnold's borrowed and partially reshaped terms and schemata (and he tends to picture himself and his contemporaries as more "tearful" than "wild") ill fit the prose and poetry of spiritual "doubt" emerging around 1850 among the self-possessed Oxonians of his own set.[21] Arnold and Clough generally, if by very different strategies, deflected the embarrassments of direct confession and revelation and were very far from sounding like either sentimental or "lawless" Germans of the *Werther-Zeit*; and they seem at least as far from the nearly catatonic generation described in "The Scholar-Gipsy."[22] Only James Anthony Froude, in *The Nemesis of Faith* (1849), wore his baffled doubt on his sleeve— and as a result gave general offense in the Arnold circle and elsewhere.[23]

II

But the *Werther* pattern offered by Goethe himself, of suffering within a context of cultural malaise, is far from accounting for even the entirety of the passage on the "one" and, more importantly, for its place in the poem as a whole. For the passage is framed by words—the one "upon the intellectual throne," "our wisest"—bearing rather different implications, which have a dense contemporary context, all of it, again, pointing to Goethe.

It is easy enough to show, first of all, that the two overlapping clusters of terms—the elevated king or monarch, a wise man or sage, seated on the intellectual or literary throne—were widespread throughout the period, and even before Carlyle (as we shall see) elaborated the notions as part of a more comprehensive polemical pattern of his own. Goethe's bitterest foes tended to impute a cruel despotism or "dictatorship" to Goethe—or a blasphemous idolatry to the public. Francis Jeffrey, in the unrelenting *Edinburgh Review*, deplored "this German idolatry,"[24] and Thomas De Quincey, in a notorious fling in 1824, spoke scornfully of the "false gods" of literature, and wondered where in "the German pantheon" we may find "the shrine of Goethe."[25] Above all, it was the critic Wolfgang Menzel who, beginning in the late 1820s, assailed Goethe on political and moral grounds; his vitriolic portrait of "the king of the muses," accepting "the royal crown" and, "even before his death, placed among the gods," became a dialectical opposite, and an inciting cause, of the haloed portrait Carlyle was simultaneously painting.[26] Intellectual enthronement was acknowledged even more freely by friendly English readers. Expectedly, we find Goethe and Schiller on the "summit" of the German Parnassus, each a candidate to become "king" on "the literary throne."[27] In his "long and uninterrupted reign," Goethe was "the undisputed sovereign of European literature," "lord of the world of art," and the "monarch of intellect."[28]

More pointedly, in the light of Arnold's usage, *Blackwood's*, as early as 1818, had found Goethe surrounded by "reverence": "Seated above competition, and fearless of

failure, he has directed and swayed the minds of two generations as if by the charm of a magician."[29] According to one
awe-struck critic, Goethe sought "to control the human intellect and the world"; he "govern[s] the understandings of his
contemporaries, as an empire of his own."[30] In 1839,
Blackwood's noted that many think Goethe "the highest and
most complete representative" of "the intellectual life of
mankind" in his age.[31] Another critic made a nearly identical
point in 1851, calling Goethe "the freshest, broadest, and most
highly cultivated intellect in Europe."[32] And in that very year,
in his *Life of John Sterling*—which Arnold is altogether
likely to have read carefully—Carlyle offered a phrase that
Arnold seems to have remembered in writing "The Scholar-
Gipsy." Although Sterling had for years nursed an "obsti-
nate" prejudice against Goethe, Carlyle explains, by the end
of his life Goethe "was in the throne of Sterling's intellectual
world."[33]

This almost universally held image of Goethe as the
supreme intellectual force of "modern" culture obviously
stands up, massively, as a central part of the immediate
backdrop of Arnold's phrase "the intellectual throne." Moreover, all the direct evidence of Arnold's career—even apart
from his own explicit statement of 1883—points to intellectual power as the least questionable area of Arnold's
response to Goethe, and at all periods. Arnold never doubted,
that is, that among the moderns Goethe and Niebuhr were—
as Arnold said in that very year 1853—"the men of strongest
head and widest culture."[34] And in that same preface, Arnold
carefully discriminates: Goethe is "the greatest poet of modern
times, the greatest critic of all times" (1:9). Similarly, in
"Memorial Verses," written three years earlier, Arnold speaks
of Goethe as "Europe's sagest head," and associates "Goethe's
sage mind" with "man's prudence" (ll. 16, 61, 59). This center
of Arnold's continuing interest in Goethe comes into even
clearer focus in 1864—in the midst of Arnold's attempts to
work out a program for "criticism"—when he pointedly
limits Goethe's status as "a great and powerful spirit" to "the
line of modern thought."[35]

It is worth noting that these other superlatives Arnold liked to apply to Goethe—sagest, strongest, widest—are of a piece with the epithet "wisest" in "The Scholar-Gipsy." On the other hand, though perhaps only different in degree, *wisdom* is not, after all, precisely the same as intellectual power or even sagacity; and the habit of viewing Goethe as the "wise man" has a discernible tradition of its own, within which Arnold's "our wisest" fits comfortably. And again, though others had already confidently placed Goethe among the "wisest,"[36] it is Carlyle who repeatedly identified Goethe as "our Greatest contemporary Man," "a living Thinker," the "grand characteristic" of whose writing is "not . . . knowledge, but wisdom" (27:401; 28:7; 23:26). Goethe, he explains, "made a New Era in Literature," in which "The true Sovereign of the world" is "the 'inspired Thinker,' whom in these days we name Poet. The true Sovereign is the Wise man" (27:376–77). In *Sartor Resartus*, the epithets emphatically applied to Goethe—"the wisest of this age," "the Wisest of our time"—are conspicuously direct precedents for Arnold's "our wisest."[37] This adulatory tone—minus Carlyle's dubious note of "suffering"—is echoed by G. H. Lewes in 1844: "He [Goethe] lived . . . a long laborious life, a wise and happy man,—one of the wisest of men; perhaps too one of the happiest."[38] And in America, the bold and penetrating Margaret Fuller, despite her doubts and ambiguities (she speaks of Goethe's "perfect wisdom and *merciless* nature"), insists that he is "the great sage."[39] The tradition reaches a fitting conclusion in 1884, when Arnold himself declares, "the work of Goethe is the greatest and wisest influence" in "the literature of our century" (*CPW*, 10:189).

III

The full resonance, however, of the passage—including the ways in which suffering is linked to wisdom and kingship—cannot be caught without reference to an even richer background in, yet again, Carlyle. As part of his own extremely influential analysis of the modern world and the modern "condition," Carlyle in the 1820s and early thirties found in Goethe's career a powerful and exemplary pattern of spiritual loss and gain. That is, the "suffering" of the Werther period, which as we saw Goethe described at length and which Arnold later referred to, becomes the purgatorial stage in a life-long process of defeat, suffering, and recovery. The pattern is applicable, in a lesser degree, to Schiller and "the rest" of the modern Germans. They are "wise and good men"; "much have they seen and suffered," and "they have conquered" the "contradictions and perplexity" of the nineteenth century. After "long trial" and "unwearied endeavour," they "have penetrated into the mystery of Nature" and wrung from Art "her secret."[40] But this sequence of experience is most fully manifest in "the great Goethe," who, "in passionate words, had to write his sorrows of Werter, before the spirit freed herself, and he could become a Man" (*SR*, p. 156).

Moving well beyond the evidence of *Weltschmertz* and restlessness in *Dichtung und Wahrheit*, Carlyle repeatedly stresses instead Goethe's "life of effort, of earnest toilsome endeavour." Goethe "struggled toughly" through "many vicissitudes" and "not a little suffering," and finally "ascends silently . . . to the supreme intellectual place" among his country-men. The ascendancy and sovereignty Goethe gains, then—his "perpetual dictatorship"—is primarily the "dominion" he gains over his own spirit. This culminating *victory* and *conquest* comes from Goethe's having mastered "the spiritual perplexities of his time," under which he had once "suffered and mourned in bitter agony"; his value to us is that he "has shown others how to rise above them," too. Carlyle claims to find this progression of Goethe's "inward life" in his works: the despair of *Werther* gives way to "the wild apocalyptic *Faust*"; the next stage is the "Pagan" affirmation of life in *Wilhelm Meisters Lehrjahre*; and finally comes the "deep all-pervading Faith" of the *Wanderjahre* and the *West-Oestlicher Divan*.[41] This image of the triumphant Goethe helps us add to the circle of interwoven terms even Arnold's phrase "the one"; for the words seem to designate not some "single" person, but a singular or exemplary figure, uniquely fitted to occupy the throne of intellect and wisdom. Goethe's movement from "doubt and discontent" to "freedom, belief and clear activity," Carlyle declares, is a model for all who seek to attain "spiritual manhood"; but Goethe's "success in this matter has been more complete than that of any other man in his age; . . . in the strictest sense, he may almost be called the *only one* that has so succeeded" (26:243; emphasis added). Even more emphatically, that Goethe "educe[d] reconcilement" out of the "woes and contradictions of an Atheistic time," is exactly what "marks him as the Strong One of his time" (27:435).

It should be noted that Carlyle did seek to delimit Goethe's alleged wisdom. Goethe's title to reign—"in undisputed sway," and "with kingly benignity"—is the fact that "The true Sovereign is the Wise Man" (27:377), and this "beautiful . . . [and] religious Wisdom" is the result of a traditional-sounding process of suffering and purgation: suffering-"one"-wise man-throne thus form a *causal* sequence. But Goethe's is precisely "the Wisdom which is proper to *this time*" (26:208; emphasis added). For Carlyle was proclaiming what C. F. Harrold calls "a new era of practical idealism."[42] The *content* of the practical wisdom he attributed to Goethe is extracted, above all, from the *Wanderjahre*, notably the notion of the "three reverences" in the Pedagogical Province of chapter 10 and the ambiguous doctrine of Renunciation (*Entsagen*) in chapter 14. Readers remain divided, even into our own day, concerning the authenticity of Goethe's late "religious" phase; and most students of Carlyle have accepted that his reading of Goethe's final works casts them in a falsely Christian, indeed Calvinistic, light.[43] In any event, it has gone unnoticed that, despite a long-standing assumption to the contrary, almost none of Goethe's fairly numerous other English readers uncritically accepted Carlyle's pragmatic but religious reading. Even an ardent defender like G. H. Lewes, deliberately I think correcting Carlyle, limits his explanation of the wisdom and happiness of Goethe's "long laborious life" to a benign, decidedly this-worldly process: "By confining himself to the knowable and attainable, and never wasting his strength on the unknowable and unattainable."[44] At one point, he thrusts even this small semblance of piety aside and almost exults in the "cruel" egotism of Goethe's "favourite doctrine of *Renunciation*": "Renounce all; endure all; but develop yourself to the utmost limit."[45]

As for the authenticity of Goethe's suffering and struggle, Carré like others insists that Goethe's career had *not* been a series of battles against doubt and pessimism, ending in victory, as Carlyle (drawing on his own experience) interpreted it. Instead, Carré says (with a new sort of piety, not unknown in modern Goethe scholarship), his "evolution" was "un lent déroulement, *Ohne Hast, aber ohne Rast*, sans précipitation, mais sans trêve."[46] But Goethe himself, as we saw in *Dichtung und Wahrheit*, did a good deal to encourage a less dignified and "evolutionary" view of his own development. Eckermann's *Conversations* with Goethe, above all, though published too late (1836, 1848) to have influenced Carlyle's earliest "construction" of Goethe, presented a more eruptive and even rather complaining Goethe. Goethe sighs, rather self-satisfiedly, recalling the Werther period: "I had lived, loved, and suffered much."[47] And in a certain mood Goethe liked to characterize his whole long life in similar terms: "I have ever been esteemed one of Fortune's chiefest favourites. . . . Yet, truly, there has been nothing but toil and care; and I may say that, in all my seventy-five years, I have never had a month of genuine comfort. It has been a perpetual rolling of a stone, which I have always had to raise anew."[48] And this is exactly the tone he adopted when he bitterly repelled the current German charges leveled against his character: pride, egotism, lack of generosity toward younger talents, sensuality, irreligiousness, and lack of patriotism. We best serve our country, he observes, by using the gifts with which we are endowed. "I have toiled hard enough," he pleads; "I can say, that . . . I have permitted myself no repose or relaxation night or day."[49] On the very eve of his death, Goethe first insists that a poet's *poetic* activities can be "confined to no particular . . . country," and then suddenly changes tack, rather plaintively redefining what "love of one's country" is: "When a poet has toiled throughout a long life, to assail mischievous prejudices, to remove illiberal notions, to enlighten the spirit of his people, to purify their taste, and to ennoble their thoughts and feelings—what better than this can he do?—are these not patriotic exertions?"[50]

Thus the two sides of the Goethe conundrum come together, and the conjunction explains some of the running confusions about Goethe in the period. In effect, Goethe himself answered the charges of egotism and indifference precisely by promoting the image of the sage, toiling on despite the "persecutions" that had "embittered" his life.[51] No doubt Goethe's self-serving views (his and Eckermann's eyes were firmly fixed on posterity), though falling short of Carlyle's claims of spiritual "victory," contributed to the comparatively benign view of the "wise" Goethe conceded even by some of his detractors. Still, not all accepted even the *fact* of Goethe's suffering and toil: as the coolly skeptical *Saturday Review* put it, Goethe "loved to believe that he has at various times of his life suffered deeply, and the delusion is one of the commonest among thoroughly selfish men."[52]

IV

Arnold was of course fully alive to the shifting cross-currents of English opinion regarding Goethe. And other Arnold poems of the period that we have not yet looked at confirm the identification (if that is still necessary) and help us locate the portrait in "The Scholar-Gipsy" along the spectrum of contemporary opinion. Arnold more heartily accepted Goethe the "sage" in "Stanzas in Memory of the Author of 'Obermann'," written in the autumn of 1849. There, Goethe "the strong much-toiling sage" (1. 50) is one of the three moderns (the others are Wordsworth and Senancour himself) who have "see[n] their way" (1. 48). But Arnold shows Goethe's "way" to be unattainable in the very act of seeming to make him a model:

> . . . Goethe's course few sons of men
> May think to emulate.
> For he pursued a lonely road,
> His eyes on Nature's plan;
> Neither made man too much a God,
> Nor God too much a man.
> Strong was he, with a spirit free
> From mists, and sane, and clear;
> Clearer, how much! than ours—yet we
> Have a worse course to steer. (11. 55-64)

For he grew up in a tranquil time, whereas

210

David J. DeLaura

> Too fast we live, too much are tried,
> Too harass'd, to attain
> Wordsworth's sweet calm, or Goethe's wide
> And luminous view to gain. (ll. 76-80)

Something similar if more casual takes place later in "Epilogue to Lessing's Laocoön" (written perhaps in 1864–65), a dialogue in which the speaker and his "friend" agree that

> ... nobly perfect, in our day
> Of haste, half-work, and disarray,
> Profound yet touching, sweet yet strong,
> Hath risen Goethe's, Wordsworth's song. (ll. 26-29)

(Still, only Homer and Shakespeare survive the test at the very end.)

Though "sweet" and "touching" are unexpected epithets, the two passages present an otherwise familiar if bland version of the Carlylean pattern: the emphasis here is on the spiritual result, through a process less of suffering and struggle than of quiet, steady effort. The lonely-but-strong toiling sage of elevated vision is the Goethe whose life, for Carlyle, is one of "effort, earnest toilsome endeavour"; in his "strength" he is "mild and kindly and calm."[53] The sane and clear spirit, free from mists, attaining to a wide and luminous view, is Carlyle's "the clearest, most universal man of his time," who attained "freedom, belief, and clear activity"—a "mind working itself into clearer and clearer freedom" (27: 371; 26:243; 27:430). And the figure with his eyes on Nature's plan is evidently one of Carlyle's "wise and good" Germans who "have penetrated into the mystery of Nature" (26:66).

But even this, Arnold's most unclouded homage to Goethe, though unquestionably sincere, both falls short of Carlyle's "religious" reading of Goethe's wisdom and makes his clarity and freedom a state of mind that "we" more harried moderns cannot attain. By contrast, the wearily "dejected" figure in "The Scholar-Gipsy" fills out the Carlylean pattern with a strong sense of suffering; but Arnold goes out of his way there, by silence and by raising an eyebrow, to bring the completeness of Goethe's actual spiritual "victory" into question. By in effect denying Goethe the serenity and strength that are in the

211

Carlylean pattern both the reward and the proof of victory, even the wisdom and intellectual ascendency that *are* acknowledged become problematic. Goethe is made to stand, dialectically, over against the Scholar-Gipsy himself,[54] and "This for our wisest!" not only suggests doubts, but places Goethe *within*—if exceptionally elevated and dignified within—the camp of the exhausted and hopeless moderns. The effect is to leave Goethe just outside the select circle of the spiritually regenerate: for Arnold was increasingly demanding of his supreme models an inwardness, an emotional warmth, a "fortifying" view of life, and even a religious "joy" which I believe he never found fully achieved in Goethe—despite Carlyle's asseverations.[55] (On the other hand, it should be noted, the portrait in Arnold's poem remained anonymous, partly perhaps because as a portrait of Goethe it left out certain positive elements that Arnold did ascribe at times to the man Goethe.)

And so there is indeed a deep-running irony in the passage in "The Scholar-Gipsy," but it is far from being (as some have thought) scornful praise directed against a plainly inappropriate figure like Tennyson.[56] It is instead a more complex and highly personal questioning of a man from whom Arnold continued to learn certain essential lessons, a man about whom the most immoderate claims had been made (alongside ferocious attacks), and a man from whom Arnold always withheld any final "consent." Arnold, a master of "withholding," knew well how to parcel out praise and blame, especially when it came to the key figures of his own development: for example, Carlyle, Emerson, Newman—and Goethe. Thus, when Arnold implies that this is the best that "our wisest" can do, Goethe is certainly being put in his place, even if a privileged and elevated place, but not in a merely debunking spirit. Indeed, the poem, grimly reactionary under its mellifluous Keatsian surfaces, involves a thoroughly Arnoldian gibe at the very notion of a "modern" and in some ways specifically "Goethean" wisdom—and Goethe is inevitably caught up in the general rejection.[57] For the poem is deliberately and "systematically" ironic: it embodies a universal bafflement, in which *all* representative positions are undermined. Even the example of the Scholar-Gipsy is finally unavailable to "us," as the less complete model offered by Goethe is unavailable in "Obermann." More damagingly, the Scholar-Gipsy's perfected consciousness—his "one aim" or "business," in effect a state of hopeful and perfectly attuned receptiveness—remains incompatible with a life of participation in society or indeed of any human interaction, as even the very limited "correction" of the coda shows.[58] It is a "deadlock" situation common in Arnold's best and most uncompromising early poetry, in which the actual is intolerable and the ideal unattainable or barely imaginable.

The poem represents the deepest impasse of Arnold's career, as he moved from the most alienated phases of his career to a reluctant and rather stiff-necked accommodation to his own society. In aid of the process, Arnold immediately hardened himself against his own temptations, praising "Sohrab and Rustum" and rather ungraciously turning back Clough's praise of "The Scholar-Gipsy": "What does it *do* for you? Homer *animates*—Shakespeare *animates* ... the Gipsy Scholar at best awakens a pleasing melancholy." The "complaining millions of men," the more public Arnold now says, want "something to *animate* and *ennoble* them—not merely to add zest to their melancholy or grace to their dreams" (*LC*, p. 146; 30 November 1853).

V

Although Arnold remained fruitfully divided on the issues, there was a pitiless and costly movement detectable in his career from about 1849 to 1853 and beyond. He sought to put behind him the Romantic yearning he associated with such figures as Byron, George Sand, Senancour, and even the early Goethe, as well as the pose of the high, detached, "inexperiential" Goethe-like poet presented in some of his earliest poems like "Shakespeare" and "Resignation."[59] He sought, that is, to remake himself into a benign sage on the pattern of the later Goethe—somewhat like the figures of wide vision and balanced soul in "To a Friend" (1848), or the muchtoiling, sane, and wise Goethe himself of the first Obermann poem. On the other hand, as H. F. Lowry once noted, the melancholy persists despite the attempt to achieve an almost static self-possession: "He opens his Goethe, but forgets to close his Byron" (*LC*, p. 32). In any case, Goethe's example remained a central, informing thread through these rapid changes and tergiversations, and Arnold's understanding of the stages of Goethe's career guided him in making his own painful decisions. It is consistent with Arnold's new "objective" and would-be classical poetic that the Preface of 1853 should reject the "doubts" and "discouragement" of a Hamlet or a Faust for their disabling embroilment with "modern problems"—specifically "the dialogue of the mind with itself" (*CW*, 1:1).[60] This view is also quite compatible with the doubt implied in "The Scholar-Gipsy" regarding the wisdom acquired during Goethe's suffering Werther period, and the rejection of the "divided aims" and half-belief that are the reality of the enervated "modern" experience.[61]

But two important letters of the period suggest a continuing internal discord. Arnold's sympathy for the suffering and vulnerable Goethe is evident in January 1851, when, in the midst of his own *Sturm und Drang*,[62] he extols Goethe's correspondence with Lavater because it "belongs to his impulsive youthful time, before he had quite finished building the Chinese Wall round his *inneres* which he speaks of in later life."[63] The second comes in December 1852, when Arnold had already begun constructing a Chinese Wall round himself—or as Auden once put it, thrusting his gift in prison. Even in disowning the poems of the *Empedocles* volume ("I feel now where my poems [this set] are all wrong, which I did not a year ago"), and wondering "whether I shall ever have heart and radiance enough to pierce the clouds that are massed round me," Arnold lashes back at the disapproving Clough, unrepentantly: "But woe was upon me if I analysed not my situation: and Werter[,] Rene[,] and such like[,] none of them analyse the modern situation in its true *blankness* and *barrenness*, and *unpoetrylessness*" (*LC*, p. 126; 14 December 1852). This is Arnold's central and immitigable perception of "these . . . damned times" (*LC*, p. 111), a kind of bedrock conviction upon which any spiritual and cultural rebuilding must be based, and with which such rebuilding must be compatible. It is by this standard that even the sympathetic suffering Goethe of the Werther-period falls short of an adequate wisdom: the letter of December 1852 thus becomes a direct commentary on the subject-matter of the controverted passage in "The Scholar-Gipsy."[64]

Goethe, then, was not only an inadequate positive or fortifying model (he lacked the "glow" that comes with "positive convictions and feeling," though these may be "illusions": *LC*, pp. 142–43); in a crucial sense, he fell short even as a "negative" critic of the modern scene also. The letter of December 1852, the 1853 Preface, and "The Scholar-Gipsy" itself all imply that both *Werther* and *Faust* are weak versions of suffering that *soften* the grim reality of the modern situation. And this convergence of evidence is strengthened by the fact, seemingly not noted before, that when Arnold aligns Goethe with Wordsworth, for different purposes, the effect is in varying degrees deflationary for *both* figures. The first Obermann poem notes that we, besides being born too late, cannot attain Goethe's wide view because his is "a lonely road," and judges, more severely, that Wordsworth achieved his sweet calm by averting his eyes "From half of human fate" (1. 54). Within a few months, in "Memorial Verses" (April 1850), Arnold again in effect accuses Wordsworth, the nominal hero of the poem, of having "put by" the "cloud of mortal destiny" (ll. 68–70); but this time he far more severely charges Goethe with being indifferent to the suffering and turmoil of modern European history, which he diagnoses with clear vision but from a position of lofty aesthetic isolation.[65] In 1864, the two figures are put side by side again, this time to Wordsworth's seemingly distinct disadvantage. The poetry of the English Romantics, including Wordsworth's, we are told, "did not know enough," whereas "the long and widely-combined critical effort of Germany" was the very condition of Goethe's achievement (*CPW* 3:262–63). In the same period, moreover, Arnold praised Goethe's Spinozistic "profound and imperturbable naturalism," as the central quality of "the modern spirit" (*CPW*, 3:109–10), and that view remained a basis of Arnold's later thought and set some of its limits. This was Arnold's more or less permanent "decision" regarding Goethe, after his own most tortuous years of "mental strife," when Goethe had helped provide standing-room. And Arnold remained grateful: "My voice shall never be joined to those which decry Goethe" (*CPW*, 3:110).

Still, those fundamental doubts remained about Goethe's qualifications for leadership in the modern world; and almost every reference to Goethe, even when favorable, tends—and this is a familiar tactic in Arnold—to put Goethe "in his place," granting *this* and withholding *that*. For in this very period of the early 1860s, Arnold began to move beyond the position of stoic impassibility to which he had resigned himself for a decade—a mood and a discipline to which the Preface of 1853 is a stony monument. As early as September 1853, in the very letter in which he found Goethe wanting in the "positive" qualities of "a perfect artist," Arnold lamented the "curse" of the "frigidity" of the modern critical intellect and spoke wistfully of the "energy and creative power," the *"warmth,"* that came for those "on the old religious road"— however beset that was with "illusions" (*LC*, p. 143).[66] In November, as we saw, he rather hopelessly repudiated his own regressive "Scholar-Gipsy" ("this is not what we want"), in favor of a poetry that *animates* and *ennobles* (*LC*, p. 146). A decade later he firmly puts behind him those other revered masters of the mind, stoics like Epictetus and Marcus Aurelius, for their "constraint and melancholy" and their lack of "a joyful and bounding emotion" (3:134). By this standard, again, Goethe, though "the greatest poet of modern times" (*CPW*, 1:9), inevitably was found wanting. Goethe was the hero of Arnold's earliest poetic, an "aesthetic" mode of detached *seeing* and *knowing*—*"Not deep the poet sees, but wide"* ("Resignation," l. 214; *LC*, p. 99). In the sixties, Arnold moved toward a standard of warmth and feeling, and a measure of participation in society: "heart and imagination" were raised to a position at least as high as "the senses and the understanding" (*CPW*, 3:225-31). The Goethe who found a questionable happiness in merely *knowing* the terror and distress of modern Europe was permanently less central to Arnold's gradually evolving program.

Something of vital importance of course remained. Arnold adopted the manner of the Goethean sage in criticism, he continued to appeal to Goethe's authority on a host of isolated matters, and Goethe, "the greatest critic of all times" (*CPW*, 1:9), was central in the formation of Arnold's doctrine and method of criticism up to about 1865. But Goethe did not become, for reasons I have been outlining, a model for the *substance* of Arnold's ethically and socially deepened doctrine of culture later in the sixties, of his religious writings of the seventies, or of the religiously-colored humanism of the later literary and social essays. And as I suggested, that frequent pairing of Goethe and Wordsworth helps explain Goethe's disqualifications for Arnold's new purposes. The "widely combined critical effort" of Goethe's Germany ensured that *his* naturalism was in Arnold's view more adequate than Wordsworth's nature-philosophy, which trailed a good many theologic clouds. But it seems evident that, from that same point of view, Goethe—as much as Wordsworth—"did not know *enough*." *Both* men, after all, had achieved their acclaimed unity of being by remaining comparatively innocent, optimistic, and (in a crucial sense) pre-modern figures.[67] From the first and on metaphysical grounds, Arnold corrected and "demythologized" the *joy* that Wordsworth found in nature; but even Goethe's more thoroughgoing organicism assumed, by Arnold's early lights, an equally illegitimate optimism about the cosmic process.[68] If Wordsworth blamably put by "the cloud of mortal destiny" and averted his eyes from "half of human fate," the "knowing" and "seeing" Goethe, differently but perhaps more blamably, also at some point averted *his* eyes from the fullness of the truth that Matthew Arnold, on *this* side of the down-slope of modern history, knew.[69]

The moderate and conciliatory Goethe could offer a stable ethical and emotional basis, during Arnold's time of transition, through his example of a clear mind and an aloof self-sufficiency. But Goethe, absorbed in his own self-development and indifferent to the modern agony, had purchased his calm, elevation, and wisdom by avoiding the necessary extremes. On the one hand, Goethe, even the Goethe of the *Sturm und*

Drang, refused to explore the full metaphysical barrenness of the modern situation, lest it disturb his cherished self-possession. At the other extreme, and for similar reasons, Goethe had in effect refused to move beyond his own "culture" or *Bildung,* despite some hints in his later works and the assertions of Carlyle, and to undergo the further transformation that is the necessary basis for positive spiritual and social reconstruction. He had, in short, refused the invitation to become one of "The Children of the Second Birth."[70] After 1863, though his voice continued to resonate in some not quite regenerate corners of Arnold's own heart, Goethe, was, in a surprisingly complete sense, "not what we want."

1. J. S. Blackie, *Foreign Quarterly Review* 16 (January 1836): 360. On the early and mid-Victorian controversy over Goethe, see my "Heroic Egotism: Goethe and the Fortunes of *Bildung* in Victorian England," forthcoming in Proceedings of the Comparative Literature Symposium, Texas Tech University, vol. 13.

2. The phrases are from Margaret Fuller, "Bettine Brentano and Her Friend Günderode," *Dial* 2 (January 1842): 314; cited here from rpt. ed. (New York, 1961).

3. In *The Reception of Classical German Literature in England, 1760-1860,* ed. John Boening, 10 vols. (New York, 1977). Because the format makes determining the exact page in the original difficult, I refer to the original source as a whole, and then give the precise page in Boening, thus: *Foreign Quarterly Review* 14 (1834): 131-62; Boening, 7:236.

4. "The Scholar-Gipsy," ll. 182-91. All citations from Arnold's poetry are from *The Poetical Works of Matthew Arnold,* ed. C. B. Tinker and H. F. Lowry (London, 1950).

5. Two other candidates have received little support: Carlyle (A. T. Quiller Couch, in *The Poems of Matthew Arnold, 1840*-1867 [London, 1920], p. 451), and Leopardi (J. C. Maxwell, *Review of English Studies,* n.s. 6 [1955]: 182-83).

6. *The Poems of Matthew Arnold,* ed. Kenneth Allott and Miriam Allott, 2d ed. (London, 1979), p. 365 n. Hereafter cited as "Allott." Tinker and Lowry, in *The Poetry of Matthew Arnold: A Commentary* (London, 1940), pp. 209-11, first pressed the case for Tennyson, though they end by suggesting that the passage may have "blended Arnold's reflections" on both figures.

7. Her discriminating study, "Rugby 1850: Arnold, Clough, Walrond, and *In Memoriam*" (1953), rpt. in *Mid-Victorian Studies* (London, 1965), pp. 180-203, hesitates to assert the Tennyson identification.

8. Frederick W. Robertson, *Lectures, Addresses and Other Literary Remains*, New Edition (London, 1906), p. 94. From lectures delivered in 1852; apparently first collected in 1858.

9. *Christian Remembrancer* 17 (January 1849): 229.

10. This is the approach of R. H. Super, *The Time Spirit of Matthew Arnold* (Ann Arbor, Mich., 1970), pp. 100-101. F. L. Lucas, *Tennyson: Poetry and Prose* (Oxford, 1947), pp. 162-62, had also suggested an "ironic" reference.

11. In fact, the closest Tennysonian parallel to the "wisest" and the "sad experience" of Arnold's passage occurs in "Locksley Hall" (1842), ll. 143-44, where the alienated speaker characterizes the sensitive modern oppressed by the "world": "Knowledge comes, but wisdom lingers, and he bears a laden breast, / Full of sad experience, moving toward the stillness of his rest." *The Poems of Tennyson*, ed. Christopher Ricks (London, 1969), p. 697. Perhaps not wholly irrelevant is an 1849 notebook passage regarding Tennyson by F. T. Palgrave, who had known Arnold and Clough at Balliol: "A noble, solid mind, bearing the look of one who had suffered;—strength and sensitiveness blended." Gwenllian F. Palgrave, *Francis Turner Palgrave* (London, 1899), p. 41.

12. The phrase is Andrew Farmer's, in "Arnold's Gipsy Reconsidered," *Essays in Criticism* 22 (January 1972): 73.

13. *Worcester Spy* (Mass.), 29 November 1883; cited by Chilson H. Leonard, "Two Notes on Arnold," *Modern Language Notes* 46 (January 1931):119

14. *Letters of Matthew Arnold*, ed. George W. E. Russell, 2 vols. in 1 (New York, 1900), 1:11. Misdated 1848 by Russell: see V. E. Horn, *Notes & Queries*, n.s. 18 (1971): 248-49. Hereafter cited as *Letters*.

15. *Unpublished Letters of Matthew Arnold*, ed. Arnold Whitridge (New Haven, Conn., 1923), p. 56. For a fuller discussion, see my *Hebrew and Hellene in Victorian England: Newman, Arnold, and Pater* (Austin, Tex., 1969), pp. 93-94.

16. *Complete Prose Works of Matthew Arnold*, ed. R. H. Super (Ann Arbor, Mich., 1960-77), 1:1. Hereafter cited as *CPW*.

17. *Matthew Arnold and Goethe* (London, 1979), p. 41; he cites a Carlyle passage I also use: "a man who . . . ascends silently," etc. Simpson's study, by far the fullest about the relationship, is richly informed on the German sources. But his brief survey of the English response to Goethe (pp. 2-16) deals largely with early material; my own reading of Arnold's career is quite different, and my approach here is to interpret the poems by "situating" them within the range of contemporary opinion. James Bentley Orrick's frequently cited "Matthew Arnold and Goethe," *Publications of the English Goethe Society*, n.s.4 (1928; rpt. 1966), dealing largely with the later "prose" Arnold and lacking Arnold's indispensable letters to Clough, draws far too sweeping conclusions from scanty evidence. For example, he is one of the many who assume Arnold's views are simply "derived . . . from Carlyle's idea of Goethe" (p. 52).

18. I draw my citations from *The Auto-Biography of Goethe: Truth and Poetry*, trans. John Oxenford, 2 vols. (original ed., 1848; London, 1872).

19. I cite Carlyle from the 30-volume Centenary Edition (1896-99); rpt.

New York, 1969, by page and volume number alone. The evidence in this section is largely drawn from the extensive account in "Goethe," 1828 (26:211-24). On pp. 220-24, Carlyle presents some of the key passages from *Dichtung und Wahrheit*, already cited; the effect was precisely to highlight those aspects of Goethe's life for later readers. The important passage on *Werther*, cited just below, is from "Goethe's Works," 1832 (27:430-31).

20. Carlyle's analysis is even more emphatically the basis of the intricate categories developed by Arnold in "Stanzas from the Grande Chartreuse," written during these same years.

21. For an attempt to capture the tone of that literary moment, see my "The Poetry of Thought," in *The Mind and Art of Victorian England*, ed. Josef L. Altholz (Minneapolis, Minn., 1976), pp. 35-57, 179-84. Wertherian agonies had been pretty much laughed off the stage in England, well before 1800; see chapter 2 of Stuart Pratt Atkins, *The Testament of Werther in Poetry and Drama* (Cambridge, Mass., 1949).

22. It may be argued that the "hero" of Clough's *Amours de Voyage* (written 1849) is "fluctuating" and vacillating to a fault. But the poem is made bracing by Clough's own detached point of view; and even the hero Claude, far from being worn out or weakly despairing, exhibits a continuous play of self-directed irony far from the spirit of Arnold's strangely "dated" description of his contemporaries.

23. See, e.g., *The Correspondence of Arthur Hugh Clough*, ed. Frederick L. Mulhauser (Oxford, 1957), 246-47, 251, and *New Letters of Thomas Carlyle*, ed. Alexander Carlyle (London, 1904), 2:59.

24. *Edinburgh Review* 42 (1825): 409-49; Boening, 9:109. "Dictatorship": *Edinburgh Review* 57 (July 1833): 371-403; Boening, 7:221.

25. *London Magazine* 10 (1824): 189-97; Boening, 9:100. Even in his entry on Goethe in the seventh edition of the *Encyclopaedia Britannica* (finished 1842), De Quincey scarcely concealed his disdain for Goethe's "supremacy of influence wholly unexampled" and for the admirers (Carlyle obviously among them) who had "enthroned" him "on the same seat with Homer and Shakspere." *De Quincey's Collected Writings*, ed. David Masson (Edinburgh, 1890), 4:396,420.

26. Wolfgang Menzel, *German Literature*, trans. Thomas Gordon (Oxford, 1840), 3:327, 353-54. The first two German editions of Menzel's work appeared in 1828 and 1836. As Goethe's admirer J. S. Blackie put it, Menzel, like Heine, is "a ringleader of that bold sect which has ventured to call in question the title of Göthe to the kingly seat on the German Parnassus." *Foreign Quarterly Review* 16 (1836): 1-26; Boening, 3:41. Longfellow, too, in his "German" romance *Hyperion* (1839), book 2, ch. 8., spoke a bit nervously of those "who would fain have dethroned the Monarch of Letters." Like many Americans, he could not quite decide whether Goethe was "The Many-sided Master-mind of Germany," or "Old Humbug, Old Heathen, Magnificent Imposter." Cited here from Orie William Long, *Literary Pioneers* (Cambridge, Mass., 1935), p. 182

27. R. P. Gillies, "German Playwrights," *Foreign Review and Continental Miscellany* 3 (1829): 97-98; Abraham Hayward, *Quarterly Review* 53 (1835): 215-29 (Boening, 2:456). John Russell, *A Tour of Germany and Some of the Provinces of the Austrian Empire, in the Years 1820, 1821, 1822*

David J. DeLaura

(Boston, 1825), p. 52 (there were two Edinburgh editions), notes that, when Goethe dies, "in the literature of Germany there will be a vacant throne." An American in the *Democratic Review*, in 1846 and 1847, notes that writers are hard pressed to assign Goethe "his true place on the literary Olympus,— to measure the height of his throne"; cited from Martin Henry Haertel, *German Literature in American Magazines, 1846 to 1880*, Bulletin of the University of Wisconsin (Philology and Literature Series, 4, no. 2), 1908, p. 68.

28. For the four phrases in sequence: *Fraser's Magazine* 36 (1847): 481-93 (Boening, 7:33); J. S. Blackie, *Foreign Quarterly Review* 18 (1836): 1-30 (Boening, 9:259); Jane Sinnett, *Dublin Review* 11 (1841): 477-505 (Boening, 9:436); Elizabeth Rigby, *Foreign Quarterly Review* 17 (1836): 391-417 (Boening, 3:58).

29. *Blackwood's Magazine* 4 (November 1818): 211-13; the article is a response to Palgrave's notorious attack in the *Edinburgh Review* 26 (1816): 304-37.

30. *Monthly Review*, 3d ser. 6 (1827), 25-32; Boening, 9:28.

31. *Blackwood's Magazine* 46 (1839): 475; Boening, 9, 237. A climax in this uncritical adulation is reached in an essay on Shelley by J. M. Mackie, in the *Dial* 1 (April 1841): 490, which finds the modern "tendency towards individual independence strikingly illustrated in Goethe, who, having laid under contribution all the improvements of the age in building up his lofty genius, at last reposed on the summit of modern civilization in all the sufficiency of Jupiter on Olympus."

32. *Literary Gazette* 33 (1851): 60-62; Boening, 9, 301.

33. 11:126. In "Carlyle and Arnold: The Religious Issue," in *Carlyle Past and Present*, ed. K. J. Fielding and Rodger L. Tarr (London, 1976), pp. 139-40, I suggest that Carlyle's presentation of Sterling provided central elements of Arnold's strangely incomplete and incompletely sympathetic portrait of Clough in "Thyrsis."

34. *CPW*, 1:14. Allott, *Poems of Matthew Arnold*, p. 670 n, correctly sees that Arnold was "struck by Niebuhr's pessimistic letters in 1830 about the future of Europe." Niebuhr reads the future as "retrogression towards barbarism" and "the flight of the sciences and Muses": *The Life and Letters of Barthold George Niebuhr* (London, 1852), 2:389; and his letters of the period are strewn with a rhetoric of degeneration, destruction, annihilation, barbarism, devastation, despotism, "universal ruin," the loss of all "free institutions," "hopeless confusion," and "the dissolution of the present order of things." Arnold would also have been attracted by Niebuhr's paralleling modern with Roman revolutions, as well as Niebuhr's sad insistence on the decline and degeneration of England (2:390 n, 397; 362, 364, 370). That Arnold should call the author of such panicked apocalypticism a man "of widest culture" says much about his own alienated state of mind in 1853.

35. *Letters*, 1:278; 22 September, 1864.

36. F. D. Maurice, *Athenaeum*, 23 January 1828, pp. 49-50, included Goethe with Lessing, Coleridge, Wordsworth, and Godwin "among the wisest and the greatest of our age."

221

37. *Sartor Resartus*, ed. Charles Frederick Harrold (New York, 1937), pp. 67, 191; hereafter cited as *SR*. Harrold notes that a reference to "the Wise Man" (*SR*, p.247) has a source in Goethe. Moreover, Carlyle's declaration in *Past and Present*, "'The great event for the world is, now as always, the arrival in it of a new Wise Man,'" occurs in a context hailing "Poet Goethe and German Literature" (10, 236).

38. *British and Foreign Review* 18 (1844): 51–92; Boening, 8:441. In *BFR*, 14 (1843): 78–135 (Boening, 7:319), Lewes spoke of Goethe as "a consummate incarnation of intellect."

39. *Memoirs of Margaret Fuller Ossoli*, ed. R. W. Emerson, W. H. Channing, and J. F. Clarke (1884; rpt. New York, 1972), 1:117, 119. Arnold read, and largely admired, the memoirs, in the spring of 1853; see *Letters*, 1:36, and *The Letters of Matthew Arnold and Arthur Hugh Clough*, ed. Howard Foster Lowry (London, 1932), pp. 132–33. The latter is hereafter cited as *LC*.

40. These phrases are from "State of German Literature" (1827).

41. This last and most explicit statement concerning Goethe's writings occurs in "Goethe's Works" (1832): 27:430–31. But the bulk of the phrasing cited in this paragraph is from the 1827 Preface to *Meister* and, especially, the essay "Goethe" (1828). My inference from all the evidence is that, almost in the act of establishing the pattern for Goethe's career that culminates in the famous three-part sequence in *Sartor* (finished 1831), Carlyle ceased to apply it with much conviction to the *man* Goethe and his "inward life"— that is, he ceased to find in Goethe himself an adequate model of life.

42. *SR*, p. 192 n. Harrold's introduction and notes remain the best treatment of Carlyle's relationship to Goethe in these matters.

43. There are some partial exceptions. Harrold, throughout his edition of *Sartor*, especially on pp. 192–93, treats Goethe's later "Christian" phase with some respect, as does W. H. Bruford, in chapter 4 of *The German Tradition of Self-Culture: 'Bildung' from Humboldt to Thomas Mann* (London, 1975).

44. *British and Foreign Review* 18 (1844): 51–92; Boening, 8:441.

45. *British and Foreign Review* 14 (1843): 78–135; Boening, 7:318.

46. Jean-Marie Carré, *Goethe en Angleterre* (Paris, 1920), p. 158.

47. Johann Peter Eckermann, *Conversations with Goethe*, trans. John Oxenford, Everyman's Library (London, 1930), p. 34; 2 January 1824. On the "unspeakable regret" Goethe felt in leaving Italy in 1788, see George Henry Lewes, *The Life of Goethe*, 2d ed. (London, 1864), pp. 300, 309.

48. Eckermann, p. 38; 27 January 1824. Carlyle reports the story of the French diplomat who said of Goethe's face: "*Voilà un homme qui a eu beaucoup de chagrins*," and Goethe's correction: "here is a man who has struggled toughly" (26:209; 1828).

49. Eckermann, pp. 359–60; 14 March 1830.

50. This is the translation in the *Athenaeum* 14 (1841): 187–88 (Boening, 3:184); see Eckermann, p. 425 (March 1832).

51. Eckermann, p. 360.

52. *Saturday Review* 7 (1859): 187–88; Boening, 8:150.

David J. DeLaura

53. The qualities of Goethe's mind are: calmness, beauty, vastness, and unmeasured strength: 23:23.

54. One of the few to see the "contrast" in the two figures is Allott, pp. 365-66.

55. For Arnold's treatment of such models, see my "Arnold and Literary Criticism: Critical Ideas," in *Matthew Arnold*, Writers and Their Back-Ground, ed. Kenneth Allott (London, 1975), pp. 147-48.

56. In "The Future of Poetry," in *Carlyle and His Contemporaries*, ed. John Clubbe (Durham, N.C., 1976), pp. 168-75, I argue in outline that Tennyson's "The Palace of Art" (1831-32) is itself in a sense "about" a caricature of Goethe current in the period, especially at Cambridge.

57. It is significant that in September 1853, just after finishing "The Scholar-Gipsy," Arnold wrote Clough on the need for "positive convictions and feeling" in poetry, and cited precisely Goethe on the need to avoid "the unnatural and unhealthy attitude of contradiction and opposition—the *Qual der Negation*." He goes on: "I think there never yet has been a perfect literature or a perfect art because the energetic nations spoil them by their illusions and their want of taste—and the nations who lose their illusions lose also their energy and creative power. Certainly Goethe had all the *negative* recomendations for a perfect artist but he wanted the *positive*— Shakespeare had the positive and wanted the negative." *LC*, pp. 142-43. This is a perfect example of Arnold the judicious "Goethean" critic using Goethe's own statements to fix Goethe himself in his limitingly "modern" place.

58. In *Victorian Prose: A Guide to Research* (New York, 1973), pp. 282-85, I summarize this and other issues that have engaged the poem's numerous critics.

59. I have discussed the implications of Arnold's predilection for such "elevated" creative figures in "A Background for Arnold's 'Shakespeare,'" in *Nineteenth-Century Literary Perspectives*, ed. Clyde de L. Ryals (Durham, N. C. 1974), pp. 129-48.

60. Although her reading of the "before" and "after" of Arnold's career differs markedly from mine, Josephine Maillet Barry, "Goethe and Arnold's 1853 Preface," *Comparative Literature* 32 (1980): 151-67, usefully shows the "artificial" and "mechanical" neoclassicism of the Preface as deriving from Goethe's "narrow and prescriptive" views of one period, the 1790s.

61. In *On the Study of Celtic Literature* (1866-67), Arnold speaks of the cult of melancholy in *Werther* and *Faust*, and concludes: "The German *Sehnsucht* itself is a wistful, soft, tearful longing, rather than a struggling, fierce, passionate one" (*CPW*, 3:371).

62. The phrase is A. Dwight Culler's in *Imaginative Reason: The Poetry of Matthew Arnold* (New Haven, Conn. 1966), p. 116. His account of Arnold's early development, and Kenneth Allott's in "A Background for 'Empedocles on Etna,'" *Essays and Studies 1968*, ed. Simeon Potter (London, 1968), pp. 80-100, are in my judgment the soundest we have.

63. *Letters*, 1:18; to his sister Jane.

64. The italicized language of this letter seems to me to match the extremity of "Dover Beach" in *its* insistence on the starkness of the modern

situation (neither joy, nor love, nor light, nor certitude, etc.). Begun perhaps as early as June 1851 (Allott), the poem joins the December 1852 letter, "The Scholar-Gipsy," and the "Grande Chartreuse" as bitter, "late," unregenerate eruptions of Arnold's deepest personal convictions concerning the *unworthy* modern world—although these are sentiments Arnold was increasingly attempting to suppress in public and probably in himself.

65. Arnold's tangled early relations with Goethe cannot be fully understood apart from "Memorial Verses" and *its* immense context in contemporary commentary; but there is no space to pursue the topic here. It should also be noted that the "Grande Chartreuse," written between 1851 and 1855 and perhaps Arnold's most defiantly alienated poem, involves a complicated quarrel with his own "masters of the mind," including implicitly Goethe.

66. Allott, p. 277, cites an even clearer passage, from the Yale MS, perhaps dating from the late 1840s: "I cannot conceal from myself the objection which really wounds and perplexes me from the religious side is that the service of reason is freezing to feeling, chilling to the religious mood. And feeling and the religious mood are eternally the deepest being of man, the ground of all joy and greatness for him."

67. For the Wordsworth relationship, see U. C. Knoepflmacher, "Dover Revisited: The Wordsworthian Matrix in the Poetry of Matthew Arnold," *Victorian Poetry* (1963): 1:17-26.

68. Erich Heller, in a notable study, "Goethe and the Avoidance of Tragedy," in *The Disinherited Mind* (New York, 1959), pp. 37-63, provides the link between Goethe's philosophy of nature and his "helplessness" in the face of "evil and sin." Arnold shows virtually no interest in Goethe's scientific views, and that silence is itself significant; but the rest of his extensive comments in Wordsworth and Goethe lead me to the conclusion I draw here. Of the other major figures of Arnold's early development, only Emerson promulgated a benign nature-philosophy, and Arnold again is notably indifferent to the subject; moreover, Emerson's never fully consistent views are more comfortably moral that Goethe's.

69. For the topography of such historical "positioning," see my "Matthew Arnold and the Nightmare of History," in *Victorian Poetry*, Stratford-upon-Avon Studies 15 (London, 1972), pp. 37-57. Regarding Wordsworth, Allott aptly cites (p.138) Arnold's "Heinrich Heine" (1863): Wordsworth "plunged himself in the inward life, he voluntarily cut himself off from the modern spirit" (*CPW*, 3:121).

70. See "Obermann," 1. 143; and *LC*, pp. 109-10 (23 September 1849), an important letter for tracing out the evolution of Arnold's deepest convictions about his own inward development.

X

JEROME H. BUCKLEY

The Identity of David Copperfield

DICKENS CLAIMED TO BE SURPRISED WHEN JOHN FORSTER TOLD him that David Copperfield's intitials reversed his own. Yet, as he reveals himself in the autobiographical fragment and in his letters, Dickens has long been partly identified with David—with the child suffering humiliation in the warehouse of Murdstone and Grinby and with the infatuated young lover courting Dora as he himself once wooed Maria Beadnell. There are other parallels, too, in David's experiences, and many reflections of personal attitude and emotion. But no one at all familiar with Dickens's temperament and career could mistake the characterization of David as a full and accurate self-portrait of David's creator.

Some recent readers have also seen Dickens, no doubt considerably distorted, in Mr. Dick, who of late seems to have become the very type of the alienated Romantic artist.[1] If Mr. Dick is indeed that, I should be tempted, remembering that his full name is Richard Babley, to identify him not with Dickens but with Richard Dadd, the mad painter, who in 1843 was confined to Bethlem Hospital for insane patricide. Dickens, we know, took a lively interest in Dadd's plight and, when walking with friends in Cobham Park, the scene of the murder, would reenact the tragedy.[2] Dadd's conversation, like Mr. Dick's memorial, frequently went off on irrelevant tangents; Dadd's obsession was a menacing devil; Mr. Dick's, originally "the bull in the china shop," changed at the last moment, by happy inspiration, to King Charles's head (which is not obviously to me the same as Charles Dickens's head). "'It's a mad world. Mad as Bedlam, boy!' said Mr. Dick."[3] But I am not eager to press the identification of Mr. Dick with Richard Dadd; I suggest only my reluctance to accept Mr. Dick as the novelist's surrogate and proper persona. And I have no intention of identifying David, in his divergence from Dickens, with Dadd or with any other early Victorian original.

I wish to approach *David Copperfield* as David's autobiography rather than Dickens's and to discuss David's character, his "identity," in the autonomous context of the novel. At the same time, I should not want to forget that the fiction, which in many respects transcends its time, embodies many Victorian values and assumptions, some awareness of which may help us assess its aesthetic and moral intentions.

David, Davy, Daisy, Copperfield, Trotwood—most of us are addressed in different ways by different people both within and beyond our family circle—but David's names and nicknames are so various as to signal perhaps a problem in identity. "David," we are told, was an uncommon name in England in 1850, though not in Scotland or Wales.[4] Especially in relation to "Uriah," it would have recalled the Biblical David and so possibly have offered a clue to the narrator's fallibility and mistaken impulse. But since Uriah Heep, who hovers leeringly over Agnes Wickfield, has little in common with the good soldier Uriah the Hittite, we cannot be sure what parallel, if any, we are expected to draw between the David who neglects Agnes and the adulterous king who seduced Uriah's lissome Bathsheba.

Quite apart from his name, however, the centrality of David or his distance from central focus is an issue from the very beginning of the novel. Some have complained that David never answers the question implicit in his first sentence: "Whether I shall turn out to be the hero of my own life or whether that station will be held by anybody else, these pages must show." The question may be thought to reflect the subtitle of *Vanity Fair*, "A Novel without a Hero," or even to imply some doubt that true heroism is possible in any realistic fiction. As readers we are indeed so absorbed in a multitude of vivid secondary characters that we often lose sight of David; and film versions of the novel almost invariably concentrate not on a single hero but on an amusing or lovable or grotesque yet always quite unheroic supporting cast. But Dickens—or I should say David the narrator—is less cynical than Thackeray about heroes. David as an abused child compares himself to "the hero in a story," dreaming of escape from a repressive home.[5] Of the end of his schooling, he remarks, in a passage of the manuscript later cut, that "life was more like a great fairy story, which I was just about to begin to read and of which the hero was David from the very first page."[6] (Dickens for his part reminded himself in his number plans that the first appearance of Agnes was to be the "introduction of the real heroine,"[7] which is to say, the real hero's counterpart.) *David Copperfield*, as I read it, is the first major English Bildungsroman, and as such a novel in which the Bildung of David the hero should be the primary focus of our attention. I should agree with Philip Collins that the book is "more deeply and continuously concerned with its hero's personality and development than its predecessors had been."[8] And I should demur only a little at Bert Hornback's assurance that the "meaning" of the novel as a whole lies "in the creation of David's heroic life: the life which becomes heroic as it achieves meaning and happiness."[9]

David Copperfield differs from the work of the earlier Dickens not only in its emphasis on the hero but also in its mode of "subjective" presentation as a well sustained first person narrative and so in effect as an extended dramatic monologue. David reveals himself by the way he talks, digresses, generalizes about life, by what he chooses to tell and by what he excludes from consideration. We see his character from within, and we look out through his eyes on an animated world. The illustrations by "Phiz," fine as they are, jar a little because in them for the first time we see David from the outside, perceived rather than perceiving, more restricted than the sensibility we share in as readers. The narrative impresses by its inwardness, the lyrical strain of its personal reflections, the haunting cadences of Dickens's "secret prose."

It is essentially a psychological life story, but David's method is seldom psychological analysis. Except in the untypical chapter called "Absence," he prefers to suggest rather than to probe his feelings. When Dora dies, we might wish some account of his response, but he disappoints our expectation: "This is not the time," he explains, "at which I am to enter on the state of my mind beneath its load of sorrow."[10] He registers something of his stunned bewilderment but describes no deeper emotional conflict. Though a novelist by profession, he nowhere explores motivation with the patience of a George Eliot or seeks to discriminate nuances of feeling with a Jamesian delicacy. His narrative is psychological in terms of revealing gesture and action rather than self-conscious introspection.

Sigmund Freud, as we know, greatly admired *David Copperfield*, probably for its incomparable depiction of childhood, possibly for its sheer abundance and vitality, but not necessarily, I should think, as a study in pathology. A number of Freudian critics nonetheless have given it rather ominous clinical readings. David has become an Angst-tortured introvert with a mother fixation and an overpowering guilt complex. His first affection for the two Claras, Copperfield and Peggotty, initiates a lifelong oedipal orientation.[11] He hates his dead father whom he finds resurrected in Mr. Murdstone. His marriage to Dora, who is as pretty and foolish as his dead mother, is said to be "an obvious case of neurotic selection."[12] " David blends self-criticism with conceit, using self-pity to soften intimations of guilt."[13] He is guilty, of course, of introducing Steerforth to the Peggottys and so effecting little Emily's ruin—though one reader of another critical persuasion believes Steerforth's charm well worth the price of Emily's disgrace.[14] David himself is alleged to have a homosexual attachment to Steerforth, who sometimes calls him Daisy.[15] The destructive power of the sea, we are told, is to be equated with "Steerforth's sexual instinct," but David, born with a caul, will escape drowning, which is to say, "will not be destroyed in the turbulent waters of sexual contact."[16] Nonetheless, whatever his sexual feelings, David, we learn, has a strong death urge and must come to terms with his own

Jerome H. Buckley

mortality before he can find satisfaction in writing his death-filled narrative.[17] In short, as one psychological critic sums up the case, David is "ridden by demons and controlled by memories he can neither comprehend nor dispel, haunted by images both of his past and his future."[18]

How are we to counter such conclusions? Or do they need to be countered? Most of them probably do embody at least half-truths, for the novel is wonderfully rich in texture and offers fresh suggestion to every sensitive reader—and indeed to every skilled practitioner of "misreading." If all of us in our intermittent questioning of life's purposes are to some degree neurotic, David is no exception; he, too, has his frequent doubts and misapprehensions. I should argue simply that David's autobiography is not essentially the case history of a sick psyche and that attaching labels to his affections and antipathies misrepresents rather than defines his identity. It means very little to say that David suffers an Oedipus complex, unless we can demonstrate that his early orientation makes for real psychological maladjustment in adult life. David is surely no Paul Morel miserably unable to love another woman as he has loved his too-possessive mother (indeed Clara Copperfield is not very possessive at all—she cares too little rather than too much for her son, and David, surviving his bereavement, has a succession of crushes and loves: little Emily, Miss Shepherd, Miss Larkins, Dora, and Agnes, both like and quite unlike his mother). If the child David momentarily wishes to lie down in his mother's coffin, we may assume that he desires to escape Mr. Murdstone forever and not that he hates the real father he has never known. Any child who enjoyed the company of Mr. Murdstone and his monstrous sister would be nothing short of a pathetic masochist—and I cannot think that David is that. As for Steerforth, David's attraction may be taken simply as the boy's inevitable hero-worship of a more sophisticated and accomplished older youth from a higher social sphere, and his later defence of his friend may be construed both as his continued loyalty and his reluctance to recognize the possible range of depravity in Steerforth's conduct. Similarly we may regard the name Daisy as an indication of David's ingenuous

229

freshness, possibly with a slangy overtone ("You're a real daisy!"), rather than a proof, as some readers find it, of David's effeminacy. There is no evidence I can unearth in the novel for any serious homosexual relationship with Steerforth or with any of the other characters, and there is, I think, no thematic reason why there should be. Nor, despite efforts to give David an obsession with death and a modern Angst, do we have many tokens of either a deliberate or an unconscious retreat from life. As a child David suffers but shows an admirable resilience, and as an adult, though his decisions are often mistaken, he meets most problems with a high degree of fortitude.

Whatever traumatic reaction Dickens may have had to his bondage at Warren's blacking house, David shows no permanent scars from his experience at Murdstone and Grinby's. He is, to be sure, at first a bit afraid that "some of the boys" at Dr. Strong's school will "find him out" and learn of his disgrace.[19] And he naturally does have mixed memories of his earlier childhood. In fact Aunt Betsey, acting as a sort of therapist, more sensible than some of his later critics, sends him back to Blunderstone so that he may confront his past. But he needs no therapy more radical than that. He occasionally suffers what he calls "a distempered fancy," and he is troubled at times by an "old unhappy feeling, like a strain of music faintly heard in the night."[20] Yet he has no hallucinations, and his sanity is never in question. There are certainly a number of odd or insane persons in the novel, but they are not surrogates for the hero, and beside their eccentricity or derangement David's clear reason shines forth. David has griefs and disappointments, but he never endures the frustrations of Rosa Dartle in his own story or the tormented Bradley Headstone in *Our Mutual Friend* or the deluded litigants of *Bleak House.*

I do not accept Mrs. Leavis's view of David as a merely representative early Victorian whom Dickens did not much admire, a man with commonplace reactions and no true individuality;[21] for David's powers of observation, as he himself suggests at the beginning of his narrative, are uncommonly acute and the command of the prose by which he creates his image is distinctly his alone. But I do believe that David is at pains to establish his psychological "normalcy" and that he succeeds in doing so without proving the contrary.

In *The Prelude* Wordsworth speaks of one of his unique spots of time, "It was in truth an ordinary sight." David generalizes his occasional extraordinary impressions in similar terms. He describes the *déjà vu* experience as "the strange feeling *to which, perhaps, no one is quite a stranger*" and, again, as "a feeling that comes over us occasionally" and that all of us know.[22] He presents his adult disillusion as something he "was now discovering, . . . with some natural pain, *as all men did.*"[23] He must learn to control his own "undisciplined heart," but nonetheless see that self-indulgence of some sort plagues most of the persons who are to serve as the examples, good and bad, from which he is eventually to learn self-mastery.[24] He is sometimes intrigued by his unexpected responses: his sudden sense of self-importance among his schoolmates when he and they hear of his mother's death, or his annoyance, despite his express desire to return unnoticed from Switzerland, that no one does come to meet him: "I was perverse enough to feel a chill . . . in receiving no welcome, and rattling, alone and silent, through the misty streets."[25] But we are to understand and accept both the self-consciousness and the "perversity" as ordinary, normal human reactions. A general normative psychology governs even the self-confrontation in the great "Tempest" chapter, where "something within me, faintly answering to the storm without, tossed up the depths of my memory and made a tumult in them."[26]

Though aware that his memory of concrete impressions is unusually sharp, David from the outset takes care to place his gifts of observation and recall within the higher ranges of normalcy, and when he generalizes—frankly from "my own experience of myself"—about a childlike sharpness of perception "remarkable" in some other men, he gives us an essential clue to his own temperament, his fresh responses, his unneurotic sanguinity of outlook: "I think the memory of most of us can go farther back into such times [early childhood] than many of us suppose; just as I believe the power of observation in numbers of very young children to be quite wonderful for its closeness and accuracy. Indeed, I think that most grown men who are remarkable in this respect, may with greater propriety be said not to have lost the faculty, than to have acquired it; the rather, as I generally observe such men to retain a certain freshness, and gentleness, and capacity of being pleased, which are also an inheritance they have preserved from their childhood."[27]

To David, memory reaching far back is in fact the strongest sanction of identity, for the present consciousness is constantly colored by the remembered or never quite forgotten past. The power of memory is also, of course, the central theme of the two greatest autobiographical poems in the language, *The Prelude* and *In Memoriam*. Both of these, we note, appeared in 1850 a few months before the serial completion of the novel, and either or both may have influenced the tone and symbolism of the last numbers. David Copperfield has been called "the most Wordsworthian of Dickens' novels"[28] and also "the most Tennysonian,"[29] though little has been said of its relation to *In Memoriam*. If the possible debt to Wordsworth is rather general, the similarities to Tennyson are somewhat more specific.

Robin Gilmour has reminded us of the closeness in mood of "Tears, Idle Tears" to David's musing on the past, his sense of the "old unhappy loss or want of something never to be realized."[30] I should compare the imagery of the poetical chapter "Absence," concerning David's self-exile in Switzerland, to that of another lyric from *The Princess*, the Swiss idyl "Come down, O maid, from yonder mountain height," where "the firths of ice" and rolling torrents represent sublime but inhuman isolation and the valley, echoing with shepherd's song and the calls of children, offers a return to society, "For love is of the valley, come thou down / And find him." David, setting himself apart like Tennyson's Jungfrau among the "awful solitudes" of the Alps, has sensed a lonely "sublimity . . . in the dread heights and precipices, in the roaring torrents, and the wastes of ice and snow"; but he now comes "down into a valley," where greeted by "shepherd voices," he finds a new serenity of spirit: "I admitted to my breast the human interest I had lately shrunk from."[31] The verbal echoes here seem to me too clear to be ignored.

But I should like to place the novel for a moment beside *In Memoriam*, which offers, I believe, a number of striking parallels not so much in language as in attitude and sensibility. In very general terms, if Agnes provides the resolution to the narrative, as I am convinced she does,[32] and poor Dora is to be considered a mistaken choice of immaturity, we might see a digest of the main plot in a single stanza comparing Hallam to

> one who once declined
> When he was little more than boy
> On some unworthy heart with joy,
> But lives to wed an equal mind.

The analogy here, however, is too common to much nineteenth century fiction to be seriously revealing. In reviewing his life, David resembles not the dead Hallam but the living, questioning poet. The curious wind from the past recurring throughout the novel, "the wind going by me like a restless memory," is reminiscent of the elegy's "wind / Of memory murmuring the past."[33] Both David and the poet wonder whether present dissatisfaction has led to a sentimentalizing of past "glory." David writes, "I did miss something of the realization of my dreams, but I thought it was a softened glory of the Past, which nothing could have thrown upon the present time."[34] The elegist similarly reflects on a distant glory:

> And was the day of my delight
>   As pure and perfect as I say ...
> And is it that the haze of grief
>   Makes former gladness loom so great?
>   The lowness of the present state
> That sets the past in this relief?
> Or that the past will always win
>   A glory from its being far?

David's vague sense of loss must ultimately be absorbed or reconciled, like Tennyson's indeterminate recollections:

> Something it is which thou hast lost,
>   Some pleasure from thine early years. . . .

> Such clouds of nameless trouble cross
> All night below the darken'd eyes;
> With morning wakes the will and cries,
> "Thou shalt not be the fool of loss."

The elegist is reassured of the continuity of love by reading the letters of his lost friend through the dark night at Somersby until the dawn brings the hope of a new day. David in "Absence" reads the letters of Agnes in the calm of a fading Swiss twilight until he feels "the night passing from my mind, and all its shadows clearing." Since Dickens almost certainly read *In Memoriam* soon after its publication in May of 1850 (he may actually have seen the trial edition printed in March) and did not write the "Absence" chapter till October, I see in this passage the strong possibility of a direct indebtedness to Tennyson.[35] I am less concerned, however, with literary sources than with the operation of a common Victorian psychology. Another comparison may serve as illustration. David in "Tempest" speaks of such a "jumble in my thoughts and recollections, that I had lost the clear arrangement of time and distance."[36] The poet likewise wonders whether grief has made him "that delirious man"—we should now say "schizophrenic"—

> Whose fancy fuses old and new
> And flashes into false and true
> And mingles all without a plan.

Both David and the poet, however, unlike some late celebrants of the schizoid sensibility, recognize their confusion and resist surrender to it; both cherish rational self-control. The poet at this point fears being stunned from "all my knowledge of myself." David, likewise seeking stability, later uses the same phrase; when at last he proposes to Agnes, he declares that he has finally come into "the better knowledge of myself."[37]

In the novel, as in the poem, it is self-knowledge, the ability to reconcile personal past and present that leads to the establishment or recovery of identity. And in both the calling of the speaker, the first person, becomes the measure of self-fulfillment, for each is deeply concerned with vocational responsibility. The elegist finds himself in returning to his "kind," that is, in meeting the demand for social communication as a poet. David assimilates his past and achieves integration in his career as novelist, where he may exercise his early gift of observation and his increasing command of language. In Carlylean terms, each attains his Everlasting Yea through the discovery and performance of his life's *work*. In the idiom of the modern identity psychologist, Erik Erikson, each reaches the mature state of "ego-integrity," at which "the young person, in order to experience wholeness, must feel a progressive continuity between that which he has become in the long years of childhood and that which he promises to become in the anticipated future, between that which he conceives himself to be and that which he perceives others to see in him and expect of him."[38]

David conceives himself to be the novelist and freely acknowledges his growing reputation as such. A recent structuralist describes *David Copperfield* as "a novel about a novelist writing a novel,"[39] but it is not quite that, for if we accept the fiction, as indeed we must, we should believe that David is not deceiving us when he claims here to be writing not a novel but a true autobiography. (We may, of course, argue that all autobiography partakes of fiction, but that is another matter). At all events, whatever his purposes in writing his own life history, David is by vocation a novelist. And David the novelist, as Philip Collins remarks, may be the "one successful and estimable intellectual" in the whole Dickens canon.[40] Nonetheless, many critical readers, including Professor Collins, have complained that David never discusses questions of technique or aesthetic theory or tells us much about what it means to be a novelist, except that it requires discipline and a great deal of Carlylean hard work.[41] But David, I should think, hardly needs to indulge in Jamesian speculation on the art of fiction. His popular success as a writer, his "fame," is acknowledged by other characters— Aunt Betsey, Agnes, Traddles, who cries, "And grown so famous! My glorious Copperfield!" and, in faroff Port Middlebury, Australia, Magistrate Micawber, who declares David's "lineaments, now familiar to the imaginations of a considerable portion of the civilized world" and urges the "eminent author" and companion of his youth to persist, "Go on, my dear sir, in your Eagle course!"[42] David himself confesses to his final advance "in fame and fortune" but offers few details about his books. We know only of his strenuous commitment to the labors of composition, amid the confusions of Dora's ill-managed ménage and especially during his recovery in Switzerland: "I fell to work, in my old ardent way, on a new fancy, which took strong possession of me. As I advanced in the execution of this task, I felt it more and more, and roused my best energies to do it well."[43] We must deduce his genius as a novelist from the writing of his autobiography, which he oddly describes as "intended for no eyes" but his own; and his skills are readily apparent. His method of presenting his story bears witness to his taste and talent, his capacity for sentiment, rhetoric, and vivid imagery. If we admire the "secret poetry" of the novel, Dickens expects us to accept the style as David's. There are, to be sure, similarities to Dickens's prose as we see it in the earlier third person novels, but there is also, as I have indicated, a newly personal, subjective quality, more sensitive, more reflective, more literary, less social, less hard-edged, that distinguishes David the novelist from the novelist who created him.

Though David properly claims for himself an unusual quickness and sharpness of observation, his story, some readers have objected, reveals much naiveté and a long-continued imperceptiveness of the needs and feelings of others, particularly of the patiently waiting Agnes.[44] "David's obtuseness," says John Carey, "is enough to make any girl weep. For Agnes has perfectly normal instincts, in fact, and is pointing not upwards but towards the bedroom. The inadequacy lies in David, not her."[45] But the mature David, who writes at least ten years after the last main events he describes, is surely aware of his past errors and misjudgments and fully able to appreciate the justice of his aunt's assessment, "Blind, blind, blind!"[46] His attainment of maturity has depended upon the clarification of his vision, his view not just of the vibrant world about him but also of his own private needs, weakness, and strength.

Towards the end he tells his aunt that writing, despite the pains it takes, "has its own charms." To which his aunt shrewdly replies, "Ah! I see! . . . Ambition, love of approbation, sympathy, and much more, I suppose!"[47] The "much more" to David in personal terms is the achievement of an inner discipline, the sense of self-knowledge in the control of his chosen medium, the quiet assertion of a slowly realized and always gentle but ultimately well-assured identity, the unexpressed conviction that a man, within limits, may become the hero of his own story.

1. On Dickens and Mr. Dick, see William C. Spengeman, *The Forms of Autobiography* (New Haven, Conn., 1980), pp. 128–32. Barry Westburg links Mr. Dick to Dickens and both to Charles I in *The Confessional Fictions of Charles Dickens* (Dekalb, Ill., 1977), p. 193. Robert Lougy speaks of Mr. Dick as "the artist-as-child" in his article, "Remembrances of Death Past and Future: A Reading of *David Copperfield*," *Dickens Studies Annual* 6 (1977): 87.

2. On Dickens and Dadd, see Patricia Allderidge, *The Late Richard Dadd* (London, 1974), pp. 35–36.

3. Nina Burgis, ed., *David Copperfield* (Oxford, 1981), p. 172. Hereafter cited as *DC*.

4. On David's name, see Sylvère Monod, *Dickens the Novelist* (Norman, Okla., 1968), pp. 301–2; A. E. Dyson, *The Inimitable Dickens* (London, 1970), pp. 119–26; and esp. Donald Hawes, "David Copperfield's Name," *Dickensian* 74 (1978): 81–87. On David and Uriah, see also Alexander Welsh, *The City of Dickens* (Oxford, 1971), 132–34; and Harry Stone, "Dickens and Fantasy: The Case of Uriah Heep," *Dickensian* 75 (1979): 100.

5. *DC*, p. 116.

6. *DC*, p. 233 and 233 n.2.

7. *DC*, "Number Plans" for chapter 15, p.760.

8. Philip Collins, *Charles Dickens: David Copperfield* (London, 1977), p. 13.

9. Bert G. Hornback, "The Hero Self," *Dickens Studies Annual* 7 (1978): 155.

10. *DC*, p. 659. When David says he will not go into his feelings, Collins (p. 20) pertinently asks, "Why not?"

11. Among the many who describe David's problems as "oedipal" are Mark Spilka, *Dickens and Kafka* (Bloomington, Ind., 1963), pp. 182–85; Max Vega-Ritter, in J. C. Amalric, ed., *Studies in the Later Dickens* (Montpelier, 1973); Stanley Friedman, "Dickens' Mid-Victorian Theodicy: *David Copperfield*," *Dickens Studies Annual* 7 (1978): 134; and Gordon D. Hirsch, "A Psychoanalytic Rereading of *David Copperfield*," *Victorian Newsletter* 58 (Fall 1980): 1–5.

12. Spilka, *Dickens and Kafka* p. 192.

13. Friedman, "Dickens' Mid-Victorian Theodicy," p. 128.

14. William R. Harvey, "Dickens and the Byronic Hero," *Nineteenth-Century Fiction* 24 (1969): 308-9.

15. See, for example, Christopher Mulvey, "*David Copperfield*: the Folk Story Structure," *Dickens Studies Annual* 5 (1976): 92.

16. Mulvey, "*David Copperfield*," p. 94.

17. Cf. Friedman, "Dickens' Mid-Victorian Theodicy," p. 128 (David is "obsessed with death") and Lougy, "Remembrances of Death," p. 76 ("The knowledge he seeks is the knowledge of his own death").

18. Lougy, "Remembrances of Death," p. 76.

19. *DC*, p. 195.

20. *DC*, pp. 328, 594; cf. pp. 552, 700.

21. See F. R. and Q. D. Leavis, *Dickens the Novelist* (London, 1970), p. 44f. Collins, *Charles Dickens* (p. 43) rejects Mrs. Leavis's argument that David is merely a representative Victorian. Lougy argues (p. 94) that David is really at odds with his time.

22. *DC*, pp. 326, 483 (italics added). Cf. a later passage (p. 673), describing David's waking from sleep: "I was roused by the silent presence of my aunt at my bedside. I felt it in my sleep, *as I suppose we all do feel such things*" (italics added).

23. *DC*, p. 595 (italics added).

24. The theme is ably traced by Gwendolen B. Needham, "The Undisciplined Heart of David Copperfield," *Nineteenth-Century Fiction* 9 (1954): 81-107.

25. *DC*, p. 702.

26. *DC*, p. 677.

27. *DC*, p. 11. On *David Copperfield* as "a novel of memory," see J. Hillis Miller, *Charles Dickens: The World of his Novels* (Cambridge, Mass., 1958), pp. 152-55; and Janet H. Brown, "The Narrator's Role in *David Copperfield*," *Dickens Studies Annual* 2 (1972): 199.

28. Lougy, "Remembrances of Death," p. 97.

29. Robin Gilmour, "Dickens, Tennyson, and the Past," *Dickensian* 95 (1979): 136.

30. *DC*, p. 700.

31. *DC*, pp. 697-99.

32. The last page of the novel speaks of Agnes as "my soul" and "the dear presence, without which I were nothing." Miller (pp. 156-58) and Friedman (p. 144) see Agnes as David's spiritual guide, and Spilka (p. 171) describes her as "clearly the agent of his redemption."

33. *DC*, p. 723.

34. *DC*, p. 552.

35. We know that Tennyson and Dickens maintained friendly relations throughout the 1840s, that Tennyson visited Dickens in Switzerland, that Dickens much admired a good deal of Tennyson's poetry. Gilmour (pp. 131-42) suggests similarity in mood between Tennyson and the reminiscential Dickens and, on the strength of the poet's concern with "the

eternal landscape of the past," the likelihood that Dickens read *In Memoriam* while writing *David Copperfield* (see Gilmour, "Dickens, Tennyson, and the Past." p. 142, n. 15).

36. *DC*, p. 676.

37. *DC*, pp. 738-39.

38. Erik H. Erikson, *Identity, Youth and Crisis* (New York, 1968), p. 87.

39. Lougy, "Remembrances of Death," p. 100.

40. Philip Collins, "The Popularity of Dickens," *Dickensian* 70 (1974): 18.

41. On David's practice as novelist, cf. Collins (*Dickens*, pp. 39-40) and Welsh (p. 78). Donald D. Stone perceptively notes the disparity between the intensity of Dickens and the gentler creative vision of David: "David is denied any of the Dickensian energy that would enable us to conceive of him masterfully bending the created world to his will. Dickens's strategy in denying the reader a glimpse of the power-hunger inherent in the creative process is probably prudent." Stone, *The Romantic Impulse in Victorian Fiction* (Cambridge, Mass., 1980), p. 263.

42. *DC*, pp. 704-5, 746-47.

43. *DC*, p. 699.

44. Janet Brown (p. 207) considers David imperceptive since he seems to ignore Mr. Murdstone's "sorrow at his wife's death," Dora's sense of defeat in marriage, and the fact that his engagement to Dora may have hastened Mr. Spenlow's death.

45. John Carey, *The Violent Effigy* (London, 1973), p. 171. James R. Kincaid takes a less sympathetic view of Agnes in his article, "The Darkness of *David Copperfield*," *Dickens Studies* 1 (1965): 71: "Agnes . . . has no capacity for facing life and offers to David only the schizophrenic haven of delusion." Agnes, then, would scarcely be "the real heroine" Dickens thought he had created, and David's integration would be far less successful than I should assume.

46. *DC*, pp. 430, 716.

47. *DC*, p. 735.

XI

JOHN J. FENSTERMAKER

Language Abuse in *Bleak House*: The First Monthly Installment

FOUR DECADES HAVE PASSED SINCE GEORGE ORWELL, HUMPHRY House, and Edmund Wilson published their seminal studies of Charles Dickens, offering a new portrait of the man that delineated the complex human being, artist, and social critic we have come to know today. During these years, *Bleak House* is perhaps the single work to have profited most from our new understanding of Dickens and his art; certainly more critical commentary has appeared on that novel since 1940 than on any of his others. Much of the best scholarship on *Bleak House* has examined Dickens's artistic control of his materials, with the substantial body of analysis devoted to the opening paragraphs providing a case in point. But the rich veins of the famous opening of the novel and of chapter 1 as a whole have not been exhausted[1]: generally, commentators have chosen to restrict their inquiries and have stopped short of considering the specific context of the opening chapter— i.e., as the first unit in a four chapter installment. Hence the richness of the complete "opening" of *Bleak House* remains, in part, undescribed.

The purpose and much of the force of chapter 1 continue unabated throughout the initial monthly number, which fully introduces the themes and major artistic techniques *Bleak House* will develop. In the whole of the first installment, as in the entire novel, particular images recur to create a general atmosphere of disease and decay, analogies with the "family" are established to provide a touchstone for determining what is responsible or irresponsible action, and the language used by characters or associated with institutions is carefully selected to offer the reader an accurate gauge for correctly placing them in the novel's moral scheme. Although each technique is fundamental to the presentation of his ideas in the opening number and later, little attention has been focused specifically on Dickens's use of the failure of words, of the abuse of language, as a key for understanding the social malaise he explores.

Basic to the artistry of *Bleak House* is Dickens's method of simultaneously presenting and judging the characters and principal institutions in the novel by emphasizing the way each uses language. The central symptom of much of the sickness Dickens examines is the failure of words, written and spoken, to express truth and to communicate genuine human fellow-feeling. Too often language is used, as the narrator says, "under false pretences of all sorts" to effect "trickery, evasion, procrastination, spoliation [and] botheration," creating "influences that can never come to good."[2] Exposing personal or institutional irresponsibility by demonstrating the extensiveness of such language abuse is an artistic device introduced in the first installment and repeated with variations throughout the book: misuse of language pervades each of the four public institutions Dickens indicts—Chancery (and the Law), Aristocracy (and Government), Religion, and organized Philanthropy—and the crucial private institution, the family. The concept of the "ideal family" provides the central analogy for Dickens's charge against these institutions and the characters associated with them: they fail to act responsibly with respect to their familial obligations.[3]

The impact of the novel's famous opening derives from its imagery. We are first offered a broad panoramic view of London and its environs where dogs, horses, and people are slipping and sliding in the mud and fog. The narrator quickly shifts from this overview and penetrates to the heart of the fog where, near the "leadenheaded old corporation" (pp. 5–6),

Temple Bar, sits the Lord High Chancellor in the High Court of Chancery. Inside the courtroom, "petty-bags," "Privy purses" (p. 7), and others struggle in the mire at the feet of the Lord Chancellor. The struggle inside the court, however, is fundamentally different from that taking place outside in that the "mountains of costly nonsense" (p. 6) befogging the solicitors are self-made verbal obstructions. We see the lawyers "mistily engaged in one of the ten thousand stages of an endless cause, tripping one another up on slippery precedents, groping knee-deep in technicalities, running their goat-hair and horse-hair warded heads against walls of words, and making a pretence of equity with serious faces, as players might" (p. 6). The imagery in this passage, similar to that describing the streets of London and the surrounding countryside, establishes an equivalence between the physical muck overwhelming the country and the moral corruption and decay debilitating Chancery as well as other institutions and many families.

Chancery serves as the premier instance of the sickness in the novel: as the highest court of equity, it has the most obvious familial responsibility to society's disadvantaged or deprived, such as the orphans and widows who are its wards or charges. Blinded by various kinds of pride, however, the members of Chancery, and of the other institutions Dickens examines, fail to behave responsibly, fail to administer humane charity (love) to their needy brothers and sisters in the general community; in each case the failure derives from, or is effected by, the same means: a corrupting of language that is sometimes inadvertent but more often deliberate, a fabricating of "walls of words" to trip up or impede others while "making a pretence of equity with serious faces, as players might."

Because the language of Chancery is the most abused and because that institution is the most pervasive in its influence, it is to Chancery that the reader is first introduced. The "mountains of costly nonsense" piled before the court and obstructing the path of justice—"bills, cross-bills, answers, rejoinders, injunctions, affidavits, issues, references to masters, masters' reports" (p. 6)—result from the mechanical, role-playing procedures that provide the practitioners endless opportunities to exercise their wit and ingenuity, to trip each other up over precedents and technicalities. More important, of course, this duly-recorded nonsense succeeds in removing the cause at hand ever further from its human element, obscuring or distorting the real issues and delaying indefinitely the resolution of the proper questions.

The human toll resulting from the interminable and circumlocutory Chancery practice is Dickens's major interest; hence, he interrupts his long indictment in chapter 1 to present dramatically, if fleetingly, a glimpse of three victims in court this day: the "little mad old woman" (Miss Flite), the "Sallow Prisoner," and the "man from Shropshire" (Gridley) (p. 7). The nonsense recorded in the piles of paper produced ad infinitum in the suit of Jarndyce and Jarndyce exists analogously in the worthless "documents" ("paper matches and lavender") Miss Flite carries in her reticule and in the "conglomeration" (p. 7) of the prisoner's records. Miss Flite's story is fully detailed later in the novel as she becomes a prominent character. The prisoner does not appear after chapter 1, but his victimization as a result of being inextricably caught up in "walls of words," where even personal entreaty is useless, Dickens describes precisely: "A sallow prisoner has come up, in custody, for the half-dozenth time, to make a personal application to 'purge himself of his contempt'; which being a solitary surviving executor who has fallen into a state of conglomeration about accounts of which it is not pretended that he had ever any knowledge, he is not at all likely ever to do. In the meantime his prospects in life are ended" (p. 7). When the prisoner is finally presented, the court decides that nothing can be done about his conglomeration, and he is promptly returned to his cell.

The pleas of the man from Shropshire carry to its logical extreme the dehumanization following from strict adherence to the rules and procedures of the Chancery game. While the court reduces Miss Flite to madness and incarcerates the prisoner, it literally denies the existence of Gridley: "Another ruined suitor, who periodically appears from Shropshire, and breaks out into efforts to address the Chancellor at the close of the day's business, and who can by no means be made to understand that the Chancellor is legally ignorant of his existence after making it desolate for a quarter of a century, plants himself in a good place and keeps an eye on the Judge, ready to call out 'My Lord!' in a voice of sonorous complaint, on the instant of his rising" (p. 7).

Gridley's sonorous complaint, "My Lord!," occurring three times in this short chapter and creating a very effective chorus or refrain, is the first instance of Dickens's use of direct speech to call attention to the abuse of language. Gridley's grandiloquent "My Lord," showing his vehemence, vitality, and anger, is immediately contrasted with the words that "slide out" of Mr. Tangle, who speaks when the Lord Chancellor inquires whether he has concluded his argument: "Mlud, no—variety of points—feel it my duty tsubmit—ludship . . . " (p. 9). This marvelously debased phrasing, underscoring the corruption and deterioration of the speaker and at the same time relating language to imagery ("mud" to "Mlud") in an overall indictment of Chancery, is doubly effective when contrasted with Gridley's passionate outburst. The reader finds himself changing Gridley's direct address "My Lord!" to the exasperated "My Lord!" (or My God!), precisely registering the indignation Dickens intends with his refrain.

By the end of chapter 1, Chancery stands fully indicted, though the spectre of this monster haunts virtually every chapter in the novel. The evil it does is directly related to its abuse or misuse of language, a result of pride in its practitioners, each of whom tries to out-do his fellows by increasing the verbal labyrinth imprisoning the parties in Jarndyce and Jarndyce, maddening them even to their graves.

In their fates we see ample illustration of the dictum: language misused produces "influences that can never come to good." Dickens next focuses his attention on the institution most similar to Chancery, that other leadenheaded, old, obstructionist bulwark of English society and government, the Aristocracy—represented by Sir Leicester Dedlock and his Lady.

Chapter 2, like chapter 1, is primarily expository. The imagery introducing the Aristocracy immediately links it to the world of Chancery: "Both the world of fashion and the Court of Chancery are things of precedent and usage; over-sleeping Rip Van Winkles, who have played at strange games through a deal of thundery weather. ... It [the world of fashion] is a deadened world, and its growth is sometimes unhealthy for want of air" (p. 11). The chapter proceeds to confirm this introduction, for the fashionable world we see is artificial, sterile, essentially lifeless.

The expository technique is similar to that of chapter 1. It features little dialogue or dramatic action, but through the dialogue that does occur and through the voice of the narrator, we see that pride and role-playing function here as in Chancery via the abuse of language, keeping language formulaic and stylized and in no sense a vehicle for communication of truth or honest feeling: on the part of Sir Leicester and Lady Dedlock, rendering all human contact mannered, impersonal, distanced; on the part of their retinue, reducing language to a prop or a tool for insincere flattery and deference, cloaking even in the highest-placed subordinates an allegiance solely to self.

Sir Leicester's conception of his social status and the value of his family heritage combines with his political reactionism to render him aloof and, consequently, generally out of touch with all persons and issues around him, even including at times Lady Dedlock, to whom he always tries to be solicitous. He and Lady Dedlock have only the most restricted contact with others, and they expect certain rote responses, whether of actions or of words, from those persons with whom they must deal directly. Dickens purposefully uses vague language to describe the baronet's ruminations, suggesting the shallowness of his thinking and his essentially reflexive responses to any matter dealing with government, law, or the role of the aristocracy: "Sir Leicester has no objection to an interminable Chancery suit. It is a slow, expensive, British, constitutional kind of thing. ... He regards the Court of Chancery, even if it should involve an occasional delay of justice and a trifling amount of confusion, as something, devised in conjunction with a variety of other somethings, by the perfection of human wisdom, for the eternal settlement (humanly speaking) of everything" (pp. 15-16).

Sharing with Sir Leicester the wealth, rank, and power of the Dedlock name is his Lady. In Honoria Dedlock, Dickens succinctly illustrates how the world of fashion replicates Chancery; hundreds of parasitic hangers-on survive through role-playing, dependent upon a language calculated and manipulative, phrased without relation to truth or justice—the chief prop in a lucrative game:

> She [Lady Dedlock] supposes herself to be an inscrutable Being, quite out of the reach and ken of ordinary mortals. . . . Yet, every dim little star revolving about her, from her maid to the manager of the Italian Opera, knows her weaknesses, prejudices, follies, haughtinesses, and caprices; and lives upon as accurate a calculation and as nice a measure of her moral nature, as her dressmaker takes of her physical proportions. . . . There are deferential people, in a dozen callings, whom my Lady Dedlock suspects of nothing but prostration before her, who can tell you how to manage her as if she were a baby; who do nothing but nurse her all their lives; who, humbly affecting to follow with profound subservience, lead her and her whole troop after them. [P. 14]

Just as Dickens renders dramatically through Miss Flite, the sallow prisoner, and Gridley specific instances of his general indictment of Chancery in chapter 1, so at the end of chapter 2 we find a brief, dramatic scene crystallizing the allegations against the Aristocracy and its subordinates. The chapter ends with our witnessing the principal players in the Dedlock drama acting out, except for a brief moment's surprise, their customary roles. The dutiful Dedlock solicitor Tulking-horn—"mute, close, irresponsive to any glancing light . . . [who] never converses, when not professionally consulted" (p. 14)—is sharing with Sir Leicester and Lady Dedlock some Chancery business concerning Lady Dedlock in a minor way. Through the use of the Chancery documents, Dickens achieves much in a small compass: the parallels between Chancery and the Aristocracy are underlined as we find Lady Dedlock implicated *in Chancery*, and the reader's attention remains focused upon language in two ways: Sir Leicester is listening to Tulkinghorn's reading with "a stately liking for the legal repetitions and prolixities, as ranging among the national bulwarks" (p. 16); Lady Dedlock in her perpetual haughtiness assumes her usual detachment and for a time "carelessly and scornfully abstracts her attention" (p. 16) until she is stunned by recognition of the law copier's handwriting:

> "Who copied that?"
> Mr. Tulkinghorn stops short, surprised by my Lady's animation and her unusual tone.
> "Is it what you people call law-hand?" she says, looking full at him in her careless way again, and toying with her screen.
> "Not quite. Probably"—Mr. Tulkinghorn examines it as he speaks—"the legal character it has, was acquired after the original hand was formed. Why do you ask?"
> "Anything to vary this detestable monotony. O, go on, do!" [P. 16]

Tulkinghorn, fully understanding his role, knows better than to remark what is not comprehended by his master. Throughout the scene, he remains deferential, on the surface showing little interest in Lady Dedlock even when, attracted by the handwriting, she becomes, in her own words, faint with the "faintness of death" (p. 16); he appears to accept without question (as in his part he must) Sir Leicester's explanation of her strange behavior: that the foul weather has been "extremely trying" and that Lady Dedlock "really has been bored to death" (p. 17) at the house in Lincolnshire. Tulkinghorn, like the other parasites feeding off the Dedlocks, moves through his relationship with them outwardly performing as directed, employing appropriate speech and action. He differs, however, from others affecting service to this corrupt institution—the Aristocracy. The pretence in his role-playing masks the wholly self-serving and extraordinarily dangerous nature of his motives in that his own fierce pride, every bit the equal of Lady Dedlock's, dictates a resolve to master her. He begins by secretly noting her unacknowledged recognition of the scrivener's handwriting; in the end, however, his desire for dominance will lead to both his and her death, and to the collapse of the Dedlock house.

Hence, in chapter 2, as in chapter 1, Dickens dramatizes through the use of empty, distorted, and misleading language the grounds for his charges of irresponsibility against both the individual characters and the institutions they represent. Again he focuses his concern over the irresponsibility on its potential cost in human terms: showing in the language of Lady Dedlock and Tulkinghorn the essential falseness in human relations and consequent denial of individual worth that grows logically out of a combined pride in social position and desire to dominate others; and in the language of Sir Leicester a similar inability to recognize or comprehend human need growing not out of an aggressive desire to dominate but rather out of that ignorance inhering in the complacent isolation that often attends social position.

The opening of chapter 3, the beginning of Esther's narrative, promises to disperse the fog. Esther's language here, as throughout the book, is simple, direct, sincere: she wants to communicate. She wishes us to understand her thoughts and ideas and even worries that she will be unequal to her task: "I have a great deal of difficulty in beginning to write my portion of these pages, for I know I am not clever. . . . I had always rather a noticing way—not a quick way, O no!—a silent way of noticing what passed before me, and thinking I should like to understand it better. I have not by any means a quick understanding" (p. 17). Esther's qualms about her ability to write her portion subtly emphasize Dickens's concerns with the language of truth.

Our hope for relief through Esther soon dissipates, however, as we learn in the story of her childhood that the novel is not turning in a more optimistic direction. The clarity, directness, and naiveté of her narrative merely intensify its horror. In describing Miss Barbary, her godmother, Esther introduces Religion, the third public institution to be scrutinized in the novel's opening installment. In addition, Miss Barbary is the first failed parent in the story. Her failure results from particular religious attitudes, which, fed by her own overweening pride, have denied the child Esther the love and emotional support characteristic of healthy family relationships.

Esther captures the cold, unfeeling Christianity of Miss Barbary without intentional irony, telling us that her god-mother was a "good, good woman! She went to church three times every Sunday, and to morning prayers on Wednesday and Friday, and to lectures whenever there were lectures; and never missed" (p. 17). But we understand this information correctly only after we learn that Miss Barbary was "grave" and "never smiled" (p. 17); Esther tells us too: "I had never heard my mama spoken of"; "I never went out at all"; "My birthday was the most melancholy day at home in the whole year" (p. 17); "Imperfect as my understanding of my sorrow was, I knew that I had brought no joy, at any time, to anybody's heart, and that I was to no one upon the earth what Dolly [a rag doll] was to me" (p. 19).

Nor does Esther distort the truth. We have only to hear Miss Barbary in her own voice expatiating on the subject of Esther's birthday to understand fully the nature of her pride and role-playing and the extent to which she has failed in her parental responsibilities, using language as an instrument of dehumanization:

> It would have been far better, little Esther, that you had had no birthday; that you had never been born. . . . Your mother, Esther, is your disgrace, and you were hers. The time will come—and soon enough—when you will understand this better, and will feel it too, as no one save a woman can. I have forgiven her . . . the wrong she did to me, and I say no more of it, though it was greater than you will ever know—than any one will ever know, but I the sufferer. For yourself unfortunate girl, orphaned and degraded from the first of these evil anniversaries, pray daily that the sins of others be not visited upon your head, according to what is written. . . . You are different from other children, Esther, because you were not born like them, in common sinfulness and wrath. You are set apart." [P. 19]

At the death of Miss Barbary, Esther, still a child, is provided for by John Jarndyce through the offices of Conversation Kenge. As is always the case when Jarndyce can obtain control, love flourishes unfettered, and Esther knows six happy years at Greenleaf learning and then teaching others how to perform as governesses. Ultimately, however, this arrangement brings Esther into the suit of Jarndyce and Jarndyce as a companion to a ward of the Court of Chancery and reintroduces Chancery as the principal agent of irresponsibility in the first installment. The focus remains on language abuse through Conversation Kenge, whom Esther describes: "He appeared to enjoy beyond everything the sound of his own voice . . . for it was mellow and full, and gave great importance to every word he uttered. He listened to himself with obvious satisfaction, and sometimes gently beat time to his own music with his head, or rounded a sentence with his hand" (p. 22). The description of Kenge emphasizes his use of language as the principal vehicle for his own posturing, a point masterfully presented in visual detail in the letter Kenge writes to Esther about Jarndyce's intention to secure her as a companion for his niece, Ada Clare. The letter, which holds good news for Esther, rivets our attention on the debased language characteristic of the lawyers in the novel and of those initiated into their society, a language corrupt in form and impersonal and formulaic in tone and content:

> Our c̄l̄t Mr. Jarndyce being ābt̄ to rec̄e into his house, under an Order of the C̄t of C̄h̄y, a W̄ard of the C̄t in this cause, for whom he wishes to secure an ēlḡble comp̄n, directs us to inform you that he will be glad of your s̄erc̄es in the ā̄fs̄d capacity.
>
> We have ārr̄n̄ḡd for your being forded, carriage free, pʳ eight o'clock coach from Reading, on Monday morning next, to White Horse Cellar, Piccadilly, Lon̄don, where one of our c̄l̄ks will be in waiting to convey you to our ōf̄fe as above.
>
> We are, Madam, Your obedˡ Servᵗˢ,
Kenge and Carboy.

Esther, safely arrived in a London she can barely see due to the intense fog of a "London particular," is granted the right to be Ada's companion by the Lord Chancellor who, though kind, "at his best, appeared so poor a substitute for the love and pride of parents" (p. 31). The chapter ends with important qualifications of her good fortune and an increased emphasis on the "love and pride of parents" as Esther, Ada, and Jarndyce's other ward, Richard Carstone, are accosted with "great ceremony" by Miss Flite: "'I was a ward myself. I was not mad at the time,' curtseying low, and smiling between every little sentence. 'I had youth and hope. I believe, beauty. It matters very little now. Neither of the three served, or saved me. I have the honour to attend Court regularly. With my documents. I expect a judgment. Shortly. On the Day of Judgment. I have discovered that the sixth seal mentioned in the Revelations is the Great Seal. It has been open a long time! Pray accept my blessing'" (p. 34). Concluding the chapter with Miss Flite produces several effects: her poignant language indicates that this good-hearted woman is mad; although introducing another variant of language abuse, the emphasis is not on the language of madness but on the parallels between Esther and Miss Flite as abused children and the potential loss in human terms produced by failed parents or surrogates, who offer "so poor a substitute for the love and pride of parents."

In chapter 3, Dickens begins to shift the direction of the first installment specifically to the subject of parental irresponsibility. The chapter opens with the indictment of a particular kind of Christianity common in Dickens's time as the wounded pride of Miss Barbary manifests itself in language so irresponsible and so devastating in its denial of love and warmth that Esther consciously feels that she has "brought no joy, at any time, to anybody's heart." Miss Barbary dies, however, and Esther is rescued by Jarndyce. Miss Flite's situation is analogous, save that she is not rescued. As a young ward like Esther, she needed the help and support of a surrogate parent—Chancery. But like Miss Barbary, Chancery practitioners cared nothing for Miss Flite; in their pride they cared only for the "mountains of costly nonsense" produced in their game. Miss Flite as a person was the "cost" of this "nonsense," and her youth and hope and beauty were in time reduced to madness. This focus on the cost of parental irresponsibility provides the transition to chapter 4.

Chapter 4 is entitled "Telescopic Philanthropy," and it is organized Philanthropy that becomes the fourth and final public institution charged with failure to fulfill its familial responsibilities. The vehicle for exposing the shortcomings of organized philanthropy is Mrs. Jellyby and her projects, principally her plans for the cultivation of coffee and education of the natives of Boorioboola-Gha on the left bank of the Niger.

The setting for this chapter recalls the major images already presented: the house, enveloped in fog, is cold and has a "marshy smell" (p. 39); Mrs. Jellyby sits at the center, like the Lord Chancellor, conducting her business undisturbed by the fog (in this case smoke from a fireplace that chokes Esther, Ada, and Richard). In two short sentences, of the many describing the disarray of this household, Dickens incorporates images associated with corruption, worthlessness, and dehumanization familiar from the earlier chapters: "The room, which was strewn with papers and nearly filled by a great writing-table covered with similar litter, was, I must say, not only very untidy, but very dirty. We were obliged to take notice of that with our sense of sight, even while, with our sense of hearing, we followed the poor child who had tumbled down-stairs: I think into the back kitchen, where somebody seemed to stifle him" (p. 37).

The dirty, untidy, and littered room with the forgotten and stifled child explicitly suggests Chancery. This chapter has its prisoners too: the little unnamed Jellyby whose head is caught between the bars on the staircase and Peepy who scales his crib bars to achieve freedom and, subsequently, recognition and succor from Esther.

Mrs. Jellyby is described by Conversation Kenge as a "lady of very remarkable strength of character, who devotes herself entirely to the public"(p. 35), but Richard hits upon a more salient characteristic when he observes that her "eyes . . . had a curious habit of seeming to look a long way off. As if . . . they could see nothing nearer than Africa!" (p. 37). Because she can see no nearer than Africa, Mrs. Jellyby fails utterly in her familial responsibilities to her husband, children, and household in general. As a result, Mr. Jellyby is permanently immobile and speechless, the children are often in physical danger, the servants drink and fight, and the house is chaotic.

Although a pride in role-playing similar to that seen in the Chancery practitioners, in the Dedlocks and Tulkinghorn, Miss Barbary, and Conversation Kenge is central to the presentation of Mrs. Jellyby and her philanthropic enterprises, the household is perhaps most directly analogous to Chancery: the public duty of both is the dispensation of meaningful charity. Again Dickens indicts in terms of language abuse: Mrs. Jellyby, like the Chancery lawyers, has given her life over to mechanically producing "mountains of costly nonsense." Those persons with whom she communicates in her vast public correspondence share with her a largely mechanical and formulaic speech: "presents her compliments to Mr. Swallow and begs . . . to inform him, in reference to his letter of inquiry on the African project" (p. 39). Similarly, Mr. Quale, a parasite with an eye for Caddy, flatters Mrs. Jellyby by rote, as Esther observes: "'I believe now, Mrs. Jellyby, you have received as many as from one hundred and fifty to two hundred letters respecting Africa in a single day, have you not?' or 'If my memory does not deceive me, Mrs. Jellyby, you once mentioned that you had sent off five thousand circulars from one post-office at one time?'—always repeating Mrs. Jellyby's answer to us like an interpreter" (p. 41).

Perhaps because this chapter is the last in the first installment or perhaps because here he can make his points about parental irresponsibility within an actual family group rather than through analogy as earlier, Dickens offers more than one scene which presents the horror of Mrs. Jellyby as failed parent. In certain of these scenes, Dickens does what he has not done before: he offers through Esther examples of genuine charity, of tender, self-effacing voluntary love of the type which, when it uses language at all, does so with warmth and a genuine desire to communicate and to achieve human contact.

A direct contrast of Mrs. Jellby's typically mechanical, role-playing devotion to the creation of walls of meaningless words and Esther's wordless, humane response occurs when the bruised and dirty Peepy arrives in the midst of dictation to display his injuries and to seek comfort. Mrs Jellyby greets him with, "No, Peepy! Not on any account!" She adds: "'Go along you naughty, Peepy!' and fixed her fine eyes on Africa again" (p. 39). Esther's instinctive and silent action at this juncture and the language of her own analysis clearly express Dickens's point:

> However, as she at once proceeded with her dictation, and as I interrupted nothing by doing it, I ventured quietly to stop poor Peepy as he was going out, and to take him up to nurse. He looked very much astonished at it, and at Ada's kissing him; but soon fell fast asleep in my arms, sobbing at longer and longer intervals, until he was quiet. I was so occupied with Peepy that I lost the letter in detail, though I derived such a general impression from it of the momentous importance of Africa, and the utter insignificance of all other places and things, that I felt quite ashamed to have thought so little about it. [P. 39]

Esther's quiet nursing of the suffering child at the cost of "the momentous importance of Africa"—while his own mother irrationally labels him "naughty" and then looks through and past him and his hurts—offers a powerful vision of parental responsibility juxtaposed with parental irresponsibility and its cost in human terms.

In a similar scene, Esther and Mrs. Jellyby are again contrasted, but this time Dickens underscores his condemnation of the lack of human sympathy in those persons and institutions he criticizes by focusing our attention on the appropriate mix of language, feeling, and action:

> Mrs. Jellyby, sitting in quite a nest of wastepaper, drank coffee all the evening, and dictated at intervals to her eldest daughter. She also held a discussion with Mr. Quale; of which the subject seemed to be—if I understood it—the Brotherhood of Humanity; and gave utterance to some beautiful sentiments. I was not so attentive an auditor as I might have wished to be, however, for Peepy and the other children came flocking about Ada and me in a corner of the drawing-room to ask for another story; so we sat down among them and told them in whispers Puss in Boots and I don't know what else, until Mrs. Jellyby accidentally remembering them, sent them to bed. [P. 41]

In their roles as philanthropists, Mrs. Jellyby and Mr. Quale create abstract and beautiful sentiments about brotherhood and humanity in a discussion we already know lacks the proper field of action; but how completely is their stature reduced by Esther and Ada, who are themselves playing a role for the first time—that of storyteller. These role-players, however, are too genuinely concerned about the needs of their listeners to produce a mechanical or rote recital of well-known material. They tell the tales in their own words; their attitude is warm and affectionate, and their listeners respond by seeking more stories. Such moments represent the brotherhood of humanity in action, and they deflate the abstract language and sentiments of Mrs. Jellyby and Mr. Quale.

Chapter 4, and thus the first installment, concludes by demonstrating the only viable response to the novel's various types of irresponsibility, focusing in passing on John Jarndyce and then specifically on Esther. Esther discovers that neither Ada nor Richard knows much about their Uncle John: Ada recalls her mother's words expressly commending his "noble generosity" (p. 43); Richard has seen him some five years earlier but remembers him only as a "bluff, rosy fellow" (p. 43). Both have received, in Ada's words, a "plain, honest letter" from him proposing to become their guardian and hoping that in time the arrangement might "heal some of the wounds made by the miserable Chancery suit" (p. 43). The wise, compassionate guardianship Jarndyce represents—particularly insofar as his actions serve as a foil for those of the Lord Chancellor, Sir Leicester, Miss Barbary, and Mrs. Jellyby (and many others in roles analogous to theirs)—is crucial to Dickens's own brotherhood or family theme; but it is the orphaned Esther who, without any of Jarndyce's particular promptings to set right a specific evil, instinctively recognizes and acts upon those familial claims for assistance that come her way, and it is with her selflessly extending her affection in a characteristically small number of words followed by an inversely large set of actions that the first installment of the novel ends.[4]

In the closing scene, Esther offers succor to the principal child-victim of the Jellyby regime—Caddy, Mrs. Jellyby's eldest daughter and her full-time amanuensis: "From her tumbled hair to her pretty feet, which were disfigured with frayed and broken satin slippers trodden down at the heel, she really seemed to have no article of dress upon her, from a pin upwards, that was in its proper condition or its right place" (p. 38). The key word in this description is *disfigured*. Indeed, when she shows up at Esther's door, Caddy is not only dishevelled but covered with ink, for her only occupation from daylight to dark is to write about Africa to her mother's dictation. The abuse of Caddy is similar to that of the child Esther by Miss Barbary in that, like Esther, Caddy is fed and clothed but is denied the more important child's right—a chance to develop an independent personality; each is forced to assume that specific identity required by the particular needs of a proud parent or guardian.

The pitifully desperate Caddy whom Esther comforts in the final scene is understandably bored with Africa and in despair that she possesses none of the education normally given to young ladies her age: in language charged with feeling, she bemoans the fact that she cannot dance, play music, sing, talk French, or "do geography, and globes, and needlework, and everything" (p. 44). In her frustration, she blurts out: "I wish Africa was dead" (p. 43) and later, "I wish I was dead. . . . I wish we were all dead. It would be a great deal better for us" (p. 44). Esther's gentle but firm responses calm her, and kneeling beside Esther with her face buried in her lap, Caddy finally falls asleep. With Esther's reflections as she herself drifts to sleep, Dickens suggests the ideal response to the needs of our brothers and sisters in the general human family, each of whom is endeavoring to establish a meaningful life in the social community; Esther's thoughts define a wholly unselfish dedication to helping anyone who needs her, and they show her expressing, subconsciously, the willingness to extend such assistance even at the cost of submerging her own needs and selfhood: "I began to lose the identity of the sleeper resting on me. Now it was Ada; now, one of my old Reading friends. . . . Now, it was the little mad woman worn out with curtseying and smiling; now, some one in authority at Bleak House. Lastly, it was no one, and I was no one" (p. 45).

Bleak House passionately, often stridently, urges the recognition of the brotherhood of humanity and extension of a genuine charity, like that appropriate to family members, as the basis of all human relationships. For a society to be healthy, Dickens argues, its families must be healthy, and its traditional institutions must mirror in fulfilling their responsibilities the loving fellowship that bonds a caring family. But most families in this novel are unhealthy; so also are those institutions charged with protecting society's least powerful members. The first installment exposes four major social institutions that fail in their role as wise parents or guardians. These institutions remain the focus of Dickens's thematic concerns, and, in this sense, the entire novel may be said to exist in miniature in the first installment. Such a conclusion applies equally well to matters of artistry, with repeated image patterns, analogy to the "family," and abuse of language constituting the dominant techniques in the opening installment and throughout.

John J. Fenstermaker

1. The most comprehensive analysis of chapter 1 and its relationship to the rest of the novel is that of Richard D. Altick, *"Bleak House*: The Reach of Chapter One," *Dickens Studies Annual* 8 (1980): 73-102.

2. *Bleak House*, ed. George Ford and Sylvère Monod (New York, 1977), p. 8. All quotations are from this edition; subsequent page references will be given in the text.

3. For an excellent discussion of the various kinds of responsibility, particularly legal and parental, that constitute the theme of *Bleak House*, see Robert A. Donovan, "Structure and Idea in *Bleak House*," *ELH* 29 (1962): 177-86 and, specifically for the centrality of family relationships, Trevor Blount, "The Documentary Symbolism of Chancery in *Bleak House*," *Dickensian* 62 (1966): 48.

4. We must remember that Esther narrates the events in both chapter 3 and chapter 4. She speaks less than other characters in the action of these chapters and provides most of her aid through kind deeds; yet in her concerted effort to tell the reader all that she observes and thinks and in the conversations she does have with others, we see how language should be used and we see that when used honestly, it produces influences that can never harm.

XII

JAMES R. KINCAID

"All the Wickedness in the World Is Print": Dickens and Subversive Interpretation

THE MATTER OF THIS ESSAY—THE UNSTABLE AND SHIFTING nature of a Dickens novel and of our response to it—developed as the result of a considerable instability of my own, namely, a most ludicrous confusion as to whether the subject to be addressed by a panel of which I had agreed to be a part was "Dickens in THIS Time" or "Dickens in HIS Time." I thought it was the former; it turned out to be the latter, a historical topic presenting itself to my competence about equally with particle physics and alchemy. Panic can, it seems, spur a sort of ingenuity, a puzzling over whether the HIS or the THIS made all that much difference, all of which leads naturally enough to a consideration of the relationship between a recovered context for interpretation—biographical, historical, sociological—and interpretations which ignore that context, which, in fact, flaunt it, running counter to stated authorial intentions, what might be taken as Victorian predilections, or even common sense. What about subversive readings, those antagonistic to, or ignorant of, history?[1]

During the long heyday of formalism and structuralism, historical-cultural-sociological critics often had a pretty bad time of it. Pushed into a corner by the New Critics, they had to spend a great deal of time justifying their enterprise or at least being defensive and snippy. Formalists gave an absolute authority to *the text*, that solid and objectified thing that could settle all issues by itself and that rendered superfluous or inauthentic any references (apart from linguistic ones) outside its boundaries. For formalists, historical criticism could proceed only from a rather pathetic naiveté.

Pride goeth before a fall. Formalism rested, it now appears, on a base so insubstantial that it can hardly be called theoretical at all. The loud and smug assertions about "the text" and its self-sufficiency sprang from notions about language and reading that now seem preposterous. How could we ever have imagined that language could be so securely stabilized, that we could, say, hold a Dickens novel still by talking about those unifying symbols—the railroad, prison, river—or thematic oppositions—firmness versus wetness, childishness versus the disciplined heart, and so forth? Various strategies employed in the fifties and sixties for showing how Dickens was not a writer of loose, baggy monsters but of coherent, unified novels were, after all, part of a general campaign to rescue him and make him a respectable subject for academic study. The resulting interpretations now appear not wrong but partial, naive not in terms of the sophistication or ingenuity displayed but in their total unawareness of their own partial nature, their necessarily provisional character.

Many forms of deconstructive and reader-response criticism have, then, perhaps ironically, restored historical criticism to a kind of avant-garde respectability. A return to investigations of the Dickens World is probably unlikely, but at least we can now say that historical contexts for interpretation are no more inauthentic than any other. Susan R. Horton's fine book, *Interpreting Interpreting*, provides a full-scale demonstration of the relatively identical adequacy—or inadequacy, depending on how one looks at it—of interpretations based on a variety of contexts, from the biographical and historical through the semiotic.[2] One would suppose that all we would have to do to arrive at a valid interpretation is to lay out carefully all the contexts and then combine them. But not so. It is impossible, for one thing, since each context is itself an interpretation and subject to all the pitfalls of that slippery enterprise. Furthermore, even in the unlikely event that we could all agree on what a detail in the text means, different contexts will cause different details to appear to have meaning. Thus, any attempt to put all contexts together would result in a cacophony, not a harmony. There is no way to force a text to stand still, to take account of everything, since we do not know what "everything" is. Dickens presents further difficulties, as Horton points out, in that we can never be certain exactly what mode or genre he is working in at any given point and, consequently, what framework of expectations might be appropriate. The presumed facts of the text are, thus, themselves elusive and unstable, much more so the connections we make between these facts in order to form readings or interpretations.

Let's take one example: an historical fact and a passage from a novel. The passage first: from *Barnaby Rudge*, old John Willet talking to his son Joe about how to spend his money and time in London: "The other sixpence is to spend in the diversions of London; and the diversion I recommend is to go to the top of the Monument, and sitting there. There's no temptations there, sir—no drink—no young women—no bad characters of any sort—nothing but imagination. That's the way I enjoyed myself when I was your age, sir."[3] Now the historical fact: just around the time that the novel was appearing in weekly installments in *Master Humphrey's Clock* there was a rash of suicidal leaps from the Monument—successful ones too, causing some public stir and the erection of a fence-like barricade to discourage melancholy-mad climbers.[4] What connections can we draw with certainty between the text and the fact? Is John Willet suggesting directly that his son plunge to a mangled death—or perhaps expressing an unconscious wish that such might occur? Possibly. Is Dickens merely hinting here at the ominous consequences of oppression and neglect, warning quietly of the fierce outbreak of repressed forces that erupts in both public and private arenas in the second half of the novel? Possibly. Is this merely a comic embellishment, playing on John Willet's wild sense of language and his eccentric notion of the pleasures of the imagination: a squiggle on the edge of the page noticed by Orwell and most recently by Robert Garis?[5] Possibly.

One could go on and on. The problem facing us in making

connections is that neither fact nor text remains steady before our gaze. What complex of associations would a Victorian reader at that period bring to bear on the word "Monument"— if any at all? How prominent would the suicides be and how relevant to the context in which the scene occurs in the novel? Would readers halt at all on the word, make it "mean"? History, it turns out, is itself a very complex text. We all know how complex novels are. In the passage quoted, we may read in it a reflection of the tyranny-leading-to-rebellion motif evident in the main plot—or we may not. After all, isn't murder-suicide rather a strong set of terms to associate with the Willet family and the Maypole plot? It requires taking the comedy pretty solemnly. Of course it is true that, later in the novel, things do turn solemn: Willet is manhandled and becomes a pathetic idiot as a result, and his son loses an arm in the glorious service of his country. But how does that all fit? Old Willet becomes a victim, not a victimizer; and he has never had any connection to the riots—other than denying that they are going on. Using a framework different from the oppression-revolt one, we could switch, say, to the word "imagination"—there's nothing on top of the Monument, Willet says, but imagination—and its connection with sui- cide-danger; or, perhaps, to a complex anti-Romantic gesture, in which climbing the Monument to sit vacantly and exercise the imagination parodies Romantic epiphanies—as with the ascent of Mount Snowdon and so forth. The possibilities, as we all know, are endless. And all this is not to deny the interest to be found in historical contexts for criticism. It is merely to assert that they are, as Horton says, bound to yield results just as problematic and incomplete as any other.

In reference to the more specific issue of subversive or ironic readings of these novels, readings that might be accused of being historically blind, violations of Dickens's intentions, the attitudes of his audience, or the general intellectual atmosphere of the times, *Martin Chuzzlewit* offers a rich storehouse of opportunities. To start with, Dickens said that the novel was about selfishness. Let us say, further, that there is every indication that his contemporaries took him at his word and seem to have read the novel in the moral and didactic terms provided for them. There is no question about the availability or, in its way, the validity of such a reading, then or now. One might say that there is presumptive evidence against the full satisfaction such a reading could provide: who would read—at least now—a novel whose organizing principle and dominating theme were so trite? Who wants to be shown the dominance of self-interest and its bad effects? But such carping begs the question and is dangerously close to claiming that some things are *in* the text and others are not. All interpretive models can find ways of fulfilling themselves. The question is not which one is more accurate but which ones come more closely to touching the most complex, unresolved, and mysterious parts of our response while we read the book.

As an example of a subversive reading, I will repeat a little of what I have already written on the novel,[6] a process that seems to me safe enough, since, so far as I know, not a single reader has been influenced, much less persuaded, by the argument. Briefly, it is this: if one adds to the selfish-selfless opposition a couple of others suggested throughout (or findable throughout) especially in the American scenes—nature versus artifice, restraint versus brutality, manners versus crudity, style versus barbarism—complications ensue rapidly. The oppositions do not cohere. Are the enemies in the American scenes of the same order as those in England? In one sense, yes. Both Colonel Scadder and Seth Pecksniff are undeniably selfish. But what of the disgust expressed at American eating habits, manner of dressing, vulgar speech, invasion of privacy? Isn't the problem, perhaps, that America allows human nature its fullest expression? "Some institutions develop human nature; others re—tard it" (16),[7] says one patriotic citizen. Perhaps he is right. The narrator expresses scorn for those shallow philosophers who so blandly appeal to "human nature," warning them that they may, in fact, be rousing a beast (13). What exactly do we take "Eden" to suggest? Perhaps the deadly swamp of the primeval natural? If so, do we not see an alternative in British restraint, British artfulness, even British artificiality—even British hypocrisy? Are we not expected to applaud the wholly anti-American

James R. Kincaid

Young Bailey and his constant "defiance of all natural laws" (26), not only as he skips happily on Todgers's menacing roof but as he convinces the barber Poll Sweedlepipe that he badly needs a shave, thus routing all "evidence of sight and touch" (26)? Isn't the wonderful defeat of nature managed by Bailey connected to the linguistic triumphs of Sairey Gamp and Mr. Pecksniff, the triumph of artificiality and the unnatural, selfish or not? Isn't it, as Mr. Pecksniff says of his architectural practices, really the "finishing touches" (6), not the raw designs that matter? Isn't it, finally, Mrs. Gamp who has the last word: "Ah, what a wale of grief," she says, "possessing herself of the bottle and glass"? She, with her daffy allusions to Bunyan and the more depressing parts of the Bible, provides a splendid parody of moralistic solemnity, moralistic depression, and moralistic interpretation, a parody in which she is joined by very artful and accomplished (if selfish) company. The force of this anarchic parody completely subverts the moralistic center provided by the theme of selfishness and suggests not righteous reconciliation but joyous carnival.

Or does it? Of course not; at least, to return to our presumptive evidence, one would suspect not, since no one seems to have responded to the novel in this way but me. Still, the reading, I assert, has the same validity as one more historically and biographically responsive. But that validity is really much of the same, limited kind. Turning the tables, changing Pecksniff from a villain into a kind of hero, is great fun; but it still works with the same furniture and simply redecorates the traditional reading. Many of the same assumptions are used, the most basic being that the work is controlled by thematic oppositions. One may, of course, complicate or reverse the connections between these oppositions, even with some undoubted usefulness, but one is still forced to hold certain points in the text steady, to make some things mean and others not, to maintain the fiction that an opposition at one point is the same as an opposition at another. One finds oneself blinking at glaring contradicitions in order to smooth out what is ruffled, mend together what is broken. For example, I have just said that Bailey's triumph over nature is

263

complete, as evidenced in his convincing Poll that his totally smooth face was, in fact, bewhiskered. That is what seems to be the effect of the fine comic scene in chapter 26. But in chapter 49, when Poll laments what he thinks is Bailey's death, he says that the shavings were a fully-conscious game, "only for fun," and that Bailey will never live to be shaved "in earnest." I do not believe that the latter statement can be said to take precedence over the former, but neither can one ignore it. At one point we are told that Poll is taken in; at another that he is not. Such contradictions present a considerable difficulty for thematic criticism, a difficulty which is too often overcome by ignoring the contradiction.[8]

If the counterreading offered is really not all that subversive but merely a reshuffling of the same thematic counters, perhaps a climb to the top (or bottom) of Horton's interpretive ladder and a view from the semiotic context will yield more unsettling results. Like the view from Todgers's, however, this one is dizzying: objects are not so much there by themselves as presented as "seeming" or "appearing," and their tendency to "thicken" and "expand" is likely to affect us as it does M. Todgers's lodger, making us "quite scared" (9) and anxious to rush back inside and descend the steps. Even the first few paragraphs that open the narrative proper (2) present us with a frightening excess. Take the following: the sun struggles to "look" through clouds, finally succeeds and illuminates the landscape of a rural Wiltshire village with a "glory" likened to "a sudden flash of memory or spirit" in the mind of an old man. The glory is momentary, however, and it is succeeded by the absence of light, the silencing of the birds, and the transformation of the shining church into a place that is "cold and dark." Are these details emblematic or symbolic, or just there? If they are symbolic, of what: the sun as source of meaning, God, the possibility of understanding—hinted at and then withdrawn? The more basic question is whether these details *mean* at all. Even within the first three paragraphs, from which these words are arbitrarily selected, there are a wealth of other details that might or might not be connected, might or might not be given significance or prominence. The scene between Pecksniff and his daughters that follows the descriptive opening might be seen as something like a parody of our single-minded interpretive efforts. In Pecksniff's great and comprehensive moral scheme, there is nothing without significance: "And eggs . . . even they have their moral," a dizzying possibility repeated later by Carroll's Duchess: "Everything's got a moral, if only you can find it."[9] As always, the Duchess is madly sane: everything in the novel can be invested with meaning or meanings, and it is not so hard to find them. But everything having meanings with connections among them is much the same as having no meaning at all.

Beating a fast retreat from such chaos, we may have a go at a narrower, admittedly provisional portion of the semiotic view, confining ourselves to direct signals emanating from the novel having to do with the possibility of valid or even partial interpretation, the nature of that process, and how all that will accord with our understanding of the novel as a whole— if, that is, we can ever really have an understanding of the novel as a whole.

Such an approach seems to be precisely the one Dickens takes pains at the start to waylay. Even his "Preface" opens with a heavily sarcastic commentary on those who accuse him of "exaggeration." Granting that "what is exaggeration to one class of minds and perceptions, is plain truth to another," he goes on to suggest that those who speak of exaggeration are those "whose eye for colour is a little dull." Worse, he says that those who are exactly represented from life in his fiction are the very ones who protest against the unnaturalness of the image. The suggestion here is the unencouraging one that the "class of minds and perceptions" able to see the truth he is representing is limited indeed—perhaps limited only to the author himself. Further, his anger is directed at his readers' ineducability, and he is clearly frustrated at being unable to train or form them. His "implied reader," in other words, is only implied, never realized. The first chapter continues the sneering assault on "just interpretation," on the "ingenious labour on the part of a commentator." He would seem to be writing a novel that declares itself in advance impervious to interpretation, blocking all attempts except those made by the idiotic.

And yet—with Dickens there is always an "and yet"—the narrator sometimes gives us clear, insistent signals on how to read, signals even the dullards he so detests could hardly miss. We are told, for instance, after much ironic indirection, that Mr. Pecksniff's true "genius lay in ensnaring parents and guardians, and pocketing premiums" (2). Similarly, the defect of Young Martin's character is pronounced bluntly as "selfishness" (21), and the origins of that blemish are just as bluntly laid forth (33). Sometimes, indeed, the insistence on the one right reading is pitched at shrillness: "And if ever plain truth were spoken on this occasionally false earth, Tom's sister spoke it when she said that" (9). But things are by no means always so clear, partly because the ironic mode often used takes some risks with the perspicacity of readers and allows for some openness.[10] The narrator is at one point so impatient with that openness that he adds an indignant footnote: "The most credulous reader"—that fool, and he is apparently legion, about whom Dickens is so worried—"will scarcely believe that Mr. Pecksniff's reasoning was once set upon as the Author's!!" (20). But, short of destroying the ironic effect by peppering the work with footnotes of this sort, the narrator must take his chances. Not only that, but the ironic forms used often take a peculiarly devious route, one that says, "Don't believe that; believe this." What we are told not to believe is false, but so is what we presumably are to believe, which leaves open the issue of truth: the truth lies in neither of the two formulations presented but in some mixture of their unstated opposites. Here is an example: "It must not be inferred from this position of humility, that the youngest Miss Pecksniff was so young as to be, as one may say, forced to sit upon a stool, by reason of the shortness of her legs. Miss Pecksniff sat upon a stool because of her simplicity and innocence, which were very great, very great" (2). It would, however, be misleading to suggest that the narrator strains to make words mean what he intends for them to mean and fails. Often, indeed, the narrator makes a point of his limited knowledge: of Mark Tapley's sense of the very cold comfort available in partings, the narrator says, "Perhaps he knew it from his reading, perhaps from his experience, perhaps from intuition. It is impossible to say" (14). Obvious attempts to restrict and control are evident now and then, but they are there so seldom as to act, perhaps, when they come as reminders of the impossibility of such control. The characters, at any rate, are constantly subverting the notion that language can be kept under such reins. Sairey Gamp's nitroglycerin talk allows the reader a boundless playground in which to swing and glide. "Gamp is my name, and Gamp my nater," she announces with authority and full confidence in her communicating ability, anticipating Humpty Dumpty's daffy assurance to Alice that proper names, like any other words, must carry definite meaning.[11] So much for directed reading!

We might, in fact, be tempted to run off in the other direction, deciding that the book is a dramatization of its own indecipherability. Certainly there is a vast territory for exploration here. A concordance would, I feel sure, demonstrate the unusual frequency with which words and phrases of uncertainty or imprecision are used: things often "seem" or "appear" to be; qualifiers like "maybe," "as it were," or "in effect" are employed to call attention to the oblique or approximate relationship between signifier and signified. More elaborate phrases suggest the difficult and uncertain nature of communication between two parties: "rather gave them to understand" is one of the most intriguing. Whether what is understood is what is given *for* understanding is unclear, qualified as the connection is by the foggy term "rather." Interpretation becomes sometimes a desperate effort of will, signaled by the phrase, "I look upon you as. ... " Lacking any effective medium for interpretation, one simply asserts a meaning and an interpretation, a way of looking that is sustained only by the declaration and that, again, invites comparison with Humpty Dumpty's wonderfully mad means of investing words with whatever meaning he chooses.[12]

Interestingly, the most potent and stable mode of communication, both for the narrator and for the characters, seems to be through irony, a surprising fact, since even such a resolute stabilizer as Wayne Booth is willing to recognize how slippery a medium it is.[13] Still, in the noncommunicating community of *Martin Chuzzlewit* ironists like Young Bailey are, comparatively, lucid: "I say . . . young ladies, there's soup to-morrow. She's a-making it now. An't she a-putting in the water? Oh! not at all neither!" (9). Indirection is, in a skewed world, as good as one can do.

One notices characters and especially the narrator attempting to adjust to the fog and the cockeyed obliquity by consistently describing one thing in terms of another. The effect is not one of metaphoric exuberance but of a kind of forlorn hopelessness. Pointing to the fact that language does not provide a straight route to fact or truth, the recurrence of "as if" and "as though" clauses indicates a waving toward other possible routes, as if an inexperienced driver, even on bad roads, might possibly be more likely to find his destination if given a variety of directions. The logic and the psychology are so weak here that they call attention to their own insufficiency, the lack of confidence in language, the only medium available. When the narrator does try to muster up some confidence in language, he does so, even then, in a mock-simile, a pointed refusal to go outside the subject that is being explained: Tom Pinch, he says, "was as happy as only Tom Pinch could be. There is no other simile that will express his state of mind" (12). Perhaps no other simile would do the job, but why, then, use a simile at all and then comment on it? The effect is to reinforce the notion that the approximation of simile is inescapable, even with so direct and forthright a character as Tom. The formal device overrides the character. It is not that the device gets us closer to Tom Pinch, just the reverse: Tom Pinch becomes a morsel of grammar, a poetic feature, a simile. Just as this habit of expressing things in simile distances characters and actions from the language describing them, so it distances us from any feeling that language will allow us direct access to truth.

There are repeated references to the uselessness of words, the inefficacy of language.[14] The main room at the Blue Dragon, for instance, not only is sunken, "all down-hill from the door," but is connected to the entrance by "a descent of two steps on the inside so exquisitely unexpected, that strangers, *despite the most elaborate cautioning,* usually dived in head first, as into a plunging-bath" (3; emphasis added). Parliamentary language is described as the art of being able "to use as many words as possible, and express nothing whatever" (43). It is not only Parliamentarians who possess this talent, however, for language has a way of tripping up even its most conscientious users. Plain speaking, as it turns out, is the least effective mode of address, the surest route to misunderstanding, as Tom Pinch discovers when he tries to rely on "the true and plain intention which my words professed" in speaking to Mercy Pecksniff (37). The connections between words and intentions, language and referent are so very unsteady that one is tempted to take refuge in Montague Tigg's happy cynicism: "Life's a riddle: a most infernally hard riddle to guess, Mr. Pecksniff. My own opinion is, that like that celebrated conundrum, 'Why's a man in jail like a man out of jail?' there's no answer to it. Upon my soul and body, it's the queerest sort of thing altogether—but there's not use in talking about it. Ha! ha!" (4). There is, for Tigg, no answer to be found—certainly not in or through language.

Given this fact, the narrator and characters often turn to an interpretive process that is more subtle, reading not words but gestures, glances, or "looks." Mercy Pecksniff gives Tom Pinch "a speaking look, and Tom knew what it said" (46). Mr. Moddle has eyes that speak "without the aid of language" (46). Jonas Chuzzlewit sits, "reading how he looked in Mr. Pecksniff's eyes" (18). Not only eyes speak, of course: Bailey's excessive ironic negatives, the narrator says, make his language "somewhat obscure," but his pantomime of lovers walking to a church exchanging affectionate glances manages to make his meaning clear (11). Tom Pinch makes a motion with his hand, "and all his little history was written in the action" (50). The coach-driver Bill Simmons has his looks contradict his words (13), and the physician Mr. Jobling is so skilled at shaking his head, rubbing his hands, smacking his lips, and uttering sounds like "Ah" that his patients can construct out of all this a coherent sentence: "I know what you're going to say better than you do; but go on, go on" (27).

Jonas Chuzzlewit, at one point unable to "make up his mind ... whether to call Tom Pinch his dear friend or a villain," settles the matter by shaking "his fist at him *pro tem*" (24). It may seem to be a world of mimes, with great acting troupes like Mr. Mould's company and its "performance of funerals" (19) at the center—or perhaps the Anglo-Bengalee Disinterested Loan and Life Assurance Company, which runs on the marvelous power of the Footman, who, "relying solely on his figure," exerts a potent "charm" with his very waistcoat, an emblem of the company's respectability and solidity (27).

Is it really possible, though, to devise a semiotic system more reliable than language? Even the narrator is sometimes baffled by the mime code, admitting that a nudge of an elbow from Pecksniff "Might either be construed into an indignant remonstrance or a cordial assent" (24). Worse still, characters like Chuffey give off no meaning; they are "the embodiment of nothing" (11). Some characters, vicious and virtuous alike, are able to make themselves illegible: Pecksniff at one point is "determined that the old man should read nothing" in his face (11), and Mark Tapley can manufacture a countenance that would make it impossible "for the most skilled physiognomist to determine what he was thinking about, or whether he was thinking at all" (43). Sairey Gamp's true meaning is even more difficult to determine because of her artistic versatility, her ability to produce "a face for all occasions" (19).

This last artistry raises a more fundamental issue, one that assails our basic assumption: that people and actions *should* be intelligible, that we should have access to some solidity and truth. As always in Dickens, the drive toward that which is ascertainable and accountable is countered by a feeling of artistic free play, a parody of truth-telling and truth-seeking. Interpretive accuracy is both sought for and laughed at. The dull and moralistic honest types are balanced by artists, artists who are often indistinguishable from liars. The views toward language and interpretation vary considerably between the two camps. Mrs. Gamp and Montague Tigg weave not just competing linguistic systems but competing worlds out of words. The great art-for-art's-sake character is Seth Pecksniff, whose speech is always, as the narrator says, "ornamental." It is Pecksniff who wonderfully inverts the Duchess's advice to Alice, rendering the proverb, "Take care of the sounds, and the sense will take care of itself."[15] He speaks always as if he were decorating tombstones: "And Thomas Pinch and I . . . will walk [the world] yet, in mutual faithfulness and friendship! And if it comes to pass that either of us be run over, in any of those busy crossings which divide the streets of life, the other will convey him to the hospital in Hope, and sit beside his bed in Bounty!" (5). It may be that his sentences communicate little matter, but whose do so in this novel? Besides, Pecksniff has the remarkable ability to make something out of nothing, turning tedium into "comfort":

> "A gentleman taken ill upon the road, has been so very bad upstairs, sir," said the tearful hostess.
> "A gentleman taken ill upon the road, has been so very bad upstairs, has he?" repeated Mr. Pecksniff. "Well, well!" (3)

"Anybody," the narrator continues, "would have been, as Mrs. Lupin was, comforted by the mere voice and presence of such a man."

Most characters, it is true, are engaged in the more mundane business of searching for truth and valid interpretation. It is all very well for Mrs. Gamp to insist confidently that some things "is plain enough to them as needn't look through millstones" (46), but how do we know exactly which things are plain? How do we do our own detective work in a world in which even normal associative processes have gone haywire: "Why are they merrymaking here, if there's no one dead?" (46)? Even proverbial wisdom, that bedrock of received certainty, is mocked: the "infallibility" of "early to bed, early to rise . . . " "has been for generations verified by the enormous fortunes amassed by chimney-sweepers" (5).

Language, then, is unreliable—sometimes; gestures and appearances are slightly less so—sometimes. The question is raised as to whether or not we truly desire reliability, and the answer is yes and no. Where do we go from here? One might be tempted to retreat down the interpretive ladder and reach for some thematic naturalization of all these contradictions. Surely an inviting possibility beckons in the division between the English and American scenes. Such splits are always susceptible either to thematic joining or thematic contrast, joining if one looks to the selfish-selfless theme, contrasted in the nature-art theme. From our semiotic standpoint, however, the New World, despite its smug sense of superiority—"They corrupt even the language in the old country. . . . Where was you rose?" (22)—looks very much like the Old, heightened some, certainly, but giving us no better clues as to interpretation. Language moves from a plain speech that is wildly rootless and always close to violence—eagles' talons, gore, bowie knives, gougings—to an insane sense of manipulation: Hannibal Chollop's feeling that Eden is not a swamp at all compared to English landscape (33)—to the floating language of the transcendental ladies: "Mind and matter . . . glide swift into the vortex of immensity. Howls the sublime . . . " (34).[16] At no point on the scale is language trustworthy or necessarily indicative of much of anything. Americans take refuge in pantomime nearly as much as the British, and sometimes the results are helpful: La Fayette Kettle has written on his eyes, "Now you won't overreach me: you want to, but you won't" (21), and the signals given off by American eating and spitting habits are clear enough. But much of the miming is mixed with cunning and is, thus, finally as unreliable as the language: Colonel Diver has "a singular expression" hovering in the neighborhood of his eyes, an expression "which was not a frown, nor a leer, and yet might have been mistaken at first glance for either" (16).

We might try to evade this impasse by throwing everything into some moralistic bundle, arguing, say, that there is a false language and a false appearance used to deceive the Virtuous, who are said to be commonly "incredulous and blind" (15). After all, both Pecksniff and Tigg, in relying on the "ornamental," prey on the unwarily upright, as, presumably, does Mrs. Gamp, and by much the same means. But we soon find ourselves in another trap. The idea of false and deceiving language implies the existence of a true and comprehensible one, and where in this novel are we to find that article? Plain speaking, as we have observed, is likely to be dangerous and generally incomprehensible. Further, if Virtue is blind, so are the Vicious. Jonas, much more a true villain than those listed above, has about him a cunning which, the narrator says, is absolutely transparent. Imagining that he is in hiding, he displays everything (28).

The search for coherence and a unifying principle is not usually given up so easily. One could, for instance, abandon language altogether and argue that virtue resided in silence, in privacy, citing such things as the distaste expressed at the New York newspapers—The New York Sewer, The New York Peeper, The New York Keyhole Reporter (16)—and their unwarranted, undignified search for private truths. There is also the curious figure of Nadgett, a man whose absolute privacy, his ability "to be a secret," makes all things come right in the end. We are obviously no better off here. Nadgett is more than a little mad, writing letters to himself and then burning them, and he suggests rather a bleak view of existence: no one will understand anyhow, so keep it to yourself. But waive that. The problem is that he makes all come right by, albeit reluctantly, not keeping things to himself but revealing them. It is, after all, a detective-story plot, and we, as much as The Keyhole Reporter, need to *know*.

We need to know but never can—fully—because we are never certain of *how* to know. The novel seems like the raging Atlantic Ocean, "constancy in nothing" (15) or like Tigg's dream, which features a "dreadful secret," "a secret which he knew and yet did not know" (42). Perhaps we, like visitors to the Blue Dragon, have no choice but to dive into the novel as into a plunging bath and to wallow around. Or perhaps we would be wiser to take our cue from Mr. Pecksniff, who has "scribbled" some but refrained from publishing it. But neither blank silence nor total uncertainty can satisfy what the novel itself demands: a participation in its own exploration of the means by which we understand, delude ourselves and others, attempt to reveal and to conceal.

The novel does not resist the application of interpretive models; it is openly hospitable, inviting one and all. The problem is, in the main, this openness, since no one model can yield results that account for everything and since each yields results that are often contradictory of others. We find what our model causes and allows us to find—within limits, perhaps, but with Dickens those limits are very broad indeed. As Sairey Gamp says of Young Bailey, "All the wickedness in the world is Print to him" (26). Those with piety uppermost will find that estimable quality reflected in print. Others, like Young Bailey and subversive critics, will be equally gratified.

1. Ignorance is, I will admit, not ordinarily taken as a subject for sustained inquiry in literary criticism, but I have developed a habit, a kind of career, out of exposing my ignorance to Richard Altick for profit; so it seems appropriate to do so in a volume honoring him and his work.

2. Susan R. Horton, *Interpreting Interpreting: Interpreting Dickens's "Dombey"* (Baltimore, 1979). The eight-runged interpretive ladder is presented on pp. 69-71.

3. The quotation from *Barnaby Rudge* is from The Oxford Illustrated Dickens (London, 1954), ch. 13.

4. This "fact" is doubly useful under the present circumstances since, like virtually every fact I ever have been able to display, it was dished to me by Richard Altick. I did not find it on my own, nor, to compound the confession, was I able to verify it with the certainty and clarity an historical scholar would require. I rely, then, with absolute trust on his work, not my own. Should he have nodded in this case—almost an impossibility—rendering the fact into a fiction, it really doesn't matter for our purposes. We can simply construe a larger fiction in which the smaller fiction about suicides becomes a fact.

5. George Orwell, *Dickens, Dali and Others* (New York, 1946), p. 61; Robert Garis, *The Dickens Theatre* (London, 1965).

6. *Dickens and the Rhetoric of Laughter* (Oxford, 1971). pp. 132-61.

7. All quotations from *Martin Chuzzlewit*, hereafter cited in the text by chapter number, are from The Oxford Illustrated Dickens (London, 1951).

8. This is not the only problem lying in wait for those out to create thematic coherence. Is or is not Mrs. Gamp aware of the fictional nature of Mrs. Harris? For the greater part of the novel, she may seem to regard her friend as real or perhaps to dwell in the fictional world containing Mrs. Harris, a world that is more real to her than any other. But in chapter 51, when it suits his purposes to do so, Dickens makes her quite unequivocally aware of the fraud. In the same way, much is made by Dickens—and by critics—of the mysterious location of Todgers's, its mythic nature, and the fact that its whereabouts are known and entrance available only to the initiated. Even postmen wander hopelessly in the surrounding labyrinth, and strangers have no chance. Yet in chapter 10, Old Martin, who would hardly seem to possess the qualities of the initiates, walks straight to the door. How?

9. Lewis Carroll, *Alice's Adventures in Wonderland*, ed. Donald J. Gray (New York, 1971), 9.

10. Irony is not dominant, of course; one of the problems is that we cannot locate a consistent or a dominant mode.

11. Lewis Carroll, *Through the Looking-Glass*, ed. Donald J. Gray (New York, 1971), ch. 6.

12. "When I use a word . . . it means just what I choose it to mean— neither more nor less" (*Looking-Glass*, ch. 6).

13. Wayne C. Booth, *A Rhetoric of Irony* (Chicago, 1974).

14. As always with this novel, there is no flat statement that cannot be successfully contradicted. At one point the word "home" is said not only to have meaning but to have magical meaning: "And though home is a name, a word, it is a strong one; stronger than magician ever spoke, or spirit answered to, in strongest conjuration" (35).

15. See Carroll, *Alice's Adventures in Wonderland*, ch. 9.

16. Again one is reminded of Carroll, of the White Queen pointing to a hill and remarking to Alice, "I could show you hills, in comparison with which you'd call that a valley" (Carroll, *Looking-Glass*, ch. 2).

XIII

ARTHUR A. ADRIAN

"Why was I ever a father!"
Charles Dickens as Father

"I CAN'T GET MY HAT ON IN CONSEQUENCE OF THE EXTENT TO which my hair stands on end at the costs and charges of these boys. Why was I ever a father!" Dickens's letter to George Dolby, 25 September 1868 (Berg Collection, New York Public Library).

Of all the social injustices Dickens attacked throughout his career, none so evoked his fierce indignation as parental neglect and abuse of children. No subject so dominated his emotions, his thoughts, his utterances—epistolary, journalistic, literary. Always nourished by the conviction that he himself had been a "not-particularly-taken-care-of boy,"[1] as he described his juvenile self to Washington Irving in 1841, he lashed out against the parental selfishness and outright brutality he had observed in British homes. In view of his sustained indictment of delinquent parents, it is interesting to see how Dickens himself met the responsibilities of fatherhood as he brought up his large family.

Determined to spare his children the heartaches he had experienced as a boy, he organized his home along principles that set it apart from the typically austere Victorian household. It was during their early years that he had his closest rapport with them, for he found babies irresistible. And they, even when strangers, seemed to sense his deep affection. "I

276

have often seen mere babies," his daughter Mary (Mamie) has told us, "who would look at no other stranger present, put out their tiny arms to him with unbounded confidence, or place a small hand in his and trot away with him, quite proud and contented at having found such a companion." She adds that his manner with his own children, though somewhat sterner, did not inhibit them from going to him with their problems, however trivial, and that "in him they could always find unvarying justice and love."[2] During his briefest absences from home, he missed them. "I kiss almost all the children I encounter," he told his wife, "in remembrance of their sweet faces, and talk to all the mothers who carry them."[3]

In talking to his children, Dickens used a peculiar tone of voice for each one. Even when not called by name, each knew exactly who was being addressed.[4] And in a characteristically playful mood, their father gave each of them a distinguishing nickname. Charles (Charley), the oldest, was "Floster Floby," a corruption of "Master Toby." Because of her gentle nature, Mamie was called "Mild Glo' ster." For Katey, a great favorite, "Lucifer Box" was generally descriptive because of her occasional bursts of fieriness. For Walter it was "Young Skull" because of his high cheekbones. Francis Jeffrey responded to "Chicken Stalker"; Sydney, fascinated even in infancy by the sea, was dubbed the "Ocean Spectre," sometimes shortened to "Hoshen Peck." Alfred Tennyson had two nicknames: "Sampson Brass" and "Skittles," from "something skittle-playing and public-housey in his countenance," explained Dickens. Henry Fielding, who was to prove the most dependable of the sons, was variously known as "The Jolly Postboy" and "The Comic Countryman." For Edward, the youngest, was reserved the longest combination of syllables: "Plornishmaroontigoonter," shortened to "Plorn." Each of these names, Dickens told his brother-in-law, was pronounced with "a peculiar howl, which I shall have great pleasure in illustrating."[5]

The key to winning his children's confidence was Dickens's ability to be a child among them. His love of surprise, his dramatic rendering of comic songs, and his enjoyment of the ludicrous—all appealed to the young. For any celebration, especially birthdays, his wholehearted participation was a certainty. "Even if I had an engagement of the most particular kind," he wrote his daughter Mamie before her tenth birthday, "I should excuse myself from keeping it, so that I might have the pleasure of celebrating at home, and among my children, the day that gave me such a dear and good daughter as you."[6] Nothing, not even illness, must prevent his surprising her. Once, unwell and unable to come down for her birthday, he sent for her, put his arms around her, kissed her, and wished her many happy returns of the day. Then, drawing a case from under his pillow, he presented her with a gold watch, the emerald back bearing her initials in enamel. When, after some speechless seconds, she was finally able to exclaim in delight, she turned to her father and met his tear-filled eyes.[7]

Nor did his love of surprise diminish as his children grew older. When in 1851 the family prepared to move to Tavistock House, he promised his daughters that they would have a better bedroom than they had ever had. But they were not to see their "gorgeous apartment" until all was in readiness. When the long-awaited day finally arrived, Dickens took his daughters on their first tour of inspection. Every detail had been planned with their needs and tastes in mind: the flowered wall paper, the chintz-covered bedsteads, the toilet tables, the writing tables, and the easy chairs—all in pairs—nothing had been overlooked.[8] All this when English bedrooms were generally spartan in their furnishings!

As an entertainer Dickens charmed his children almost from their infancy. One child on each knee and the others gathered round his rocking chair (acquired on his first trip to America), he would sing them comic songs at bedtime. A special favorite, which told the story of an old man plagued with a cold and rheumatism, had to be rendered to the accompaniment of sneezes, coughs, and gestures. It was so popular that the small audience demanded repeated encores. Another favorite related the history of Guy Fawkes, "the prince of sinisters,/ Who once blew up the House of Lords,/The King and all his ministers." Each stanza ended with a noisy refrain that appealed to little ears: "Bow, wow, wow, wow, ri foldi riddi, oddy, bow, wow, wow."[9]

Each year, with the approach of Christmas, Dickens became once more a child among his children. "It is good to be children sometimes," he would declare, "and never better than at Christmas, when its Mighty founder was a child Himself."[10] Usually taking the whole week off before the holidays, he personally supervised the preparations: the special foods with their tantalizing aromas, the holly-decked walls, the invitations to house guests—all excited him. The day before Christmas, as long as his family lived in London, he would take his children to a toy shop in Holborn, where they were allowed to select their own gifts and any they wished to give their friends. Though it was often an hour or more before they could make up their minds, he never begrudged them the time.[11] At the Christmas feast, climaxed by the entry of the blazing plum pudding, resplendent on its holly-decked china platter, Dickens always delivered his traditional blessing: "Reflect upon your blessings—of which every man has many—not on your past misfortunes, of which all men have some. Fill your glass again, with a merry face and a contented heart. Our life on it, but your Christmas shall be merry and your New Year a happy one."[12]

Sometimes Dickens was so carried away by his childlike enthusiasm that he took over completely a project originally intended for one of his sons. Such was the case when he and the artist Clarkson Stanfield set up a toy theater, a specimen of Drury Lane, that had been bought for Charley. So fascinated were the two men by this project that the boy could only look on as they painted, cut, and gummed.[13]

Since Charley's birthday fell on Twelfth Night, the occasion called for elaborate parties. A magic lantern, conjuring tricks, games of blindman's buff, dancing—there was no limit to the hilarity. Always it was Dickens who dominated the scene. "I have made a tremendous hit with a conjuring apparatus," he told Angela Burdett Coutts, the philanthropist who was Charley's godmother and always sent him a large cake on his birthday. Dickens reported that he had been most popular with the small fry "after cooking a plum pudding in a hat, and producing a pocket handkerchief from a Wine Bottle."[14]

As soon as the younger children could participate in the activities, they were assigned roles in the amateur theatricals staged in the schoolroom at Tavistock House. Beginning with *Tom Thumb* in 1854, the performances soon became finished productions with the addition of adult actors from Dickens's experienced troupe of amateurs. Rehearsals were serious affairs, and everyone knew there must be no trifling. According to Charley, December became one "Long rehearsal." Dickens took infinite pains to teach the children their parts, helping them individually to memorize their lines and directing their acting. Though always patient and understanding, he demanded each one's best efforts. "Do everything at your best," he would say of any undertaking. "I shall not mind if you do not succeed in what you are doing, so long as I feel sure that you have done your best." It was a principle to which he himself had adhered faithfully. "I can truly assure you that I have taken as great pains with the smallest thing I have ever undertaken as with the biggest," he told his sons.[15]

A family project viewed with considerable pride took form in 1864, when Henry (Harry) and three of his brothers organized a small newspaper recording the week's local events. Called the Gad's Hill *Gazette*, it began with one handwritten sheet, but eventually became four printed pages run off on a real printing press, the gift of W. H. Wills, Dickens's subeditor. At the peak of its success it had a hundred subscribers who paid two pence a copy for news about the Dickens family and their friends. That Dickens himself supplied some of the material for the *Gazette* is evident from a few pages of copy preserved in his handwriting. Usually he helped out when Harry, who eventually assumed sole responsibility for the paper, ran short of material. At such times he would contribute humorous letters, using fictitious names to register a complaint and denounce the paper in one number, only to come out with a strong defense of the editorial policies, contents, and format in the next. Thus a letter signed "Jabez Skinner, the Skinnery, Flintshire" would be answered by "Blackberry Jones, the Jonery, Everyshire."

For all his love of fun, occasionally displayed in ludicrous antics, Dickens could be serious, even stern, especially where orderliness and punctuality were demanded. Some of his letters, as well as the reminiscences of his son Harry, tell of his daily inspection of the boys' rooms. "Nothing is allowed to be out of place," Dickens reported during the family's stay in Boulogne. "Each in his turn is appointed Keeper for the week, and I go out in solemn procession . . . three times a day, on a tour of inspection."[16] It was a standing joke among the children that he "must be personally acquainted with every nail in the house." According to Harry, "there was a parade from time to time to check the stains of grease and dirt which had accumulated on . . . clothing; and to one boy was allotted the task each week of collecting the sticks, balls and croquet and cricket materials." On outings or picnics each one was charged with cleaning up; not a single scrap of paper or bit of waste ever escaped Dickens's sharp eye."[17]

About appearing on time for meals or keeping appointments Dickens was equally strict. One of his granddaughters has recalled an early experience at Gad's Hill. "Somebody is late for dinner," she concluded after some awkward moments, "and, I think, even the small observer in the muslin pinafore has a notion that 'Venerables' [the name Dickens preferred to *Grandfather*] does not like people to be late."[18] What punishment was meted out for an infraction of the rules is not a matter of record, though in a letter to Landor, Dickens mentions having put the twelve-year-old Walter, "a very good boy," in solitary bathroom confinement for "terminating a dispute with a nurse by throwing a chair in her direction."[19] Usually, Dickens's displeasure was sufficient deterrent to any misconduct. Moreover, special treats and prizes could always be counted on as rewards for neatness and promptness.

Ever ready to give even their small problems his sympathetic understanding, Dickens encouraged his sons and daughters to come to him for advice. At no time would he make them feel foolish, however unreasonable their requests, or snub them. Nor did he want them to feel intimidated or fearful. Even as toddlers they were never to be frightened, never to be sent against their will into the dark. "If the fixed impression be of an object terrible to the child," Dickens maintained, "it will be (for want of reasoning upon) inseparable from great

281

fear. Force the child at such a time, be Spartan with it, send it into the dark against its will, and you had better murder it."[20]

Never did the children feel their father's affection more deeply than during their illnesses. His presence in the sickroom eased their pain, quieted their raging fever, drove away their fear. "Quick, active, sensible, bright and cheery . . .," Mamie would reminisce later, "he would seize the 'case' at once, knew exactly what to do, and do it."[21] At the sound of his footsteps the little heart would beat faster and the eyes brighten as his reassuring voice greeted the invalid. There was something magnetic in his touch, a "curious life-giving power," Anne Thackeray Ritchie called it, "the combined tenderness of a woman and his own mysteriously dominant strength."[22]

To no part of his children's upbringing did Dickens devote more attention than to their education. Basically, he was concerned that it should take into account their individual aptitudes. To the headmasters of his sons' schools he wrote repeatedly about the boys' special interests, their specific weaknesses, and his own hopes for them. Charley, with his facility for languages, was encouraged to consolidate his French by attending the Parisian theaters. For learning the language in three months, he was awarded a Geneva watch. After Eton, where his father visited him regularly to check on his progress and picnic with him and his friends, he went to Germany to learn the language because he had decided on a commercial career. The boys were to consider their education a preparation for a definite calling. When they showed little aptitude for academic pursuits, they were immediately switched to practical training that would prepare them for their life's work.

Only one of the sons, Harry, attended a university. It was not that Dickens opposed higher education, but he had to be sure that the money would be spent wisely. Before sending Harry to Cambridge, he asked his headmaster whether the boy really had the "qualities and habits" necessary to marked success there. "I could by no means afford," he insisted, "to send a son to college who went there for any other purpose than to work hard, and to gain distinction."[23]

Arthur A. Adrian

As for the daughters, though preparation for a career was not the object, Dickens engaged tutors for them and encouraged them to acquire fluency in French. He urged Mamie to develop her musical talent; and Katey, because of her special aptitude for art, was enrolled for drawing lessons at Bedford College. In short, the education of his children was one of Dickens's major concerns.

Equally serious were his ideas about his children's religious training. Introduced as a boy to the rantings of a Dissenting preacher in Chatham, next door to his home in St. Mary's Terrace, he could not forget how he had been "caught in the palm of a female hand by the crown, . . .violently scrubbed from the neck to the roots of the hair as a purification for the Temple, and . . . carried off, . . . to be steamed like a potato in the unventilated breath of Boanerges Boiler and his congregation."[24] (Dickens's parents may have come under the influence of a Chapel sect while living in Chatham.) Because of his early conditioning, Dickens always opposed any form of worship which, in the words of Carlyle, had "its eye forever turned on its own navel."[25] On spiritual matters he was decidedly reticent, refusing to cheapen religion by playing on the emotions.

For his younger children, Dickens vehemently opposed any instruction in the religious mysteries that they could but "imperfectly understand." Nor would he tolerate the "frequent references to the Almighty in small matters." Why should children be made to see God as "avenging and wrathful"? It was preposterous to believe that the Creator, who in His wisdom had made them children before they were men and women, would "punish them awfully for every little venial offence" which was but a "necessary part" of their growing up. They were not to see God as a rigid judge or be imbued with the fear of death. "If God be as rigid as they are told," Dickens insisted, "their fathers and mothers and three fourths of their relations and friends must be doomed to Eternal Perdition." Under no circumstances was anyone to use such terms as "lamb of God" or some "injudicious catechising" with his children. Rather than have them enter a place of worship where they might be subjected to "religious

283

forms of restraint," Dickens would have them acquire "the principles of religion from a contemplation of nature and all the goodness and beneficence of the Great Being who created it."[26]

Exhorting his children always to follow as their guide the teachings of the New Testament, a copy of which was packed with each son's personal effects on leaving home, Dickens wrote for their exclusive study and meditation a *Life of Our Lord*, prefacing it: "My dear children, I am very anxious that you should know something about the History of Jesus Christ. For everybody ought to know about Him. No one ever lived, who was so good, so kind, so gentle, and so sorry for all people who did wrong, or were in any way ill, or miserable, as he was. And as he is now in Heaven, where we hope to go and all meet each other after we are dead, and there to be happy always together, you never can think what a good place Heaven is without knowing who he was and what he did."

How successful was Dickens as a father? For all his solicitous care, his close supervision of his children's education and religious training, his devoted love; for all his insistence on mutual trust and understanding, he was to be deeply disappointed. Though he was well ahead of his time in making himself available to his children, in offering them sympathetic understanding, in planning their careers on the basis of their aptitudes, only one of his sons, Harry, lived up to expectations.

For Charley, the first-born, the future at first looked promising because he seemed to be doing well at Eton. But, according to Dickens, he wanted "a habit of perseverance," having inherited from his mother "an indescribable lassitude of character."[27] When, after some uncertainties about his future, he decided on a mercantile career, he had all the necessary backing from his father. After several unsuccessful ventures, however, the last ending in bankruptcy, Dickens finally made a place for him as an editorial assistant on his weekly journal, *All the Year Round*. After Dickens's death the journal continued for twenty-three years under Charles's editorship and was produced by the printing firm of which he and Evans, his brother-in-law, were partners. On a tour of

America in 1888, he lectured on his father and read selections from his novels. The support of a large family (seven daughters and one son) compelled him to undertake any venture that might bolster his uncertain finances. Even so, he was not always prudent in his investments, as when he bought Gad's Hill, his father's last home, for nearly seven thousand pounds, an inflated price at the time because of its prestige. After his death in 1897, Queen Victoria granted his hard-pressed widow an annual pension of a hundred pounds.

The next child, Mamie, whom Henry James described as the "image of her father,"[28] displayed an abnormal coolness toward any suitable lover. At first indifferent to Percy Fitzgerald, one of Dickens's younger friends, she later ignored the attentions of an army officer, a William Lynch. Dickens is said to have admired him greatly and was disappointed by Mamie's attitude. Years later her brother Harry speculated on why his attractive sister had never married. "I think it was because she was so absolutely devoted to my father," he concluded.[29] One cannot help wondering whether he recognized such pathological devotion as a classic case of a father fixation. "My love for my father has never been touched or approached by any other love," Mamie herself confessed in her published recollections. "I hold him in my heart of hearts as a man apart from all other beings."[30] To Mrs. James T. Fields of Boston, she wrote an impassioned letter after her father's funeral, eulogizing him and declaring that it was a "glorious inheritance to have such blood flowing in one's veins." And, as if to dismiss any speculation about possible lovers, past or future, she affirmed her happiness at never having changed her name.[31]

Surviving Dickens by twenty-six years, she grew increasingly restless. At first she made her home with her maiden aunt, Georgina Hogarth. Then followed a succession of residences. In her last years she was a pathetic drifter, ill and lonely, "seeking escape in alcohol."[32]

Katey, the third child, fared better. Much like her father in temperament, she was a great favorite with him, as her brothers and sister quickly realized while still young when they commissioned her to ask for special favors.[33] Less awed by her father, she spoke her mind with complete candor, a frankness he respected. Ultimately, the uncomfortable situation arising from her parents' domestic rupture in 1858 led to her marriage to a man twelve years her senior, Charles Collins, Wilkie's younger brother. Collins's poor health caused Dickens much uneasiness, as is evident from his frequent references to it in his correspondence. Collins was to survive Dickens by only three years. After his death Katey married Carlo Perugini, a rising painter whom she had met through her art circle.

That Katey came closer than any of the other children to assessing her father's genius is borne out by her correspondence with George Bernard Shaw while the disposition of Dickens's letters to his wife was under consideration.[34] "You wrong me," she told Shaw, "when you think for one second that I would suggest any comparison between my father and any other artist in the world—. I believe my father to have been a man apart—as high above his fellow men—as the children of such great and exceptional men, are generally . . . below them." Such an exalted position, she felt, was not consistent with the impression too many readers carried away from Dickens's novels. "If you could make the public understand," she explained, "that my father was not a joyous jocose gentleman walking with a plum pudding and a bowl of punch you would greatly oblige me." At the same time, she made no attempt to condone her father's shortcomings, both as artist and man. Countering Shaw's suggestion that future critics would attribute the interpolated tales in such books as *Pickwick* to another author ("an abysmally inferior hand"), she argued that "all the bad in my father's work is as entirely his own as the good." He would not have tolerated others working for him, she insisted; consequently, the weaker portions of his novels, written during fatigue or without inspiration, had been allowed to "pass as worthy to be placed with the best." Then, with probing insight, she explained, "He could not have been the man he was without this weakness in his writing, *as in his character* [italics added]. They explain the man." Thus, however much she seemed to idolize her father, she had not allowed emotion to distort her

286

judgment: "My father was—as the girl in 'Caste' used to say 'a very clever man' but like all clever people he wrote and talked nonsense at times. *But that nonsense was his own.*"

For Walter, his fourth child, Dickens had no academic ambitions, finding him not "so clever as Charley," but a "steady, amiable boy, of good reliable capacity."[35] This son was to be prepared, accordingly, for a military career in India. He left England in July 1857 during the Indian mutiny. A lieutenant in the twenty-sixth Native Infantry, he died suddenly of hematemesis (the vomiting of blood) on 31 December 1863, shortly after he was to have been sent home on sick leave. Letters from his superior officer ultimately brought the sad account of accumulated unpaid debts. Temporarily halting his work on the tenth number of *Our Mutual Friend*, Dickens had to settle the "regimental part of poor Walter's wretched affairs—utterly incomprehensible, as they have always been," he complained.[36]

The next son, Francis Jeffrey (Frank), also sent to India, lacked steadiness and purpose, Dickens felt. Suffering from a painful stammer and occasional deafness, Frank, after spending some time in Germany to learn the language, had, because of his speech impediment, given up his ambition to become a doctor. A brief period with *All the Year Round* having shown him to be of little value there, he was nominated in 1863 to the Bengal Mounted Police. During his seven years in India, he proved himself an excellent officer, but decided to return to England after his father's death. Fortunately, Dickens was spared the pain of seeing him lose his inheritance through speculation and wasteful spending. Through the efforts of his Aunt Georgina and his sisters, he was offered a commission in the Canadian Northwest Mounted Police. Shortly after retiring he died in 1886 during a visit to Moline, Illinois.

The pattern of squandering money and accumulating debts, especially painful to Dickens because of his experiences with his feckless father and several brothers, was to continue with the next son, Alfred Tennyson. Though the boy had spent six years to prepare himself for a military career, he finally abandoned his goal of a cadetship in artillery or engineering. In May 1865 he sailed for Australia to take up sheep farming, leaving behind many unpaid accounts with various haberdashers. Dickens had the embarrassment of settling a succession of bills for coats, trousers, silk scarves, French kid gloves, shirts, shirt studs and sleeve links, silk umbrellas, and bottles of scent.[37] When he left Australia years later, Alfred capitalized on his father's reputation by lecturing about him in Britain and America, his performances combining personal reminiscences and dramatic readings from the novels. Having become addicted to drink like his sister Mamie, he was not received at the home of his younger brother Harry while in London.[38] During a tour in New York, he died in his hotel room on 2 January 1912 and was buried in the cemetery of Trinity Parish at 155th and Broadway.

Again the specter of extravagance haunted Dickens's household after the next son, Sydney Smith Haldimand, affectionately called "The Admiral," went to sea. So small that he "could easily have stowed himself and his wife and family of his own proportions" in his sea chest, wrote Dickens, he was a great favorite. But once on his own he succumbed to the temptation of living beyond his means. Threatened with naval disciplinary action when he could not redeem his bills, he sought help from his father. "You can't understand how ashamed I am to appeal to you again," he wrote. Confessing to "insufficient strength of mind" to shake the habit of drinking with riotous associates, the real cause of his money problems, he pleaded, "If any promise for future amends can be relied on you have mine most cordially, but for God's sake assist me now." The result of refusal, he warned, would be "utter ruination."[39] But Sydney's promises were not to be trusted. Finally, convinced that removing one financial crisis simply cleared the way for another, Dickens abandoned all hope. His last letter to Sydney informed him that the doors of Gad's Hill would henceforth be shut to him. Nothing could have been more painful than turning against this son, the deeply loved "Ocean Spectre," who had looked out so intently over the sea in childhood, the "Little Admiral," who had come home from training, "all eyes and buttons."

Toward his youngest son, Edward ("The Noble Plorn"), Dickens seemed to express his affection more freely than he had done with the others. Trotting beside his father in their country walks, the little fellow would always be a source of keen amusement and deep admiration with his childish prattle. But all his father's love could not ward off the lassitude and instability that had plagued nearly all of Edward's brothers. His general ineptitude for learning and his poor record at school persuaded Dickens to prepare him for sheep farming in Australia. Accordingly, after some training to acquaint him with life in the bush, he was sent to Melbourne in September 1868 to join his brother Alfred. It was the hardest parting of all. "He seemed to me to become once more my youngest and favourite child . . . ," Dickens wrote after seeing him off, "and I did not think I could have been so shaken."[40] His early death in 1870 mercifully spared him the pain of watching this favorite son get involved in heavy gambling losses, followed by appeals to Harry for loans that were never repaid or even acknowledged.

Only one son, Harry, the second youngest, did not disappoint Dickens. Of him Katey wrote in one of her letters to Shaw: "out of our large family of nine children, there was only *one* who ever seemed to me really quite sane."[41] Already demonstrating his steadiness and dedicated industry while still in grammar school, he appeared to be the one who would benefit from a university education. For all his dependability, however, he was not exempt from close supervision. Once he was settled in Cambridge, his father wrote him a frank, businesslike letter detailing financial matters. "We must have no shadow of debt," Dickens warned. Reminded that his father had never had any outside help since childhood and had always worked hard for his money, Harry was told again what he and his brothers had heard *ad nauseam*, "You know that you are one of many heavy charges on me." This charge, he was given to understand, could be diminished by improving the advantages of his "expensive education."[42] This admonition Harry took to heart by distinguishing himself at Trinity Hall, though Dickens's response to his honors was only an understated and terse comment of approval. Such reticence was typical, a "habit of suppression," as Dickens himself diagnosed it, "which now belongs to me, which I know is no part of my original nature but which makes me chary of showing my affections, even to my children, except when they are very young."[43] Years later Harry was to describe his father's reserve as "an intense dislike of letting himself go in private life." Though his children knew "he was devotedly attached to them, there was still a kind of reserve . . . which seemed to occasionally come as a cloud between us and which I never quite understood."[44] What a pity that Dickens did not live to follow this son's successful career as barrister and judge!

Why was Dickens to be disappointed in all but one of his sons? Surely no man ever took more seriously his paternal responsibilities. "I hope you will always be able to say in after life, that you had a kind father," he wrote in a farewell letter to Edward.[45] How had this kindness miscarried? Having played with his children when they were small, recorded their antics, and carefully planned their education, he had unquestionably been a concerned parent. Certainly no father had ever been closer to his sons and daughters in their early years. Indeed, in his love of excitement and surprise, his exuberant delight in their amusements, his sympathetic understanding of their trivial vexations, he had enjoyed complete empathy with them. It was as if, deprived of his own boyhood after the age of twelve, he was desperately trying to recapture through them his lost years. In him the child and the parent were coexistent. It must be remembered, however, that he experienced the happiest relations with his children in their early years, but seemingly never grew up with them. Actually, he dreaded the prospect of growing old, as demonstrated by his preference for being addressed as Venerables instead of Grandfather when his grandchildren came along. "Childhood is usually so beautiful and engaging," he observed in "Where We Stopped Growing" (*Household Words*, 1 January 1853), "that . . . there is a mournful shadow of the common lot in the notion of its changing and fading into anything else."

As a child of "larger growth" among his children, however, Dickens may have dominated their work and play too much. His taking over the building of Charley's toy theater has already been cited as a case in point. Such close supervision and domination also applied to the family's Twelfth Night festivities. "I found the children getting up a dull charade," Dickens reported while preparations for Charley's birthday celebration were already in progress.[46] Unwilling to see his children in an uninspired performance of their own devising, he promptly master-minded an elaborate production of *Tom Thumb,* complete with an assisting cast of adults from his own troupe. In denying the small actors the pleasure of initiating their own projects, he prevented them from using their imagination and exercising their ingenuity. Such a course inevitably saps initiative. Though in modern terms Dickens must be commended for making himself indispensable to his children, a wise parent "watches the drama of growth, but resists the desire to intervene too often."[47]

Equally unwise was Dickens's obsession with tidiness. The daily inspection of the children's rooms, the insistence that all hats and coats be kept on assigned pegs when not in use, the examination of garments for fresh stains, and the regimented routine of the household irritated the boys. However valuable their early training in orderliness, forceful imposition of tidiness may have had a negative effect. It could even explain Frank's stammer, for such a speech impediment is but a symptom of underlying nervous maladjustment.[48] And it may well have had some bearing on his boyhood sleepwalking.

That Dickens's sons sometimes regarded their father as a martinet is attested by Harry's later reminiscences. Though they dared not express their displeasure openly, "our resentment," he recalls, "took the more insidious form of deeply whispered mutterings among ourselves on the subject of 'slavery,' 'degradation,' and so forth, which, while being somewhat transpontine in their character and wholly ineffective in their results, still served as a kind of safety valve and helped soothe our ruffled feelings."[49]

In addition to orderliness, Dickens demanded peace and quiet. Under strain when he was meeting monthly deadlines, not to mention other commitments, he may not always have concealed his annoyance at the least disturbance. When he was so completely absorbed in his work and so tense that just the dropping of a spoon would pain him, the very presence of his sons in the home irritated him. To Wilkie Collins he complained of their noise: "Why any boy of that age [Walter's] should seem to have at all times, 150 pairs of double-soled boots, I don't know."[50] Even as late as 1863, he was still disturbed by unusual activity. "This place is at present pervaded by boys to a fearful extent," he again complained to Collins. "They boil over (if an affectionate parent may mention it) all over the house."[51]

Along with openly disapproving of even routine noises, Dickens constantly harped on the importance of thrift. Frequently reminded that he had worked hard for his money and that they were a heavy drain on him, all but one of the sons built up a subconscious resistance to his advice by overspending their allowance and ignoring their bills. Brought up in a home maintained on a rather lavish scale with its rich and showy furnishings and elaborate dinner parties, the boys naturally assumed they were entitled to expenditures in keeping with such opulence. Dickens's constant reminders that their personal expenditures were burdensome they soon learned to shrug off. But Dickens's annoyance continued, spilling over into complaints about his sons' impecuniousness to his reading manager.

Interspersed with such complaints were the flippant references to the size of his family. Though, as already stated, he found babies irresistible, announcing each new arrival as "a chopping boy," "a brilliant boy of unheard-of-dimensions," he became progressively less exuberant until he declared after the last, "I am not quite clear that I particularly wanted the latter." Facetiously he wrote to a Mrs. Gore of a plan to intercede with the "Bishop of London to have a little service in Saint Paul's beseeching that I may be considered to have done enough towards my country's population." And he affirmed his determination not to give her a godchild.[52] One cannot help wondering whether his children were aware of his mocking attitude, either through overhearing his remarks or listening to some of his tasteless jokes. According to one source he was not above the crudity of calling attention, with pointed allusions, to the condition of a pregnant woman, embarrassing all who heard him, including the "subject of his obstetric wit."[53]

As his sons grew older, Dickens may have let them sense his disappointment in them. Believing that their instability was inherited from their mother, he confided his pessimism about them to his friends. To Wills he complained that his boys had "a curse of limpness on them" and an "inadaptability to anything."[54] To Wilkie Collins he wrote ruefully: "I am so undoubtedly one of the sons of Toil—and fathers of children— that expect to be presently presented with a smock frock, a pair of leather breeches, and a pewter watch, for having brought up the largest family ever known with the smallest disposition to do anything for themselves."[55] When Charles Albert Fechter, the Alsatian actor, told Longfellow that all Dickens's success went for nothing because he was unhappy in his family, Mrs. James T. Fields, who overheard the remark, could not help wondering "how much too much of this the children have had to hear."[56] Whatever they did hear, or merely sensed, would certainly not have inspired them to do their best.

There is, moreover, a question about the children's capacity for achievement. Katey, for one, had no illusions about their shortcomings. "I think," she told Shaw, "the children of a very clever man who uses his brain all day long—have a very poor chance of having much themselves—and seldom if ever resemble their father in any one particular." Except for Harry, she explained, each of the Dickens children, though sane, had "a crack somewhere."[57] Convinced that they could never measure up to the demands of a genius like their father, the sons seem to have viewed their mediocrity as inevitable. As Edward was to remark in later years, "Sons of great men are not usually as great as their fathers. You cannot get two Charles Dickens in one generation."[58]

Determined to counteract in his children any early indications of the pecuniary recklessness that had ruined his father and several brothers, Dickens wanted to make his sons self-sufficient against the time when they could no longer fall back on him for support. All but dependable Harry were therefore sent from home early to find their special "groove": Sydney at thirteen; Charley, Walter, and Edward at sixteen; Frank at nineteen; and Alfred at twenty. Even as he prepared them for their ventures, Dickens kept complaining about the mounting expenses. Early discouraging reports evoked renewed laments about his sons' lassitude, "their want of perseverance, their inability to follow a fixed purpose."

One cannot help wondering whether it ever occurred to Dickens that his sons' instability might have had some connection with what he himself called the "skeleton in the domestic closet," the deepening rift between himself and his wife, which brought on the dark moods and restlessness of his middle age. According to him, the incompatibility had developed gradually, beginning soon after the birth of the second child in 1838 and becoming unbearable in the fifties. At times, if one may believe his statements, his wife's insane jealousies of various women, compounded by neurotic outbursts, had widened the rift until domestic tranquility could never be restored. Having borne ten children (one died in infancy) in fifteen years, not to mention several miscarriages, Catherine Dickens had been unable to keep pace with her energetic husband. As the Newcastle *Chronicle* would characterize her some years later (9 March 1889), she was "seemingly quite without the natural power, or spirit, or natural force of manner to guide or control such a volatile character as that of Charles Dickens." Her physical clumsiness and bulging plumpness, worsened by constant child-bearing, had often made her the butt of his tart jokes. Intellectually, moreover, she had been forced by repeated confinement to restrict her interests and social contacts, so that she had fallen behind her husband in mental breadth. With his friends and their scintillating repartee, she must have felt out of place.

How much of this domestic unhappiness erupted in the open is, of course, a matter of speculation. But there can be little doubt that some of it filtered through to the children. Close observers of their parents, according to one authority, children react emotionally. If all is well at home they feel secure and do not waste psychic energy in worry. But where they sense parental friction they feel "anxious and guilty—anxious because their home is threatened, guilty because of their actual or imagined role in the family friction. Justifiably or not, children assume that they are the cause of the domestic strife."[59] Such anxiety may well have been another underlying cause of Frank's stammer.

By mutual consent the Dickenses finally agreed to a legal separation. When Catherine left her husband's roof to live alone in London, the terms of the deed having been completed in April 1858, all the children but Charley remained with their father. Though they were free to visit their mother, they seldom did so for fear of displeasing him. This neglect of duty may have made the older ones feel guilty.

Coming at a time when the five youngest sons, ranging in age from six to thirteen, still needed the security of a normal home life, the domestic rupture set the family apart from other households. To be sure, Catherine's younger sister, Georgina Hogarth, was still in charge. Having been with the Dickenses from the age of fourteen, she had gradually made herself indispensable by taking over the early instruction of the children and the management of domestic matters. According to Dickens her nieces and nephews felt more comfortable with her than with their own mother. But when she refused to leave with her sister after the legal separation, both her family and respectable society were outraged. As she accordingly became the subject of unsavory and malicious gossip, Dickens bristled with indignation. Reverberations from the fury he unleashed against the scandalmongers and reports of his demands for public apologies may well have reached his children.

Even more damaging would have been the curious visits of Ellen Ternan, the young actress now generally believed to have been Dickens's mistress. Prevented on legal grounds from obtaining a divorce and marrying her, he settled for unrestricted access to a house he leased for her in London. The older children must have realized that this youthful beauty was more than just a good friend of the family. But perhaps, like their Aunt Georgina, they condoned their father's conduct by affirming that "a man of genius ought not to be judged with the common herd of men."[60] Such a rationale could not insulate them, however, against the harsh criticism that they must have heard occasionally in their social circle.

"There is hardly one actress in London at all young and handsome who was not scandalized by having her name associated with this affair," declared an anonymous reporter in the Newcastle *Chronicle* (4 June 1858). "But the most generally accepted version pointed to a young and clever actress in the Haymarket company, and it would not be fair to give her name in connection with what is now an exploded scandal. So far did it proceed, however, that it is said Mrs. Dickens herself wrote a letter to a member of the company stating that, though it was true she and her husband had some differences, yet she felt it her due to the lady, whose name was so freely implicated, to say that she was not the cause of them." (Catherine Dickens's letter would, of course, have been written at her husband's insistence, may even have been dictated by him.)

Since Dickens appeared in public with Ellen Ternan while traveling back and forth to France, his conduct continued to provoke censure. Typical, perhaps, was the reaction of an indignant fellow passenger on the Boulogne Packet. Having seen Dickens with "a lady not his wife, nor his sister-in-law," she deplored his "bad taste" in parading "the unwarrantable acts of his private life so as to give public scandal." She charged, further, that he lacked "the instincts of a gentleman," for he "strutted about the deck with the air of a man bristling with self-importance!" It was her conviction that "no one can afford to overlook his immoral life."[61]

Whatever the sources and the nature of the strictures directed at their father, the children must have found them disturbing. As for the younger sons, such glimmerings of the truth as they may have been capable of, together with an uneasiness over their mother's abnormal isolation, would have contributed further to their failure "to follow a fixed purpose."

Dickens's fatherhood, then, though characterized by deep affection and sympathetic concern, brought its toll in disappointments and heartaches. Some of these may be attributed to his overzealousness in seeking to spare his children the insecurity of his own boyhood. Still others may have resulted from his absorption in the world of his imagination, where his dream children were often closer to him than his real children with all their failings. In short, he may have been unable to bridge the gap between idealized and flawed children. Finally, there were the unhappy events leading to the domestic rupture, as well as the separation itself. These all left an imprint on the sons in their formative years. So, though Dickens had only the best intentions for his family and was well ahead of his time in demanding that his children be granted their rights as individuals, he was to be disappointed in the sequence of events that confirmed what must have been his own growing doubts about his adequacy as a father. Perhaps his daughter Katey was right when she told Shaw, "Men of genius ... ought not to be allowed to have children."[62] In this conviction, moreover, Dickens had already anticipated her when he exclaimed jestingly, in words that could be interpreted on several levels, "Why was I ever a father!"

1. *The Pilgrim Edition of the Letters of Charles Dickens*, ed. Madeline House, Graham Storey, and Kathleen Tillotson 4 vols. (Oxford, 1965, 1970, 1974, 1977), 2:268, 21/4/41. Hereafter cited in text as *Pilgrim*, with day of the week, month, and year given in that order.

2. Mary Dickens, "Charles Dickens at Home," *Cornhill* (January, 1855), 4:33.

3. *The Nonesuch Edition of the Letters of Charles Dickens*, ed. Walter Dexter, 3 vols. (London, 1938), 2:507, 4/11/53. Hereafter cited as *Nonesuch*, with day of the week, month, and year given in that order.

4. "Charles Dickens at Home," 4:33.

5. *Pilgrim*, 3:331, H. Austin, 25/9/42.

6. *Nonesuch*, 2:147, 27/2/49.

7. "Charles Dickens at Home," 4:38.

8. Ibid., p. 39.

9. Charles Dickens, Jr., "Glimpses of Charles Dickens," *North American Review* 160:525-26.

10. Mary Dickens, *My Father as I Recall Him* (London, 1877), p. 38.

11. Ibid., p. 46.

12. Ibid.

13. "Glimpses of Charles Dickens," 160:527.

14. Edgar Johnson, *The Heart of Charles Dickens* (New York, 1952),

15. Henry F. Dickens, *Recollections of Sir Henry Dickens* (London, 1943), p. 40.

16. Johnson, *The Heart of Charles Dickens,* p. 320, Coutts, 5/7/56.

17. Henry F. Dickens, *Memories of My Father* (London, 1928), pp. 25-26; H. Dickens, *Recollections,* p. 21.

18. Mary Angela Dickens, "A Child's Memories," *Strand Magazine* 13:73

19. *Nonesuch,* 2:486, 3/8/53.

20. "Charles Dickens at Home," 4:37.

21. *My Father as I Recall Him,* p. 13.

22. "Charles Dickens as I Remember Him," *Pall Mall Magazine* 308-9.

23. Letter in the H. E. House Collection, Cambridge, England. W. Brackenbury, 18/9/65.

24. Charles Dickens, "City of London Churches," *Uncommercial Traveller.*

25. *Past and Present,* 2:15.

26. *Pilgrim,* 2:568, Mrs. Godfrey, 25/7,39; 3:574, R. S. Starey, 24/9/43.

27. Johnson, *The Heart of Charles Dickens,* 254, Angela Coutts, 4/1/54.

28. *The Letters of Henry James,* ed. Leon Edel, 5 vols. (Cambridge, Mass., 1974), 1:16, Alice James, 10/3/69.

29. *Recollections of Sir Henry Dickens,* p. 95. For an account of Lynch see my *Georgina Hogarth and the Dickens Circle* (London, 1959), pp. 127, 132.

30. *My Father as I Recall Him,* p. 2.

31. Letter in the Henry E. Huntington Library, San Marino, Calif., Mrs. Fields, 1/9/70. Hereafter cited as Hunt. MS. This letter is quoted in my *Georgina Hogarth and the Dickens Circle,* p. 158.

32. Information supplied by the late Henry Charles Dickens, London, 1954.

33. *My Father as I Recall Him,* p. 10.

34. At Shaw's urging these letters were given to the British Museum. Katey's letters to Shaw are also in the British Museum, ADD MS 50546. Hereafter cited as BM MS ADD 50546.

35. Johnson, *The Heart of Charles Dickens,* 187, Coutts, 22/8/51.

36. Hunt. Ms., Georgina Hogarth, 12/10/64. Quoted in my *Georgina Hogarth and the Dickens Circle,* p. 86.

37. For a more detailed account of Alfred's debts see my *Georgina Hogarth and the Dickens Circle,* p. 86.

38. Information supplied by the late Henry Charles Dickens, London, 1954.

39. Letter among the documents relating to Frederic Ouvry's association with members of the Dickens family; housed at the offices of Sir Leslie Farrer, K.C.V.O., London, 19/3/69. Quoted in my *Georgina Hogarth and the Dickens Circle,* p. 123.

40. *Nonesuch,* 3:669, Fechter [9/68].

41. BM MS ADD 50546.

42. *Nonesuch,* 3:673, 15/10/68.

43. Ibid., 2:633, E. M. Winter, 22/2/55.

44. *Memories of My Father*, p. 19.

45. *Nonesuch*, 3:668 [26/9/68].

46. Johnson, *The Heart of Charles Dickens*, 257, Coutts, 2/1/54.

47. Haim Ginott, *Between Parent and Child* (New York, 1965), p. 37.

48. Leo Bartemeier, "The Contribution of the Father to the Mental Health of the Family," *American Journal of Psychiatry*, 110:277-80.

49. *Memories of My Father*, p. 26.

50. *Nonesuch*, 2:680, 17/7/56.

51. Ibid., 3:360, 9/8/63.

52. Ibid., 2:416, 17/9/52.

53. Lyndon Orr, "Charles Dickens as a Husband," *Bookman* (New York, 1906) 23:14-17.

54. Hunt. Ms, 6/6/67. Quoted in my *Georgina Hogarth and the Dickens Circle*, p. 101.

55. *Nonesuch*, 3:487, 4/10/66.

56. From the unpublished portions of Mrs. James T. Fields's diaries in the Library of the Massachusetts Historical Society, Boston.

57. BM MS ADD 50546.

58. Mary Lazarus, *A Tale of Two Brothers* (Sydney, 1973), p. 110.

59. Ginott, *Between Parent and Child*, p. 37.

60. See K. J. Fielding, "Charles Dickens and His Wife," *Études Anglaises*, 8:216, for a persuasive argument supporting the authenticity of the letter from which this is quoted.

61. Julia Byrne, *Gossip of the Century* (London, 1982), pp. 255-57.

62. BM MS ADD 50546.

XIV

GEORGE J. WORTH

Of Muscles And Manliness:
Some Reflections On Thomas Hughes

IN FEBRUARY 1858, TEN MONTHS AFTER THE PUBLICATION OF *Tom Brown's School Days*, a writer in a respected British quarterly referred to it as "a work which everybody has read, or means to read."[1] The early publishing history of Thomas Hughes's novel seems to confirm this characterization: by the time the remark appeared in print, *Tom Brown's School Days* had already attained its sixth edition in England and come out under two different titles in the United States.[2] Reviewers, as well as readers, found the novel to be highly pleasing and highly instructive,[3] and throughout the rest of the century there was no doubt about its status as a minor classic.

In our own day, however, it can claim no such distinction. Though obviously one cannot say that *Tom Brown's School Days* is "a work which *nobody* has read," there is considerable evidence to indicate that the book is ignored by that elusive creature, the late twentieth-century common reader. To be sure, the 1981 American and British *Books in Print* do list nine currently available editions of *Tom Brown's School Days*, but closer inspection reveals that these are by and large intended for the juvenile market, bearing such imprints as Puffin Books and Dent's Illustrated Children's Classics. The suspicion that adult readers of Victorian fiction, most of whom these days seem to inhabit universities and colleges, disregard *Tom Brown's School Days* is reinforced by a perusal of the recent annual bibliographies in *Victorian Studies*: during the entire decade of the 1970s, for instance, these show only two brief articles concentrating on Hughes's novel, and one of these was published in the journal *Children's Literature in Education*.

Contemporary scholars have not totally overlooked *Tom Brown's School Days*, of course; but on the whole they have viewed it less as a novel worthy of consideration—let alone enjoyment—in its own right than as a document in the history of something: public-school fiction, or the public school itself, or physical fitness, or the revival of the chivalric ideal.[4] Even more striking is the fact that modern critics with no visible pretensions to scholarship but with ready access to highly regarded periodicals for the expression of their opinions have heaped on *Tom Brown's School Days* a kind of abuse that can have had few parallels in the long and honorable tradition that induces men and women of letters to subject cherished books to periodic reassessment. And so Richard Usborne has exclaimed in the *Spectator* "What a thoroughly unpleasant book *Tom Brown's Schooldays* is!" and gone on to dismiss it as "generally being painful, or mawkish, or snobbish."[5] Not to be outdone, Kenneth Allsop, writing in *Encounter*, calls Hughes's novel "humid drivel" brimming over with "cruelty, conformity, and homosexuality," and Hughes himself a fool or a knave (it is impossible to be sure which) afflicted with "thick-headed self-satisfaction, fluctuating between a facetious smugness and a creepy piety."[6]

Why this neglect? Why this abuse? Such questions are, of course, impossible to answer conclusively, but there are several possible explanations. For one thing, *Tom Brown's School Days*, like the rest of Hughes's writings, is obviously dated, heavily didactic, and clumsily constructed; but then so are many other mid-Victorian novels that we continue to read, or at least to teach, and to write about with every indication of affection and respect. A more promising line of inquiry might lead us away from aesthetics into the even trickier terrain of twentieth-century British social and political history to examine the following hypothesis: because many British intellectuals, especially of the Labor and lately the Social Democratic persuasions, deplore the effect that they are sure the public schools have had in perpetuating the class system and perverting the communal life of their country, and because *Tom Brown's School Days* can be shown to have played a major role in elevating the public schools to a prominent place in the national consciousness, Hughes's modest little novel makes an irresistible target for them—all the more so because his religious convictions happen to be quite unfashionable among the majority of those who mold opinion in postwar, post-Imperial, post-Christian Britain.

This brings me to my own thesis. I shall not defend the artistic merits of *Tom Brown's School Days* (though I believe they are considerable), and I shall avoid sociopolitical pronouncements (though I am sorely tempted to slip them in). Rather, my task is a much more restricted one: I shall argue that one important reason for the low esteem in which Hughes is generally held today is that *Tom Brown's School Days*, and by extension the rest of his work, is closely associated with two interrelated mid-Victorian concepts that few now take seriously and many ridicule or condemn: "muscular Christianity" and "manliness"; that Hughes did indeed deal with both concepts, frequently and respectfully; but that he regarded them in ways that are quite different from, and much subtler than, the simpleminded attitudes often ascribed to him by those who have read him with certain biases, a long time ago, or not at all.

I

The phrase "muscular Christianity" appears to have been coined by the author of a February 1857 review of Charles Kingsley's novel *Two Years Ago*: "We all know by this time what is the task that Mr. Kingsley has made specially his own—it is that of spreading the knowledge and fostering the love of a muscular Christianity. His ideal is a man who fears God and can walk a thousand miles in a thousand hours— who, in the language which Mr. Kingsley has made popular, breathes God's free air on God's rich earth, and at the same time can hit a woodcock, doctor a horse, and twist a poker round his fingers."[7] Two months later, *Tom Brown's School Days* was published, and it was not long before reviewers of this novel began to link Hughes's work with that of his close friend. The *Literary Gazette,* for example, pointed to "the remarkable affinity" between *Tom Brown's School Days* and "the writings of Mr. Kingsley," particularly in its celebration of "the true Saxon delight in exercise, combat, and every manifestation of physical strength."[8] The *Times,* going further, applied the label "muscular Christianity" to the ideas of both novelists, but, in a generally favorable notice, did take Hughes to task for his praise of the spiritual dimensions of fighting: "We cannot but regret that everything high and holy should be invoked to the aid of the vulgar instinct of pugnacity, and that what Christianity commands should be so recklessly confounded with that which it prohibits."[9] Writing about the novel in the *Edinburgh Review,* James Fitzjames Stephen took a somewhat different line. Though he called *Tom Brown's School Days* "a very charming book" and "heartily congratulate[d] Mr. Kingsley on a disciple who reproduces so vigorously many of his own great merits," Stephen worried about one aspect of the Kingsleyan doctrine it professed: "not content with asserting the value of bodily strength, it throws by implication a certain slur on intellectual strength, which, when all is said and done, is much more important."[10] Such misgivings about the allegedly irreligious or anti-intellectual tone of its muscular Christianity did nothing to diminish the acclaim with which Hughes's novel was initially greeted, but they were indicative of much that was to come in its subsequent critical history.

Hughes had certainly given ammunition to censorious critics, of his day or ours. There is no question about it: when Tom Brown arrives at Rugby School at the age of ten,[11] he is a little animal, much more partial to outdoor sports and games and physical exercise than to studying.[12] Even earlier, he is fascinated by "the noble old game of back-sword" that is still in vogue in his native Berkshire. As Allsop reminds his readers in 1965, the players' object "is simply to break one another's heads" with the "good stout ash stick" each of them wields (1:2). Among Hughes's frequent sermon-like digressions (in

themselves objectionable to post-Jamesian students of fiction), the most notorious in the eyes of Allsop and like-
minded critics is his widely quoted praise of fighting: "After
all, what would life be without fighting, I should like to
know? From the cradle to the grave, fighting, rightly understood, is the business, the real, highest, honestest business of
every son of man" (2:5).

But reading to prove a point and selective quotation fail to
do justice to Hughes or to *Tom Brown's School Days.* That
Tom is, and to a large extent remains, a physical rather than a
spiritual or an intellectual being is undeniable. It is equally
clear from a judicious reading of the novel, however, that—
under the tutelage of Thomas Arnold, of the teachers at
Rugby (especially the one referred to as "the young master"),
and even of his fellow-pupils—Tom does develop in significant ways spiritually, intellectually, and morally while at the
school, and that he goes up to Oxford with a social conscience
as well. The nature of that social conscience may be beyond
our comprehension today, combining as it does a full-blown
Carlylean hero-worship of Arnold with an incipient Christian
Socialism; but this does not alter the fact that it is manifestly
there. A close look at the last two chapters of the novel should
remove any doubts on that score.

As to the supposedly brutal game of back-swording, it is
necessary to do two things if Hughes's feelings about it are to
be properly assessed: to place his more hair-raising remarks in
context, and to understand that he himself viewed this sport
with considerable ambivalence.

The picture of back-swording as relentless mutual blud-
geoning that Allsop paints with such relish is appreciably
modified if one reads on beyond the point where he chooses to
stop quoting. In Hughes's text, the phrase "to break one
another's heads" is followed by a colon and not by a period as
in Allsop's *Encounter* piece; the sentence continues: "for the
moment that blood runs an inch anywhere above the eyebrow,
the old gamester to whom it belongs is beaten, and has to
stop." And the next sentence, omitted by Allsop, reads: "A
very slight blow with the sticks will fetch blood, so that it is by
no means a punishing pastime, if the men don't play on

purpose, and savagely, at the body and arms of their adversaries" (1:2).

They do not in fact ordinarily play in order to inflict pain, either in *Tom Brown's School Days* or in Hughes's second novel, *The Scouring of the White Horse* (1858), but rather to demonstrate their remarkable agility. And they are doing more than that. Back-swording and wrestling are traditional amusements in the Vale of the White Horse, where Tom Brown spends his early childhood and which the protagonist of Hughes's next novel visits to his great edification; by the second quarter of the nineteenth century, such diversions are indulged in ritualistically at the great feasts that periodically draw the entire community together in fellowship, and they are rich in historic associations, which the participants carry on into an age that is too rapidly becoming commercialized and in a society that is increasingly held together by a cash-payment nexus rather than by more meaningful bonds.

These celebrations, the Parson in *The Scouring of the White Horse* insists, are essentially religious observances: God intended them to be "feasts for the whole nation—for the rich and the poor, the free man and the slave." The games that have, he concedes, given rise to considerable controversy play an important role in such divinely sanctioned festivals. "The object of wrestling and of all other athletic sports is to strengthen men's bodies, and to teach them to use their strength readily, to keep their tempers, to endure fatigue and pain. These are noble ends, my brethren. God gives us few more valuable gifts than strength of body, and courage, and endurance—to you labouring men they are beyond all price. We ought to cultivate them in all right ways, for they are given us to protect the weak, to subdue the earth, to fight for our homes and our country if necessary."[13]

But these sports need to be more strictly regulated, the Parson goes on to stress. Under the surveillance of resolute umpires, the participants must subordinate their animal instincts to rules that guarantee fair play. To suppress such drives, which are necessary and healthy, would turn them into less than men; to give these impulses free rein, on the other hand, by resorting to excessive violence or outright brutality, would lead to anarchy. In this sense, the stage where back-swording and wrestling contests are held is not really very different from the playing fields of Rugby or, for that matter, from the arena in which the social and political life of the nation runs its course.

Like those contests between aging rustics, the fighting between schoolboys that Hughes depicts is also something quite distinct from what critics have read into his work. The locus classicus is chapter 5 of part 2 of *Tom Brown's School Days*, where Tom comes to the aid of his frail young friend George Arthur after the smaller boy is picked on by "Slogger" Williams, one of the duller and more brutish members of their class. Tom manages to battle this bully to a draw in a free-form contest that combines bare-knuckle boxing with West Country wrestling before Dr. Arnold's arrival on the scene puts a stop to the proceedings. Far from being an everyday event, however, this is in fact "Tom's only single combat with a school-fellow" during his nine years at Rugby; "it was not at all usual in those days for two School-house boys to have a fight."

Before the battle begins, Hughes makes the famous statement about fighting being "the real, highest, honestest business of every son of man" that hostile critics like Allsop have held against him. But Hughes's next sentence makes it clear that according to his definition "fighting" means far more than fisticuffs or brawling, taking in moral as well as physical combat and sometimes combining the two, as in patriotic or Abolitionist fervor. (If the former is in ill repute in the 1980s, the latter certainly is not.) "Every one who is worth his salt has his enemies, who must be beaten, be they evil thoughts and habits in himself, or spiritual wickednesses in high places, or Russians, or Border-ruffians, or Bill, Tom, or Harry, who will not let him live his life in quiet till he has thrashed them."

Far from advocating physical combat for its own sake, Hughes takes pains to point out that it should normally be avoided, but that there are situations in which there is no acceptable alternative. When the Slogger lays violent hands on the smaller and weaker Arthur, Tom must rescue him, even if this means a fight, or else stand by and watch Arthur absorb a beating that he has done nothing to deserve. Those who accuse Hughes of arguing in favor of blind pugnacity need to look again at the final paragraph of the chapter:

> As to fighting, keep out of it if you can, by all means. When the time comes, if it ever should, that you have to say "Yes" or "No" to a challenge to fight, say "No" if you can—only take care you make it clear to yourselves why you say "No." It's a proof of the highest courage, if done from true Christian motives. It's quite right and justifiable, if done from simple aversion to physical pain and danger. But don't say "No" because you fear a licking, and say or think it's because you fear God, for that's neither Christian nor honest. And if you do fight, fight it out; and don't give in while you can stand and see.

As Mark Girouard has noted recently,[14] one of Hughes's immediate predecessors in his praise of fighting was Carlyle; like Hughes, he gave the term a broad, and at least largely unobjectionable, meaning. In *Past and Present*, a book Hughes read while an undergraduate at Oriel and much admired,[15] Carlyle had written: "Man is created to fight; he is perhaps best of all definable as a born soldier; his life 'a battle and a march,' under the right General. It is forever indispensable for a man to fight: now with Necessity, with Barrenness, Scarcity, with Puddles, Bogs, tangled Forests, unkempt Cotton;—now also with the hallucinations of his poor fellow Men."[16] That Thomas Hughes—the school and college athlete, the outdoorsman, the boxing and gymnastics coach at the London Working Men's College, the vigorous man of action—should be thought of as an advocate of mindless bodily strength and pugnaciousness is understandable, though wrong; to think of his idol and inspiration Thomas Carlyle, the perpetually ailing Sage of Chelsea, in that light is ludicrous.

Like Kingsley,[17] Hughes was uncomfortable wearing the mantle of the muscular Christian. In his view the term was unfortunate because it carried, then as now, certain misleading connotations. If this designation is to be applied to him, Hughes urges more than once, let it at least be defined appropriately and distinguished from that which it is not. In the eleventh chapter of *Tom Brown at Oxford*, for instance, he

307

sets down some wry observations on the confusion that has arisen regarding the whole subject of muscular Christianity:

> Our hero on his first appearance in public some years since, was without his own consent at once patted on the back by the good-natured critics, and enrolled for better or worse in the brotherhood of muscular Christians, who at that time were beginning to be recognised as an actual and lusty portion of general British life. . . . I am speaking of course under correction, and with only a slight acquaintance with the faith of muscular Christianity, gathered almost entirely from the witty expositions and comments of persons of a somewhat dyspeptic habit, who are not amongst the faithful themselves. Indeed, I am not aware that any authorized articles of belief have been sanctioned or published by the sect, Church, or whatever they may be. . . .
>
> But in the course of my inquiries on the subject of muscular Christians, their works and ways, a fact has forced itself on my attention, which . . . ought not to be passed over. I find, then, that, side by side with these muscular Christians, and apparently claiming some sort of connexion with them . . . have risen up another set of persons, against whom I desire to caution my readers and my hero. . . . I must call the persons in question "musclemen," as distinguished from muscular Christians; the only point in common between the two being, that both hold it to be a good thing to have strong and well-exercised bodies. . . . Here all likeness ends; for the "muscleman" seems to have no belief whatever as to the purposes for which his body has been given him, except some hazy idea that it is to go up and down the world with him, belabouring men and captivating women for his benefit or pleasure, at once the servant and fomenter of those fierce and brutal passions which he seems to think it a necessity, and rather a fine thing than otherwise, to indulge and obey. Whereas, so far as I know, the least of the muscular Christians has hold of the old chivalrous and Christian belief, that a man's body is given him to be trained and brought into subjection, and then used for the protection of the weak, the advancement of all righteous causes, and the subduing of the earth which God has given to the children of men. He does not hold that mere strength or activity are in themselves worthy of any respect or worship, or that one man is a bit better than another because he can knock him down, or carry a bigger sack of potatoes than he.

Described in this way, seriously but not solemnly, muscular Christianity actually sounds rather engaging. Though it may be difficult for us to accept it, it should be even more difficult to rail against it or ridicule it.

II

Walter Houghton and other chroniclers of "the Victorian frame of mind" have correctly identified manliness as an important mid-nineteenth-century touchstone of virtue. Houghton himself conceives of it as part of the tradition "of the English squirearchy, both at home and at the public schools and universities, with its cult of games and field sports, and its admiration for physical strength and prowess," and calls *Tom Brown's School Days* "the classic text" of manliness.[18] There are, however, several difficulties here.

In the first place, that numerous band of Englishmen to which an admiring Hughes refers collectively as "The Brown Family" in the title of the opening chapter of *Tom Brown's School Days* contains representatives of several classes, and so one cannot really say, as Houghton does, that "the Browns are the squires of England." Second, games, field sports, and displays of physical strength and prowess, though undeniably important in *Tom Brown's School Days* and elsewhere in Hughes's work, are not all-important, as we have seen. And finally, an examination of *Tom Brown's School Days* itself reveals that Hughes's use of the terms *manly* and *manliness* is neither frequent nor specific.

Hughes calls the village boys—certainly not members of the squirearchy—with whom Tom Brown plays before he begins his schooling "fully as manly and honest, and certainly purer, than those in a higher rank" (1:3). Old Brooke, the sixth-form hero during Tom's early days at Rugby, admonishes the younger boys in their house that, though they " 'get plenty of good beer here,' " " 'drinking isn't fine or manly' " (1:6). In one of Hughes's numerous asides, he urges "boys who are getting into the upper forms" to remember that their juniors will view them as what we now call role models: "Speak up, and strike out if necessary, for whatsoever is true, and manly, and lovely, and of good report" (1:8). In another, he remarks on the beneficent influence of "Arnold's manly piety" (2:1) in so softening the mood of the school that boys were no longer ashamed of being seen and heard to say their prayers kneeling at their dormitory bedsides. Tom's "young master" tells him as he is about to leave Rugby that the headmaster's goal had been to enable Tom to acquire "manliness and thoughtfulness" (2:8).

My list of five examples may not be complete, but it is

certainly representative, and it suggests that for Hughes in *Tom Brown's School Days* manliness may be equated with such general concepts as moral virtue and strength of character.[19] Though its first syllable doubtless grates on the ears of some, the term could conceivably be applied to right-living girls and women as well as to right-living boys and men, and it certainly goes beyond mere bodily strength or athletic prowess much as the muscular Christian excels over the mere muscleman.

Those who question Hughes's conception of manliness sometimes read back into *Tom Brown's School Days* the title, if not the contents, of a somewhat disconcertingly named work he published twenty-two years later, *The Manliness of Christ*. They might find instructive a little confession that one writer inserted into a review of *The Manliness of Christ* shortly after it appeared. Having been put off by the title, this critic went ahead and read the book anyway, and was much relieved to discover that "our feeling of dislike has entirely passed away" and that "'manliness' is not the old 'muscular Christianity,' only under a new name; but that it is humanity at its best."[20]

Despite its relatively late date, *The Manliness of Christ* is worth bringing into the present discussion because it is the one place where Hughes provides an extended definition of manliness as he understands it.[21] Having begun by praising Jesus for displaying courage and manliness, Hughes devotes some twenty pages to differentiating between those terms before launching into the chronological account of Christ's life and ministry that comprises the body of the work. Put simply, manliness is more comprehensive than courage, and neither attribute is necessarily connected with physical strength or athletic skill. Manliness, which includes such ingredients as "tenderness and thoughtfulness for others,"[22] is a distinctly human quality, though it does bear out the fact that mankind at its best both reflects and aspires to divinity. Ordinary physical courage, on the other hand, admirable and necessary though it may be at times as a component or accompaniment of manliness, is really "an animal quality" (p. 22). As for "athleticism," with which Hughes has so often been identified, he insists that it is worthless in itself—"a good thing if kept in its place," but one that "has come to be very much over-praised and over-valued among us" (p. 24)—and that, unlike manliness, it can be turned to vicious purposes: "a great athlete may be a brute and a coward, while the truly manly man can be neither" (p. 26).

There are three other important characteristics of manliness, in Christ or in the ordinary mortals for whom he serves as the supreme example. The first and most obvious is the readiness to bear pain or even death—not in the form of self-gratification we call masochism, but unselfishly, for the sake of one's fellow humans. A second attribute of manliness is unswerving loyalty to truth, which is, according to Hughes, "the most rare and difficult of human qualities," especially when we are forced to bear this witness, as Christ did, not only against the establishment but also "against those we love, against those whose judgments and opinions we respect, in defence or furtherance of that which approves itself as true to our inmost conscience" (pp. 34-35). Finally, manliness is marked by the subordination of the human will to one's sense of duty, ultimately duty to one's God: " 'to do the will of my Father and your Father'" (p. 40).

Though the subject and the aim of *The Manliness of Christ* are clearly loftier than those of Hughes's three novels, it is not difficult to see how the definition of manliness it articulates is implicit in those earlier works, as they deal with Tom Brown's development at school and at college or with Richard's growth during his Berkshire holiday in *The Scouring of the White Horse*. Clearly, there is far more involved in all four books than "games and field sports," than "physical strength or prowess."

III

At the end of *The Healthy Body and Victorian Culture*, Bruce Haley points out that the "manly ideal" was a product of the Victorian age but also that "Victorian intellectuals initiated the protest against it. They did so, not because it equated health and manliness, but because it envisioned both of these so narrowly."[23] *The Manliness of Christ* could hardly be called a "protest" against "the manly ideal," but certainly it is an attempt—a largely successful one, I would maintain—to broaden it, in much the same way that *Tom Brown at Oxford* contains a telling attempt to correct and expand the popular perception of muscular Christianity.

Our understanding of what a mid-Victorian like Thomas Hughes meant by muscular Christianity and manliness is necessarily much cloudier than that of his contemporaries, partly because some of our recent reading has befogged rather than clarified our thinking and partly because in these *autres temps* we observe *autres moeurs*. To the extent that we believe we comprehend those old-fashioned ideals, many of us regard them as naive, objectionable, or risible. We are, after all, products of a culture in which a series of novels by George Macdonald Fraser celebrating the later exploits of Flashman, the odious arch-bully at Tom Brown's Rugby, has achieved considerable popularity since the late 1960s. In a few strategic places, this outrageous anti-hero openly expresses his profound contempt for Hughes, for Arnold, for Arnold's school, and for the "manly" set there, and all of his ultimately triumphant misadventures implicitly mock their values.

Thomas Hughes did indeed praise muscular Christianity and manliness, the former reluctantly and the latter with increasing precision as his career continued. If we are to read *Tom Brown's School Days* and his other work aright, we must try to free those terms of the overtones and connotations they have taken on over the past century and a quarter, by doing what we can to recover the meanings that he himself assigned to them. If we are successful at this task, a return to, or a first acquaintance with, his writing should yield some pleasant surprises.

1. "Arnold and His School," *North British Review* 28 (February 1858): 139.

2. Edward C. Mack and W. H. G. Armytage, *Thomas Hughes* (London, 1952), p. 294.

3. See, for example: "Tom Brown's Schooldays," *Spectator* 30 (2 May 1857): 477–78; "Books of the Week," *Examiner*, 2 May 1857, p. 278; "*Tom*

Brown's School Days," *Literary Gazette,* 20 June 1857, pp. 587-88; "Tom Brown's School Days," *Saturday Review* 4 (3 October 1857): 313-14; *"The Book of Rugby School, Its History and Its Daily Life* and *Tom Brown's School Days by an Old Boy,"* *Quarterly Review* 102 (October 1857): 330-54; and *"Tom Brown's School Days* (Third Edition)," *Times,* 9 October 1857, p. 10.

4. John R. Reed, *Old School Ties: The Public Schools in British Literature* (Syracuse, 1964), pp. 17, 26-27; cf. Reed's "The Public Schools in Victorian Literature," *NCF* 29 (1974): 67-69; David Newsome, *Godliness & Good Learning* (London, 1961), passim; Bruce Haley, *The Healthy Body and Victorian Culture* (Cambridge, Mass., 1978), pp. 145-55; and Mark Girouard, *The Return to Camelot: Chivalry and the English Gentleman* (New Haven, Conn., 1981), pp. 166-68.

5. Richard Usborne, "A Re-reading of 'Tom Brown,'" *Spectator* 197 (17 August 1956): 229.

6. Kenneth Allsop, "A Coupon for Instant Tradition: On 'Tom Brown's Schooldays,'" *Encounter* 25 (November 1965): 60-63. Allsop was answered by A. L. LeQuesne in "Defending Tom Brown," *Encounter* 26 (June 1966): 93-94; and by A. J. Hartley in "Christian Socialism and Victorian Morality: The Inner Meaning of *Tom Brown's School-days,"* *Dalhousie Review* 49 (1969): 216-23. I agree with both LeQuesne and Hartley, but my discussion of muscular Christianity and manliness goes considerably beyond them. (There may be some significance in the fact that, unlike Usborne and Allsop, neither LeQuesne [an Australian] nor Hartley [a Canadian] is English.)

7. "Two Years Ago," *Saturday Review* 4 (21 February 1857): 176.

8. *Literary Gazette,* 20 June 1857, p. 587.

9. *Times,* 9 October 1857, p. 10.

10. James Fitzjames Stephen, *"Tom Brown's Schooldays.* 4th edition," *Edinburgh Review* 107 (January 1858): 193.

11. The time scheme of *Tom Brown's School Days* is neither clear nor consistent. In the first chapter of part 1, the reader is told that Tom "went first to school when nearly eight years of age," but two chapters later Tom is shown setting out for that establishment, a private school, "when he was nine years old." If the second statement is correct, Tom would have to be ten when he goes to Rugby, for he leaves his first school "in the middle of his third half-year, in October, 183-" (1:3) and is sent to Rugby almost immediately, "in the early part of November 183-" (1: 4). The statement that Tom has "grown into a young man nineteen years old" when he leaves Rugby occurs in 2:8, but the text yields no persuasive evidence that nine years have in fact passed since his arrival there. Subsequent quotations from *Tom Brown's School Days* will be documented parenthetically, with part numbers followed by chapter numbers.

12. Tom's "boyishness" is defined as consisting of "animal life in its fullest measure, good nature and honest impulses, hatred of injustice and meanness, and thoughtlessness enough to sink a three-decker" (1:7).

13. "The Sermon Which the Parson Sent to Mr. Joseph Hurst, of Elm Close Farm, in Fulfilment of His Promise," *The Scouring of the White Horse* (Cambridge, 1859), pp. 203 and 210.

14. Girouard, *The Return to Camelot*, p. 130.

15. Mack and Armytage, *Thomas Hughes*, p. 35.

16. *Past and Present*, ed. Richard D. Altick (Boston, 1965), p. 191.

17. Robert B. Martin, *The Dust of Combat: A Life of Charles Kingsley* (London, 1959), p. 219.

18. *The Victorian Frame of Mind 1830-1870* (New Haven, Conn., 1957), p. 202.

19. In *Tom Brown at Oxford*, Hughes works from essentially the same definition. For instance, in chapter 15, while sliding into an irresponsible affair with a barmaid, Tom hears "the still small voice appealing to the man, the true man, within us, which is made in the image of God—calling on him to assert his dominion over the wild beast" and bringing out his better nature, his "true strength, and nobleness, and manliness." I find Henry R. Harrington's equation of Tom's emerging manliness with sublimated sexual energy interesting but reductive and ultimately unpersuasive. See his "Childhood and the Victorian Idea of Manliness in *Tom Brown's Schooldays*," *VNL* 44 (Fall 1973): 13-17.

20. "Mr. Hughes on the Manliness of Christ," *Spectator* 53 (3 April 1880): 437.

21. Mention should be made here of a curious volume of extracts from Hughes's writings that was published in the United States a year after *The Manliness of Christ: True Manliness*, ed. E. E. Brown (Boston, 1880). Except for a fifteen-page autobiographical letter by Hughes, prefaced with a "Preliminary Note" by his friend James Russell Lowell, to whom the letter had been written, the book contains nothing that had not previously appeared in print. It seems clear that the American publisher, who included *True Manliness* in his uplifting "Spare Minute Series," was trading on the popularity of *The Manliness of Christ*, from which long passages are included. Hughes had nothing to do with the publication of *True Manliness* and apparently did not even see a copy until 1894. See Mack and Armytage, *Thomas Hughes*, pp. 289-91.

22. Thomas Hughes, *The Manliness of Christ* (London, 1879), p. 21. Subsequent quotations from *The Manliness of Christ* will be documented parenthetically.

23. Haley, *The Healthy Body and Victorian Culture*, p. 261.

XV

ANDREW WRIGHT

Trollope Transformed, or
The Disguises of Mr Harding and Others

ADAPTATION—THAT IS, ABRIDGMENT, SIMPLIFICATION, DRAMA-tization, and translation—of literary classics is not peculiar to the twentieth century, but it has taken new as well as old forms, and all have cultural significance—or at least all provide food for thought: they indicate the strengths and possibly the limitations of the works adapted, together with the surroundings in which they have been produced.[1] That there is a morality of adaptation is a matter of common sense: the very integrity of the writer is in the balance; and the range may be from slight adjustment to facile debasement. Accord-ingly, readers of a volume devoted to a scholar who has done more than any other to make us conscious of the social significance of the rise of literacy may like to consider the subject, and I propose to do so in reasonably economical compass: Trollope, for all that he was prolific, has not been treated to the pullings and haulings of which Dickens has been so notoriously the victim, often to be sure by his own connivance, indeed by his own agency. Nor is Trollope a cult figure to the top of anyone's bent like Jane Austen (or for that matter like Dickens): he has therefore been spared some of the more egregious transformational efforts, but there have been enough to make analysis useful.

Indeed, Trollope adaptations are more numerous than might at first be supposed, but comparatively speaking the number is modest and so is the range. It is no surprise that *The Warden* and *Barchester Towers* have been treated much more frequently than any of the other titles, but adaptations of all the Chronicles of Barsetshire and all those in the Palliser series have also appeared, as well as adaptations of a number of other works. The following, for instance, have been produced on the BBC: *The Claverings, Cousin Henry, Dr. Wortle's School, Is He Popenjoy?, John Caldigate, The Prime Minister, The Vicar of Bullhampton,* and *The Way We Live Now.* In book form there have been adaptations of a number of the foregoing and of still other titles, including *Ayala's Angel, North America, South Africa,* and *The Three Clerks.*

Although all kinds of adaptation invite attention, translations to foreign languages raise questions that are less germane here than those posed by abridgment, simplification, and dramatization: in any event translation raises issues directed at least as much to the language into which the work is translated as to the work itself. The questions deriving from native adaptation are at any rate sufficiently varied to make foreign excursions a luxury that need not be afforded in the present essay.

To consider first of all the question of abridgment, Trollope, it will be remembered, was no friend of short-windedness. When he was asked by his publisher to shorten *Barchester Towers* he said, "I do object to reducing the book to two volumes—not because I am particularly wedded to three, but from a conviction that no book written in three can be judiciously so reduced," and Gordon Ray has shown that Trollope regarded bulk and worth as near allied.[2] To be sure, in 1878 Trollope did reduce the length of *The Duke's Children* considerably, but this was at a time when his popularity was on the wane; his willingness indicates a clear-eyed recognition of the actualities of public expectation as his life drew to a close rather than the late acquisition of an affection for brevity. Because I have dealt with the question of the abridgment of *The Duke's Children* elsewhere, I shall not rehearse that unique departure here:[3] the point is that amplitude rather than compression was for Trollope the desideratum. When, therefore, compression takes place, his own sense of himself as an artist is unquestionably threatened.

Of course, all adaptation of a classic involves loss, unless the adapter is a person whose genius and perhaps boldness are at least equal to those of the author of the original. Trollope has never been adapted by the likes of Shakespeare or Robert Lowell; and the fact of loss, though there is a considerable range, remains a constant: no one blots Trollope's lines with artistic impunity. Yet overall appraisal, although irresistible here and there in the present essay, may be less useful because more difficult to illustrate comparatively than the more precisely focused analysis of representative passages. From *The Warden* the three passages I have chosen are the first five paragraphs of chapter 1 ("Hiram's Hospital"), the archdeacon's address to the bedesmen in chapter 5 ("Dr. Grantly Visits the Hospital"), and Mr. Harding's parting words to his charges in the penultimate chapter ("Farewell"). The first passage consists of the combination of narrative and narrator's comment characteristic of Trollope; the second, of a combination of dialogue and comment; the third, of almost unencumbered speech.

In laying out the evidence, I shall begin with the abridgment by Lord Hemingford.[4] The advertised slightness of the abridgment makes examination of the issues convenient; it also minimizes the necessity of repetition: what Lord Hemingford omits is also what others have tended to omit. In a preface the sparing approach is set forth as follows: "Some words and phrases have been simplified, but there are not many. Various passages have been omitted, but these do not affect the plot" (p. xi). I have departed a little from the usual practice favored by analytical bibliographers, in order to emphasize the nature and extent of the alterations: Trollope's own words are indicated in the typeface employed throughout the present volume; his own words are also indicated in **boldface** type in the specimen passages, but boldface type is used for words that are omitted in the abridgment; where underscored words are adjacent to or near italicized words, the latter are substitutions introduced by the abridger. Italics are also used for larger-scale substitutions. The text of *The Warden* is that of the Oxford Trollope.

Chapter 1: Hiram's Hospital

The Rev. Septimus Harding was, a few years since, a **beneficed** clergyman residing in the cathedral town of ----; **let us call it** Barchester. **Were we to name Wells or Salisbury, Exeter, Hereford, or Gloucester, it might be presumed that something personal was intended; and as this tale will refer mainly to the cathedral dignitaries of the town in question, we are anxious that no personality may be suspected.** Let us presume *suppose* that Barchester is a quiet town in the West of England, more remarkable for the beauty of its cathedral and the antiquity of its monuments *age of its buildings* than for any commercial prosperity; that the west end of Barchester is the cathedral close *cathedral is at the west end of Barchester* and that the aristocracy *leading people* of Barchester are the bishop, dean, and canons, with their respective wives and daughters *families*.

Early in life Mr. Harding found himself located *placed* at Barchester. A fine voice and a taste for sacred music had decided the position in which he was to exercise his calling *follow his profession*, and for many years he performed the easy but not highly paid duties of a minor canon. At the age of forty a small living in the close vicinity of the town *the charge of a small parish near the town* increased both his work and his income, and at the age of fifty he became precentor of the cathedral.

Mr. Harding had married early in life, and was the father of two daughters. The eldest *elder*, Susan, was born soon after his marriage; the other, Eleanor, not till ten years later. At the time at which we introduce him to our readers he was living as precentor at Barchester with his youngest *younger* daughter, then twenty-four years of age; having been many years a widower, and having married his eldest *elder* daughter to a son of the bishop, a very short time before his installation *appointment* to the office of precentor.

Scandal *Talkers* at Barchester affirmed *declared* that had it not been for the beauty of his daughter, Mr. Harding would have remained a minor canon; but here probably Scandal *talkers* lied, as she *they* so often does *do*; for even as a minor canon no one had been more popular among his reverend brethren **in the close,** than Mr. Harding; and Scandal *talkers*, before she had reprobated *they blamed* Mr. Harding for being made precentor by his friend the bishop, had loudly blamed the bishop for having so long omitted to do something for his friend Mr. Harding. Be this as it may, Susan Harding, some twelve years since, had married *the bishop's son,* the Rev. Theophilus Grantly, son of the bishop, archdeacon of Barchester, and rector of Plumstead Episcopi, and her father became, a few months later, precentor of Barchester Cathedral, that office being, as is not usual, in the bishop's gift. *was appointed, by the bishop, a few months later, precentor of Barchester Cathedral.*

Now there are peculiar circumstances connected with the precentorship which must be explained. In the year 1434 there died at Barchester one John Hiram, who had made money in the town as a woolstapler, *wool-manufacturer*, and in his will he left the house in which he died and certain meadows and closes *fields* near the town, still called Hiram's Butts, and Hiram's Patch *Fields* for the support of twelve superannuated wool-carders *retired workmen*, all of whom should have been born and bred and spent their days in Barchester; he also appointed *enjoined* that an alms-house *a hospital* should be built for their abode *dwelling*, with a fitting *suitable* residence for a warden, which *and that the* warden was also to *should also* receive a certain sum annually out of the rents of the said butts and patches *these fields*. He, moreover, willed, having had a soul alive to harmony, that the precentor of the cathedral should have the option of being also *might also be* warden of the alms-houses *hospital*, if the bishop in each case approved.

By omitting the long dash (impossible, alas, to indicate typographically) and "let us call it" before Barchester the abridger is subtracting at least three elements from the original: first, the no doubt deliberately languid ostentatiousness of the narrator in declaring his control over his materials; second, the concomitant sense that he is embarking on the telling of a tale rather than the representation of actuality: here is to be a novel rather than journalism or history; third, the universalizing force of the long dash, so that "Barchester" stands not for one cathedral town but for Wells, Salisbury, Exeter, Hereford, and Gloucester—to mention only those cathedral towns which Trollope himself names in the following sentence, but which the abridger omits.

By employing simpler diction than that in the original— "suppose" for "presume," "age of its buildings" for "antiquity of its monuments," "follow his profession" for "exercise his calling," "blamed" for "reprobated," and so forth, the abridger has virtually withdrawn an element that is important in establishing the relationship between story-teller and reader as one between equals of a sort, reasonably cultivated men of the world who know what they can say to one another and what can be left unsaid. In fact, the over-all effect of the abridgment in the passage under examination is of the near-extinction of the character of the narrator, surely a dubious, even dangerous, enterprise.

Readers of Henry James's cavils in two essays published in *Partial Portraits* (1888), namely "Anthony Trollope" and "The Art of Fiction," will remember the strongly-worded view expressed there that Trollope should have been more self-effacing in his novels, especially in the matter of calling attention to the fictiveness of his fictions; but James never argued that Trollope the narrator should have been tamed as the Oxford abridger has tamed him.

Chapter 5: Dr. Grantly Visits the Hospital

As the archdeacon stood up to make his speech, erect in the middle of that little square, he looked like an ecclesiastical statue placed there, as a fitting impersonation of the church militant here on earth; his shovel hat, large, new, and well-pronounced, a churchman's hat in every inch, declared the profession as plainly as does the Quaker's broad brim; his heavy eyebrows, large open eyes, and full mouth and chin expressed the solidity of his order; the broad chest, amply covered with fine cloth, told how well to do was its estate; one hand ensconced within his pocket, evinced the practical hold which our mother church keeps on her temporal possessions; and the other, loose for action, was ready to fight if need be in her defence; and, below these, the decorous breeches, and neat black gaiters showing so admirably that well-turned leg, betokened the stability, the decency, the outward beauty and grace of our church establishment.

The archdeacon—a man of heavy eyebrows, large eyes, strong mouth and chin, and broad chest—stood up to make his speech, erect in the middle of that little square.

'Now, my men,' he began, **when he had settled himself well in his position;** 'I want to say a few words to you. Your good friend, the warden here, and myself, and my lord the bishop, on whose behalf I wish to speak to you, would all be very sorry, very sorry indeed, that you should have any just ground of complaint. Any just cause of complaint on your part would be removed at once by the warden, or by his lordship, or by me on his behalf, without the necessity of any petition on your part.' Here the <u>orator</u> *speaker* stopped for a moment, expecting that some little murmurs of applause would show that the weakest of men were beginning to give way; but no such murmurs came. Bunce, himself, even sat with closed lips, <u>mute</u> *silent* and unsatisfactory. 'Without the necessity of any petition at all,' he repeated. 'I'm told you have addressed a petition to my lord.' He paused for a reply from the men, and after a while, Handy plucked up courage and said, 'Yes, we <u>has</u> *have*.'

'You have addressed a petition to my lord, in which, as I am informed, you express an opinion that you do not receive from Hiram's estate all that is your due.' **Here most of the men expressed their assent.** 'Now what is it you ask for? What is it you want that you haven't got here? What is it—'

'A hundred a year,' muttered old Moody, with a voice as if it came out of the ground.

'A hundred a year!' ejacula̲t̲e̲d̲ *exclaimed* the archdeacon **militant, defying the impudence of these claimants with one hand stretched out and closed, while with the other he tightly grasped, and secured within his breeches pocket, that symbol of the church's wealth which his own loose half-crowns not unaptly represented.** 'A hundred a year! Why, my men, you must be mad! And you talk about John Hiram's will.'

The remainder of the speech, except for one or two small substitutions—"weak" for "infirm," "rich men" for "gentlemen"—is adhered to by the abridger. The seriousness of the omission of the narrator's account is the more fully realized when the characterization of Dr. Grantly as a whole is taken into account: he is, specifically and at large, worldly, self-seeking, power-hungry, authoritarian, insensitive; the greatness of the portrait resides in the presentation of him in such a way as to elicit affection for him despite all his faults. In order to bring off this small miracle, Trollope has to "go behind": the observer scamped by the abridger pretends, but only pretends, to be describing the clergyman before him, but the force of the words is such as to reveal a vanity that is sufficiently ludicrous, self-deluding, and ineffectual as to be amiably venial.

Chapter 20: Farewell
'My dear old friends,' said he [Mr. Harding], 'you all know that I am going to leave you.'

There was a sort of murmur ran round the room, intended, perhaps, to express regret at his departure; but it was b̲u̲t̲ *only* a murmur, and might have meant that or anything else.

'There has been lately some misunderstanding between us. You have thought, I believe, that you did not get all that you w̲e̲r̲e̲ e̲n̲t̲i̲t̲l̲e̲d̲ *had a right* to, and that the funds of the hospital have not been properly disposed of. As for me, I cannot say w̲h̲a̲t̲ s̲h̲o̲u̲l̲d̲ b̲e̲ t̲h̲e̲ d̲i̲s̲p̲o̲s̲i̲t̲i̲o̲n̲ o̲f̲ t̲h̲e̲s̲e̲ m̲o̲n̲e̲y̲s̲, *how these funds should be disposed of*, or how they should be managed, and I have therefore thought it best to go.'

'We never wanted to drive y̲o̲u̲r̲ r̲e̲v̲e̲r̲e̲n̲c̲e̲ o̲u̲t̲ o̲f̲ i̲t̲,' *you out of it, sir*,' said Handy.

'No, indeed, y̲o̲u̲r̲ r̲e̲v̲e̲r̲e̲n̲c̲e̲,' *sir*,' said Skulpit. 'We never thought it would come to this. When I signed the petition—that is, I didn't sign it, because—'

'Let h̲i̲s̲ r̲e̲v̲e̲r̲e̲n̲c̲e̲ *the warden* speak, can't you?' said Moody.

'No,' continued Mr. Harding; 'I am sure you did not wish to turn me out; but I thought it best to leave you. I am not a very good hand at a lawsuit, as you may all guess; and when it seemed necessary that our ordinary quiet ~~mode~~ *way* of living should be disturbed, I thought it better to go. I am neither angry nor ~~offended~~ *displeased* with any man in the hospital.'

Here Bunce uttered a kind of groan, very clearly expressive of disagreement.

'I am neither angry nor displeased with any man in the hospital,' repeated Mr. Harding emphatically. 'If any man has been wrong—and I don't say any man has—he has erred through wrong advice. In this country all <u>are</u> <u>entitled</u> <u>to</u> <u>look</u> <u>for</u> <u>their</u> <u>own</u> <u>rights</u>, *have a right to care for their own* *interests*, and you have done no more. As long as your interests and my interests were <u>at</u> <u>variance</u>, *in conflict*, I could give you no counsel on this subject; but the connection between us has ceased; my income can no longer depend on your doings, and therefore, as I leave you, I venture to offer to you my advice.'

The men all declared that they would from henceforth be entirely guided by Mr. Harding's opinion in their affairs.

'Some gentleman will probably take my place here very soon, and I strongly advise you to be prepared to receive him in a kindly spirit and to raise no further question among yourselves as to the amount of his income. <u>Were</u> <u>you</u> *If you were* to succeed in lessening what he has to receive, you would not increase your own allowance. The surplus would not go to you; your wants are <u>sufficiently</u> *adequately* provided for, and your position could hardly be improved.'

'God bless <u>your</u> <u>reverence</u>, <u>we</u> <u>knows</u> <u>it</u>,' *you, sir, we know it*,' said Spriggs.

'It's all true, <u>your</u> <u>reverence</u>,' *sir*,' said Skulpit. 'We <u>sees</u> *see* it all now.'

Here the abridger has seen fit to alter the spoken words of Mr. Harding not sufficiently to change the sense of the speech to the pensioners but—ever so slightly—the character of the old clergyman himself. When he says "had a right to" for "were entitled to" and "have a right to care for their own interests" for "are entitled to look for their own rights," and "in conflict" for "at variance," he is made somewhat less mild than in the original. None of these paraphrases alters the picture more than a little, but together they efface something of the tenderness of manner that contrasts with the effective force of his decision to resign the wardenship. Furthermore, the suppression by the abridger of the habitual mode of address by the pensioners to Mr. Harding—"your reverence"— diminishes the sense of antique respect in which he is held. Still, it cannot be said that the alterations compromise Trollope's intention as a whole.

Andrew Wright

Now, to consider a couple of extremes: the first is the abridgment of *The Warden* issued by the Mellifont Press in London in 1947. Opposite the title page is an introductory note, the last paragraph of which reads: "In this edition certain longueurs inherent in Trollope's style have been sensitively minimised for the modern reader." But so little has been excised that it is impossible to refrain from wondering why there should have been any tampering at all, especially as *The Warden* is not a long novel by Victorian standards. In the first passage there is merely the substitution of the words "younger" for "youngest," and in the second "eyebrow" for "eyebrows" (hardly "longueurs"). At the end of the archdeacon's speech, the following sentence is omitted: "They stared grimly upon his burly figure, but did not express, by word or sign, the anger and disgust which such language was sure to give rise." The paragraph as written by Trollope is the stronger because the less sentimental. From the warden's farewell nothing is omitted.

By contrast, and to move away from mere abridgment, there is the retelling of the works in entirely, or almost entirely, new words. The genre is that of the simplification. Here most poignantly the question of morality arises. Charles and Mary Lamb at least did not pretend that their tales were Shakespeare. In *The Warden of Hiram's Hospital*, however, H. Oldfield Box wisely signals in the retitling of the novel that something is afoot, and on the title page he equally conscionably proclaims the scope of his efforts and his intended audience: "Retold for Young People by H. Oldfield Box." The volume belongs to Crowther's "Introduction to Good Reading" series and was issued at Bognor Regis in 1946. (Although I question the desirability of such versions as this one, I do not want to abuse H. Oldfield Box, who is a hero of Trollopian adaptation as I shall shortly demonstrate.)

Chapter 1 [The chapters are untitled in this version]
If you look at a map of England to discover Barsetshire, you will not be able to find it. For Barset is an imaginary county, created by Anthony Trollope as a background for six novels about English country life in the 'fifties and 'sixties of the last century. But the life that was lived there was so typical of English country life at that time—and especially in the south-western part of the country—that Barset is in at least one sense a real county.

323

To those who have read and loved Trollope's stories it seems very real indeed.

The story which follows is taken from the first of these six Barsetshire novels.

Now in 185- there lived in Barset, in its cathedral city of Barchester, an elderly clergyman, the Rev. Septimus Harding. He was well known and much loved for his kindly, tolerant and Christian nature. He had for long been Precentor of Barchester Cathedral, and he was also warden of Hiram's Hospital, a position to which he had been appointed many years before by his friend the Bishop of Barchester, a truly pious and lovable old man. The Bishop was Mr. Harding's senior by a number of years, and his son, Archdeacon Grantly, rector of Plumstead Episcopi, had married the warden's elder daughter, Susan, so the ties between the two families had become very close.

Hiram's Hospital was not a hospital in the modern sense. It was an almshouse, founded in the fifteenth century by a certain John Hiram, a successful woolstapler in the town, who had left his house and certain lands near the city for the support of twelve old woolcarders whom age had forced to retire from their work. . . .

Where is Anthony Trollope? Where is Mr. Harding?

Chapter 4 [for 5]

'Listen,' my men, 'began the Archdeacon, when they were all assembled. 'I want to speak a few words to you. You know what I've come to speak about?'

A low muttering from his audience indicated that they did know.

'Very well,' continued the Archdeacon. 'We won't beat about the bush. If you had any just grounds of complaint they would be removed at once. But understand that you have no such grounds. I hear that you have actually addressed a petition to his lordship, the Bishop. Is this so?'

Handy, plucking up courage, murmured that they wanted their hundred a year.

'A hundred a year!' echoed the Archdeacon scornfully. 'My men, you must be mad.'

The archdeacon presented here is less sympathetic than in the original: Trollope's satiric strokes are such as to intensify the depiction of Dr. Grantly as an outrageously worldly divine (though not any kind of hypocrite), the outrage stemming at least in part from his unconsciousness of the contest in himself between God and Mammon. Box omits the whole of the paragraph describing the archdeacon's appearance as he stands before the bedesmen, and the retelling presents him in a simpler, harsher light. There is no reason to think him so lacking in sympathy as he is in understanding; indeed, in the original a certain sympathy—patronizing it may be, but genuine—is expressed. Also the vulnerable naiveté of his expectation of a favorable response to "without the necessity of any petition on your part" is passed over. Nor can it be said that Box improves on Trollope when he puts into the arch-deacon's mouth " 'We won't beat about the bush' " and revises the response to the request for a hundred a year to " 'A hundred a year!' echoed the Archdeacon scornfully," omitting also all the Trollopian commentary that comes before " 'Why, my men, you must be mad.' "

Chapter 10 [for 20]

It was with great grief that he took leave of his old pensioners. Just before his departure from the Hospital he assembled them all in his drawing-room for a last glass of wine.

'We never wanted to drive your reverence out,' said Abel Handy, now truly repentant; and the rest with tears in their eyes, and knowing that their friend and protector was soon to leave them, could only echo his words. Poor old men! It was not their fault that they had been misled into expecting riches that could never be theirs. The Warden comforted them as best he could with an assurance of his continued friendship and a promise to visit them from time to time.

The reader is denied the amplitude of this sentimental scene, one that must be expected in the novel Trollope wrote, and over which a certain leisureliness of presentation makes for the sense of satisfaction produced by the concluding pages of the novel.

On the BBC *The Warden* has been performed at least eight times since the early years of the Second World War and once on television—not counting repeats. The range is from the single-episode dramatization by H. Oldfield Box in 1942 to the six-part television version by Cedric Wallis in 1951, incorporation into *The Barchester Chronicles* in 1973, and an abridgment by Ronald Russell read by Paul Rogers in 1977. Not all the manuscripts of these versions survive; those that do afford abundant evidence that the BBC has been commendably conscientious in making the classics available to its listeners.

There is other evidence as well. Predictably, each version bears the marks of the time in which it was produced. Thus the 1948 version of *The Warden* by H. Oldfield Box—which, I have reason to believe, is a revision of the lost wartime versions of 1942 and 1945—opens with the following words of a narrator: "Happy Barchester! No German planes, or indeed any planes, ever roared over your quiet Cathedral precincts. Here is a mid-Victorian cathedral town, set in a West-of-England county, a city where it seems always afternoon." When the play was revised for broadcast in 1951, the bombers were made to disappear but the note of nostalgia rang a little louder: "Barchester! Happy Barchester! An old cathedral town in the mid-Victorian era,—an age of security which seemed as set and enduring as the ancient cathedral itself. (*Organ* music) Barchester! a city where it seemed always afternoon." The play itself is duly respectful of Trollope's language and, though much abbreviated, a worthy effort to capture the spirit of the original. The leisurely exposition of the first chapter is replaced by an evocation of atmosphere: a tenor voice chants the Litany, a choir joins in the responses, and the narrator declares (in 1948), "Our story does not deal with battle. . . ." There follows a condensed retelling of the circumstances set forth at the beginning of the novel. In the archdeacon's speech to the pensioners, the modifications are very nearly identical to those in the Box version for young people. Mr. Harding's farewell is a shrewdly cut version of the original.

In the six-part black-and-white television version of 1951, written by Cedric Wallis and produced by Campbell Logan, there is a commendable fidelity to the original, especially in the matter of dialogue, though inevitably certain compressions are to be observed. What is reduced drastically is narration (always, as has been seen, regarded as the most dispensable element in the novel). There is, besides, a strong infusion of what may be called the nostalgia effect. Thus, the very introduction of the piece is pictorially and verbally constructed to elicit the sense of a sweet past now irremediably gone:

Andrew Wright

NARRATOR: The year is eighteen hundred and fifty; the place, Barchester, a quiet and peaceful town, nestling close to its ancient Cathedral. Life was gentle and slow in those days, permanent it seemed, and unbroken. People went about their business as their fathers had done before them, and their sons would after them, in the shadow of the Cathedral, to the changeless rhythm of their lives; they were born, they married, they died: and upon the whole they were happy.

Virtually nothing of Trollope's first chapter remains, though the narrator does offer a brief exposition, in different words from Trollope's, of the circumstances of Hiram's Hospital and its warden. But the archdeacon's address to the bedesmen and the warden's farewell are both, though abridged, adequately representative of the dialogue in the original. The narrator's characterization of the archdeacon is no doubt rightly scamped: visually it must have been possible for Lockwood West, who played the part of Dr. Grantly, to embody what the narrator describes.

In the BBC radio series called *The Barchester Chronicles* of 1973, *The Warden* is treated almost entirely in the first two of twenty episodes, the second concluding—with due dramatic effect—at the parting after the interview between Sir Abraham Haphazard and Mr. Harding, in which the clergyman gives unequivocal notice of his intention to resign the wardenship (having discovered that he can actually do so). The final words are spoken by Godfrey Kenton, who as "Trollope" reports:

"Mr. Harding was sufficiently satisfied with the interview to feel a glow of comfort as he descended into the small old square of Lincoln's Inn. *He had done what he believed was right, and if the attorney-general regarded him as little better than a fool he did not mind. But as he approached his hotel, he knew his work for the night was not yet over. He had still to tell Archdeacon Grantly.*"

There is no farewell to the bedesmen in this dramatization, but at the beginning of the third episode is a version of Mr. Harding's interview with the archdeacon in which the decision to resign is timorously but firmly communicated. There follows the account by "Trollope" of Mr. Harding's being

327

appointed to the living of St. Cuthbert's by the bishop. Then this episode of *The Barchester Chronicles* turns to the matter of the beginning of *Barchester Towers*, namely the decline and death of the bishop and the archdeacon's hope of succession.

Of the abridgment for broadcast of 1977, read in ten twenty-five minute parts, it is probably desirable to be somewhat charitable in view of the constraints imposed by broadcasting and the necessity of reading aloud. At all events, the opening of the first chapter is shorn of discursiveness and wholly without the narrator's sense of himself as a narrator. What remains is a plain account, almost altogether in Trollope's words, of the facts of the case—who Mr. Harding is, the offices he holds, the relationship between past and present at Hiram's Hospital. Likewise the speech of the archdeacon to the pensioners is without narrative comment; the speech itself, though abbreviated, employs the words which Trollope himself invented for the purpose. The third passage, except for the omission of a single clause at the beginning ("but it was but a murmur, and might have meant that or anything else") is identical to the original. All in all it is a respectably faithful piece of work, and as Paul Rogers reads extremely well, the adaptation can be regarded as successful.

There is, finally, the practice, ranging from the defensible to the egregious, of offering "notes" which, despite disclaimers, serve as a substitute for the real thing. Students of Trollope may be able to turn with profit to such crutches as Kathleen Goad's *Anthony Trollope: The Warden* (London: Brodie, 1957) and Kenneth M. Lobb's book of the same title published by Hulton in 1966, where various treatments of the author and the novel are offered, together with questions that may be considered in connection with the novel (and, if one is lucky, asked in examinations). But the anonymously issued *Notes on The Warden and Other Works* (London: Coles, 1968) is another kettle of fish. Though it is not in the catalogue of the British Library, it is readily obtainable down the road at Dillon's University Book Shop: its ninety-five pages include a short biography of Trollope, a couple of pages on the background of the novel (quotations from the *Autobiography* and Michael Sadleir), a three-page plot summary, a categorical statement of the themes ("conscience . . . also . . . politics"), a few pages on the setting, character summaries, a disquisition on character portrayal in general in Trollope, treatment of Trollope's style, humor, irony, the structure of the book, "Trollope's Literary World," "Typical Review Questions," and a selected (and very inadequate) bibliography. But the center of the book is a chapter-by-chapter summary of the novel, of which I shall offer but a single sample: it is the beginning.

Chapter 1: Hiram's Hospital

The Reverend Septimus Harding, a widower, is a clergyman in the town of Barchester, remarkable for the beauty of its cathedral and the antiquity of its monuments. At the age of 50, he had become precentor of the cathedral; he had married early in life and was the father of Susan and Eleanor. When the story opens it is 10 years after his appointment as precentor, and his eldest daughter, Susan, has been married to the son of the bishop, Archdeacon Theophilus Grantly, for a number of years. Soon after the marriage, her father was given the job of precentor and with it the right to be warden of Hiram's Hospital. John Hiram had died in 1434 and in his will left the house and lands for the support of twelve superannuated woolcarders who "should have been born and bred and spent their days in Barchester."

Literacy is a good thing—of course: even when the term is understood in a minimal sense, reading and writing a little are obviously better than to be able to do neither at all. Likewise, the higher the level of literacy the better. There remain, however, vexed questions when literacy and culture come together, as they inevitably (and properly) do. Classics being by definition the best that a culture produces, how should they be put before the readers within the culture? If there are difficulties, how far should they be explained? Should some or all of the difficulties be removed or made less formidable? Should the works be rewritten altogether in a simpler language that can be wholly understood—by the young and inexperienced or by the culturally deprived? A separate and rather sad question is suggested by the existence of versions for young readers such as that of H. Oldfield Box: when so much has been omitted and smoothed away, is not what remains so different as no longer to be considered whatever it was originally (a rhetorical question indeed)?

When does Anthony Trollope's *The Warden* cease to be *The Warden*? As for the possible effect of such dilutions when swallowed by Third World readers: is it conscionable to allow them to suppose that they are reading the real thing? Is western culture thus presented unacceptably imperialistic as well as indisputably altered? Will Richard Altick tell us?

1. With one exception (to be noted in due course), all the published adaptations of Trollope mentioned in this essay are in the British Library. To Challice Reed of the BBC Script Library, Allan Ferris of the BBC Play Library, Irene Basterfield of the BBC Television Script Unit, and Jacqueline Kavanagh of the BBC Written Archives Centre I am grateful for having helped me find the unpublished scripts and for having allowed me to examine them. All treated here are available on microform at the Written Archives Centre at Reading.

2. To William Longman, 20 December 1856, *Letters*, ed. Bradford A. Booth (London, 1951), p. 25, Gordon Ray, "Trollope at Full Length," *Huntington Library Quarterly* 31 (1968): 313-40.

3. "Trollope Revises Trollope," in *Trollope Centenary Essays*, ed. John Halperin (London, 1982), pp. 109-33.

4. *The Warden* (London, 1950).

XVI

WENDELL V. HARRIS

An Anatomy of Aestheticism

THE PURSUIT OF THE DEFINITIVE DEFINITION OF LITERARY TERMS like romanticism, realism, and aestheticism is very much like the pursuit of the Grail undertaken by Arthur's knights. The endeavor is likely to distract us from the slaying of historical dragons and the redressing of critical wrongs to follow will-of-the-wisps fruitlessly through swamps and across deserts. One suspects that the literary historian valiant, dedicated, and pure enough to be allowed to look on, let's say, romanticism bare, would be snatched up to the heights of Helicon, and like Galahad, never seen again. Nevertheless, ever and anon such quests beckon all of us.

That prolegomena is by way of explaining the trepidation with which I enter upon the attempt to anatomize nineteenth-century aestheticism. The immediate cause of my interest is a discovery I made in the card catalog (soon to be but a lamented relic) of the forty-eight late nineteenth-century volumes edited by Peter Stansky and Rodney Shewan and reprinted under the title "The Aesthetic Movement and the Arts and Crafts Movement."[1] Initially I saw nothing strange in the linking of the two movements: the one has always led easily to the other in my own class lectures on Victorian culture—but the more I thought about the links between them, the more fragile they seemed to become. Bemused, I turned to Linda Dowling's valuable little bibliography, *Aestheticism and Decadence*.[2] But as I recognized that the bibliography focuses on the last twenty years of the century, I began to ask myself what violence was done to the aesthetic movement by thus severing the latter from the earlier part. That drove me back to a half-remembered article by Ruth Temple that appeared in *ELT* in 1974. Her "Truth in Labelling: Pre-Raphaelitism, Aestheticism, Decadence, Fin-de-Siècle" deserved to be better remembered.[3] Opening with the announcement that "the general misuse and misapprehension" of these labels "constitutes a scandal in literary history" and that the "confusion in this subject is such as to rock the reason" she goes on to illustrate that confusion at length and offer helpful suggestions toward its rectification. She distinguishes the two phases of Pre-Raphaelitism, and the period of the original brotherhood and the later loose confederation of Rossetti, Morris, and Burne-Jones, and defines decadence as the end-of-the-century product of romanticism. "Aesthetic," she says, "as a label for a literary movement had better be discarded. There was no movement."

Probably not, if we define "literary movement" narrowly. And certainly we are led into confusions if we do not differentiate between "aestheticism" and the "aesthetic movement," that Professor Temple, for all her care in threading her way through other conflations, does not do. But of course there *was* something called an aesthetic movement. Can we doubt not only Du Maurier, *Patience*, F. C. Burnand, and later Beerbohm, but Walter Hamilton's 1882 *Aesthetic Movement in England*, that *omnium gatherum* of literary and aesthetic gossip of the day? Nor of course was Ruth Temple the first to note the all-embracing use of the term by the end of the century. Writing in the *Pall Mall Magazine* in 1895, five months before the Wilde scandal, Thomas Plowman reported that "In the popular mind, Pre-Raphaelites, Medievalists, Queen-Annites and China-maniacs jostle each other in a common crowd, in which Rossetti, Morris, Burne-Jones, Swinburne, and Oscar Wilde mainly stand out as recognizable personalities. They are collectively labelled 'aesthetes,' without regard to species, and are credited with an equal share in the floating and direction of a sort of joint-stock company for the regeneration of things in general and art in particular."[4]

When and how such a movement began of course depends

on how we define it. Walter Hamilton opens his account with the founding of the Pre-Raphaelite Brotherhood in 1848. Some eighty years later John Dixon Hunt's carefully researched *The Pre-Raphaelite Imagination* claims for the movement a breadth of influence pretty much continuous with what Hamilton describes, except that with the advantage of writing after the end of the century, Hunt is able to annex the 1890s as well. But on the other hand, it is possible for Elizabeth Aslin, writing in 1969 and focusing on theories of design and decoration and their preparation for art nouveau, to trace the beginning of the aesthetic movement not to the P. R. B. but to complaints of the 1830s and 1840s that English manufacturers had no understanding of the art of design.[5]

The significant question here of course is not the exact date or point of origin, but whether a view of the aesthetic movement that emphasizes the role of the craftsman and the desire to reform the economic structure of society is really compatible with one that emphasizes preoccupation with the picturesqueness of medievalism, introspection, realistic detail, and woman—at least the Pre-Raphaelite image of woman—as a symbol of the soul's desires. What are we to make of a situation in which Hamilton's 1882 and Hunt's 1968 analyses largely dismiss Whistler because he is not clearly in the line of descent from the P. R. B., while Elizabeth Aslin assigns him a major role because of his influence on decorative art as well as painting, though he again scarcely appears in Gillian Naylor's 1971 *The Arts and Crafts Movement* because, despite his influence on decoration, he was not important in enunciating the theories of either design or craftsmanship as the arts and crafts movement understood them?[6] Or again, what is the true role of Ruskin who seems to stand always at the elbow of Morris and the leaders of the arts and crafts movement like Lethaby, Gimson, Day, and Ashbee, but who appears in J. D. Hunt's Rossetti-dominated volume only to rescue the hardpressed Pre-Raphaelites with that timely letter to the *Times*? Or, more briefly, is Oscar Wilde a paradigm or parody of the aesthetic movement? Whether or not we have a scandal in literary history, we certainly have a potpourri of emphases and interpretations.

What I should like to propose is neither a set of definitions nor a challenge to the views of any particular critic or critics. The tangled situation appears to me so complex after the interweavings of a century of critical commentary that it is hardly likely to yield to any such assault. What I propose then is simply an alternative way of regarding the really very curious mixture of theories, events, influences, and results which are gathered together under the rubric "aesthetic movement." I suggest six tendencies from which are blended the various submovements. They are the medievalizing, the botanical, the ornamental, the omnibeautiful, the demand for art for the artist's sake, and the dreamily melancholic.

The love of selected aspects of the middle ages from the 1830s on is so familiar that I need give but barest mention of it. Walter Hamilton indeed defines the aesthetic movement in his preface as a renaissance of medieval art and culture. A rich topic for excursus is suggested by the concept of a renaissance of the medieval, but I shall confine myself to pointing out that we are confronted with the medieval as a source of picturesque subject matter, as a period when artists were faithful to nature, as a time when religious faith was not only strong but imbued the social structure with greater humanity, and as an exemplification of the rightful place of craftsmanship. Clearly there is something there for Pugin, Ruskin, Rossetti, Hunt, Millais, Morris, Wilde, Cobden-Sanderson, and Ashbee—but not the same thing in each case. Medievalism appears to have been at any man's service. Nor is it easy to find consistency in the simplest manifestations. The flowers and leaves Ruskin admires on the capitals and crockets of medieval cathedrals are suggested by nature; Rossetti's lilies are suggested by Christian symbolism; the flowers beside Millais's Ophelia are suggested by Shakespeare; and those crushed by Holman Hunt's Hireling Shepherd appear there either because they were growing in the field where Hunt placed his models or with equal likelihood because of symbolism that I have not penetrated. Wilde takes his lily either from Rossetti or, as anecdote would have it, from the name of the charming actress to whose door he carried what was in fact an enormous amaryllis—a confusion I will not pause to untangle. The appeal of his green carnation is of course that it is unnatural. Where the ubiquitous sunflower came from heaven only knows.

The example leads me into the second tendency, which I call the botanical. The term has a peculiar sound in this context perhaps, but certainly anything which will help us to distinguish among the multifarious senses of the word "nature" seems an improvement. The point I wish to make is that although in the beginning Ruskin was dedicated to asserting the accuracy of the representations by his favorite contemporary painter of all of nature—mountains, sky, sea—his recommendation of the forms of trees, plants, and flowers as the basis for the most noble decoration was what, as it were, took root. We find the love of vegetation of course in that best known of all Ruskin, the chapter on "The Nature of Gothic." "There is, however, one direction in which the Naturalism of the Gothic workmen is peculiarly manifested; and this direction is even more characteristic of the school than the Naturalism itself; I mean their peculiar fondness for the forms of Vegetation." Thus in the highest forms of Gothic, writes Ruskin, "the stony pillar grew slender and the vaulted roof grew light, till they had wreathed themselves into the semblance of the summer woods at their fairest." And finally, "The proudest architecture that man can build has no higher honour than to bear the image and recall the memory of that grass of the field which is, at once, the type and support of his existence: the goodly building is then most glorious when it is sculptured into the likeness of the leaves of Paradise; and the great Gothic spirit, as we showed it to be noble in its disquietude, is also noble in its hold of nature."[7] One hardly need repeat the program of the Pre-Raphaelite's *Germ*, "an entire adherence to the simplicity of nature."

The association of love for vegetative forms with medievalism lasted long and strongly enough for it to be of service to Gilbert in the lyric of *Patience* as Bunthorne sings of "the sentimental fashion for a vegetable passion." But by then the leading spokesmen for the arts and crafts movement were in fact inclined to take the vegetative forms and let the medieval associations go. Though in general medieval art and decoration is given no pride of place in that movement, the forms of plants, trees, and flowers are offered again and again as the most essential of models in the spate of manuals on design that appeared in the 1880s and 1890s. "Nature is our one and constant model," writes Lewis Day, author of a series of textbooks of design published between 1892 and 1900. The passage from *Nature in Ornament* continues: "The question is as to how freely or how painfully, how broadly or how literally, how individually or how slavishly, we shall render the model before us, how much of it, and what of it, we shall depict." More telling perhaps is the very career of Christopher Dresser, who described himself as "an architect and ornamentist by profession"—and thus it is not surprising that three of his books on ornament and design are reprinted by Stansky and Shewan—but who also served as lecturer on botany and master of the botanical drawing classes at the South Kensington Museum, which led him to publish three books on botany. The title of one of these botanical volumes, *Unity in Variety, as Deduced from the Vegetable Kingdom*, sums up the relation between botany and ornament.

The third tendency is toward the ornamental. By this I mean the application of a design, or pattern, or representation of anything from the gods to a human scene to landscape to the recognizable outline of animal, vegetable, or mineral—the application of any of these to any functional object from a cathedral to a teapot. Interest in reform of the design of all things functional begins in the 1830s, one more evidence that more than the first reform bill and Queen Victoria's coronation make that decade a great watershed. As Sir Herbert Read and then Gillian Naylor pointed out,[8] Peel was supporting in 1832 the foundation of a National Gallery on the grounds that it would improve English manufacture. And of course in 1835 there was appointed a Select Committee to "inquire into the best means of extending a knowledge of the arts and principles of design among the people (especially the manufacturing population) of the country." Henry Cole founded his Summerly Art Manufacturers in 1847 partly as a corrective to public taste, to which he added the *Journal of Design and Manufacture* in 1848. He went on to be one of the leading figures in the organization of the Crystal Palace Exhibition, which, as he came to recognize, established the importance of good design by exhibiting masses of bad.

Again, Pugin not only held strong views about the kind of ornament appropriate to architecture—"all ornament should consist of enrichment of the essential construction of the building"—but prescribed, like Ruskin, that ornament should be based on forms found in nature and appropriate to the object (thus staircase turrets are not to be used for inkstands or gable ends hung on handles or pillars assigned to support a lamp), that wallpaper patterns should be two-dimensional as should any design used on a floor ("Nothing can be more ridiculous than . . . highly relieved foliage and perforated tracery for the decoration of a floor"). It is thus not only in Dickens's depiction of utilitarianism in *Hard Times* that one encounters such prohibitions; they begin early and continue to the end of the century. They will be found for instance in Ralph Wornum's "On the 1851 Exhibitions as A Lesson in Taste" and Christopher Dresser's 1862 comments on the carpets in the International Exhibition: "Nothing can be more uncomfortable to walk over than a rough and uneven surface of sand and water, bestrewed with bushes and other large objects which cast massive shadows."[9]

Now what is fascinating in this, from my point of view, is not that there was concern about the quality of English design and ornamentation, but the degree of preoccupation with ornamentation or decoration as something added to function. The interpretation of design as the masterly control of line and mass rather than the incorporation of pattern or decoration into the surface of an object was long in arriving. Ralph Wornum's essay on the Crystal Palace Exhibition, the winner of the *Art-Journal* prize competition, states the matter rather straightforwardly: "When manufacturers have attained a high mechanical perfection, or have completely met the necessities of the body, the energy that brought them to that perfection must either stagnate or be confined in a higher province—that of Taste; for there is a stage of cultivation when the mind must revolt at mere mechanical utility. So it is a natural propensity to decorate or embellish whatever is useful or agreeable to us."[10] Thus the ornamentation of everything, machinery as well as objects intended to sit decoratively on a side table. (I cannot forbear here giving one of my favorites from among the descriptions accompanying the engravings in the *Art-Journal Catalogue* of the Crystal Palace Exhibition: "The large engraving is from a PERFUME VASE, in which the handles are not less distinguished by novelty than by good taste, though they may here seem somewhat too large; the body is ornamented with an embossed running pattern of ash-leaves, acorns, aqueous plants, and fish; the lid is surmounted by a vulture, which seems ready to pounce on the prey beneath.")[11]

Some of us also have a hard time reconciling our admiration of what William Morris and his firm were trying to accomplish with painted panels on chests and sideboards. And it is even more a surprise to find how single-mindedly the concept of ornamentation permeates the writings of the spokesmen for the arts and crafts movement of the 1880s and 1890s. Lewis Day's books include *The Application of Ornament, The Anatomy of Pattern, Instances of Accessory Art* (subtitled "Original Designs and Suggestive Examples of Ornament with Practical and Critical Notes") as well as the *Nature in Ornament* already mentioned. Christopher Dresser produced *Modern Ornamentation: Being a Series of Original Designs* "with the hope that it may be of service to Manufacturers who are engaged in the production of Figured Objects, and to Architects and Designers who have to produce the Patterns which Manufacturers require."[12] Fifty years after Pugin and more than thirty years after the lessons of the Great Exhibition, writers like Day and Dresser continue to write as though pattern and design are to be conceived separately and superadded to the functional object, though if directly challenged they would likely have agreed with Morris that one strength of the medieval craftsman had been that "as he fashioned the thing he had under his hand, [he] ornamented it so naturally and so entirely without conscious effort, that it is often difficult to distinguish where the mere utilitarian part of his work ended and the ornament began."[13]

The fourth tendency I would call the omnibeautiful. By this I mean simply the preoccupation with infusing the entire society with taste and surrounding it with beauty. Pugin's *Contrasts* of course mingles emphasis on the greater beauty of the medieval city, and the presumed beneficial result thereof, with social and religious satire. Ruskin warred continually on the propositions that the upper class could distinguish the beautiful from the ugly, that the middle class really desired the ugly, and that the poor deserved it. The less exalted goals of the already mentioned Select Committee of 1835 in investigating means of improving the workingman's taste in order to increase the value of English goods has already been mentioned. Morris's concern to raise the standards of taste and decoration requires no comment. Eloquent testimony to the undiminished concern for this goal is again to be found in the selection of volumes reprinted under the editorship of Shewan and Stansky.

These fall into a number of categories. First, there are quite a few volumes of ambiguous intention that appear to be addressed equally to practitioners and amateurs desirous of improving their taste. This is true of the series of essays edited by Cobden-Sanderson entitled *Art and Life and the Building and Decoration of Cities* and Walter Crane's *The Bases of Design* ostensibly addressed "to the students of the Manchester Municipal School of Art" but rather too general to be of much use to practicing craftsmen. Dresser's *Development of Ornamental Art in the International Exhibition* combines chapters on the general principles of ornamentation with comments on various exhibits at the International Exhibition of 1862. And then there is the flood of quite practical advice addressed to men and women aspiring to achieve beauty in furnishing their own surroundings: *Artistic Homes; or, How to Furnish with Taste* (1881), the ubiquitous Lewis Day's *Every-Day Art*, subtitled "Short Essays on the Arts Not Fine," which begins with general chapters on ornament and goes on to discussion of decorations appropriate for each kind of room and how to arrange pictures on one's walls, W. J. Loftie's *A Plea for Art in the House*, Rhoda and Agnes Garrett's *House Decoration*, and Mrs. Loftie, Mrs. Orrinsmith, and Lady Barker writing respectively on *The Dining Room*, *The Drawing Room*, and *The Bedroom and The Boudoir*.

The fifth tendency I have called "art for the artist's sake"—a concept which I think had a great deal more power in England throughout the century than that of "art for art's sake." One might say that "art for art's sake" was the French, "art for the artist's sake" the English, position. Once more one thinks first of Ruskin and Morris whose positions on the role of the craftsman need not here be rehearsed. But the tradition continues strongly through the end of the century in active visionaries like C. R. Ashbee, who followed the example of Ruskin and Morris fully enough to found the Guild of Handicraft in which a group of craftsmen worked cooperatively to produce household furnishings under what they hoped could be made ideal conditions. The emphasis here is distinctly the same as Ruskin's: the goal of such a system of manufacture is the reformation of society. "We have reached a stage in our social development," writes Ashbee in an 1894 volume significantly titled *A Few Chapters in Workshop Reconstruction and Citizenship*, "when it behooves us to ask what is to be our Ideal of Citizenship? How far are we to look for the formation of the citizen in our modern system of industry—the workshop—how far in education provided by the State?" Ruskin had written as early as 1849 that "I believe the right question to ask, respecting all ornament, is simply this: Was it done with enjoyment—was the carver happy while he was about it?" Morris's "That thing which I understand by real art is the expression by man of his pleasure in labour" is one of a multitude of similar affirmations in his lectures.[14] Ashbee holds this doctrine of art for the artist's sake strongly enough to argue that "the standard of artistic excellence must depend ultimately upon the pleasure given, not to the consumer, but to the producer."[15] He is naturally therefore much concerned with the role of machinery in production; like Ruskin he wishes machinery confined to those things that cannot be adequately done by hand; unlike Ruskin, having found that moral exhortation will not stop the advance of machinery, he calls for its regulation so that its use in place of handicraft will be prohibited.

All in all, Ashbee's volumes are fascinating as they wrestle with commonplace ways of bringing about the conditions of manufacture that Ruskin had envisioned—unfortunately in commonplace prose. Where Ruskin argued that ways must be found to prevent the rate of wages from varying with demand for labor and to maintain workmen at such fixed rates of wages and with such security that they will have a permanent interest in their establishment (is anyone investigating the influence of Ruskin on Japanese industry?), Ashbee calls directly for a minimum wage. So earnest is he in this that he would forbid the economically secure (the lady who likes to do a little painting or the gentleman who likes to do a little woodwork on the side) from selling what they produce for less than an established minimum rate. And, of course, like Ruskin and Morris, Ashbee sees the return of manufacture to the craftsman working by hand from his own designs at a guaranteed wage as the means of reestablishing quality. "Standard"—with a capital S—which Ashbee prefers to the word quality, is a vague but haunting ideal always before him.

All of this comes together in the volume *Craftsmanship in Competitive Industry* (1908). "What I seek to show is that this Arts and Crafts movement, which began with the earnestness of the Pre-Raphaelite painters, the prophetic enthusiasm of Ruskin and the titanic energy of Morris, is not what the public has thought it to be, or is seeking to make it: a nursery for luxuries, a hothouse for the production of mere trivialities, and useless things for the rich. It is a movement for the stamping out of such things by sound production on the one hand, and the inevitable regulation of machine production and cheap labour on the other. My thesis is that the expensive superfluity and the cheap superfluity are one and the same thing, equally useless, equally wasteful, and that both must be destroyed. The Arts and Crafts movement then, if it means anything, means Standard, whether of work or of life, the protection of Standard, whether in the product or in the producer, and it means that these two things must be taken together."[16] But like Morris, Ashbee found that whether because of the very nature of post-Renaissance society or the difficulties of transforming the whole of society altogether and at once so that the craftsman would be paid well enough to afford the work of other craftsmen, his and other workshops could be patronized only by the rich. Gillian Naylor quotes a pathetic self-indictment from his unpublished memoirs: "We have made of a great social movement, a narrow and tiresome little aristocracy working with great skill for the very rich." [17] His recognition of that apparent anomaly is finally much more devastating than Veblen's gibe at the way the arts and crafts movement led to "the exaltation of the defective." [18]

Finally, then, whence came the languorous attitudes, the aesthetes parodied by Du Maurier, the immoral poetry which aroused Robert Buchanan's alarm? These began in the sixth and last tendency, which gathers force in the work of the Pre-Raphaelite Brotherhood and which I would call simply the dreamy melancholic. The P. R. B. has always been singularly difficult for critics to deal with. Shortly after announcing their program of "an entire adherence to the simplicity of nature" they fell asunder, only Rossetti and Holman Hunt contining to keep before the public works with distinct features that seemed to deserve some such explanatory term as Pre-Raphaelite. Yet the one came to be known by many primarily as the fleshly poet while the other devoted himself to an amalgamation of natural detail and religious symbolism so painstaking and in some ways so unrewarding that our mental image of Hunt is all too apt to fuse with that of the unhappy animal he painted under the title "The Scapegoat." So thin has the P. R. B. center proved that critics have been fain to draft Morris and Burne-Jones, Rossetti's comrades and erstwhile disciples in the Oxford Union fresco project, into the ranks to give it substance. And again, though the P. R. B. is frequently cited as the source of the aesthetic movement, as Jerome Buckley noted long ago, "Far from being 'aesthetic,' they set out consciously to attack artifice and calculated design. . . . Like Wordsworth half a century before, they pled for a simpler language of emotion. And in their various media they worked conscientiously toward a closer truth to nature" while each detail was to stand "as a symbol of some spiritual force above sense perception." [19]

The key figure here is Rossetti, and the clue to the most

central contribution of the Pre-Raphaelite movement to the century is not, I think, to be found in any formal pronouncements, but rather is suggested by John Heath-Stubbs' argument that what Rossetti wrote is best described as "dream-poetry."[20] To put *The House of Life* against Meredith's *Modern Love* is to see just how dreamy, filled with misty abstractions and, despite Rossetti's love of detail, essentially vague Rossetti's sonnets finally are. The sonnets and poems as varied as "The Blessed Damozel," "The Portrait," "The Staff and Scrip," and "The Orchard-Pit" all are compounded of equal parts of introspection and abstraction, mingling three very different poets whose power Rossetti helped proclaim: the visionary quality of Blake, the love of lyric imagery in Keats, and the pessimism, though not (perhaps unfortunately) the irony of Edward FitzGerald.

John Dixon Hunt has argued that one of the central characteristics of the Pre-Raphaelites (by which he essentially means Rossetti–ites) was "their celebration of the noumenous; the search for a dialectic of symbolism subtle enough to convey their apprehension of a meaningful world beyond exterior description and rational habits of mind."[21] But I must challenge the word "noumenous" if by it is meant an ultimate reality not apprehensible by the senses but understood to underlie the phenomenal world. I find no evidence for anything so philosophically definite in Rossetti—rather simply a penchant for elaborate dreaming, partly self-explanatory, partly escapist. G. K. Chesterton, who was thinking primarily of Rossetti, called the aesthetic movement "the romance from the South." "It is," he said, "that warm wind that had never blown so strong since Chaucer, standing in his cold English April, had smelt the spring in Provence."[22] I have been fascinated by that description since I first read it, though I now think that that warm wind came from a region to be found on no map of the known world. The sensuality Buchanan decried loses whatever noxiousness it might have had in this strange atmosphere. Much of Morris's poetry, certainly the longer narrative poems, and indeed much of the Swinburne of *Poems and Ballads*, is similarly insulated.

Shocked though Buchanan was, the stir even Swinburne's poems created was in fact mild enough. Why not, when lines such as

> Thou were fair in the fearless old fashion,
> And thy limbs are as melodies yet,
> And move to the music of passion
> With lithe and lascivious regret.
> What ailed us, O Gods to desert you
> For creeds that refuse and restrain?
> Come down and redeem us from virtue,
> Our Lady of Pain.

lose their seduction in lack of subtlety and are cleansed of passion by their musicality? Thomas Plowman's description of such verse as "pessimistic amativeness" is cogent, as is his characterization of the associated paintings of maidens with "faces full of the sad weariness of love-lorn languor."[23]

Rossetti's "Hand and Soul," which had as much influence on one current of the short story as his poetry on succeeding poets, is similarly dreamy, distanced not only in time but by the low pressure of its telling. William Morris's early stories are cast in this same smoothly flowing but nerveless prose, which we meet also in Walter Pater's *Imaginary Portraits* and again in Arthur Symons' *Spiritual Adventures*. What in essence the dream world of both prose and poetry presented was an escape from Crystal Palaces and Coketowns, mills Satanic and Mills utilitarian, questions of secret ballot and deceased wives' sisters.

These are, I think, the ingredients that combine in various proportions in the aesthetic movement, the arts and crafts movement, and finally the "decadence" of the 1890s. And it is at this point perhaps that we can say why Whistler's relationship to the aesthetic movement is so curious. The medieval was not of interest to him; as for the botanical, "The Ten O'Clock" lecture tells us, "To say to the painter, that Nature is to be taken as she is, is to say to the player, that he may sit on the piano"; "ornament" was not a term one much associates with Whistler, except perhaps if coupled with "spare" and "elegant"; "The Ten O'Clock" decisively dismisses the omni-beautiful goal; and I doubt that anyone ever thought of the butterfly with a sting in his tail as dreamily melancholic. Where Whistler does meld with, and paradoxically at the same time stand apart from, the aesthetic movement is in his own personal interpretation of *l'art pour l'art,* which for him means precisely that the creation of art is for the pleasure of the artist, it being always understood that mere workmen, even craftsmen, are no artists.

We tend to think not of these six tendencies or ingredients in themselves but of their combination in powerful personalities. We speak of the poetry of the Pre-Raphaelites and cite Rossetti. We speak of art for art's sake and we cite Swinburne. We speak of aesthetes and cite Wilde.

And when we come to speak of Wilde, we ought to recognize that he managed not so much the debut of aesthetic consciousness as the dissolution of its complexity. Brilliant in forecasting some of the directions criticism was to take eventually, Wilde was essentially a master *bricoleur* (to use the favorite term of the early structuralists): while distilling essences from Ruskin, Rossetti, Morris, Whistler, and Pater, he transmogrified them all. What dropped out were the dimension of art for the artist so far as that concerned the ordinary worker or craftsman and the technical side of ornamentation that went along with it. What Wilde was disentangling had in fact essentially been knotted together first by Ruskin. One might indeed say, if one were, like Pater, looking for the moment that combines the greatest and most complex assemblage of "forces parting sooner or later on their ways," that the brief moment encapsulating the aesthetic movement was Ruskin's defense of the Pre-Raphaelites. Finding the brotherhood championing a return to nature and evincing a delight in the pre-Renaissance past, Ruskin comes to their defense, confounding the botanical and medieval tendencies with the ornamental, the omnibeautiful, and the artist-centered, and incidentally and unknowingly sweeping up the dreamily melancholic as well.

That moment when Ruskin becomes the champion of a Rossetti, Hunt, and Millais who have not yet separated to go their ways, and to a lesser extent that summer of 1856 when Rossetti, thanks to Ruskin's good offices, is allowed to paint what he thinks are frescoes on the Oxford Union walls and acquires Morris and Burne-Jones as disciples, are the moments when the disparate tendencies are most clearly intertwined. The most stable balance this amalgamation achieves is to be found in William Morris. But by the late 1870s, the tenuous relationship between these tendencies so fortuitously brought together has elsewhere begun rapidly to dissolve. One notes that Mallock's *New Republic* of 1877 makes no one in the house party he satirically assembles at all interested in the questions of the life of the workman, the creativity of the craftsman, the presumed coherence of the medieval society, or the way all art from ornament to architecture reveals the moral worth of a society. Then in 1878 came both the apostasy of a shift back toward greater admiration for the Renaissance sponsored by Pater and the Whistler-Ruskin trial. In the last two decades of the century, Whistler's and then Wilde's wit and showmanship, potent reagents, were turned on one of our six tendencies after another, dissolving or transforming them.

By 1881 and 1882, when certain aesthetic ideals are being embodied in the irregular brick sunflower-ornamented cottages of Bedford Park, Wilde is pursuing his witty progress through American lecture halls, F. C. Burnand's parody of aestheticism, "The Colonel," is on the boards, *Patience* is opening at the new Savoy Theatre, Du Maurier is beginning to tire of his *Punch* cartoons depicting aesthetic follies, Morris is enlarging his business by the addition of the tapestry workshop at Merton while moving toward the Socialist party, Rossetti's *Ballads and Sonnets* are appearing while his health is breaking, and Wilde's *Poems* are achieving print—by these early autumn years of the Victorian era, the aesthetic movement has disintegrated, though the individual tendencies that Ruskin had briefly conflated continued to and through the end of the century.

1. The series is described as: "The Aesthetic Movement and the Arts and Crafts Movement. Edited by Peter Stansky and Rodney Shewan. Forty-Eight of the Most Important Books, Reprinted in Thirty-Eight Volumes, Including over One Thousand Illustrations" (New York, 1977–79). It has

Wendell V. Harris

seemed unnecessary to include bibliographical information on volumes in this series (hereafter cited as AMACM) that I mention only by title.

2. Linda Dowling, *Aestheticism and Decadence: A Selective Annotated Bibliography* (New York, 1977).

3. Ruth Temple, *English Literature in Transition* 17, no. 4 (1974): 201-22.

4. Thomas Plowman, "The Aesthetes," *Pall Mall Magazine* 5 (January 1895): 27.

5. Walter Hamilton, *The Aesthetic Movement* (London, 1882); John Dixon Hunt, *The Pre-Rephaelite Imagination* (Lincoln, 1968); Elizabeth Aslin, *The Aesthetic Movement: Prelude to Art Nouveau* (New York, 1969).

6. Gillian Naylor, *The Arts and Crafts Movement* (Cambridge, Mass., 1971).

7. John Ruskin, *The Works of John Ruskin*, ed. E. T. Cook and Alexander Wedderburn, 39 vols. (London, 1904) 10:235, 238, 239.

8. See Naylor, *Arts and Crafts*, pp. 15-16.

9. A.W.N. Pugin, *The True Principles and Revival of Christian Architecture* (Edinburgh, 1895), pp. 1, 22, 23; Wornum, in *The Crystal Palace Exhibition Illustrated Catalogue* (London, 1851 [Published in Connection with *The Art-Journal*]; rpt. New York, 1970), see p. 20 of the appended essay; Christopher Dresser, *Development of Ornamental Art in the International Exhibition* (London, 1862; rpt. AMACM), p. 72.

10. Wornum, *Crystal Palace*, p. xxi.

11. *Crystal Palace Exhibition Illustrated Catalogue*, p. 283.

12. Christopher Dresser, *Modern Ornamentation* (London, 1866; rpt. AMACM).

13. *The Collected Works of William Morris*, 24 vols. (London, 1910-15), 23:113.

14. John Ruskin, *The Seven Lamps of Architecture*, ed. Cook and Wedderburn, (London, 1903), 8:218; Morris, "The Art of the People" in *Hopes and Fears for Art*, rpt. *The Collected Works of William Morris* (London, 1914), 22:42.

15. C.R. Ashbee, *A Few Chapters in Workshop Reconstruction and Citizenship* (London, 1894; rpt. AMACM), pp. 9, 16.

16. C.R. Ashbee, *Craftsmanship in Competitive Industry* (Campden, 1908; rptd. AMACM), pp. 9-10.

17. Naylor, *Arts and Crafts*, p. 9.

18. Thorstein Veblen, *Theory of the Leisure Class* (London, 1899; rpt. New York, 1953), p. 115.

19. Jerome Buckley, *The Triumph of Time* (Cambridge, Mass., 1966), p. 164.

20. John Heath-Stubbs, *The Darkling Plain* (London, 1950), pp. 156-57.

21. John Dixon Hunt, *The Pre-Raphaelite Imagination*, p. xii.

22. G.K. Chesterton, *The Victorian Age in Literature* (New York, n.d.), p. 188.

23. Thomas Plowman, "The Aesthetes," p. 33.

BIBLIOGRAPHY OF THE WRITINGS OF RICHARD D. ALTICK

Books

Richard Owen Cambridge: Belated Augustan (Ph.D. diss., Philadelphia, 1941).

Preface to Critical Reading (New York: Henry Holt & Co., 1946. Revised editions, 1951, 1956, 1960, 1969. Sixth edition, revised by Andrea Lunsford, 1983.) Excerpts of various lengths reprinted in numerous textbooks and anthologies.

The Cowden Clarkes (London and New York: Oxford University Press, 1948; rpt., Westport, Conn., Greenwood Press, 1973).

The Scholar Adventurers (New York: Macmillan Co. 1950. Paperback editions, Macmillan Paperbacks, 1960; Free Press, 1966). Chapters or shorter excerpts reprinted in "Literary Scholars in Business Suits," *American Scholar* 19 (Autumn 1950): 471-79; "A Milk-Toast Hawthorne," *Omnibook Best-Seller Magazine* (July 1951), pp. 55-58; *Bouillabaisse for Bibliophiles*, ed. William Targ (World Publishing Co., 1955), pp. 101-25; Nathan Comfort Starr, *The Pursuit of Learning* (Harcourt, Brace, 1956), pp. 169-76; *The Uses of Prose*, ed. Ernest Earnest (Harcourt, Brace, 1956), pp. 232-45; *Bibliophile in the Nursery*, ed. William Targ (World Publishing Co., 1957), pp. 167-92; J. Hooper Wise et al., *The Meaning in Reading*, 5th ed. (Harcourt, Brace, 1960), pp. 231-42; *Our Century in Prose*, ed. Ernest H. Winter (Macmillan of Canada, 1966), pp. 303-21; Richard E. Hughes and P. Albert Duhamel, *Rhetoric: Principles and Usages*, 2d ed. (Prentice-Hall, 1967), pp. 259-64; Alice Chandler, *The Prose Spectrum* (Allyn & Bacon, 1968), pp. 225-39; James M. McCrimmon, *From Source to Statement* (Houghton, Mifflin, 1968), pp. 92-102; *The Historian as Detective: Essays on Evidence*, ed. Robin Winks (Harper, 1969), pp. 104-26.

The English Common Reader: A Social History of the Mass Read-

ing Public 1800-1900 (Chicago: University of Chicago Press, 1957; Phoenix paperback edition, 1963; Midway reprint, 1983). Excerpts reprinted in *Mass Leisure*, ed. Eric Larrabee and Rolf Meyersohn (Free Press, 1958), pp. 43–53; *Backgrounds to Victorian Literature*, ed. Richard A. Levine (Chandler, 1967), pp. 203–21.

The Art of Literary Research (New York: W. W. Norton & Co., 1963. Revised editions, 1975, 1981, the latter by John J. Fenstermaker). Excerpt reprinted in *The Norton Reader*, ed. Arthur M. Eastman et al., rev. ed. (Norton, 1969), pp. 658–70.

Lives and Letters: A History of Literary Biography in England and America (New York: Alfred A. Knopf, 1965; rpt., Greenwood Press, 1979). Excerpt reprinted in *Twentieth Century Interpretations of Boswell's "Life of Johnson"*, ed. James L. Clifford (Prentice-Hall, 1970), pp. 104–11.

With James F. Loucks II, *Browning's Roman Murder Story: A Reading of "The Ring and the Book"* (Chicago: University of Chicago Press, 1968).

To Be in England (New York: W. W. Norton & Co., 1969).

Victorian Studies in Scarlet (New York: W. W. Norton & Co., 1970; London: J. M. Dent, 1972). Excerpt reprinted in *The Pleasures of Murder*, ed. Jonathan Goodman (Allison & Busby, 1983), pp. 20–25.

Victorian People and Ideas (New York: W. W. Norton & Co., 1973; London: J. M. Dent, 1974).

The Shows of London (Cambridge, Mass., and London: Belknap Press of Harvard University Press, 1978). Excerpts reprinted in "Snake Was Fake but Egyptian Hall Wowed London," *Smithsonian Magazine* 9, no. 1 (April 1978): pp. 68–77; "Technology for the Million" ("London's National Gallery of Practical Science" and "London's Royal Polytechnic Institution"), *New Scientist* (London), 78 (29 June 1978): 912–14, and 79 (6 July 1978): 36–38.

Editions
Thomas Carlyle: *Past and Present.* Riverside Edition (Boston: Houghton, Mifflin, 1965; rpt., New York University Press, 1977).

Robert Browning: *The Ring and the Book.* Penguin English Poets (Harmondsworth: Penguin Books 1971; rpt., English Poets Series, New Haven, Conn.: Yale University Press, 1981).

Bibliographies and Bibliographical Essays
"[Nineteenth-Century] Newspapers and Magazines," *The Cambridge Bibliography of English Literature* 5 (Supplement) (Cambridge: Cambridge University Press, 1957), pp. 678–87.

Bibliography of the Writings of Richard D. Altick

With William R. Matthews, *Guide to Doctoral Dissertations in Victorian Literature, 1886-1958* (Urbana: University of Illinois Press, 1960; rpt., Greenwood Press, 1973).

With Andrew Wright, *Selective Bibliography for the Study of English and American Literature* (New York: Macmillan Co., 1960. Revised editions, 1963, 1967, 1971, 1975).

Bibliographical supplement to Samuel C. Chew, *The Nineteenth Century and After*, in Albert C. Baugh, *Literary History of England* (New York, 1967). [78 pages.]

"General Materials," *Victorian Fiction: A Second Guide to Research*, ed. George H. Ford (New York: Appleton-Century-Crofts, 1978), pp. 1-20.

Articles

"Mark Twain's Despair: An Explanation in Terms of His Humanity," *South Atlantic Quarterly* 34 (October 1935): 359-67.

"Pranks and Punishment in an Old Pennsylvania College," *Pennsylvania History* 4 (October 1937): 241-47.

"Humorous Hogarth: His Literary Associations," *Sewanee Review* 42 (April-June 1939): 255-67.

"The Ephrata Cloisters in 1759," *Pennsylvania History* 6 (October 1939): 241-45.

"Mr. Sherlock Holmes and Dr. Samuel Johnson," *221B: Studies in Sherlock Holmes*, ed. Vincent Starrett (New York: Macmillan Co., 1940; rpt., Baker Street Irregulars, Morristown, N.J., 1956), pp. 109-28.

"Average Citizen in Grub Street," *South Atlantic Quarterly* 41 (January 1942): 18-31. [On Christopher Morley.]

"Toryism's Last Stand," *South Atlantic Quarterly* 41 (July 1942): 297-312. [On Charles Whibley's "Musings Without Method."]

"Mr. Cambridge Serenades the Berry Sisters," *Notes & Queries* 183 (12 September 1942): 158-61.

"Mr. Pope Expands His Grotto," *Philological Quarterly* 21 (October 1942): 427-30.

"Was Lowell an Historical Critic?", *American Literature* 14 (November 1942): 250-59.

"Maryland Haymaking," *South Atlantic Quarterly* 42 (July 1943): 243-51.

With Helen K. Altick, "Square-Rigger on a Modern Mission," *College English* 5 (November 1943): 75-80. [On H. M. Tomlinson.]

Bibliography of the Writings of Richard D. Altick

"The War of Nerves: Campus Version," *Journal of Higher Education* 14 (December 1943): 477-82.

"When Did Keats Meet Leigh Hunt?", *Notes & Queries* 187 (7 October 1944): 159-62.

"The Marvelous Child of the English Stage," *College English* 7 (November 1945): 78-85. [On "the Infant Roscius."]

"'Conveyers' and Fortune's Buckets in *Richard II*," *Modern Language Notes* 61 (March 1946): 179-80.

"Symphonic Imagery in *Richard II*," *PMLA* 62 (June 1947): 339-65. Reprinted in Japanese translation by Toshiko Oyama, Tokyo, 1957; in *The Tragedy of King Richard the Second*, ed. Kenneth Muir (Signet Classic Shakespeare; New American Library of World Literature, 1963), pp. 199-234; *Twentieth Century Interpretations of "Richard II*," ed. Paul M. Cubeta (Prentice-Hall, 1971), pp. 66-81; and *Shakespeare: "Richard II": A Casebook*, ed. Nicholas Brooke (London: Macmillan & Co., 1973), pp. 101-30.

"A Neglected Source for Literary Biography," *PMLA* 64 (June 1949): 319-24. Reprinted in *Autograph Collectors' Journal* 2 (January 1950): 13-16.

"Dickens and America: Some Unpublished Letters," *Pennsylvania Magazine of History and Biography* 73 (July 1949): 326-36.

"Robert Browning Rides the Chicago & Alton," *New Colophon 1950*, pp. 78-81.

"*Cope's Tobacco Plant*: An Episode in Victorian Journalism," *Papers of the Bibliographical Society of America* 45 (4th Quarter 1951): 333-50.

"Fifty Years of Literary Scholarship," *The Past Half-Century in Literature: A Symposium* (Ohio College English Association, 1952), pp. 39-47.

"The Private Life of Robert Browning," *Yale Review* 41 (Winter 1952): 247-62. Reprinted in *The Browning Critics*, ed. Boyd Litzinger and K. L. Knickerbocker (University of Kentucky Press, 1965), pp. 247-64.

"Nineteenth-Century English Periodicals," *Newberry Library Bulletin*, 2d ser. no. 9 (May 1952): 255-64.

Introduction to James Morier's *The Adventures of Hajji Baba of Ispahan*, Modern Library edition (New York: Random House, 1954), pp. v-ix.

"English Publishing and the Mass Audience in 1852," *Studies in Bibliography* 6 (1954): 3-24.

Bibliography of the Writings of Richard D. Altick

Biographical introductions and (some) headnotes in the Romantic and Victorian sections of Albert C. Baugh and George W. McClelland, *English Literature: A Period Anthology* (New York: Appleton-Century-Crofts, 1954).

"*Hamlet* and the Odor of Mortality," *Shakespeare Quarterly* 5 (Spring 1954): 167-76.

"The Scholar's Paradise," *College and Research Libraries* 15 (October 1954): 375-82.

"Browning's 'Karshish' and St. Paul," *Modern Language Notes* 72 (November 1957): 494-96.

"From Aldine to Everyman: Cheap Reprint Series of the English Classics, 1830-1906," *Studies in Bibliography* 11 (1958): 3-24.

"The Literature of an Imminent Democracy," *1859: Entering an Age of Crisis,* ed. Philip Appleman et al. (Bloomington: Indiana University Press, 1959), pp. 215-28.

"Charles Lamb," *Encyclopedia Americana*, 1959 edition, 16: 663-64.

"English Lives and American Scholars," *Nation* 188 (24 January 1959): 73-74.

"Browning's 'Transcendentalism,'" *Journal of English and Germanic Philology* 58 (January 1959): 24-28.

"Dion Boucicault Stages *Mary Barton*," *Nineteenth-Century Fiction* 14 (September 1959): 129-41.

"Another Victorian First," *Victorian Newsletter* 16 (Fall 1959): 34-36. [On the *Guide to Doctoral Dissertations in Victorian Literature*.]

"Four Victorian Poets and an Exploding Island," *Victorian Studies* 3 (March 1960): 249-60.

"Delia Salter Bacon," *Ohio Authors and Their Books*, ed. William Coyle (Cleveland: World Publishing Co., 1962), pp. 24-26.

"The Sociology of Authorship: The Social Origins, Education, and Occupations of 1,100 British Writers, 1800-1935," *Bulletin of the New York Public Library* 66 (June 1962): 389-404. Reprinted in *Authorship*, vol. 10 of *Literary Taste, Culture and Mass Communication*, ed. Peter Davison et al. (Chadwyck-Healey, 1978), pp. 47-62.

"Memo to the Next Annotator of Browning," *Victorian Poetry* 1 (January 1963): 61-68.

"'A Grammarian's Funeral': Browning's Praise of Folly?", *Studies in English Literature* 3 (Autumn 1963): 449-60. Reprinted in

Robert Browning: A Collection of Critical Essays, ed. Philip Drew (Methuen, 1966), pp. 199-211.

"The Symbolism of Browning's 'Master Hugues of Saxe-Gotha,'" *Victorian Poetry* 3 (Winter 1965): 1-7.

"'Our Gallant Colonel' in *Punch* and Parliament," *Bulletin of the New York Public Library* 69 (September 1965): 424-45. [On the eccentric politician, Colonel Sibthorp.]

"Education, the Common Reader, and the Future," *A. L. A. Bulletin* 60 (March 1966): 275-82.

"Lovers' Finiteness: Browning's 'Two in the Campagna,'" *Papers on Language and Literature* 3 (Winter 1967): 75-80.

"The Scholar's Workshop: The Academic Library and the Generation of Knowledge." [Brochure.] *Dedication of the University Library,* Bowling Green, Ohio, 1968, pp. 8-18.

"'Andrea del Sarto': The Kingdom of Hell is Within," *Browning's Mind and Art,* ed. Clarence Tracy (Edinburgh: Oliver and Boyd, 1968), pp. 18-31.

"Nineteenth-Century English Best-Sellers: A Further List," *Studies in Bibliography* 22 (1969): 197-206.

"Charles Dickens," *World Book Encyclopedia,* 1969 edition, 5: 154-56.

"The Emergence of Popular Reading and Scholarly Activity in the Eighteenth and Nineteenth Centuries," *Forum* (University of Houston) 7, no. 2 (Spring 1969): 9-14.

"Victorian Readers and the Sense of the Present," *Midway* (University of Chicago), 10 (Spring 1970): 95-119.

"The Reading Public in England and America in 1900," *Literature and Western Civilization,* ed. David Daiches and Anthony Thorlby, vol. 5: *The Modern World II: Realities* (London: Aldus Books, 1972), 547-68.

"Librarianship and the Pursuit of Truth," Richard H. Shoemaker Lecture, 1972. [Brochure.] (New Brunswick: Rutgers University Graduate School of Library Science, 1974).

"Education, Print, and Paper in *Our Mutual Friend,*" *Nineteenth-Century Literary Perspectives: Essays in Honor of Lionel Stevenson,* ed. Clyde de L. Ryals et al. (Durham, N. C.: Duke University Press, 1974), pp. 237-54.

"*Past and Present*: Topicality as Technique," *Carlyle and His Contemporaries: Essays in Honor of Charles Richard Sanders,* ed. John Clubbe (Durham, N. C.: Duke University Press, 1976), pp. 112-28.

Bibliography of the Writings of Richard D. Altick

"Borrioboola-Gha, Bushmen, and Brickmakers," *Dickensian* 74 (September 1978): 157-59.

"Anachronisms in *Middlemarch*: A Note," *Nineteenth-Century Fiction* 33 (December 1978): 366-72.

"Afterword," Dickens: *Little Dorrit*, Signet Classic edition (New York: New American Library, 1980), pp. 804-16.

"Varieties of Readers' Response: The Case of *Dombey and Son*," *Yearbook of English Studies* 10 (1980): 70-94.

"*Bleak House*: The Reach of Chapter One," *Dickens Studies Annual* 8 (1980): 73-102.

"An Uncommon Curiosity: In Search of the Shows of London," *Quarterly Journal of the Library of Congress* 38 (Winter 1981): 12-23.

"Victorians on the Move; or, 'Tis Forty Years Since," *Dickens Studies Annual* 10 (1982): 2-21.

Reviews and Review-Articles

(Excluding reviews in *New York Times Book Review*, 1944-45, 1966; *New York Herald Tribune Books*, 1952-63; *Chicago Sun-Times*, 1971-74; *London Review of Books*, 1980-.)

Letters of Thomas Hood, ed. Leslie A. Marchand, *Modern Language Quarterly* 7 (September 1946): 366-67.

Dr. Campbell's Diary of a Visit to England in 1775, ed. James L. Clifford, *Modern Language Quarterly* 9 (September 1948): 368.

"On the Poets Called Romantic," *Virginia Quarterly Review* 26 (Spring 1950): 311-16.

Leigh Hunt's Dramatic Criticism, 1807-1831, ed. L. H. Houtchens and C. W. Houtchens, *Modern Language Quarterly* 13 (September 1952): 311-12.

Strathearn Gordon and T. G. B. Cocks, *A People's Conscience*, *William and Mary Quarterly* 10 (October 1953): 648-50.

Robert Browning: A Bibliography 1830-1950, comp. L. N. Broughton et al., *Papers of the Bibliographical Society of America* 48 (2d Quarter 1954): 212-14.

Robert K. Webb, *The British Working Class Reader*, *Papers of the Bibliographical Society of America* 50 (1st Quarter 1956): 97-100.

Leigh Hunt's Literary Criticism, ed. L. H. Houtchens and C. W. Houtchens. *Victorian Studies* 1 (September 1957): 85-87.

Leon Edel, *Literary Biography*, *Victorian Newsletter*, 13 (Spring 1958): 9-10.

Thomas Kelly, *George Birkbeck: Pioneer of Adult Education,* *Journal of the History of Medicine* 14 (April 1959): 256-57.

Alvar Ellegård, *Darwin and the General Reader, Gazette: International Journal for Mass Communication Studies* (Leiden, Holland) 5 (1959): 275-76.

Marchette Chute, *Two Gentle Men,* and Catherine Drinker Bowen, *Adventures of a Biographer, Nation* 189 (19 December 1959): 470-71.

Arthur H. Nethercot: *The First Five Lives of Annie Besant, Modern Philology* 58 (February 1961): 220-22.

Royal A. Gettmann, *A Victorian Publisher: A Study of the Bentley Papers, Library Quarterly* 31 (April 1961): 192-93.

Amy Cruse, *The Victorians and Their Reading, South Atlantic Quarterly* 63 (Winter 1964): 137-38.

Robert D. Mayo, *The English Novel in the Magazines, 1740-1815, Library Quarterly* 34 (January 1964): 131-32.

Louis James, *Fiction for the Working Man 1830-1850, Journal of English and Germanic Philology* 63 (July 1964): 529-31.

J. W. Saunders, *The Profession of English Letters, Modern Philology* 64 (August 1966): 90-92.

Thomas Kelly, *Early Public Libraries: A History of Public Libraries in Great Britain Before 1850, Library Quarterly* 36 (October 1966): 337-38.

G. B. Tennyson, *"Sartor" Called "Resartus," Journal of English and Germanic Philology* 65 (October 1966): 734-35.

The Wellesley Index to Victorian Periodicals, 1824-1900, vol. 1, *Nineteenth-Century Fiction* 21 (March 1967): 381-83.

Charles Dickens, *Oliver Twist* (Clarendon Press edition, ed. Kathleen Tillotson), *Victorian Studies* 11 (March 1968): 415-16.

Herbert L. Sussman, *Victorians and the Machine: The Literary Response to Technology, Journal of English and Germanic Philology* 68 (January 1969): 192-94.

E. D. H. Johnson, *Charles Dickens: An Introduction to His Novels, Dickensian* 66 (January 1970): 59.

Mary Rose Sullivan, *Browning's Voices in "The Ring and the Book," Modern Language Quarterly* 31 (June 1970): 260-62.

John Gross, *The Rise and Fall of the Man of Letters, Victorian Studies* 14 (September 1970): 93-94.

The New Cambridge Bibliography of English Literature, vol. 3

Bibliography of the Writings of Richard D. Altick

(1800-1900), *Journal of English and Germanic Philology* 70 (January 1971): 139-45.

The Letters of Charles Dickens (Pilgrim edition), vols. 1 and 2, ed. Madeline House and Graham Storey, *Dickens Studies Newsletter* 2 (June 1971): 34-37.

The Letters of Robert Browning and Elizabeth Barrett Barrett, ed. Elvan Kintner, *Modern Philology* 69 (August 1971): 76-77.

Lionel Madden, *How To Find Out About the Victorian Period*, *Dickensian* 68 (January 1972): 62-63.

The Stature of Dickens: A Centenary Bibliography, ed. Joseph Gold, *Nineteenth-Century Fiction* 27 (June 1972): 107-10.

"Crossing the Andean Range" [on *Horace Walpole's Correspondence with Sir Horace Mann*, vols. 9-11 (Yale Edition of Walpole's Correspondence)], *Virginia Quarterly Review* 48 (Autumn 1972): 613-16.

Tim Chilcott, *A Publisher and His Circle: The Life and Work of John Taylor, Keats's Publisher*, *Comparative Literature Studies* 10 (September 1973): 270-72.

The Wellesley Index to Victorian Periodicals, vol. 2, *Nineteenth-Century Fiction* 28 (September 1973): 239-41.

Robert Collison, *The Story of Street Literature: Forerunner of the Popular Press*, and Leslie Shepard, *The History of Street Literature*, *Library Quarterly* 44 (July 1974): 282-84.

William Irvine and Park Honan, *The Book, the Ring, and the Poet: A Biography of Robert Browning*, *Victorian Poetry* 12 (Autumn 1974): 297-300.

The Letters of Charles Dickens (Pilgrim edition), vol. 3, ed. Madeline House et al., *Dickens Studies Newsletter* 6 (March 1975): 17-19.

David Buchanan, *The Treasure of Auchinleck: The Story of the Boswell Papers*, *Modern Language Quarterly* 36 (September 1975): 316-18.

Horace Walpole's Correspondence, vol. 39, *Philological Quarterly* 54 (Fall 1975): 1,067-68.

John R. Reed, *Victorian Conventions*, *Clio* 5 (Winter 1976): 253-57.

J. J. Tobias, *Prince of Fences: The Life and Crimes of Ikey Solomons*, and David D. Cooper, *The Lesson of the Scaffold: The Public Execution Controversy in Victorian England*, *Victorian Studies* 19 (March 1976): 416-17.

Louis James, *Print and the People 1819-1851*, Publishing History 1 (1977): 135-36.

Mary S. Hartman, *Victorian Murderesses*, Criticism 20 (Winter 1978): 87-89.

Alan J. Lee, *The Origins of the Popular Press in England, 1855-1914*, Library Quarterly 48 (January 1978): 102-103.

K. M. Elisabeth Murray, *Caught in the Web of Words: James A. H. Murray and the "Oxford English Dictionary,"* Modern Language Quarterly 39 (March 1978): 85-87.

Dorothy Eagle and Hilary Carnell, *The Oxford Literary Guide to the British Isles*, and Robin W. Winks, *An American's Guide to Britain*, Ohio Journal 4 (Summer 1978): 46-47.

The Letters of Charles Dickens (Pilgrim edition), vol. 4, ed. Kathleen Tillotson, Dickens Studies Newsletter 9 (September 1978): 84-86.

"The Nature-Loving Victorians" [on *Nature and the Victorian Imagination*, ed. U. C. Knoepflmacher and G. B. Tennyson], Virginia Quarterly Review 54 (Autumn 1978): 748-54.

H. E. Meller, *Leisure and the Changing City, 1870-1914*, Journal of Library History 13 (Fall 1978): 471-72.

"This Will Never Do" [on Margaret C. Patterson, *Literary Research Guide*], Review 1 (1979): 47-60.

Geoffrey Tillotson, *A View of Victorian Literature*, Journal of English and Germanic Philology 78 (January 1979): 142-43.

George Boyce et al., *Newspaper History from the Seventeenth Century to the Present Day*, Sociological Review (University of Keele) 27 (May 1979): 385-86.

Peter Bailey, *Leisure and Class in Victorian England: Rational Recreation and the Contest for Control*, American Historical Review 84 (October 1979): 1055-56.

The Wellesley Index to Victorian Periodicals, vol. 3, Nineteenth-Century Fiction 34 (December 1979): 371-73.

Robert L. Patten, *Charles Dickens and His Publishers*, South Atlantic Quarterly 79 (Winter 1980): 107-108.

Frederick A. Pottle, *Pride and Negligence: The History of the Boswell Papers*, Modern Language Quarterly 43 (March 1892): 87-89.

"All About Tennyson" [on *Lady Tennyson's Journal*, ed. James O. Hoge, and *The Letters of Alfred Tennyson*, ed. Cecil Y. Lang and

Bibliography of the Writings of Richard D. Altick

Edgar F. Shannon, Jr.], *Virginia Quarterly Review* 58 (Summer 1982): 507-13.

Victorian Science and Victorian Values: Literary Perspectives, ed. James Paradis and Thomas Postlewait, *South Atlantic Quarterly* 81 (Summer 1982): 345-46.

Park Honan, *Matthew Arnold: A Life*, *Modern Philology* 80 (November 1982): 211-14.

NOTES ON CONTRIBUTORS

ARTHUR A. ADRIAN is Professor Emeritus of English at Case Western Reserve University. His studies in Victorian biography include *Georgina Hogarth and the Dickens Circle* (1957) and *Mark Lemmon: First Editor of Punch* (1966). The essay included here is a shortened version of a chapter from his forthcoming *Charles Dickens and the Parent-Child Relationship*.

JEROME BEATY is professor of English at Emory University. He is the author of *"Middlemarch" from Notebook to Novel* (1960); coauthor of *Poetry from Statement to Meaning* (1965); and editor of *The Norton Introduction to Fiction* (1973, 1981) and *The Norton Introduction to the Short Novel*.

JEROME H. BUCKLEY is widely known for his studies of literary and intellectual history, *The Victorian Temper* (1951) and *The Triumph of Time* (1966). He is the author of *Tennyson: The Growth of a Poet* (1961) and *Season of Youth: The Bildungsroman from Dickens to Golding* (1974). He is Gurney Professor of English Literature at Harvard University.

JOHN CLUBBE has been an NEH and Guggenheim Fellow. He has written essays on Byron and edited *Carlyle and His Contemporaries* (1976) and *Froude's Life of Carlyle* (1979). He is the author of *Victorian Forerunner* (1968), a critical biography of Thomas Hood, and is professor of English at the University of Kentucky.

ROBERT A. COLBY is Professor of Library Science at Queens College, City University of New York. His special interest in the social history of reading taste is reflected in *Fiction with a Purpose* (1967) and *Thackeray's Canvass of Humanity* (1979). He has been a Guggenheim and Newberry Library Fellow.

361

Notes on Contributors

PHILLIP COLLINS is Emeritus Professor of English at the University of Leicester. Best known for his work on Dickens, such as *Dickens and Crime* (1962), *Dickens: the Critical Heritage* (1971), and *Dickens: the Public Readings* (1975), he has lately been writing also on Tennyson, Thackeray, Trollope, and Hardy.

DAVID J. DeLAURA is Avalon Foundation Professor of Humanities and professor of English at the University of Pennsylvania. He has been a Guggenheim and NEH Fellow, and won the first William Riley Parker Prize of the Modern Language Association (1964). He is the author of *Hebrew and Hellene in Victorian England: Newman, Arnold, and Pater* (1969) and the editor of *Matthew Arnold: A Collection of Critical Essays* (1973) and *Victorian Prose: A Guide to Research* (1973).

JOHN J. FENSTERMAKER is professor of English at Florida State University and chairman of the English department. He is the author of *Charles Dickens, 1940–1975: An Analytical Subject Index to Periodical Criticism of the Novels and Christmas Books* (1979). A former student of Professor Altick, he has revised the third edition of *The Art of Literary Research* (1981).

GEORGE H. FORD is former president of the Dickens Fellowship and the author of *Dickens and His Readers* (1955). He is the editor of authoritative editions of *Hard Times* (1966) and (with Sylvère Monod) *Bleak House* (1977). He is coeditor of *The Norton Anthology of English Literature* (1974) and editor of *Victorian Fiction: A Second Guide to Research* (1978). At the University of Rochester he is Joseph H. Gilmore Professor of English.

DONALD GRAY is professor of English at Indiana University, Bloomington, where he has served as chairman of the English department. A former student of Professor Altick, he is the editor of an authoritative edition of *Alice in Wonderland* (1971) and coeditor of *Victorian Literature: Poetry/Prose* (1976). An active member of the National Council of Teachers of English, he edits *College English*.

WENDELL V. HARRIS has written on the short story and various topics of Victorian thought. He is the author of *British Short Fiction in the Nineteenth Century* (1979) and *The Omnipresent Debate: Empiricism and Transcendentalism in Nineteenth-Century English Prose* (1981). A former National Endowment for the Humanities Fellow, he is professor of English at Pennsylvania State University.

Notes on Contributors

JAMES R. KINCAID is a former Guggenheim Fellow and serves on a number of professional boards. He is the author of *Dickens and the Rhetoric of Laughter* (1971), *Tennyson's Major Poems: The Comic and Ironic Patterns* (1975), and *The Novels of Anthony Trollope* (1977). A former colleague of Professor Altick at Ohio State, he is currently Professor of English at the University of Colorado.

U. C. KNOEPFLMACHER is professor of English at Princeton University. He has been a Guggenheim and National Endowment for the Humanities Fellow. He has coedited collections of essays on Romantic and Victorian topics, is the author of *Religious Humanism and the Victorian Novel* (1965), and he has written about the nineteenth-century novel in *Laughter and Despair* (1971) and *George Eliot's Early Novels: The Limits of Realism* (1968).

ALBERT J. KUHN is professor of English at Ohio State, where he has served as department chairman and provost of the University. He is the author of essays on English intellectual history of the eighteenth and nineteenth centuries and the editor of *Three Sentimental Novels* (1970).

ALEXANDER WELSH is professor of English at the University of California, Los Angeles. A former editor of *Nineteenth-Century Fiction*, he has explored special topics in fiction in *The City of Dickens* (1971) and *Reflections on the Hero as Quixote* (1981). He is the editor of *Thackeray: A Collection of Critical Essays* (1968) and a former Guggenheim Fellow.

GEORGE J. WORTH is professor of English at the University of Kansas and former longtime department chairman. His studies include *James Hannay: His Life and Works* (1964), *William Harrison Ainsworth* (1972), and *Dickensian Melodrama* (1978). He is coeditor of essays on nineteenth-century thought and the writer's relation to his audience.

ANDREW WRIGHT is professor of English at the University of California, San Diego. His work on the novel includes *Jane Austen's Novels: A Study in Structure* (1953), *Joyce Cary: A Preface to His Novels* (1958), *Henry Fielding: Mask and Feast* (1965), and *Anthony Trollope: Dream and Art* (1983). He has been a student and colleague of Professor Altick at Ohio State and with him has coauthored six editions of the *Selective Bibliography for the Study of English and American Literature* (1960–79). He is a Fellow of the Royal Society of Literature.

INDEX

Adler, Alfred, 115 n.2
Adrian, Arthur A., 28 n.60, 298 nn.31, 39, 54
"Aesthetes," 332, 342, 345
Aestheticism, 197, 331-47; medievalism and, 334-35; melancholic tendency of, 342-44; William Morris and, 332, 334, 338-39, 340, 341, 342, 344, 345; omnibeautiful tendency of, 338-39; ornamental tendency of, 336-38; Pre-Raphaelitism and, 332, 342, 344, 345
Aikin, John, *Evenings At Home*, 53
Ainsworth, Harrison, 63; *Ainsworth's Magazine*, 64
Allott, Kenneth, 198, 199, 221 n.34, 223 nn.54, 55, 62, 224 nn.66, 69
Allott, Miriam, 170, 171, 182
Allsop, Kenneth, 301, 303, 304
Altick, Richard D., 31, 67, 74, 75-77, 257 n.1, 274 n.4
Amadis de Gaul, 46
Amis, Kingsley, 3
Annan School, 124
Anti-Delphine, 50
Antinovels, 50-51, 70 n.8
Apostles, Society of, (Tennyson and), 158-60
Arnold, Matthew, 62, 88, 124, 133, 147, 159, 160, 164, 165 n.17; and Goethe, 197-224; and lecturing, 6, 14, 15, 17-18, 19, 21, 24; "Balder Dead," 123; "Dover Beach," 223 n.64; *Empedocles*, 214; "Epilogue to Lessing's Laocoön,"
211; Preface to *Poems* 1853, 170, 199, 202, 214, 215, 216; "Memorial Verses," 205, 215, 224 n.65; "On Literature and Science," 159; "On Celtic Literature," 223 n.61; "Resignation," 213, 216; "Shakespeare," 213; "The Scholar-Gipsy," 197-218, 224 n.64; "Stanzas from the Grande Chartreuse," 220 n.20, 224 nn.64, 65; "Stanzas in Memory of the Author of 'Obermann'," 210, 213, 215, 224 n.70; "Thyrsis," 221 n.33; "To a Friend," 213
Arnold, Dr. Thomas, 151, 156, 163, 304, 306, 312
Ashbee, C. R., 340-41
Aslin, Elizabeth, 333
Atherstone, Edwin, 78
Auckland, Earl of, 90
Auden, W. H., 148, 158, 160, 165, 214
Aurelius, Marcus, 216
Austen, Jane, 49, 70 n.9, 152
Austin, Alfred, 65
Autobiography, spiritual, 59, 183-84

Babbage, Charles, *On the Economy of Machinery and Manufactures*, 36-42
Bailey, P. J., 78
Ballads, 86-87; *Iliad* as, 132-36
Barrett, Eaton Stannard, *The Heroine*, 50
Barry, Josephine M., 223 n.60
Behn, Mrs. Aphra, 50
Belgravia, 66

Index

Bell, Currer. *See* Charlotte Brontë
Bellew, Reverend John, 7, 9
Bentham, Jeremy, 53; on copying, 32-34, 36, 38, 43
Bentley's Standard Novels, 57, 171
Besant, Sir Walter, *The Art of Fiction*, 47; 66, 67, 69
Bethlem Hospital, 225
Bewick, Thomas, 188
Bible, 129, 132, 133, 153, 154
Bildungsroman, 62, 227
Biography, exemplary, 54, 67
Black, Adam, 64
Blackie, J. S., 220 n. 26
Blackwood's Magazine, 170, 171, 172, 204, 205
Blake, William, 122, 343
Block, Andrew, 195 n. 14
Booth, Wayne, 268
Botanical bent, in Aestheticism, 335-36
Bowdoin College, 22, 26
Box, H. Oldfield, 323-25, 329
Braddon, M. E., 66, 67
Bradlaugh, Charles, 7, 9
Bradley, A. C., 160
Bradley, Granville, 151, 160
Bright, John, 9
BBC, (adaptations of, Anthony Trollope) 316, 325-28
British Library, 328
British Museum, 55
Brontë, Branwell, 95
Brontë, Charlotte, 110; *Jane Eyre*, 68, 105; as "fictional autobiography," 168-96; *Shirley*, 57; *Villette*, 62
Brontë, Emily, *Wuthering Heights*, 104
Brontës, 110, 152, 168
Brooke, Henry, *The Fool of Quality*, 181
Brougham, Lord Henry, and Society for the Diffusion of Useful Knowledge, 52-56, 69
Broughton, Rhoda, 66
Brown, Janet H., 239 n. 44
Browning, Elizabeth Barrett, 92 n. 3; *Aurora Leigh*, 123
Browning, Robert, 77, 123, 152
Buchanan, President James, 15
Buchanan, Robert, 342, 344
Buckingham, James Silk, 10
Buckingham Palace, 15
Buckley, Jerome H., 342
Buller, Charles, 141
Bulwer, Sir Edward. *See* Lytton, Sir Edward Bulwer
Bunn, Alfred, 13
Bunyan, John, *The Pilgrim's Progress*, 53, 178, 183

Burgis, Nina, 44
Burn, W. L., 164
Burnand, F. C., "The Colonel," 332, 346
Burne-Jones, Edward, 332, 342, 346
Burney, Fanny, 110; *Evelina*, 48
Burns, Robert, 137
Bush, Douglas, 133
Butler, Montague, 149
Byron, Lord, 77, 95, 121, 153, 203, 213
Byron, Medora Gordon, 50
Byronic convention of the novel, 168, 172, 173, 174, 178

Cabau, Jacques, 131
Calder, Grace, 136
Cambridge University, Tennyson at, 153-60; 282, 289
Campbell, Thomas, *Gertrude of Wyoming*, 79; 92 n. 3
Canadian Northwest Mounted Police, 287
Carey, John, 236
Carlyle, Jane Welsh, 76, 149
Carlyle, Thomas, 10, 68, 76, 150, 220 n. 20, 235, 283, 307; on Goethe, 205-12; as epic historian, 119-45; and the *Iliad*, 123-36; "Biography," 122; "Boswell's *Life of Johnson*," 125; "Corn-Law Rhymes," 138, 140; *Cromwell*, 131; "The Diamond Necklace," 126; *Early Kings of Norway*, 145 n. 35; *French Revolution*, 119, 120-22, 126, 130, 131, 136, 144 n. 27, 145 n. 33; "On Heroes and Hero-Worship," 103, 138, 145 n. 33; Journal, 127; *History of Friedrich II*, 142; *Latter-Day Pamphlets*, 120, 135, 136, 141, 142; *Lectures 1838*, 134; *Life of Sterling*, 204, 205; *Past and Present*, 120, 134, 136-42, 222 n. 37, 307; *Sartor Resartus*, 125, 130, 137, 170, 206, 207, 222 n. 41
Carré, Jean-Marie, 209
Carroll, Lewis, 265, 275 n. 16
Cary C., "Beauties of the Poets," 53
Cervantes, Miguel de, 50, 149
Chancellor's Prize Essay, 66
Chapman, George, 129, 153
Charles I, in *David Copperfield*, 43
Chartists, 89
Chatham, Dickens at, 283
Chaucer, Geoffrey, 49, 343, *Troilus and Criseyde*, 46; *Wife of Bath's Tale*, 117 n. 15
Chesterton, G. K., 343
Children's Literature in Education, 301
Christian Socialism, 304
Cicero, 153, 155

Index

Civil War, American, 4, 7
Clare, John, 78, 153
Coates, Thomas, 54
Cobham Park, 225
Clarke, Samuel, 144 n. 18
Clive, John, 90
Clough, Arthur Hugh, 8, 123, 203, 213, 214, 219 nn. 11, 17, 221 n. 33; *Amours de Voyage*, 220 n. 22; *Dipsychus*, 163
Cobden-Sanderson, T. J., 339
Coffin, Robert P. Tristram, 165 n. 1
Colby, Robert A., 196 nn. 16, 17
Cole, Henry, *Journal of Design and Manufacture*, 336
Coleridge, Samuel Taylor, *Biographia Literaria*, 34-35, 36; 133, 144 nn. 26, 221 n. 36
Collins, Charles, 286
Collins, Philip, 227, 235, 237, n. 10, 238 n. 21
Collins, Wilkie, 7, 9, 11, 16, 47, 286, 292, 293
Combe, George, 10
Commonwealth, English, 119
Corelli, Marie, 66
Corn Laws, 138
Coutts, Angela Burdett, 279
Craigenputtoch, 120, 125, 126, 127, 128, 130, 131
Craik, Dinah Mulock, *John Halifax*, 65
Craik, George L., *The Pursuit of Knowledge*, 54, 67, 68
Crane, Walter, *The Bases of Design*, 339
Cromwell, Oliver, 140
Cross, Mary Ann Evans Lewes, 112
Crowther's series, 323
Crystal Palace Exhibition, 336, 337, 338, 344
Culler, A. Dwight, 147, 223 n. 62
Cuthbertson, Misses, 51

Dadd, Richard, 225, 226
Dante, 132, 149
Darwin, Charles, 123, 136
David (biblical), 226
Davidson, John, 78
Day, Lewis, 336, 338-39
"Decadence," 332, 344
Defoe, Daniel, 66, 183; *Journal of the Plague Year*, 55; *Robinson Crusoe*, 53
Deloney, Thomas, 47
Dent's Illustrated Children's Classics, 300
DeQuincey, Thomas, 133, 204, 220 n. 25
Derrida, Jacques, 45 n. 6

Dickens, Catherine, 294-96
Dickens, Charles, 47, 60, 61, 121, 171, 187, 315; critical approaches to, 258-61; as father, 276-99; and lecturing, 4, 7, 13, 15, 20, 21, 25; *All the Year Round*, 284, 287; *American Notes*, 12, 27 n. 22; *Barnaby Rudge*, 260-61; *Bleak House*, 33, 230, language abuse in, 240-57; *David Copperfield*, Mr. Dick's copying, 43-45, 151, 195 n. 11; as David's autobiography, 68, 225-39; *Great Expectations*, 53; *Hard Times*, 57, 164, 337, 344; *Household Words*, 290; *Life of Our Lord*, 284; *Martin Chuzzlewit*, 12, 27 n. 22, ironic or subversive reading of, 261-74; *Master Humphrey's Clock*, 260; *Oliver Twist*, 55, 196 nn. 19, 27, and *Jane Eyre*, 178-82; *Our Mutual Friend*, 287; *Pickwick Papers*, 11, 286
Dickens children's careers, Charles Jr., (Charley), 284-85; Mary (Mamie), 285; Kate (Katey), 285-86; Walter Landor, 287; Francis Jeffrey (Frank), 287; Alfred Tennyson, 287-88; Sydney Smith (The Admiral), 288; Henry Fielding (Harry), 289-90; Edward (The Noble Plorn), 288-89
Dickinson, Lowes, 156
Diderot, Denis, 125
Disraeli, Benjamin, 119, *Coningsby*, 173; *Contarini Fleming*, and *Jane Eyre*, 172-78, 181, 187, 195 n. 15; *Sybil, Tancred*, 173; *Vivian Grey*, 57
Disraeli, Isaac, 153
Dolby, George, 276
Donovan, Robert, 257 n. 3
Dowling, Linda, *Aestheticism and Decadence*, 331
Doyle, Conan, 9, 11
Doyle, Frances, 86
Dresser, Christopher, on ornamentation, 336, 337, 338, 339
Du Maurier, George, 332, 342, 346
Dunbar, George, 124
Dunbar Mechanics Institution, 52
Dunlop, John Colin, *History of Prose Fiction*, 47-48, 63

Eagles, John, 172, 195 n. 8
Eckermann, J. P., 209, 210
Edgeworth, Maria, 49, 50, 70 n. 9, 110; *Moral Tales*, 53
Edinburgh Review, 55, 80, 81, 125, 303
Elgin Marbles, 54

367

Index

368

Index

Index

Index

Sterling, John, 205
Stevenson, Robert Louis, 66
Stone, Donald D., 195 n.12, 239 n.41
Strabo, 46
Sturm und Drang Movement, 200, 203, 217
Suetonius, 153
Sullivan, Sir Arthur, 13
Summerly Art Manufacturers, 336
Swift, Jonathan, 62
Swinburne, Algernon, 77, 92 n.3, 332, 345; *Poems and Ballads*, 343-44
Symons, Arthur, *Spiritual Adventures*, 344

Tacitus, 153
Tavistock House, 278, 280
Temple, Ruth, 331
Tennyson, Alfred, 7, 9, 77, 94, 212; as "an educated Victorian mind," 146-67; at Cambridge, 153-60; and science and religion, 159-65; and Dickens, 232-34, 238 n.35; "Lines on Cambridge," 157; "Charge of the Light Brigade," 86; *Enoch Arden*, 78; *Idylls of the King*, 123; *In Memoriam*, 158, 161, 198, 199, 232-34; "Locksley Hall," 219 n.11; "Locksley Hall: Sixty Years After," 164; "Morte d'Arthur," 123; "The Passing of Arthur," 86; "Northern Farmer," 153; "The Palace of Art," 158, 198; *The Princess*, 198, 232; "Tears, Idle Tears," 232
Tennyson, G. B., 131
Tennyson, Dr. George, 152, 166 n.24
Tennyson, Hallam, 149, 151
Ternan, Ellen, 295, 296
Thackeray, William Makepeace, as lecturer, 5, 8, 9, 16, 20, 22, 23, 25; 46, 61, 121, 148, 164; *The English Humorists*, 4; *Henry Esmond*, 63, 64, 121, 123, 185; *History of Pendennis*, 68; *The New-comes*, 66; "On Some French Fashionable Novels," 62; *Vanity Fair*, 65, 68, 151, 226, 227
Thomas, Dylan, 3
Thomson, J. A. K., 119
Thoreau, Henry David, 121
Thucydides, 90
Thumb, "General" Tom, 15
Tillotson's Fiction Bureau, 66
Tillotson, Kathleen, 170, 198
Tillyard, E. M. W., 143 n.13
Times, 40, 66, 333
Tom Thumb, 280, 291
Tonna, Charlotte E., 60

Tractarianism, 160
Travel fiction, 62
Treatises, 67
Trevelyan, George Otto, 81
Trilling, Lionel, 17
Trimmer, Mrs., *Tales*, 53
Trinity Parish, 288
Trollope, Anthony, 4, 24, 26 n.2, 46, 50, 64, 121; adaptations of, 315-30; of *Barchester Towers*, 316, 328; of *The Barchester Chronicles*, 325-27; of *The Warden*, 317-30; *Autobiography*, 151 329; *North America*, 13; "On Prose Fiction," 64-65; *The Way We Live Now*, 61
Trollope, Mrs. Frances, 13, 47, 60; *Michael Armstrong*, 56
Tupper, Martin, 10, 18
Turner, Frank, 135
Turner, Paul, 148
Thwing, Charles F., 73 n.47
Twain, Mark, 11
Two Cultures, 148, 164
Tyndall, John, 7, 163

University of Cincinnati, 146
University of Richmond, 146
Uriah, the Hittite, 226
Usborne, Richard, 301
Utile dulci principle, 48

Vale of the White Horse, 305
Varnhagen von Ense, K. A., *Memoirs*, 133, 134
Veblen, Thorstein, 342
Versailles, Court of, 63
Victoria, Queen, 15, 52, 61, 111, 285, 336
Virgil, 153, 155; *Aeneid*, 138, 140
Voltaire, F. M. A. de, 132
Voss, J. H., 127, 129, 144 n.18

Wallis, Cedric, 325, 326
Ward, Mrs. Humphry, *Robert Elsmere*, 59
Watson, William, 77
Watts-Dunton, Theodore, 92 n.3
Waugh, Evelyn, *Decline and Fall*, 150
Wellington, Duke of, 99
Wells, H. G., *Tono-Bungay*, 121
Wesley, John, 107, 181
West, Lockwood, 327
Westminster Abbey, 8
Wheatley, Vera, 71, 16
Whewell, William, 154-55
White House, 15
Whitman, Walt, 6, 23

373